Also by David Falkner

The Last Yankee
Nine Sides of the Diamond
The Short Season
Sadaharu Oh: A Zen Way of Baseball
Joe Morgan: A Life in Baseball (with Joe Morgan)
L.T.: Living on the Edge (with Lawrence Taylor)

Great Time Coming

The Life of Jackie Robinson, from Baseball to Birmingham

DAVID FALKNER

A Touchstone Book
Published by Simon & Schuster
New York   London   Toronto   Sydney   Tokyo   Singapore

TOUCHSTONE
Rockefeller Center
1230 Avenue of the Americas
New York, NY 10020

First Touchstone Edition 1996

TOUCHSTONE and colophon are registered trademarks
of Simon & Schuster Inc.

Designed by Irving Perkins Associates, Inc.

Manufactured in the United States of America

1   2   3   4   5   6   7   8   9   10

Library of Congress Cataloging-in-Publication Data
Falkner, David.
Great time coming: the life of Jackie Robinson, from baseball
to Birmingham/David Falkner.
p.   cm.
Includes index.
1. Robinson, Jackie, 1919–1972.   2. Baseball players—United States—
Biography.   3. Afro-American baseball players—Biography.   4. Civil rights
movements—United States.   I. Title.
GV865   R6F35   1995
796.357′092—dc20
94–44876
CIP
[B]
ISBN: 0-671-79336-5
0-684-82348-9 (Pbk.)

for Judy Siff

Great
Time
Coming

PROLOGUE

August 29, 1947, Ebbets Field, sixth inning. The Giants were in for the first of three games. It was one of those Friday nights in Brooklyn, remembered now by fewer and fewer living souls but recorded in that time capsule of baseball moments: the Giants coming across the river to play the Dodgers, the pennant on the line, and Jackie Robinson, in his rookie season, on the base paths.

Shoehorned into the ballpark were 34,512 fans screaming, banging cowbells, stomping their feet. Jackie Robinson, the major leagues' first black player in the twentieth century, was on third base, dancing back and forth, threatening to steal home. Who could measure the dreams of those who watched him: all those fans; the gallery of writers hung from the upper deck; the executives, including Branch Rickey; the thirty-seven-year-old veteran pitcher Joe Beggs?

Beggs went into his windup, his head twisted slightly toward third to keep the mote in his eye from completely blinding him. From that vantage point, he saw the dance man in his cream-white flannels suddenly streak plateward. The crowd noise hit him with almost concussive force as he hurried his pitch. And then Robinson, three-quarters of the way to home plate, stopped as though within the engine of his body he possessed an unknown gear that could throw all of his two hundred forward-hurtling pounds instantly into nimble-footed retreat. He was back at third, his hands on his hips, before the Giants' startled catcher, Walker Cooper, could make up his mind to throw either to third or back to the mound. Cooper glumly tossed the ball back to Beggs.

As Beggs looked in to get his sign for the next pitch, Robinson again pranced off third, and the wave of crowd noise rose. Beggs, looking at Robinson, then to the plate, delivered his pitch. But this time the streaking Jackie Robinson, halfway, three-quarters of the way down the line, did not stop. He came all the way, flying on pigeon-toed, spindly legs, arms flopping, his head a bauble above the dust as he slid beneath the tag applied by Walker Cooper. And as quickly as that, still enveloped in the dust cloud he had raised, he was on his

feet, trotting back to the dugout, the explosion of cheering telling him what he already knew: for the third time in this epochal opening season of his, he had stolen home, had dismantled that invisible barrier confronting base runners of any size, shape, or color standing at third base; he had dismantled it as he had only months before dismantled a century of bigotry that had seemingly permanently sealed America's Pastime. A reporter that night went to Branch Rickey, the architect of this greater dismantling, to ask him about the smaller one that had just taken place on the field.

"Who taught him to do things like that?" the reporter inquired.

"Primarily God," Mr. Rickey answered.

Robinson, though, had another answer. When he was on third base and broke for the plate the first time, he said, he counted how many seconds it took for the pitcher to get the ball to the plate from that exact point on the base path where he stopped. He numbered inwardly, "One-two-three-four"—and told himself he had enough time.

He was just doing what it took to get the job done.

Part 1
Black Boy

CHAPTER ONE

Before Albany, Georgia, became a civil rights flashpoint in the early 1960s, it was simply a small southern city, segregated as any other, but special in the sense that it was (and had been since its founding over 130 years before) a gateway to the lower part of the state. The way from Albany to the sea, through the scrub pine and sandy loam of the eastern coastal plain, is popularly referred to as the Velvet Corridor—not because of its slow, lazy climate, its vistas of heavy summer haze hanging on broad, open fields and snaking rivers, but because it is plantation country. For the better part of a hundred years, powerful and wealthy white families established themselves throughout the corridor. The postal registry reads like pages from the Social Register: Rockefeller, Morgan, Mellon, Whitney, Vanderbilt, Windsor.

There was another side, of course, to those vistas of wealth and easy living. In the shadows of the great main houses lay the shacks and cabins of former slaves, sharecroppers and tenant farmers, those whose dependency on the great families had not changed even with the end of slavery.

For anyone born to a sharecropper's cabin, as the members of Jackie Robinson's family were at the beginning of this century in Cairo, a town in the southern part of the Corridor, the look of the area was doubly formidable. The Corridor was more newly settled than other areas but less likely, because of its geography, to permit mobility or escape. To the east the land was bordered by the thick, impenetrable reaches of the great Okefenokee Swamp; to the west by a dense wall of overgrown Alabama forest; to the south by the sea; to the north by the Piedmont Plateau and the Appalachian Mountains. From spring to fall it was punishingly hot, with days of blazing sun and carpet-thick air, relieved only by inundating rainstorms followed by pestilential swarms of insects.

The difficult life of a southern black sharecropping family in the first decades of this century—and especially in an area such as the Velvet Corridor—is today nearly beyond the reach of imagination, white or black. W. E. B. Du Bois, the editor of the NAACP's magazine, *Crisis,* felt he had come upon the landscape of another planet when he traveled through Georgia south of Albany. The area, Du Bois knew from his studies, was the very center of the so-called black belt. "No other state in the Union," he wrote in 1903, "can count a million Negroes among its citizens—a population as large as the slave population of the whole Union in 1800." The apex of this country was Albany. And then south of it, going through the heart of the Corridor, Du Bois wrote, "the whole land seems forlorn and forsaken. Here are the remnants of the vast plantations of the Sheldons, the Pellots, and the Rensons; but the souls of them are passed. The houses lie in half ruin, or have wholly disappeared. . . . Yonder stretch the wide acres of Bildad Reasor . . . and now only the black tenant remains; but the shadow-hand of the master's grand-nephew or cousin or creditor stretches out of the grey distance to collect the rack-rent remorselessly, and so the land is uncared-for and poor. Only black tenants can stand such a system, and then only because they must. Ten miles we have ridden today and seen no white face."

To Du Bois, a northerner, this landscape demonstrated the dividing line between white and black: the veil, a symbol that expressed the many-sidedness of racism. "The problem of the twentieth-century," he wrote then, "is the problem of the color line."

The division between white and black, as Du Bois saw it, was total: it was economic, social, psychological. Its centuries-old history reached back to Africa and Europe, forward to the Caribbean and Latin America, and it could no longer be understood in terms of laws passed or annulled, wars won or lost. More formidable, more subtle than a barrier or wall, which could after all be dismantled, the veil promoted visual distortion even as it created separation. On one side there was light, visibility, and on the other side darkness and obscurity. Half a century before the novelist Ralph Ellison wrote *Invisible Man,* Du Bois understood that the common experience for persons of African descent living in the United States was to be caught in the grip of stereotype and assumption. The ordinary expectation of being treated as a human being—the birthright of almost any white—was impossible. The consequences of such a profound social disconnection went beyond slavery and Reconstruction to all the miseries of contemporary racism: poverty, segregation, repression, resistance, self-deception, and self-doubt.

The Robinson family, living in the heart of the Corridor when Jackie, the fifth and last surviving child, was born on January 31, 1919, was as representative as any other. The Robinsons lived in a sharecropper's cabin—a log-cabin structure with an open "dog track" hallway—on the Jim Sasser Plantation. The chimney of that cabin still stands, without a marking plaque or memorial of any kind.

As sharecroppers, the Robinsons worked the land for the Sasser family in exchange for their cabin and provisions. The arrangement, all too typical, was little more than slavery surviving in another form. For the labor provided by the family—husband, wife, and children— the Robinsons received, in the form of "chits" that could be redeemed only at the Sasser Plantation store, the equivalent of three dollars' worth of goods a week. (This was better than what most families received; a typical weekly wage at the turn of the century, according to Du Bois, was a dollar and a half.) Credit was always extended and always further bound those who used it to the system. Memories of those times are fuzzy; few in the area now remember the company store, but there are those who recall that Old Jim Sasser was once nearly electrocuted in its building. As the story goes, he came in out of a thunderstorm one day and was leaning against a wall in the store when it took a bolt of lightning that lifted Old Jim clear off the floor. Old Jim, strong as a horse and ornery as an alligator, survived to resume his command.

The kind of farming done in the area then was punishing. In addition to the basic crops of corn and potatoes, Cairo was a center for sugar cane; boosters eventually nicknamed Cairo "Syrup City" because of its production of cane syrup. In the first decades of the century, the cultivation of cane was perhaps the most physically dangerous form of farming known.

The Sasser farm was one of the most productive in the area. A private family history described the typical annual output of the plantation:

"It was said that . . . Jim Sasser . . . took home-cured ham, bacon, and beef and cattle to Cairo to sell by the two-horse wagon loads. One load was reported to have weighed over 1000 pounds. A report of yield on South Grady County farming gave the rundown on a 10-acre field that belonged to him. The field made 20 bushels of corn, followed by a crop of 50 bushels of various beans and among the beans was penders [peanuts] that produced more than 100 bushels per acre; also

15

an acre and a half of potato patch produced 1000 pounds of potatoes with more than 1000 bushels left for the hogs. In the same year he used this patch for collards and realized seed at the rate of 200 dollars per acre—so that is figured that the yield was 700 dollars per acre for the year.

"In addition, Jim Sasser was one of the first farmers in the area to use a steam-rig for his syrup making. His farm was referred to as a model farm."

Jerry Robinson was little more than a hired serf. Shortly after he married Mallie McGriff in 1909, he had to borrow fifteen dollars against his next year's wages from Old Jim. Of that fifteen dollars, he gave his wife five to care for their first Christmas together. Periodically, the landowner permitted a hog kill on his property; the share-croppers were invited to join the hunt, but were allowed to bring home only the internal organs—the intestines, kidneys, livers—of the beasts they killed. The good meat went to the owner or filled the two-horse wagonloads heading for town. Mallie McGriff complained bitterly that her family was being so penalized.

Both the Robinsons craved more from their life on the Sasser farm. Mallie Robinson understood that sharecropping wages were intolerable and unfair; her husband was a good, strong worker—why not have a wage to show for it? She pushed him to demand a half-crop. In half-cropping, a tenant farmer got to keep for himself half of what he cultivated. Instead of receiving a flat wage from the landowner, he received whatever cash he could get on the open market. He became, in however limited a way, an entrepreneur.

Sasser at first resisted—and resented—Mallie Robinson's efforts on behalf of her husband, but eventually gave in. Jerry Robinson was one of his best workers, and Sasser understood his value to the farm.

As a result, the Robinson family income suddenly went from around $134 a year to over $350, more money than they ever had before: money to pay off debts, and also money to spend.

The family's change of fortune was a mixed blessing. Jerry Robinson began looking around—to the pleasures of Cairo and beyond. With money, he discovered that the backbreaking life of the field was not for him. While the exact trigger for his decision is unknown, Jerry Robinson abandoned his wife, one day boarding a train for Florida with another man's wife. The family had no further word about him until a telegram, years later, informed them of his death.

Mallie Robinson, according to all her children, was a woman of powerful religious faith, devoted to making a better life for her family. What awaited them, she knew, was only what unceasing labor could bring. After Jerry Robinson left in 1919, the Robinson family remained for a time on the plantation. Mallie Robinson later said that Old Jim offered to call out the sheriff to get Jerry back. She told Sasser that her husband was "a free man, free to do what he wanted." Angered by her haughtiness, Sasser forced the family to move to smaller quarters. To support her children Mrs. Robinson subsequently got work in town as a domestic. When it became clear that she could never make enough for the family to survive, she too began looking over the hill.

The era was unsettled. The Great War had just ended. Changes were afoot everywhere. Old arrangements and assumptions were as much war casualties as the dead and wounded. In the United States, the changes in the black community had been under way for years. In the South, with the increasing establishment of official segregation and with the sharecropping system creating a new form of serfdom, migration became common. Blacks by the thousands had been moving to the Midwest and northern cities in the first decades of the century. This dislocation was also driven by an ever-increasing and violent resistance to even the minimal gains of freedom by former slaves and their descendants. The rise of the Ku Klux Klan, a phenomenon of Reconstruction, was in full swing with the beginning of the new century; by 1920 there were at least 4 million members. It was impossible in those years to be elected to any important office in the deep South without Klan support.

At the same time, in response to the growing violence and repression, organized black resistance was beginning. The failed Populist movement of the 1870s, '80s and '90s, which envisioned unity between the races, was superseded by the Niagara Movement of 1905, led by W. E. B. Du Bois, which merged, in 1910, with the new NAACP. During the war years, racial divisions led to at least one major riot—in St. Louis—in which homes were burned and at least forty blacks lost their lives. Following the war, with a steep rise in unemployment and the fear of hard times everywhere, race riots broke out all across the country, North and South. The old order, it turned out, was no sturdier than a house of cards, even if those who dealt the cards remained the same.

During the war period, Mallie Robinson's brother, Burton, had moved from Cairo to California, and his accounts of life there, hard but relatively open and receptive to black migrants, were enticing. When Burton returned to Cairo for a visit, he brought his stories, along with a deceptive look of prosperity. Mallie Robinson and other family members were bruised and impressed enough to follow him back to California.

"There were thirteen of us who went, I don't remember everyone," recalled Jackie's sister Willa Mae Walker, who was four at the time. "Aside from my mother and her five children, there was my auntie Cora and my uncle Sam Wade, and they had two children, then there was William Wade, who was a friend not a relative, and there were a couple of others too."

The trip west was punishing and depressing. The army of travelers remained packed in segregated cars. "All I can remember is that the cars were dark and crowded and the seats were very uncomfortable," Mrs. Walker said. "I think they were metal or something, but all I know is they were very uncomfortable."

When the group arrived in California, they all shared a small, cold-water flat in Pasadena. Within the week, Mrs. Robinson looked for and found work as a domestic, almost the only kind of job available to a black woman. In California, the dream of El Dorado was a little different for those on the other side of the veil. For whites, Pasadena, especially before the advent of smog and freeways, was a little patch of paradise on the other side of the San Gabriel Mountains: million-aires' mansions, elegant boulevards, exotic flowering shrubs, the sweet and beguiling odors of eucalyptus, roses, and oranges were everywhere. For those in the shadows of this luxury, life was always bittersweet. It wasn't paradise but survival that was most on Mallie Robinson's mind when she sought and found a job soon after the family's arrival.

CHAPTER TWO

Pasadena in the twenties and thirties comes to us today in flickering frames, lights and shadows from old silent movies. Once a farming community, it became linked by rail to Los Angeles in the mid-1880s and then, with the birth of the automobile, by road, so that by the beginning of the century, the pristine climate and the open, luxuriant spaces transformed the community into an alluring playground for those with money enough to escape the harsh eastern winters. Some of its current residents still remember the original look of the great mansions along Orange Grove Boulevard—the Wrigley Mansion, the almost surreal grandeur of the Ritz-Carlton, the Huntington Hotel.

Even though Pasadena was "northern" and no segregation laws were on the books, the separation of races was nearly as strict as it was in the South. Facing a rigidly controlled job market and educational system, blacks lived apart from whites, unable to use the same public facilities or able to use them only under limited conditions. (The public swimming pool in Brookside Park, for example, was open to blacks only one day per week; movie theaters had separate sections, downstairs for whites, balconies or side sections for blacks.) At almost every point of daily contact, a person of color in Pasadena was made to understand that doors were closed and life was limited. (As late as the 1950s, a huge uproar occurred over the naming of a Rose Queen who turned out to be black. The woman, very light-skinned, had been elected by the judges who assumed she was white. When her husband later appeared at a Civic Auditorium ceremony honoring the Queen and her Princesses, officials became suspicious. The day of the Rose Parade, when the Queen traditionally rides a float along the parade route, she was not to be seen. The official explanation was that that year, because of too many requests, the number of floats had to be limited.)

The impact of those first years on Jackie Robinson is hard to measure because they took place beyond the reach of memory, part of a chain of events, like his Georgia origins, that touched him deeply but came to him only through stories.

This much was told: Mrs. Robinson, able for a time to support her family with domestic work, soon lost her job when her employers moved. As before, she was out on the street looking for work, once more racing the clock for food.

In making her rounds one day, she turned up at a welfare office and was given a supply of clothing and the promise of regular support. The encounter at the welfare office is noted in Robinson's early autobiography, done with Carl Rowan, but in a way that adds a component of magic:

"Soon Mrs. Robinson's first employer left town and she was in desperate need of work. Someone told her about the advertisements domestics could place in the newspaper, so she left her children and set out to walk the several miles in search of the *Pasadena Star News*. When she had difficulty finding it, she stopped to ask directions in a building where she saw a huge sign saying, WELFARE. When she explained to the woman behind the desk what she sought to do, the woman smiled and said, 'This is as far as you need to go.' She opened the door to a room with great piles of clothing and said to Mallie, 'Go on in and dress yourself up and pick out some clothing for your children.' "

She returned to her family wearing a fur-trimmed outfit (Mallie's sister recalled, "Why, I started not to let you in the house. I looked out the window and saw you coming and I said who on earth is this colored lady and what's she coming up here for?"). But the good news of clothing and support from welfare, as the narrative went, was immediately supplanted by better news: a few days later, there was a new job.

Some seventy years later, Willa Mae Walker emphasized something else: welfare, she said, was never part of the equation. "As my mother always said, the Lord took care of us. Because when we get to thinking back, it sure was the Lord because we couldn't get on welfare. Yes, there may have been clothing, but other people, even relatives, whole families and their children, could get on welfare, but somehow not my mother, even though she had five children and no husband to support her. My mother did it all without welfare."

The different versions of the story, with some twisting of the lens, can be reconciled. But what no one contests, what all those who were too young to know directly but found out later, is that Mallie Robinson was the family's center in those crucial, early years. Her labor, energy, and wages sustained her family.

For a time, the Robinsons and the Wades continued to share space and to pool their resources. Within a year and a half, the group moved to somewhat larger quarters in the home of Mallie's brother, Burton, on Glorietta Street in the town's poorer northwest section. Two years later, there was another move, one fraught with both risk and opportunity.

A house on Pepper Street, also on the northwest side but in a modest all-white neighborhood, became available. The usual made-for-publication accounts of this move have Mallie Robinson purchasing the house outright, out of savings from her work as a domestic. There was more to it than that.

The house at 121 Pepper Street, with several bedrooms upstairs and downstairs, had been standing empty for some time. The house was owned by a black woman who had apparently purchased it without calculating the hostile response of white neighbors. Subsequently, the woman chose not to live there. She contacted a real estate agent, a man named Harrison, one of the few black professionals in the San Gabriel area, and asked him to help her at least get her money back. Harrison had a better idea: since the black community was small, he knew about the Robinsons and the Wades. Why not let them have the space they sorely needed, he reasoned, letting them take over monthly payments on the place while they straightened out their living situation, and meanwhile, with a Noah's ark of black folks suddenly docking in the neighborhood, whites would panic and come forward willing to buy the house at twice or three times its value. The arrangement, shady but inventive, went forward.

"There was definitely a little fixing up in the deal," Willa Mae Walker recalled with a laugh, "but me being smaller, I don't know all of it, but the deal was they would get in there . . . find a place for us to stay, you know, and they did . . . so all of us moved in."

But the Great White Buyer never came forward. As the only black families on Pepper Street, the Robinsons and Wades were initially taunted by neighbors. Stones were thrown, the property was vandalized. On one occasion, remembered Willa Walker, a cross was burned on the front lawn. "It was in the first year we were there. It wasn't in the middle of the night, either; it was in the evening when everybody was awake. My oldest brother, Edgar, went outside and put the fire out."

When the older children went to school (where they were invariably isolated in class), they were often jeered at by passing motorists. In school they were blamed first for any disturbances. White friends visited them at home but would never in turn invite them to their houses. The injuries, small and large, formed a pattern in the veil each of the children came to know well and from which they formed their own view of the world.

Mrs. Robinson worked as a domestic five days a week, fifty-two weeks a year. Numerous accounts by different members of the family make clear just how demanding her life as a single parent was. "My mother got up before daylight to go to her job," Jackie Robinson recalled shortly before his death, "and although she came home tired, she managed to give us the extra attention we needed. She indoctrinated us with the importance of family unity, religion, and kindness toward others." The portrait of Mrs. Robinson, given by relatives and friends, has a saintly, almost unearthly quality to it. In a recent biography of Robinson, Harvey Frommer quotes a close childhood friend of the family:

"Mallie Robinson was not only a supportive mother for her own children, but 'she was motherly to all of us kids in the neighborhood,' recalls Sidney Heard, Robinson's childhood friend. 'We'd come over to the house and she'd be good to us, share with us what she had. She remembered certain parts of the slavery times that had been told to her by her folks. She had no bitterness, though—maybe a little, but not enough to notice.' "

The tendency to romanticize Mallie Robinson has actually served to obscure the kind of influence she had within the family. Poverty drove the family. In order to eat, Mrs. Robinson and eventually the children as well had to work. Some days they all went without. Sometimes meals came in the form of leftovers Mrs. Robinson brought back from her employers, or meals were sugared bread soaked in water or milk. The Robinsons were referred to by others in and around the neighborhood as the "Robinson Crusoe family."

Work kept Mallie Robinson away from the house and her children for long periods, leaving the children on their own. To be sure, marching orders were left that she expected to be carried out. Each of the children, according to his or her age, was responsible for looking after the next youngest sibling. The oldest child, Edgar, was referred to as "Papa," and he was generally the one to whom the others deferred. Edgar, physically the most imposing, whipped himself around the neighborhood by bike and roller skates with the sort of skill and energy that terrified neighbors and delighted siblings. He was also the most religious of the children, closest to the strict and formal churchgoing practices of his mother.

Willa Mae, because she was second youngest, generally looked after Jackie. When schooltime came, before he was old enough to go to school, she simply took him along with her. There were no provisions for day care or regular baby-sitting, so Willa Mae, eight years old but responsible beyond her years, worked out an arrangement with her teacher whereby she was allowed to sit near a window in class and look out at her brother, who had been placed in a playground sandbox with some toys. If it rained, she brought him into the school building. If she saw that he was getting himself into difficulty, she was allowed to go to his aid. It was her view then and now—taken directly from her mother—that kindness was stronger than fear and prejudice.

Still, the children were exposed to the hostility of their white neighbors. The Careys, a family directly across the way from them, were particularly menacing and provocative. In all likelihood, Willa Mae believed, "it was Mr. Carey that burned the cross in our yard."

Jackie, barely of school age, remembered cries of "nigger, nigger, nigger," as he walked in the street. He ignored the advice of his mother, his brother Edgar, and his sister Willa Mae to close his ears. "Cracker, cracker, cracker," he shouted back—and when the rocks came flying, small as he was, he picked them up and flung them back.

His older brother Mack likewise remembers that winning a couple of fistfights, rather than cheek-turning, helped clear the air: "We just kicked some white ass," he told Maury Allen almost three-quarters of a century later. "Kids aren't so tough when you can knock them down with a punch."

Adults, however, require a different kind of persuasion. Edgar chopped wood and did small favors for a widow who lived next door, a woman who was reputedly the wealthiest person on the block. When a petition was circulated by neighbors trying to drive the Robinsons out, this woman's support was considered crucial, but she remembered Edgar's generosity and refused to go along. Her opposition to the petition and her unwillingness to attempt to buy out the Robinson family was, said Willa Mae, a real turning point.

On the weekends, Mallie was more directly involved. Sundays belonged to the Lord. All the children dressed up and went to Sunday school and church. While there were activities such as card-playing and trips to the movies during the week, none were permitted on Sundays. Paying respect to the Lord represented both spiritual sustenance and collective survival in a social order ruled by racism and poverty.

The mother's teaching was by example. Mrs. Robinson refused to be broken or even limited by circumstances. Her notion of the Lord included a worldly spirit that would always be ready to combat evil through goodness and effort.

The children all understood that their mother's dream was for them to receive, as she had not, a real education. Evenings, when she was home, meant pulling up a chair around a wide oaken table in the kitchen and doing homework. They were expected to bring home passing grades from school, and to show those who meant them harm that, though they might cross the room or cross the yard to avoid conflict, they would not go away.

Her example also included opening her front door to whoever came through. "Their door was never locked," said one family friend. "You could go in any time, day or night, help yourself to anything in the kitchen—everybody in the neighborhood knew that." Family or friends looking for a temporary place to stay referred to the Robinson's house as "the castle" or "the hotel."

Mrs. Robinson came from a large family—fourteen children—and she kept in touch with them. Within several years of the move into the house on Pepper Street, two other sisters and their families moved from the South and eventually found houses in the neighborhood. Another sister and her husband came to California but separated after the birth of a daughter; the husband returned to the South while Mallie's sister, Marylou, briefly moved in with the family. When Marylou collapsed and died one day at work, her infant daughter, Jessica, became a permanent member of the Robinson family, a sixth child in the house—where she remained, except for a brief period when she was eighteen, until she married and moved out in her twenties.

This sixth child, Jessie Maxwell Wills, vividly recalled the hold Mallie had over her children. It was based on a powerful sense of right and wrong. There were "whippings" when there was wrongdoing, but "there wasn't that much actual whipping, that wasn't really the way Mama got to you," Mrs. Wills recalled. "She brought us up believing in God, knowing there was a God and also a true hell."

The "true hell," Mrs. Wills said, in a child's mind included "devils and pitchforks" but something else as well. Each day, before school, Mallie Robinson dressed and groomed her daughters before they left the house. "In getting me ready for school, she'd have to fix my hair, and while she was doing my hair, I was a captive audience. If you had done something wrong the previous day, you were told about it. And I mean there were times when I felt I would rather have had a whipping. Mama's real idea of hell was consciousness. And that stays with you longer than a switch."

At eighteen, when she briefly left the house to live "independently," Jessie Wills recalled that, most of all, she looked forward to doing "what I wanted to do," but found that impossible. "I discovered I wasn't free to do what I wanted because my conscience wouldn't let me. Even though I was not living at home, I still was not free."

As she grew older, Mrs. Wills understood that her mother's idea of hell was even deeper than conscience. "My view now is that hell is being shut off from God," Mrs. Wills said. "I don't dwell on that, but I do know that what Mama was teaching all along was to be in the will of God."

It was this spiritual notion that best explained how Mallie Robinson could be out of the house so much while still maintaining a powerful influence on her children. Living according to the will of God was an active, not an abstract, principle. Faith sustained the family when reason provided little support. From day to day, being in the will of God meant a lifestyle that opened rather than closed the house. With bedrooms on both floors, there was always a cousin, an uncle, or a family lodging with them. With the front door always open, people in the neighborhood came and went as they pleased. The Robinson family was one of the first on the block to have a telephone. The phone was placed on a small table in an alcove under the front stairs, and, said Mrs. Wills, "people from the neighborhood came in all the time and used it, and you know what—they never ran up any long-distance calls either.''

Generosity—even when you were without—was intimately bound up with living in the will of God, which meant that the Robinsons were obliged to do more than return hate for hate.

Willa Walker described the evolution of the family's relationships with their neighbors:

"There was this baker up the street. The bakeries weren't open on Sundays in Pasadena, so one day he told my mother that on Saturday at closing time to have the boys come up with their wagon and that he'd give us bread that he couldn't sell. And he did—including sweets and cookies. We came every week. And sometimes we'd get so much, we gave some of it away. My mother fixed up boxes for people on the street because it was more than we could use. At first, when we went to them, they couldn't figure it out, but then that changed them. They changed towards us. Sometimes the milkman would leave four or five gallons for the Robinson Crusoe family—and we would pass that around the neighborhood too—the poor looking after the poor.''

But the God that demanded respect for others especially demanded self-respect.

Mallie Robinson fit no one's stereotype. She crossed the continent for her children; she crossed the street for no one. She demanded iron discipline; she opened her home. She was, so simple biographical fact says, a mother with a large family, god-fearing, churchgoing, long-suffering. There is a portrait of her in the 1950 movie *The Jackie Robinson Story* that is a period cliché, in keeping with the sanitized picture of her celebrated son.

By most accounts, Mrs. Robinson was not a demonstrative, outgoing woman at all. Though physically imposing, she had a look that could at times seem almost ethereal. In a family picture of her taken when she was in her midthirties, her face, smooth and oval, seems to reflect sensitivity more than durability, youthfulness more than age or experience. The picture of her playfully wrapping herself in cast-off furs is against type, but perhaps closer to the physical truth. So too is the brief sketch of her given years ago by her son Mack:

"We were raising some horses for a man, and I took a horse by the house one day. My mother came out. She got up there and rode the horse sidesaddle. She rode the horse better than I did, and I was astride the horse. She went galloping up the street. I would assume she was about forty years old at the time.''

More than anything, what she transmitted was the sense that the spiritual life she demanded from her children came first from herself. All her children, and especially Jackie, took up the challenge she posed for them in their own way. In the case of her youngest son, that way led through a wilderness with more promise of trouble than reward.

CHAPTER THREE

The re-creation of Jackie Robinson's childhood long ago was shaped by what he later became. There is a folklorish, if unspoken, assumption that those early years have an exotic connection to what followed, much as if his life had been molded by fate, as though Jackie Robinson, the hero with a perfect hero's name, was only waiting for the great time that was surely coming. Nothing could have been further from the truth.

The overriding reality of Robinson's early years was that, for black youth, the future was closed. Simple as that. It didn't take a sociologist or a Jim Crow sign to tell him that schools, jobs, opportunities, careers were severely limited.

What is missing in the Jackie Robinson story as it has been handed down is the period in his life when the principal effect of his mother's teaching was not that the future would work out, but that it would not; when he saw standing up for himself not so much in terms of the church on Sundays but of the street, at any hour of day or night.

According to one friend from his days at Cleveland Elementary School, Robinson was never a sharp student but was better than others at sports. "He could do things in games and sports that other kids could not do," said Sidney Heard.

One of the games played at school was dodgeball, a game requiring quick starting and stopping. The specific moves of the game suggested to Heard an origin for Robinson's later baserunning skills as a major league ballplayer—but in those days it was only child's play, energy to burn. And that is what Jackie Robinson seemed most to have.

He went to and from school, often without food in his belly, sometimes accepting portions of lunch given to him by his teachers; but he seemed to live only for hours of rough and tumble on the streets and playground. His siblings and friends remember that he spent little time indoors. It was home and then out again, into the streets, to the neighboring vacant lots and fields where he could take up any game, anytime.

"When marble time came, he played marbles," Sidney Heard recalled. "We would get up early in the morning and play marbles from eight o'clock to five o'clock. He didn't even take his lunch. We used to draw a big circle, which we used to call a 'Boston.' We would draw a little circle and put the marbles in it and put the agates in. Those were petrified wood almost crystallized and harder than rock. Those were precious marbles—almost like diamonds in those days. We used to put several diamonds, as we called them, in the middle of the circle surrounded by marbles, until we cleaned them out and got to the agates. Boy, that dude Jackie, he cleaned us out. He could concentrate. He could concentrate better than any of us."

Ray Bartlett, another childhood friend and schoolmate at Cleveland Elementary, remembers that Robinson was also outstanding at soccer and handball.

"At lunchtime, we'd have a little time and get into these games. Was he good? He was good at any game he took up. I think maybe soccer and handball required these moves everybody later saw in baseball, but I don't know. He was just an outstanding athlete from the start."

If Robinson was a precocious athlete, he was also bound by his time and place. When he left his house and walked to school, he was conscious that his hometown was full of invisible lines that were not to be crossed.

Yoshi Hasagawa, a junior-high schoolmate of Robinson's, was acutely conscious of these boundaries.

"There weren't signs in the neighborhoods or anything, but you didn't need them. If you were black or Japanese or Mexican, you just made it a point to stay out of those neighborhoods."

The nearly all-white schools reinforced the sense of isolation.

"The teachers were prejudiced, but you just accepted it. We all knew it, but there were so few of us, what could you do?" Hasagawa said. "The way they would do it varied. They would just exclude us from things sometimes, other times they'd blame you for something first, before anyone else. Very often they were just plain rude—or they wouldn't pass us in a course, they'd leave us behind to repeat a grade—they didn't use racial epithets or anything, but they didn't have to."

Everyday prejudice was Robinson's silent companion wherever he went, to and from school, to the neighboring parks, to the segregated movie theaters, to the curbside "markets" where the Bond-bread truck, the vegetable truck, the milk truck, sold their wares because most local food merchants refused to welcome nonwhites in their stores.

"I remember, even as a small boy, having a lot of pride in my mother," Robinson recalled. "I thought she must have some kind of magic to be able to do all the things she did, to work so hard and never complain and to make us all feel happy. . . . My pride in my mother was tempered with a sense of sadness that she had to bear most of our burdens. At a very early age I began to want to relieve her in any small way I could. I was happy whenever I had money to give her."

But sensitivity to his mother's plight and a willingness to lighten her load were not at all the only ways, or even the most important ways, in which Robinson reacted to life in Pasadena:

"Along with a number of other children in the neighborhood, I had a lot of free time, and a lot of freedom. Some of it I put to good use— I had a paper route, I cut grass and ran errands when I could. The rest of the time, I stole—all sorts of small things from stores, particularly food—and I was a member in good standing of the Pepper Street gang."

Much has been made of Robinson's early membership in a youth gang. It has been fairly pointed out that street gangs then and now have little in common. But the idea, conveyed by a number of Robinson's biographers, that a street gang then was only a social club with some rough edges is also misleading.

The Pepper Street gang didn't have a clubhouse where they opened bottles of soda pop, they didn't carry secret badges or compose letters in code. They had fun together, say the surviving members—but their "fun" inevitably brought them into contact with the police.

The gang, just for kicks, diverted or stopped traffic in their neighborhood by pelting passing cars with rocks or clods of dirt; they knocked out local streetlamps, smashed windows, raided local orchards—orchards that were regularly patrolled by armed guards. One time, the gang tarred the lawn of a homeowner who had taunted them with racial epithets. Robinson's mother, when she found out about the incident, forced her son and his friends to clean up the gummy mess down to the last blade of grass.

The gang, led by Jackie, used to secret themselves alongside the fairways of local golf courses so they could steal balls from the course and then sell them back to unsuspecting or unresisting golfers in the midst of play. There is a story, told by Sidney Heard, where a passing golfer, accosted in the middle of a fairway by Jackie looking to sell him back his own ball, challenged Jackie to finish out the hole. If the golfer won, Robinson would return the ball; if Robinson won, he could keep the ball and win an additional dollar. Robinson agreed. The golfer handed him a putter and took a seven iron for himself. Robinson, who had never played golf in his life, won by nearly holing out.

But the fun and games had another side. The police were never very far behind them, and the principal target of their interest among gang members was always Jackie Robinson. Jackie was known to be nervier, more impulsive, more heedless of authority. Jack Gordon, a childhood friend, remembers that he and Jackie regularly went to the movies together, and invariably Robinson started trouble of one kind or another.

"Whenever there was a newsreel of Joe Louis," Gordon said, "Jackie would start up going *Wham! Bam! Pow!* stuff like that—man, he would just carry on, you couldn't stop him. And sure enough, they'd come over and ask us to leave."

And then, whenever they were in a segregated theater, Robinson insisted on switching seats as soon as the lights went down. "I'd go right along with him," Gordon said. "We'd go over and sit in the other section, they'd come over and get us to move . . . and they had cops in those days, they'd call them the minute there was any kind of trouble."

There was trouble even in the one theater in town that was patronized almost exclusively by minorities, a theater Gordon said was referred to derisively by whites as "The Garlic Opera House." "With Jack, we even had trouble there, that theater of all places!"

In junior high school, as his athletic abilities were becoming more widely known, Robinson used to playfully tease other students on the way home from school. Yoshi Hasagawa, two years younger than Robinson, remembers him chasing her and a girlfriend one afternoon after school: "He picked both of us up in his arms and deposited us in a trash can, you know, like with our legs sticking out! He was just having a good time with us."

Jack Gordon remembered a time around July Fourth somewhat

later on, when Robinson and several friends rode into downtown Los Angeles one evening, and the friends got more "fun" than they had bargained for:

"We rode in this old raggy pickup truck—the padded seat was a box, you know. We went up to Valverty first, there wasn't much doing, there was a swimming pool, the place was dusty. Jack loved firecrackers and he wound up getting some there, and then we went on into L.A. There must have been five or six of us. We came in along Central Avenue, which is like One Hundred and Twenty-fifth Street. I'll never forget it, this guy was standing on the street corner wearing one of these real sharp zoot suits, his hand was on the post, he was real fat and jolly, the whole thing—and Jack took a firecracker and tossed it. The thing not only scared the guy half to death, it blew a hole in his suit, you could see the smoke on his jacket—and then when he cursed us out, Jack just laughed his head off. And then we returned to Pasadena. Before we got home, though, Jack lit another firecracker and tossed it in the back of the truck where all the other guys were. *Boom!* Just like that! He was so mischievous, he was more mischievous than anything."

"Devilish more than anything," said Gordon's wife, Rudi, who also grew up with Robinson in Pasadena.

Robinson never planned trouble or particularly looked for it, he just let his moods carry him. Jack Gordon remembers that he and Robinson used to frequent a local Woolworth's and would sometimes go over to the lunch counter for something to eat.

"They'd never wait on us, you know. There was no law or anything, they just wouldn't serve us, so Jack would just want to sit. He'd insist on it, until they came over and finally served us. No matter how long it took. I told my sister a few years ago, 'Ya know, we were sitting in and we didn't even know what the hell we were doing.' "

When local swimming pools were opened for blacks one day a week (the day the water was changed), Robinson, said Gordon, used to climb the highest diving board and cannonball himself into the pool, over and over again, "making these splashes that were like explosions, so that the guards had to come over and put a stop to it."

And then, during the heat waves, Robinson induced his friends to swim in the local reservoir. Ultimately, the police learned of this and surrounded the reservoir and flushed out Robinson and his companions, who went scurrying naked into the hillside underbrush. As Robinson related the story to Carl Rowan, a sheriff's deputy taunted them, "Look there, niggers swimming in my drinking water." And then, when the youths were arrested and taken to jail, one of the sixteen, crowded into a small cell, pleaded that he he was hot and thirsty. The sheriff said, "The coon's hungry. Go buy a watermelon." According to the story, watermelon was then actually purchased and sliced and handed to Robinson and his friends, who were mockingly photographed by the police as they ate the fruit.

During Robinson's teens, he was increasingly singled out by police. Whenever there was trouble of any kind in the streets involving youth, he was brought into the station house for questioning. A local police captain named Morgan, said to be sympathetic to young people and their problems, was—according to several accounts of Robinson's life —the one person who stood between Robinson and jail. Yet even this Captain Morgan fueled an already gathering resentment in young Jackie.

"The Pepper Street gang included boys of Mexican, Japanese, Negro, and Caucasian background," wrote Carl Rowan, "and Morgan would call each racial group in separately for his lecture. Afterwards, the boys would compare notes with great laughter. Morgan would say to the Japanese: 'If you keep associating with these Negroes, they're going to get you into trouble'; and to the Negroes: 'If you keep running around with these Japs, you're going to wind up in the reformatory'; and to the Caucasians: 'A white boy is just asking for trouble when he keeps running around with these colored fellows.' "

The one person who assuredly did help keep Robinson from a reformatory was his mother. Jackie, like his siblings, had a roster of chores to do along with his homework and Sunday obligations. He, like his cousin Jessie, knew the meaning and reality of hell. Then, midway through Robinson's teens, a new Pasadena minister, Karl Downs, arrived on the scene.

Downs was unlike any other minister Robinson knew. For one thing, he was young, in his twenties, not so far removed from the gang members he reached out to. A red-haired African-American—like Malcolm X—with a strong, athletic build, he was much like the street youths himself. Downs knew the humiliations of prejudice as well as

33

any of them—only his answer had been to become a minister. He appeared one day on a street corner near Morton and Mountain, the favorite hangout of the Pepper Street gang, and asked for the youngster he knew was the leader of the gang.

"Is Jackie Robinson here?" he asked. No one answered, least of all Robinson, who eyed Downs with suspicion and curiosity. In time, the Reverend Mr. Downs, who had made it a point to check with local authorities, school officials, and neighborhood people about the condition of young people in the city, induced Robinson and the others to give his church program a try—just that, no more—so they could see for themselves that he was offering them team sports, a good time, and someone who was always willing to listen.

"Red" was a basketball player, a softball player, a man who would have been an athlete himself if he had not first turned to the ministry. Above all, he turned out to be a friend. He helped young people find jobs, secured parcels of aid for their families, provided counseling for anyone anytime. Downs eventually got members of the Pepper Street gang to help build a youth center in the church. The center became for Robinson, said one friend, "a place where he could always go to get straightened out." After a time, Robinson became a volunteer Sunday-school teacher in Downs' church.

Perhaps more than anything, more than his mother's influence or that of Karl Downs, what moved Jackie Robinson away from trouble and even crime was sports. It was his enormous good fortune to have been born, like his brothers and sisters, with a talent that separated him from others. From junior high on, his prowess on the playing field became apparent far beyond his immediate circle of friends and classmates. He was confronted with possibilities and challenges that he would not otherwise have had, but because of that, the way ahead was anything but simple. In fact, the growing awareness in Robinson of his ability only made the future seem darker, more threatening. He had to look no further than his brother Mack, four and half years older than himself, gifted beyond calculation, to understand that prodigious talent matched to black skin could mean nothing at all.

CHAPTER FOUR

"If there was one person Jack idolized growing up, it was his brother Mack," Willa Mae Walker said. Mack Robinson was a star in Jack's eyes. Long before Mack joined organized games in school, before he joined teams and programs, Mack had speed and ability—and a reputation.

Years later, Mack remembered that early period. "We used to play a game as kids called Chase the Fox," he told a reporter. "We'd all stand around in a circle until somebody broke out, and then everybody tried to catch him. When I was the fox, I was pretty hard to catch."

Initially Jackie, just a tag-along youngster, never tried to catch the fox. He was a delighted observer. Later, when Mack was a standout player on various softball, basketball, and baseball teams, Jack, because he was so good himself, joined in.

When Mack reached junior high, a major change occurred in his life. With a promising athletic career opening before him, a heart murmur was discovered in a routine physical. Further testing confirmed the finding, and school authorities then banned him from all sports. Mack was devastated—and unwilling to accept the verdict. He badgered his mother until she went to school to plead for him. School officials ultimately allowed Mack to participate in noncontact sports only—which meant track. Mrs. Robinson had to sign a letter absolving the school of responsibility if anything should happen.

Mack became a local legend at his sport, first for Washington Junior High, then for Muir Tech and Pasadena Junior College. As an eighth-grade sprinter and hurdler, Mack set a statewide junior-high-school record in the high hurdles that lasted for over a quarter of a century. At Muir, he was an undefeated state champion in the 100-yard dash. At Pasadena, he dominated the school's track team. He was an unmatched short sprinter, but was even better in the 220 and 440. In 1937, he set a national AAU record in the broad jump at 25' 5½".

What Mack is most remembered for, what he himself cherished, was being a member of the 1936 Olympic team and finishing second to Jesse Owens in the 200-meter dash at the Berlin Games.

"The games were broadcast on the radio, and all of us used to sit up in the kitchen at three o'clock in the morning listening because that was the time the Games came on. We were all so excited—especially Jack," Willa Mae Walker recalled.

Mack came into the Games determined and fit. There is a picture of him from that era that would be appropriate for a Grecian urn. He has a lean, powerfully built, almost perfect athlete's body. His shoulders are broad, his waist narrow, his strong upper thighs taper to long-muscled lower legs. He is all sinew and grace, his face dark and handsome, a glowering mask of ambition and accomplishment. He looks like the hero he was.

The Games were a turning point for him—and in retrospect for his brother too.

To the world, Mack's second-place finish to Jesse Owens was anything but noteworthy. Owens's four gold medals were the sports story of the year. Owens' accomplishments became an inspiring (if ironic) symbol of the era—democracy standing up to Hitler's nightmare vision of Aryan supremacy.

Mack, however, believed he should have won the gold in the 200, not Jesse Owens. "I led Jesse all the way in the trials until he nipped me in the last stride," he told a reporter years later. He also confessed that he had been wearing an old pair of spikes that day, spikes that pinched his feet. He said that if he had been able to afford a new pair, he would have beaten Owens. "I told Jesse the same thing," he said.

Mack's closest friends and relatives knew something else. When they saw the films of the race, they noticed that Mack looked over his shoulder coming down the stretch, a fatal mistake.

"The funny thing about that," Jack Gordon said, "was that Mack always used to tell the guys in school when he came there, 'Don't look around, it costs you steps.' At the 200 meters, he had Jesse Owens beat—and he looked around! When he came back home, I said, 'Mack, why did you look around?' He said, 'I don't know.' "

Marty Glickman, the sportscaster who was a teammate of Mack's and later a friend of Robinson's, believed there was something in Mack that made him a second-place finisher—second to Jesse Owens, second to Jackie. Glickman was also aware that the pressure of internal politics on the track team was significant and not very pretty.

At the Randall's Island trials for the 1936 Games, Mack was expected to qualify in a number of events. It did not work out that way.

In the 100-meter dash, which some observers thought he might win, he finished dead last in the final heat. That complicated his opportunities in other races and undoubtedly weighed on his confidence. He qualified in the 200-meter race, but a question arose over his placement on any of the relay teams. Originally, the sprinters who finished fourth, fifth, sixth, and seventh in the 100-meter, which would have included Mack, were going to run relay. But in Berlin, when the Americans heard that the German team had "hidden" their top sprinters for the relays, changes were made. Glickman and Sam Stoller, because they were Jewish and because host sensibilities came first, were excluded. Mack, who had run so poorly in the trials, was also taken off the relay team.

"The morning of the day we were supposed to run," Glickman recalled, "the seven sprinters, Mack being the seventh, were called into a meeting, and we were told [Sam and I] were going to be replaced by Jesse [Owens] and Ralph [Metcalfe]. We were told there was a rumor that the Germans were hiding their very best sprinters to save them to upset the team in the four-hundred-meter relay. The guys were upset. Mack didn't say anything. Sam and I spoke up because we were brash eighteen-year-olds and what did we know? When Jesse tried to say something, he was told to shut up and do as he was told. That was the way it was then. Mack was not even considered for the relay because he had done so badly in the one hundred."

The Americans eventually won the 400-meter relay, but none of the members of the team ever forgot the arbitrary treatment they received—and the reasons for it. For a pair of young Jewish athletes, what had been decided was raw, ugly, and irreducible. For Mack Robinson, the issue was more complicated and, in some ways, even more painful.

Race—that is, skin color—played a role in the American victory in the 400.

"We won the race by at least fifteen yards," Glickman said. "The Germans were fourth. If you see Leni Riefenstahl's film of the Games, there's no one else at the finish line except Frank Wyckoff. In a race like the 400, that kind of lead was just amazing. But that hides another part of the story. Wyckoff was not our fastest finisher—Metcalfe was. But they wanted a white guy, a southern-California white guy there at the finish. Jesse, of all people, was the starter, and he had a bad start. He was absolutely mediocre at that position."

Mack Robinson, said Glickman, was surly and private through those Olympic days. He seemed to have no friends. After the Games, the American Olympic team toured Europe. Everywhere the team went, according to newspaper accounts, there were convincing victories—Mack ran a record-tying 200-meter race in Paris—and the runners were accorded all the respect of Olympic champions. That is, until they arrived in the United States.

"There were no ticker-tape parades, no plaques, no nothing," Mack remembered years later. "The first night home we were segregated by color in different hotels."

The Germans and Hitler made little impression on Mack. Compared to his white countrymen, they seemed almost benign.

"As far as I can remember," he said, "not one of the eleven Negro athletes on the Olympic track team ever mentioned Hitler's name during the Games. He was the head of state, not the one handing out medals. We were treated very well by the Germans."

The fact that the German press carried virulent, racist cartoons depicting the black athletes apparently went unnoticed by Mack. It was American racism he was born to and American racism waiting for him as soon as he checked through customs in New York.

"I just said to myself 'the hell with it' and went home. But it wasn't any different in Pasadena. They didn't do anything either."

To those who knew him best, Mack was a profoundly changed man when he came back. "It was like he was two different people," said Willa Mae Walker. "You couldn't talk to him, it was like he had gotten so swell-headed, so full of himself. He had this leather Olympic jacket and he would never take it off. My mother used to joke that Mack must have gotten crazy from being so high up in the airplane he traveled on."

In Pasadena, as elsewhere, the Depression was in full swing. Mack's silver medal no more qualified him for a job than his Pepper Street address. When he did finally locate something, it was as a streetsweeper, working the midnight shift.

The job was demeaning as well as punishing. Because it was a night job, it interfered with his training, as it did with his fondness for good times. He was soon to be married to the first of five wives. Absenteeism and the discovery that he sometimes spent the night elsewhere after checking into work led to his eventual firing.

The future, as Mack saw it, seemed to hold little more than extending an amateur running career for a few more seasons, perhaps into the next Olympics. And then, with the coming of world war, when the Games were indefinitely suspended, that hope faded too. What was left was anger and bitterness.

Sometime after the Olympics, Jack Gordon recalled, Karl Downs organized a group of runners from the Pasadena area, loaned them a car, and sent them to a meet in Prairie View, Texas. Mack was the pickup team's adviser and coach. Uppermost in his mind, Gordon realized, was not how well the team would do but who Mack Robinson was.

"We got down there, it was so funny," Gordon said. "Mack was the spokesman. And who's there but Ralph Metcalfe, coaching one of the college teams at the meet. Metcalfe, of course, knew Mack well, and after we had run against a freshman team from USC, I think, Mack goes off to this meeting and comes back to tell us that we aren't going to be allowed to run. He says we can only run exhibition. We were supposed to run in the 880 relay against Loyola, a top-notch team; they went on to the Penn Relays, and if we beat them, maybe we would have had a chance. But now it's only exhibition and because of that, Mack says, okay, he's going to run, he's going to anchor. Well, it so happens that he had entered and won the broad jump, and in the process he had pulled a hamstring. That didn't stop him. He was still gonna run, said it was only exhibition. I said to him, 'Mack, how can you do that, you've even got a bad leg?' Mack just wanted the glory. Everybody there was pulling for us, too—and we lost by a hair, we lost just because Mack wanted to anchor."

The person most directly affected by Mack's life change was Jackie. Because he had idolized him, learned from him, worshiped him, saw him as a role model for his own athletic career, Robinson was forced to rearrange his thinking. As he had in the past, he vied with Mack in track; from the time Jack was in high school, they ran and jumped, flip-flopping first and second places in local meets. Only now, Robinson understood that winning or losing could provoke feelings in his brother Robinson had not perceived before.

"Mack was jealous of Jack," Willa Mae Walker said, "and he let him know it. Jack couldn't understand any of it."

Within a year of his return from the Olympics, after he had lost his job with the city, Mack had another opportunity—this time to go to the University of Oregon on an athletic scholarship. He accepted. There would be a few more months, a season, perhaps two, to keep his skills honed.

For Jack, especially with Mack away from Pasadena for a while, the future looked somewhat different. Jack had no illusions about where an athletic career might lead, but at least now he no longer had to live in the shadow of his gifted brother. When Jackie Robinson set foot in Pasadena Junior College in the fall of 1937, he was on his own. Left to himself, Robinson was about to become the most accomplished all-around athlete this nation ever produced.

CHAPTER FIVE

By the time he entered junior college, Jackie Robinson had been earning his own reputation for some time, in all sports, not just one. With astonishing energy he went from one to the other, almost as if what he did became markers for the seasons in California's perennial summer.

He had been a baseball star since grade school:

"I was in the ninth grade then, he was in the seventh, and we were on different teams," recalled Shigeo Takayama, who, like Jack Gordon, attended McKinley Junior High. "We were shortstops on our respective teams and we played against each other. He just amazed me. I thought I was a hotshot, other people said I was good. But he was just outstanding, he humbled me. His team was the best in the area, but only because of him. He was the team."

It was the same story in other sports. At Muir, Robinson's game-breaking ability as a runner made the school a powerhouse, and other teams turned nearly criminal in their efforts to stop him. In a conference championship game against Glendale High in 1936, played in the Rose Bowl, he was blindsided early in the game after a whistle had blown. The hit was deliberate, breaking two of his ribs, forcing him to the sidelines, after which Glendale went on to win.

In basketball, he was the leading scorer, rebounder, passer. In track, Jack's schoolmates, who knew all about Mack, learned early that Jackie was something more than a younger rival and shadow:

"We used to have these pentathlons for all the junior high classes," Shigeo Takayama said. "Every student had to go through these events; we had to run fifty yards, high jump, broad jump, do different things, and after you acquired a certain number of points, you competed to see who would have the highest total. I don't remember if he won everything, he probably did, but I remember the broad jump. I thought I was good in that, but he consistently outjumped me by a foot, a foot and a half. And he was no bigger than me then. I was five two, five three, he was no taller."

Jackie, like Mack, was not bashful about letting others know how

41

good he was. But his whirlwind drive, intensity, determination to win, more than any itch for recognition, powered him. Like Mack, his talent—and the fact that he was a black star in the Milky Way— isolated him, or at least made him cautious whenever he reached out beyond the immediate circle of his friends and neighborhood. Impulse, the flash of anger, and his own skill combined to project him constantly into danger or accomplishment.

In junior high school, Jack Gordon was a second-string quarterback for McKinley, a rival of Washington, Robinson's school. Gordon, like any other youngster in the area, had heard a lot about Jackie, but had not yet met him. He was at choir practice one day ("That's the way you met everybody in small towns then," he said), and Robinson suddenly appeared before him:

"We were scheduled to play each other, it was going to be a really big game. So I'm standing there with my wife-to-be, not yet a girl-friend—there were a couple of girlfriends—and Jack walks up. Out of a clear blue sky. Didn't say hello, didn't introduce himself or any-thing. Just walks up and says, 'I hear you were lucky in your last game. How are you gonna go ninety-eight yards for a touchdown against us?' And he walked away. They went out and beat us six to nothing, they were bigger, stronger, faster. Didn't say a word to me during the game. We didn't talk after that till we both got to junior college together."

Mack's reputation as a big-time athlete continued to push Jackie. Between the fall of 1937 and the spring of 1939, Robinson became perhaps the most widely followed athlete in the area. He was the standout on a football team that lost only two games and that was undefeated in eleven games in his final season. He was the top scorer on his basketball team, the best player in the conference; he led his baseball team to a conference championship in 1938, the same year he broke Mack's national junior-college AAU record in the broad jump.

The breaking of that record is one of the foundations of the legend Robinson built around himself before he was even out of his teens. The meet was scheduled on the same spring day that the baseball team was playing its championship game, forty miles away. Robinson had an old Studebaker, and a friend drove it, first to the track meet in Pomona, then to the baseball game in Glendale.

"I don't remember whether I drove or it was my wife's brother,

Johnny Burke," said Jack Gordon. "But we went out there, me, my wife and her brother, and Jack, and we got a flat on the way. So we're standing out there on the road, and a guy pulled up—John O'Mara, he was the dean of students—and it turned out his spare tire fit Jack's car! So that's how we got there. Of course he never got the tire back. Whenever we saw him on campus, we'd go the other way!"

At the track meet, Robinson had no time to take warm-ups, he simply took his four competitive jumps, making his record 25' 6½" leap on his final try.

Back in the car, Clark Kent changed uniforms and emerged in Glendale in midgame, to contribute a couple of hits and a stolen base in his team's title victory. Jack Gordon remembered the game and, particularly, the stolen base:

"Jack was on first, had got a hit. I remember this because the day was really windy, kicking up dust all over the place. Jack took his lead, then bent down and kept picking up handfuls of dust, which he'd toss in the air. The wind blew the dust from first to third, right in the pitcher's eyes, so he had to keep brushing it away. That's when Jack stole the base. He was so smart. Even then."

Duke Snider, then an area schoolboy, claimed Robinson was his idol growing up. He too knew some tales from the planet Krypton. "I saw Jackie when he was in Pasadena Junior College and I was in junior high school," he said in his autobiography. "Five or six of us kids saw him play a baseball game, leave in the middle of it with his uniform still on to trot over to compete in the broad jump in a track meet, and then run back and finish the baseball game just as if nothing unusual had happened. That's how great and versatile he was, and how bright the fire of competition burned in him.

"I have another early memory of Jackie Robinson. I was in the eighth grade when he was playing football for Pasadena, the big rival of our own school, Compton Junior College. I was in the stands when he took a kickoff, reversed his field three times, and returned it for a touchdown. It was as dazzling a piece of broken-field running as you could ever hope to see."

As spectacular as these accomplishments were, there is almost a misleading ease in the telling, because the way was never so easy. As Mack's career so richly illustrated, talent coupled to race created conditions that could always keep hope in check.

In Jackie's first weeks at Pasadena J.C., he turned up for football practice, expecting a place on the team as a starting tailback, only to find a near boycott by a group of white players from Oklahoma who had been recruited into the program by the coach, Tom Mallory. At an initial practice, the conflict between the white players and the team's three black players was so severe that the practice was canceled.

Jack Gordon, playing basketball at a court adjoining the field, saw the players coming off. "I said, 'What, are you guys through already?' Jackie answered, 'Naw, they don't want to play with us.' "

For a while it appeared there could be no reconciling the split. The Oklahoma players, according to Gordon, "I don't think they had ever been out of Oklahoma, their talk was just thick, thick, thick southern drawl. Man, you knew where they were coming from!"

But a truce was eventually established by the coach, and largely through the insistence of Jackie and Ray Bartlett, the players, black and white, became a unit. (Jackie's determination to see something through was later to impress Branch Rickey when he was doing research on Robinson's background.)

But those first days, Robinson's peculiarly ambiguous position as a star athlete but also just another black youth manifested itself in another way. During a scrimmage one afternoon, he twisted an ankle. The injury was so painful he had to leave the field limping, but no one on the coaching staff, from the head coach to the trainer, thought to have the injury evaluated. He could walk, he was not making much of it, it was assumed he had a sprain of some kind. His ankle was bandaged and he was told to go on about his business. A day or so later, after he had continued to play on it, his friend Jack Gordon noticed that he was in obvious pain. The pair had gone to a local movie house and Robinson kept fidgeting and grimacing in pain, finally acknowledging, "It's my ankle, it's killing me."

Because it was the weekend, Gordon said, no school facilities were open, so the pair visited the emergency room of a local hospital. Robinson's ankle was X-rayed and turned out to be broken. The break did not require a cast, but it had clearly been exacerbated by the initial neglect in permitting him to walk and even play on it. The injury, to one degree or another, affected him for the rest of his life.

In Robinson's second year, the football team had a scheduled game

44

against a junior college in Phoenix. When the team arrived in Arizona, the black players expected to be housed with their teammates. They discovered instead that the accommodations were segregated.

"We weren't allowed to stay in the same hotel with the rest of the team, with the white players," Ray Bartlett said. "We had to stay in a place that was like a house converted to a hotel. I remember the name of it well: the Rice Hotel."

The coaches denied knowing that the team was going to be segregated, but no one believed them. Robinson, Bartlett, and two other players, Larry Pickens and Jim Wright, were so upset they refused to take the rooms offered them.

"I don't remember any of us going to bed. I think we just sat up and talked in the lobby area and maybe we slept sitting up in the chairs," said Ray Bartlett.

The humiliating reminders of boundaries and unequal treatment were as obvious to Robinson and his friends as the air they breathed. James Baldwin, a little less than two decades later, wrote, "I can conceive of no Negro native to this country who has not, by the age of puberty, been irreparably scarred by the conditions of his life." The scarring in Robinson's case, like that of his brother Mack, formed a peculiar pattern with medals and honors.

At Pasadena, Jackie and two other athletes were the first blacks ever named to the student honor society, the Lancers. In all, the society consisted of about twenty members, and Robinson and his friends later joked that they were the ones who "integrated" the group. But as Lancers, aside from the characteristic black sweaters they wore with their vividly emblazoned letters, they were aware that their privileges were ambiguous.

On Friday nights, when there were no games at the Rose Bowl, there were events—concerts, movies—at the Civic Auditorium. Seating there, though never mandated by race, was segregated in practice. Robinson and his fellow black Lancers prowled the balcony where black students habitually sat, urging them to get up and go downstairs —to no avail.

Robinson regarded academics lightly. He was, at best, a barely passing student, not because he was incapable of doing better but because he had, like Mack, decided on some fundamental level that there was little for him to get from school beyond sports.

On the weekends, during vacation time, and in the summer, there were games in Brookside Park, nights on the loose up at Mountain and Morton, or car rides down to L.A. He had a girlfriend, Bessie, who "ran" with the Pepper Street gang, but it was hard to say Robinson was actually serious about her or anyone then. He gave little thought to the future beyond games and good times that could, in a flash, become something else.

As a competitor, Robinson's temperament was as widely known as his ability. Because other teams keyed on him, because he was an on-field target from grade school on, he learned early to fight back. He never knowingly permitted an opponent to get away with anything.

In one notorious encounter between Long Beach State and Pasadena in basketball, the word had gone out that Jackie Robinson was going to be stopped—one way or another.

"I ran into Jack's brother, Frank, and a cousin of theirs, Van Wade, and they said there was liable to be real trouble at this game," Jack Gordon said. "Frank had a tire iron with him. I said to him, 'What are you doing with that?' He says that Long Beach plays dirty basketball. And sure enough, the guy guarding Jack keeps sticking his fingers in his face, right in his mouth. Well, he does it one more time, puts his finger in Jack's mouth—and this time Jack nearly bit it off. After that, everybody came out of the stands. *Boom!* It was like somebody had thrown a match. Everybody was out there and it seemed like they were all carrying pipes! It was so bad they wound up canceling all future competition between the schools."

In another game, a shouting match between Jackie and opposing players degenerated into a running battle of foulmouthed epithets that could be heard all over the gym—to the point where, afterward, Robinson was reprimanded by his own coach. On his way to becoming a junior-college all-American in football in 1938, an all-conference basketball player, and a national-record holder in track, Jackie's competitive fury boiled over again and again. Whether it came to blows, giving back harder than he got, or unleashing torrents of verbal abuse, everyone had by then learned that Robinson's game was set to a hair trigger.

Jackie's friends knew that his moods away from the playing field were equally volatile and unpredictable. The good-natured rides down to L.A. continued. Often Robinson and his friends went down to Third

Street, to catch a movie, drop in on the Follies. Robinson had a fondness for cowboy movies, said Jack Gordon, particularly those that included Ralph Cooper, the only well-known black cowboy of the era. The Follies featured strippers and comics such as Joe Ewell, Mickey Rooney's father. Before the shows, if anyone had money, they would stop and buy clothing at one of the bargain stores on Third and Main.

Before and after, anything could happen. One night, Gordon remembered, they were riding along and Jackie picked up a luggage strap that was in the car, whipped it out the window, and snagged a passing bicyclist, pulling him to the ground—just for laughs.

Then there was a postmidnight stop at a fruit stand. Jackie noticed there was only one attendant in the place. The friends, spurred on by Jackie, piled out of the car, went into the market ostensibly to buy ten cents' worth of fruit—but actually to pilfer what they could carry—until the clerk confronted them. The fruit was laughingly returned before serious trouble developed.

There was no fun at all in an incident that boiled over following a softball game one October evening in Brookside Park. Ray Bartlett remembered that Robinson and he were in a car together and that a white motorist trying to pass them shouted out racial insults. "Called us a bunch of niggers, I think, something like that," Bartlett said. "Anyway, I was on the side of the car and I hit the guy with my glove, and then I don't know exactly what happened. We pulled over, he pulled over—and I withdrew because I was afraid of what my mother might do. But Jack, he just kept at it, you couldn't stop him."

In no time, the area was flooded by neighborhood people—and then by police. Jack Gordon, who was also one of the passengers in Robinson's car and who was closer to the melee than Bartlett, noticed that one of the policemen, obviously fearful, reached for his gun.

"This cop was surrounded by blacks—we called them 'colored' in those days—and so he starts for his gun and this guy Woodrow Cunningham, I'll never forget it, puts his hand on the guy's holster and says, 'No, no, don't do that, you're wrong.' But then the next thing we knew, they had Jack and they took him off to jail."

What had begun as an altercation between motorists had blossomed into a near race riot, and Jackie Robinson was the one who was going to answer for it. He was hauled in and booked for blocking a street,

47

suspicion of robbery, and resisting arrest. Those who had followed to the jail tried to intercede, to no avail. Because of the continuing tension, the excessive jitteriness of the police, or just their determination to assert authority, Robinson, following his booking, was immediately placed in a cell for the night and, according to one report, was refused permission to make his single telephone call until the following morning.

Robinson's cell was on the top floor of the jail, and for a time his friends remained in the street below. Jackie shouted down to them, they to him. He asked that his old baseball coach at Pasadena be called to help out. Jack Gordon remembers making the call to Thurman himself, telling him what happened.

"[Thurman] just blew his top. 'What the hell is Jack doing this time? What's he in jail for?' I explained it to him as best I could, and then I had to go off to my job," Gordon said.

Robinson was released on bond the next morning. But a condition of his bail was an implicit acknowledgment of the charges against him —which were still pending.

It is not clear who counseled him or interceded on his behalf. One report names Coach Thurman and other officials at Pasadena, another says that unidentified persons at UCLA were the ones—but in any case, the advice Robinson got was to skip his scheduled court hearing, pay a small fine, and rest assured that the incident would quietly be expunged from the record.

Instead, on October 19, 1939, the *Los Angeles Times* carried a skewed and highly prejudicial account of the episode and of the fact that Jackie had skipped out on a scheduled court appearance, thereby forfeiting his bond. Far from having the charges "disappear," a single count of blocking a street was entered against him, a permanent part of his record. Even beyond its personal significance, the event carried extra weight because by then Jackie Robinson, barely a month on campus, was the spectacular new star of the UCLA Bruins' football team.

CHAPTER SIX

Jackie Robinson's arrival at UCLA in the fall of 1939 was not nearly as direct a transition as geography would suggest. The distance between Pasadena and Westwood was short, but the road was tortuous and filled with unforeseen turns. It was almost as if fate, not choice, was guiding the way.

In his final year at Pasadena Junior College, from which he graduated in the spring of 1939, Jackie had become one of the most highly recruited athletes on the West Coast. His exploits had drawn representatives from four-year schools one after the other to his home on Pepper Street. There were major offers from Washington and Washington State, remembered Ray Bartlett, who also received offers from those schools. "We thought we might get an even break up there, but the weather was no good," he joked. Jackie received other offers, though. One recruiter not only offered him a full scholarship, but a designated girlfriend as well, along with a fully paid apartment near campus for Jackie's mother. Another recruiter simply tossed the keys to a brand-new Dodge on Robinson's front porch as he left the house following a visit.

Mack Robinson tried, he said, to induce Jackie to think of Oregon, his school, and noted, "I also tried to persuade Oregon to offer Jackie a scholarship. I told them he could make any team on campus. But I guess they just thought I was trying to get a free ride for my brother. They ignored him."

But Oregon's indifference was unusual. Among the offers that poured in was one from UCLA, a school Bartlett believed "would give us a better chance as Negroes than we would get at USC." The director of athletics at the time, Bill Spaulding, later told Dodger executive Arthur Mann that he wondered whether it had been right to take Jackie because "he was so good at everything, I was afraid our four coaches would start fighting among themselves."

So convinced were UCLA recruiters of Robinson's special athletic gifts that they were willing to pay his tuition and expenses at a four-year school outside the state if he chose not to accept their scholarship offer—just to keep him from the clutches of competing schools.

For a variety of reasons, UCLA wound up with the inside track. Robinson had never lived away from home for any length of time and was not eager to do so now. In addition, his brother Frank, who had become his number one fan and something of a self-appointed career counselor, favored the UCLA bid.

Jackie's relationship with Frank was most important at this time. Frank, several years older than Jack, was the least athletic of the Robinsons, though he was reported to have possessed more than ordinary skills in track and field. His build was slight, he was shorter than his more famous brothers, and his temperament was milder, without Jack's fire or Mack's boastfulness. But he was intense, loyal, and devoted. He attended all of Jackie's games and meets. He was a regular on Friday nights at the Rose Bowl when as many as thirty-five thousand people (the entire population of Pasadena then was only slightly more than fifty thousand) turned up for PJC games. Where Mack was Jack's rival, Frank was simply his brother.

Frank watched Jackie closely and memorized his moves, his mistakes, his opportunities. He scouted opposing teams and continually sought ways to enhance his brother's skills—and Jackie in turn not only listened and tried to apply Frank's teaching, but confided in him. Because Frank was so clearly devoted and bright, Jackie reached out to him as he did not to anyone else.

But on May 10, 1939, Jackie was at the home of a neighborhood friend, playing cards, when another friend, Carl Anderson, suddenly turned up and said there was a phone call at his house and that Jackie should come immediately. Robinson was told that Frank had been in a motorcycle accident. There was no word about injuries, but the local police might know more.

When Robinson got to the police station, he was sent on to the hospital. At the hospital, he found his brother in critical condition. He lay in agony in his hospital room, begging anyone who would listen just to turn him over and let him die. The sight of his brother in such pain, wrote Carl Rowan, was more than Jackie could bear: "Jackie dashed out of the hospital sobbing. He ran home and fell into bed, pulling the pillows over his head." The next day, after Frank had died, Jackie sat with his mother in the kitchen of their home, listening to her numbly recite again how she should have turned her son over "and let him die like he wanted to."

The death of Frank, who was married and had two young children, ironically determined for Robinson where his future lay. He accepted the UCLA scholarship not because it was better than any other but because he wanted to be near both Mallie and Frank's family.

Jackie went to UCLA as a commuter and was one of approximately thirty black students out of several thousand on campus. He traveled to and from Pasadena by bus or in his old Studebaker. He, like Ray Bartlett, who also accepted a scholarship at the school, worked to support himself. In later years, the only job Jackie acknowledged having was as a valet at Warner Brothers—in one early account he had the job as busboy in the studio cafeteria—but there were probably others. One reason that no certain résumé exists in Jackie's case is that, contrary to the image presented in most records of his life, he did not willingly take to menial labor.

Jack Gordon remembered that Robinson once had a potato-picking job. "Jack didn't do much picking," he said, "but he picked some of the other guys' potatoes. Jack never did any hard work that I can recall. He sold papers once, used to have a little steel wagon with wheels, and boy you could hear 'em come with the *Sunday Examiner* and the *Times,* and what the guys told me was, as soon as they got through with their route, they would go gamble. Shoot dice, the whole thing. Jack was in the middle of it." Another source of income, Jack Gordon remembered, was ticket scalping. Robinson regularly got an allotment of tickets for home football games, which he turned over to Gordon, who then sold them for what he could get, splitting the proceeds.

In any case, there was not enough to take care of his own needs, let alone those of his mother and of Frank's family.

"It was always tougher on us after football season," Ray Bartlett said, "because during football we had a training table. That was our main meal. Listen, we were poor, we didn't have any money, I want to tell you that right now. We didn't have any money in our pockets and we looked forward to training table because they fed us very well, steaks and all the good heavy meat and potatoes stuff."

Training table continued for Robinson during the basketball season, but there was none for track or baseball, which may in part account for the fact that he paid less attention to those sports as a collegian.

The Bruin football team, though traditionally a losing one, was in transition when Robinson arrived in the fall of 1939. The school, in a rush to catch up with its competitors, was one of the few predominantly white major colleges in the country that openly courted black players. The established stars of the 1939 team were Kenny Washington and Woody Strode, both seniors, who were shortly to go on and enjoy precedent-shattering careers in the NFL with the Los Angeles Rams.

The inclusion of black athletes, even before Robinson's arrival, hyped attendance and created local interest as never before. Home games at the Coliseum, which seated one hundred thousand, were usually sold-out and—according to Woody Strode—approximately "forty thousand of them would be black."

The career of Kenny Washington in particular had drawn national attention to UCLA. A local product, from Los Angeles, Washington had been the most talked-about local athlete in the area since his high school days. Like Jackie, he was multitalented; a superb baseball player, he hit over .454 one season for UCLA and might easily have been a candidate to break the color barrier in the majors had he not done it in professional football following his years in the military during the war. (There had been two black players in the early days of the NFL, Duke Slater and Smokey Joe Lillard, both of the Chicago Cardinals. But from 1933, when Lillard quit, until 1946, no black players had been accepted.) Washington also had notable ability as a boxer, though less in track and field.

Washington's football skills and exploits made him an instant hero. He was UCLA's leading rusher and passer for three seasons prior to Robinson's arrival. Not only was he quick and speedy from the line of scrimmage, but he was powerful. Though he played left halfback in a single-wing attack, he was a natural fullback, a two-hundred-pounder who ran straight ahead with devastating effectiveness. His ninety-one-yard run from scrimmage is still a Los Angeles Rams' team record. As a passer, he could throw for distance as well as accuracy. On one play against USC—some say it was then the longest recorded pass in the history of college football—Washington threw a ball from his own 15-yard line to the opponent's 23—sixty-two yards in the air, seventy-two yards when the play was completed. So strong was his arm, Woody Strode remembered, that Washington, just fooling around, came close one day to tossing a ball from the playing field right out of the Coliseum.

"We used to have contests in the Coliseum to see if anybody could throw a football clear out of the bowl," Strode said. "We'd bet to see who could throw the farthest. Kenny got seventy-eight rows; there are about eighty rows altogether. Try that with a baseball sometime; I'll bet you only get halfway."

Coming into a program where he would be called on to play second fiddle could not have been easy for Robinson. And he and Kenny Washington carried themselves very differently.

Washington, by nature, was warm and outgoing, a perfect match for athletic stardom. Teammates, teachers, ordinary fans as well as friends, seemed to adore him. He was bright and modest at the same time, and he was a gifted speaker. "As far as the general public was concerned, I mean the local yokels," said Strode, "Kenny was it. He was the main drawing card. He became quite a celebrity; people would stop him on the street to say hello. He was a handsome, clean-cut kid. He had a broad nose, warm, kind eyes, and a smile that lit up his whole face. He had a really good sense of humor. People loved to hang out with the guy."

By contrast, only close friends hung out with Jackie Robinson. He was noticeably angry and withdrawn. On campus he was a loner. Woody Strode, like many other area residents who read the papers, remembered the near race riot in Brookside Park that resulted in Robinson's arrest. Strode thought, beyond any damage to Robinson's reputation, it might have put him on his guard when he arrived on campus.

Because he was a senior, Strode did not know Robinson that well. "We were only together that one year. But Jackie was a very intelligent and good-looking young man. He had a very dark complexion with thin, straight features. He had a perfect white smile and steely hard eyes that could flash angry in a heartbeat. To be honest, Jackie Robinson was not well-liked when he was at UCLA. He would never believe there would be a statue of him sitting out there right now, at the baseball stadium UCLA named after him.

"Jackie was not friendly. He had been in a few scuffles in Pasadena with the law, minor trouble. When he came to UCLA, he was very withdrawn. Even on the football field, he would stand off by himself. People used to ask me, 'Why is Jackie so sullen and always by himself?' '' Strode and others had no answer.

But on the field, Robinson provided answers that more than satisfied his coaches. He was the missing piece of the puzzle for the football team. In 1939, for the first time ever, UCLA went undefeated, winning six, tying four, coming within an eyelash of a Rose Bowl invitation. The ties cost the team a trip to the Bowl, and three of the four ties, coming in the final three games of the season, coincided exactly with another ankle injury that Robinson sustained in a scrimmage. The team's final game that year was a tie against archrival USC, a team that had never lost to UCLA and had, only three years before, beaten them 72–0. This time they battled to a 0–0 tie, and because that meant that USC closed out its own undefeated season with one fewer tie, they and not UCLA got the Rose Bowl bid.

Nevertheless, Robinson was the key to a spectacular season. Against Stanford, whom the Bruins tied 14–14, Jackie had a 52-yard run from scrimmage one way and a 51-yard run on an intercepted pass the other. Following the game, the Stanford coach, Tiny Thornhill, called Robinson "the greatest backfield runner" he had seen in twenty-five years of coaching. In a 16–6 win against Oregon, Jackie caught a touchdown pass from Kenny Washington and later scored on an 81-yard run from scrimmage. Against Washington State, Robinson led UCLA to a 24–7 win, scoring on a 35-yard run and on a 25-yard pass. He also took a punt return sixty-five yards to the 5-yard line against Washington in a game won by UCLA, 14–7.

Because Kenny Washington was the team's principal running back (the ball, in the single-wing formation, was snapped directly to him on every play), Robinson's stats on first glance are deceptive. The team's coach, Babe Horrell, used Robinson primarily as a decoy, theorizing that he drew at least two defenders with him wherever he moved on the field, opening running lanes for Washington and another running back, Leo Cantor. Nevertheless, Robinson ran for a total of 519 yards —or 51.9 yards per game, good enough to rank tenth in total offense in the Pacific Coast Conference. But behind those numbers is an even more telling one: Robinson's yardage came from handling the ball only forty-two times. His average gain from scrimmage was an incredible 11.28 yards per carry.

People who saw him play invariably describe his running style as distinctive. He had the capacity to stop and start, feint one way, move another, twist, squirm, then explode so that it was virtually impossible to defend against him. He could be double- and triple-teamed, but it did not seem to matter. If he got running room, the other team was in trouble. Five yards behind the line of scrimmage in the single-wing, he had that running room; on punt returns he had more, and as a pass receiver it varied. "He was the greatest open-field runner I ever saw," Ray Bartlett said, "and that includes guys right up to today."

But the key to Robinson was never in numbers; it was inside him. As great as his skills were, his desire to win, his intensity and his fury —the very qualities that seemed to isolate him from others—made him an ultimate team player. Ray Bartlett, his friend and teammate, described one play in the course of a game that seemed to epitomize Robinson. He and Jackie, both in the defensive backfield, together went to intercept a pass in the SMU game. They collided, Bartlett said, "and the guy from Southern Methodist, who was lying on the ground, just had the ball literally drop into his lap for a reception." Rather than shrug it off, it made Jackie sick, Baretlett said. The inadvertent error was intolerable, inexcusable. Robinson could not forgive himself. In the USC game, when a trip to the Rose Bowl hung in the balance, the tie, said Carl Rowan, left Robinson deaf to the cheers that followed him off the field. Making certain the shower was running so no one would hear him, Robinson, "the tough Bruin halfback," wept inconsolably, "sick with disappointment."

After barely catching his breath from what he felt was the failure of the football season, he was at it full tilt in basketball. In his first season with the Bruins, he was the leading scorer in the Pacific Coast Conference, Southern Division, averaging better than twelve points a game—a Jordanesque figure considering that usual team totals for a game then were somewhere between thirty and forty points.

Robinson played right forward in a time when the game was slower, more patterned, nearly always below the rim. He was quick, deceptive, a superb passer, a deadly outside shooter. He led his team on a highly successful East Coast tour that year, a tour that concluded with a welcome home from a wildly cheering crowd at Union Station. He ran neck and neck for conference scoring honors with Ralph Vaughn of USC, one of the top names in California and the nation in college basketball. The race between Vaughn and Robinson dominated local sports headlines through the latter part of the basketball season, but also ultimately provided further evidence of Jackie's determination to win games before personal honors.

Toward season's end, UCLA had a key game against Stanford. The late Wilbur Johns, the UCLA coach, once recalled Robinson's game against Stanford and their own high-scoring star, Don Williams:

"Jackie had another great night. He could rise to the occasion in uncanny fashion against our so-called traditional rivals, and he always played his head off against Stanford. This night his floor work was breathtaking. His speed, passing, and deception sent our fans wild with joy. Stanford often put two men on him, and they held him to twenty-three points, but he ran rings around Williams and outscored him. But that's not the unforgettable part.

"We all knew that Vaughn was going well up at Berkeley. The ticker in the press box said so. We knew that Jackie had to keep scoring to keep pace with Vaughn. He knew it too.

"Yet with the score close and time running out, he deliberately held on to the ball several times, instead of shooting. He'd set himself, draw the defense down near the Stanford goal, and then pivot and dribble down the court to freeze the ball, rather than risk a chance of a Stanford score by shooting, and losing possession of the ball. . . . The whole gallery was yelling for him to shoot and pile up his record against Vaughn. But Jackie thought of the score and the team. Nothing else counted."

For Wilbur Johns, one of the four coaches Athletic Director Spaulding feared would fight over Robinson, Jackie's first season was proof of what he already knew: "If Jackie hadn't played football, he might have been the greatest of all basketball players. His timing was perfect. His rhythm was unmatched. . . . He always placed the welfare of his team above his chance for greater stardom."

And then there was baseball. Without a training table or anything like the investment in the other major sports, it was almost an afterthought. Robinson went out for the team, made it, and played for it— as a shortstop—but with not nearly the success he enjoyed elsewhere. In his first game, on March 10, 1940, he got four hits and stole four bases, including home, in a 6–4 loss to Los Angeles City College. That, almost literally, was it. He had only two more hits in the ten games following the opener, winding up with a season average of .097. He committed ten errors in those games, finishing with a low .907 fielding percentage. There was no one then talking up his skill, much less his future, in the sport.

With the completion of the baseball schedule, however, he went immediately to outdoor track, winning broad-jump titles in the NCAA nationals and in the Pacific Coast Conference Meet, where he set a record at twenty-five feet even.

In his later years, Robinson came to believe that his commitment to all sports as a collegian, far from creating opportunity, was a liability, in that the punishment his body took eventually made him old before his time and almost certainly shortened his career in professional baseball.

Even more certain is that he had no illusions about where his career as a collegiate athletic star might lead. He rode up and down the coast and across the country as he might never have been able to do otherwise, and he was surrounded by hullabaloo and public acclaim unknown to the vast majority of aspiring athletes, black or white, but he understood the future was closed.

During the week before the big Rose Bowl–deciding game against USC, Woody Strode remembered, the team practiced in great secrecy. If anyone was caught spying, "they took them out to fraternity row. The kids out there shaved UCLA in their hair, painted them blue and gold, and sent 'em home. . . . There was always a pregame rally that was held around a huge bonfire, which, if you look it up, means 'fire of bones.' We didn't burn any bodies; we built a structure out of telephone poles set about thirty feet apart. The week prior to the game, all the kids would search the city of Los Angeles looking for wood to fill this structure. . . . The night before this game, they would set off this fire and the flames would shoot hundreds of feet into the sky. . . . The kids would stand around and dance while the yell leaders stood on a platform and said whatever they could think of to get the crowd worked up."

Across town, USC had bonfires of their own in which they burned Kenny Washington, Jackie Robinson, and Woody Strode in effigy. "That wasn't racial, that was fear," Strode said. No one knows what thoughts Jackie brought into that game.

The night before the game, the UCLA players were housed at the

Beverly Hills Hotel. "The Beverly Hills," said Strode, "is probably one of the three fanciest hotels in the city. That's where all the actors and movie producers stay, out there on Sunset Boulevard. Being seen by their pool or sipping drinks in their Polo Lounge is as classy as you can get.

"I remember sitting in the Polo Lounge with Jackie, Leo, Kenny, and Ned. We were shining in our best clothes. I wore a dark blue wool suit, double-breasted with big lapels, and a red silk tie. We sat there all quiet and respectful, sipping water and eating apples, listening to Don Nova sing."

But Robinson was never taken in by his status on campus. He was, despite his accomplishments, a shy person, determined to live his own life. He neither smoked nor drank, nor ever wished to push himself forward. He was suspicious of praise, whether it came in the form of newspaper columns or social invitations from the opposite sex. He was reticent with women, especially white women, whose interest in him was not surprising but put him on his guard.

"When I was at UCLA," he told Roger Kahn decades later, "more white women wanted to go to bed with me than I wanted to go bed with white women. . . . Everybody thinks it's the other way."

Hardly a saint, Robinson kept to his old friends. A group of five or six of the Pasadena crowd found his friendship helpful in finagling their way into UCLA sorority parties. "These girls used to have midnight parties, you know, and five or six of us would go up to the door," Jack Gordon said. "Jackie'd kind of hang back. I'd be standing there and they'd say, 'You can't come in here.' I'd say, 'Whaddaya mean we can't come in here? We got Jackie Robinson.' They'd say, 'Jackie Robinson can come in, but you guys can't.' I'd say, 'Okay, if we don't go in, Jack don't go in.' That's the way it was. We got to be very popular!"

There is another snapshot of Robinson in the land of plenty from this period: The Cardsharp.

"UCLA made us dress up when we traveled, and we rode the trains everywhere," Woody Strode remembered. "It was a great way to travel that no one even thinks about doing anymore. The school would lease a whole railroad car for the team, and we'd raise hell—water fights, food fights, pillow fights, all that crazy stuff. Some of the guys played cards. Jackie Robinson was quite a cardplayer; he beat the guys out of a lot of money. I never played cards. I was too afraid to gamble in those days.''

The fear of gambling, in Robinson's case, was offset by the competitive excitement of it and by the hard, compressed awareness that he was good at it and had a chance to pick up some needed cash.

He was twenty years old as he hurtled through his first brilliant year at UCLA, but he was already old, old in the ways that James Baldwin would say any young black man was old growing up in America. He had already been marked so that he knew all too well where he was and was not going as the train rocketed along the track.

CHAPTER SEVEN

In his second year at UCLA (with two years in junior college, he was now a senior), Robinson found himself the unchallenged star of the football team. Kenny Washington, Woody Strode, and other key players from the 1939 squad had graduated, and the way was open for him. But the 1940 Bruins were clawless, winning only one of ten games.

Robinson's stats were again somewhat misleading. While he was second in the PCC in total offense for the 1940 season (440 yards rushing and 435 passing), his rushing average of 3.64 yards per carry was only ninth in the conference. As the third-ranked passer, his completion mark of .418 was not outstanding, and he had five of ninety-eight passes intercepted—not bad, but not memorable.

Robinson's brilliance, though, came precisely from the fact that he played for a poor team. He did not have the kind of offensive line in front of him that allowed for much running room. Where he could create his own space, he more than made himself known. He returned nineteen punts for 399 yards that season, an average of 21 yards a return, a national record at the time (broken seven years later). With no line protecting him—and with no experience either—he was the third-leading passer in the far West. Above all, he was a football player who created excitement wherever he went. Almost single-handedly, he made a season out of it for his team.

UCLA lost its opening game of the season at home, 9–6, to SMU. The single UCLA touchdown of the game came on an 87-yard zigzag punt return by Robinson that had Coliseum fans on their feet.

The Stanford game, normally a huge one for UCLA, was off the books that year. Stanford, which wound up the season undefeated, fielded one of the most powerful college football teams of the era. Featured was the great Frankie Albert at quarterback and huge Norm Standlee at fullback. UCLA was going to be little more than a Rose Bowl tune-up.

Instead, largely because of Jackie Robinson, the game turned into a war in the trenches, eventually won by Stanford, 20–14. The closeness of the game, however, could not disguise the fact that beyond Robinson, UCLA had nothing.

In the weeks that followed, Jackie's amazing solo high-wire act continued. Against Washington State, he was personally responsible for three touchdowns in a game won by the Bruins, 34–26. He passed for UCLA's first touchdown of the afternoon, then later had a 60-yard run from scrimmage for another score. In the last quarter, with the game very much in doubt, Jackie ran an off-tackle slant from his own 25-yard line, going seventy-five spectacular yards for the game-breaker.

He finished the season by keeping UCLA close in the traditional crosstown match with USC. UCLA lost 28–14, but not before Robinson had run for one score and passed for another.

The basketball team also fielded a bus-and-truck cast, with Robinson as the marquee attraction. While UCLA won only two of twelve conference games, Jackie was the PCC Southern Division scoring champ, averaging 11.08 points a game. In the season finale, USC whipped UCLA 52–37—with Robinson, however, contributing twenty points. But the single most important thing that happened to him that year had little to do with numbers. He fell in love—almost.

For weeks, in the student lounge in Kerckhoff Hall, he had seen Rachel Isum come and go. As there were only a handful of black students on campus, they belonged to an insular group. But even as he had noticed her, been attracted to her, wanted to meet her, he held back. His friend Ray Bartlett had an easier time talking to women; he seemed to have no problem talking to Rachel, and he knew that Jackie wanted to meet her.

"It was a casual thing, in an area where we just used to gather and talk," Bartlett said. "He liked Rachel and how she looked and all, but he was so bashful, so I said, come on, I'll introduce you."

At the time, Isum was a freshman. A scholarship student from south Los Angeles, she was not only pretty, she was smart—a straight-A student thinking of going into nursing. Though she was anything but loud or boastful, she had, certainly more than Robinson, a determined view about the future. She did not think in terms of limitations or exclusions. Though her family's circumstances were no better than Robinson's—her mother also worked as a domestic, and her father, ill with a heart condition, was housebound—she never thought of her family as poor or her horizons as narrow. She had opinions about herself, her family, the future, and, it turned out, about Jackie Robinson.

She, like many people in the area, had heard of him. She knew about him, or thought she did, before he ever got to UCLA. On at least one occasion, she watched him play football for Pasadena Junior College. She noticed more than his football skills: there was the way he stood on the field, his hands on his hips, his head held at a certain angle. She knew, without having met him, that he was cocky, arrogant, and conceited, and later on she told him so.

When they did meet, finally, there was a physical attraction and a certain ease in each other's company. Robinson found that he could talk to her, that she listened, and that she had opinions. Robinson felt comfortable enough to replay uncomfortable parts of games with her. She was bright enough never to make light of how hard he took winning or losing.

"You can't replay a single minute and change anything except your temper," she told him once, stressing that he could only make matters worse for himself by getting so worked up.

But intimacy and trust neither came easily nor all at once. In the beginning, Robinson was a Big Man on Campus, someone whose stature seemed matched to an aloofness that did seem arrogant. It took time to see that he was shy, and that his shyness did not come so much from inexperience as from mistrust.

As Jackie later confided to Carl Rowan, he was wary of women who fawned over him—white and black. He was on guard against white women he met and who were attracted to him because he had seen firsthand how sexual attraction had been used exploitatively in Pasadena. He recalled the way the city had found excuses to fire black employees in Pasadena who had joined in efforts to desegregate local swimming pools. "When they couldn't find a legitimate excuse for firing some Negroes," he told Carl Rowan, "they got some white girls to tempt them, to give them the old come-on. First thing these Negroes knew, they were out on their fannies, accused of making insulting passes at white girls."

But black women too were caught up in racial gamesmanship. As if the standards of attractiveness had been set by whites, black women also often looked at black men according to the shade of their complexion, the lighter-skinned ones being looked upon with more favor, the more dark-skinned—like Jackie Robinson—with less. Or at least so Jackie believed, growing up. While he had one "steady" girlfriend, Bessie Renfro, he generally, said Carl Rowan, had acquired an armor by which he "could fend off the subtle prejudices that had permeated Negro society."

Because Rachel seemed intelligent and sympathetic as well as attractive, he let his guard down enough to let her see that he was interested. He invited her to the 1940 Homecoming Dance at the Biltmore Hotel in downtown Los Angeles, one of the biggest social events on the school calendar.

Rachel accepted. She bought a special dress for the occasion, and a hat—a little black hat with fox trim. Her excitement was barely sated. She wanted more fur than that, she told her mother. Mrs. Isum lent her a prized black Alaska-seal coat that belonged to her mother and offered it to her for the evening.

"I was thoroughly excited over going to a dance at the Biltmore," Rachel said. "Although I tried to hide this at the time, I was also very proud to go with Jackie Robinson. I'm sure I must have been quite a comical character in that huge fur. We danced to 'Star Dust,' 'Mood Indigo,' 'I'll Never Smile Again,' and all those tunes that were popular at the time."

Rachel's parents were less taken with Jackie Robinson. Rachel acknowledged that her father could not shed a typically protective attitude toward his daughter, a view that inevitably cast Jackie, the big-time campus athlete, as a common lothario. But, apparently, there was more to it than that.

"Rachel's father didn't like Jack because he was too black—and Jack understood that very well," Jackie's sister, Willa Mae, said.

Robinson continued to see Rachel over the next months. Clearly he was drawn to her, but he was also still on his guard. He could not get free from the idea that where he came from was not quite where she came from. Their directions in life, whatever he felt for her, were very different—she at the beginning not at the end of her college years, he about to finish and, as yet, with no idea of what he was going to do, without the optimism and confidence about the future that she seemed to exude.

When basketball season ended and with it the training table and other perks of the major programs, Robinson felt far more pressed about how to make a living than whom he was dating. Graduation loomed. He could not begin to figure what advantage that would hold for him. His most urgent need, he believed, was a real job. Frank's widow and children still needed to be looked after. Mack had recently married and was living at home, so his needs were now part of the picture as well.

Robinson hoped that somehow his athletic abilities might be parlayed into some kind of work with children, perhaps as a coach. Additionally, if he was careful, there might be a few extra dollars in semiprofessional and professional sports as well as what he might pick up here and there at the card table or the track.

As he tried to balance the scales, there was an overload. Sometime toward the end of basketball season, before spring baseball and track, Jackie decided to quit UCLA. The decision, which he shared with those close to him, was not open to revision, though his mother and Karl Downs tried to dissuade him.

Mallie and Downs argued that he was so close to graduation that it made no sense for him to quit; there was no advantage that wouldn't be waiting for him in a few weeks. At one point, school officials, urging him to stay, offered to help pay his expenses through graduation. Only Rachel, who had been ardent about the importance of a college degree, seemed to understand—albeit reluctantly. In the end, no arguments could sway him; he could not be convinced that a college degree would really mean that much, or that his principal skills—in physical education—would be more useful later than now.

In the spring of 1941, with the country not yet at war and the effects of the Great Depression still very much present, the best hope for a job came from the many New Deal government programs that were still running.

The National Youth Administration had programs for young people and needed coaches, athletic counselors, and assistants. Through Pat Ahearn, the athletic director at the NYA, Robinson received and accepted a position at an NYA camp at Atascadero, about halfway between Los Angeles and San Francisco. He left home for the first time in his life and had no idea when he would return.

His NYA job initially was to play shortstop for the camp baseball team. They played other agency and semipro teams primarily for the entertainment of campers and staff. In between games, Robinson worked with groups of youngsters, most of them from broken homes and backgrounds of poverty, though the racial breakdown of the campers is unknown.

A fellow assistant director, Lippman Duckat, who had played second base alongside Robinson on the baseball team, became the camp MC for different entertainments. One night, when he was to MC, he noticed Robinson lying around the bunkhouse and asked him to come along. Jackie declined, saying he didn't want to create trouble. Duckat, unable to believe that there could be any kind of difficulty relating to color at the camp, finally persuaded him to come along. If there was any question about Robinson's attendance, Duckat said he would quit as MC.

To Duckat's utter amazement—but not at all to Robinson's—the two men were stopped at the door and Jackie was refused admission, precipitating Duckat's refusal to take part in the show.

For Robinson, the event was barely worth mentioning. There was nothing new in it. The only question for him was the steadiness of his paycheck, which turned out to be not steady at all.

Within months of his arrival, the camp, along with many other government programs, was shut down, and Robinson, like legions of others in prewar America, was again out of work. What made him different, however, was that he was not just anyone; he was, according to the local papers at the time he made his decision to leave UCLA, one of the greatest athletes ever, someone with more all-around ability than Joe Louis, Jesse Owens, Paul Robeson, Jack Johnson, and others—"the Jim Thorpe of his race." While Robinson never had his head turned by praise, he could see how established he had become in the public eye. Within weeks of the camp's closing that summer, Robinson received—and accepted—an invitation to play in that year's *Chicago Tribune* all-star game against the NFL champion Chicago Bears. Among other things, the invitation meant another three weeks with all expenses paid.

The game was a rout by the Bears—37–13—but Robinson scored one of the collegians' touchdowns on a pass reception and generally handled himself well enough to be noticed in the press box and among the more than ninety-eight thousand fans who filled Soldier Field. And there was an incidental benefit: another job, this one with a nomadic professional football team, the Los Angeles Bulldogs (soon to be the Honolulu Bears). For $100 a game and the promise of a construction job, Robinson, along with his friend Ray Bartlett, set sail for Hawaii in September 1941.

Bartlett and Robinson shared a duplex. Their construction job, which Bartlett said "didn't interest Jack much," paid for their expenses. Because of the heat, the team practiced and played its games at night. The Honolulu Bears' season ended in early December, and Bartlett decided he wanted to learn more about the construction business and stayed. On the morning of December 5, Robinson boarded a steamship for the voyage home.

Because the ship, the *Lurline,* took several days to reach the mainland, it was at sea when Pearl Harbor was bombed. Over the years, as layers of myth, like Nile Valley silt, have settled on the details of Robinson's life, these few days have often been given a symbolic fertility they probably did not have.

One account of his life has him peering out a porthole to catch the bombing itself, mistaking it for a winter thunderstorm; another account pictures him as virtually the only passenger on board who turned down the offer of a life jacket because "there was something about authority that brought out the iconoclast in him." The reality was that Robinson, engrossed in a game of poker that morning, was unaware of any danger aboard until he was summoned on deck with everyone else and told that the Japanese had bombed Pearl Harbor. Passengers were offered life jackets, which Robinson declined, not because he mistrusted authority but because, as he told Carl Rowan, he was shaky and superstitious, the way a person might be taking out insurance before a plane trip. On the day of the bombing Robinson said he noticed that the windows of the ship were painted black. He was, Carl Rowan said, "a most uneasy man during the rest of the zigzag blackout trip home."

With little idea of what he wanted to do, Robinson fell into another time-killer at home. A semipro basketball team, the Los Angeles Red Devils, invited him to play. Stuck for personnel—no more than eight players were on the Red Devils' squad—the team accepted whatever games they could. They played a pro team from Sheboygan one night at the Coliseum. Sheboygan featured the six-foot-ten-inch, all-American center George Mikan, and Robinson, according to Jack Gordon, "had a real hurtin' put on him."

Basketball, though, was only a brief interlude. With the passage of a Selective Service Act extension by one vote in the House of

Representatives in August, 1941, another kind of future opened. The draft had been on Robinson's mind since 1940, when the law was first passed, but he had been comfortable with a deferment based on economic hardship. He was listed with the draft board as the sole means of support for his mother. With the coming of war, however, his status soon came under challenge.

His military service is another phase in Robinson's life enmeshed in mythmaking. Given what he later became, the retelling of his story almost demands that questions of red, white, and blue never be confused with those of color. Rowan, working with Robinson on his autobiography *Wait Till Next Year* in 1960, is unclear about the sequence of events from the time Jackie returned from Hawaii to the time he received his draft notice in the spring of 1942. Rowan makes no mention at all of Robinson's playing professional basketball. The first event noted was a "joyful reunion" with Rachel, "who, again, chided him for leaving UCLA before getting his degree, and for staying in Hawaii so long."

Then Robinson tells her—and us—that the draft board had raised some questions about his civilian status, notably about his being the sole support of his mother. Rachel expresses concern that Robinson might, in some inadvertent way, be using the matter of support to keep from being drafted.

"You aren't pressing that point, are you?" she asks.

"No—in fact that's not the big issue. It's that old business of an athlete being in a touchy spot where the draft is concerned. I'm still bothered by a broken ankle I got in junior college. The doctors say there are bone chips in it and that they really doubt I'm qualified for military service."

"Well, just remember how the public feels about these things, Jack. If anybody gets the notion you're using that ankle injury to avoid service, there'll be a huge blowup about how a big strong halfback is shirking his duty to his country."

Robinson then assures her that he is not about to ask for any special favors on the basis of his ankle.

This exchange, whatever may be said for its cue-card stiffness, indicates that Robinson, at that time, was serious about Rachel, and that by the time of the writing he was probably concerned about the way later generations would interpret his relationship to the military. That part of the story did indeed become complicated.

CHAPTER EIGHT

On March 23, 1942, the day that an induction order was issued for Jackie Robinson, a banner headline in the Communist *Daily Worker* read, " 'Get After Landis, We'd Welcome You,' Sox Manager Tells Negro Stars." The day before, the Chicago White Sox, training for the upcoming season at Brookside Park in Pasadena, allowed two black players to work out with them. One of the players was Nate Moreland, a pitcher who had spent a season with the Negro League Baltimore Elite Giants and an additional season with a Mexican League team. The other player was Jackie Robinson.

The *Worker,* alone in the white press, had been campaigning for years to integrate professional baseball. The Negro press, particularly the weekly *Pittsburgh Courier,* had been just as active, sometimes in uneasy partnership with the *Worker.* But the details of this significant moment along the way to Robinson's eventual breaking of the color barrier are unclear. Who arranged the tryout or, more to the point, who persuaded a journeyman player with no future and another who was about to go into the army to ask for the tryout also remains unclear.

In any case, the tryout, even given the weighted ideological interests of the *Worker,* was more than a curiosity. Sox manager Jimmy Dykes went on record supporting the idea of integration: "Personally, I would welcome Negro players on the Sox, and I believe every one of the other fifteen big-league managers would do likewise. As for the players, they'd all get along too." Though not directly quoted, Dykes was reported to have said that Robinson was easily worth $50,000 to any of the current ball clubs.

What is odd is that Robinson nowhere mentions this tryout—not in his several autobiographies nor the different magazine retrospectives he wrote nor the early biography by Arthur Mann, which was completed with Robinson's obvious assistance.

This may indicate the involvement of the Communist Party, a group Robinson might not have needed to shield himself from at the time, but which, a few years later, was a national concern bordering on obsession. It is also possible that he simply put no stock in the tryout, regarding it as a fraud and a waste of time.

But there was another reason for keeping mum. The impressive display of his talents on the eve of his being taken into the army inevitably raised the question of his physical condition. Rowan's and the other early life stories all report, as a matter of fact, that Robinson entered the military with a designated "limited service" qualification due to his old ankle injury from football. No such qualification is in the official service record.

The record of the induction physical at Fort McArthur in Los Angeles on April 3, 1942, makes no mention of an ankle problem. On page two of the record, under the heading "Current Enlistment," is the subheading "Physical defects at enlistment." Next to it are typed the words, "Fixed bridge serviceable. Right 12. Kline negative." Nothing else.

This discrepancy is important because Robinson's nearly three-year career in the army remains one of the most controversial and intriguing periods of his life.

Upon passage of his physical, Robinson was dispatched to Ft. Riley, Kansas, for three months of basic training. He did well in basic, receiving high marks for his character and his ability to handle a rifle. His score of 196 with an M1 on the gunnery range qualified him officially as an "expert marksman." Eventually he was assigned to a cavalry unit where his day-to-day responsibilities were menial chores in and around the stable area. He lived in a completely segregated unit.

Perhaps because conditions for segregated draftees were so poor, and perhaps because he wanted to make up for the army's decision to disallow a special Class E support allowance of $22 a month that his mother had been receiving, Robinson applied for Officer Candidate School. He was turned down. No reasons were given.

But in one of those strokes of fate that seemed to shadow Robinson throughout his life, Ft. Riley soon had a new and very distinguished soldier on temporary transfer assignment: heavyweight boxing champion Joe Louis.

Louis discovered that Robinson, also a celebrated athlete, was on base and looked him up. A lifelong friendship followed, initiated then by some afternoon rounds of golf. While golfing, Robinson told Louis that he had been turned down for OCS. Louis responded by making a few telephone calls—one to Truman Gibson, a special civilian assistant to the secretary of war, to inform him of the situation black recruits were facing at Ft. Riley. Gibson responded by flying out to Kansas to meet with Louis, Robinson, and other black soldiers; within days of the meeting, Robinson and several others who had been turned down were admitted to OCS.

Robinson entered OCS in early November 1942 and was commissioned as a second lieutenant, cavalry, on January 28, 1943. He thereafter became a morale officer for a unit of black soldiers. Morale in a black unit inevitably centered around relations with whites, and Robinson, even as an officer, was no more immune to the insults and injuries he was assigned to mediate than he had been as a recruit.

Early in the spring of that year, he walked over to the baseball field, having heard there was a particularly good squad of players, one of whom was Dixie Walker. Another was Pete Reiser, who remembered Robinson's sudden appearance:

"One day a Negro lieutenant came out for the ball team," Reiser told Donald Honig. "An officer told him he couldn't play. 'You'll have to play with the colored team,' the officer said. That was a joke. There was no colored team. The lieutenant didn't say anything. He stood there for a while, watching us work out. Then he turned and walked away. I didn't know who he was then, but that was the first time I saw Jackie Robinson. I can still remember him walking away by himself."

A more fractious moment came in the fall when the camp football team tried to recruit him. The team's coach, a senior officer, had a son on the team and was looking to strengthen the squad any way he could, even if it meant recruiting black players. He personally asked Robinson to join the team, letting him know that he would have to sit out a couple of games against southern schools. But Robinson knew the score even better than his army coach. He declined the invitation to join the team—but only after first wangling a two-week furlough for himself. His maneuver angered the coach, who inevitably complained about him to higher-ups.

Base brass had to contend with him in his official capacity as well. Robinson's job brought him nose to nose with the racism that was a part of the order and discipline of army life. Preferential treatment in the use of toilets, drinking fountains, restaurants, and recreational facilities was the regular and wearying staple of complaints received and passed on. As a responsible officer, Robinson made it his business to speak up for his men.

One particularly forceful complaint involved an incident at a base canteen where black soldiers were forced to line up ten deep for the few stools and tables available to them while white soldiers came and went as they pleased. Robinson promised the GIs who complained to him that he would intercede. He telephoned the provost marshal of the base, a Major Hafner, to demand that changes be made.

The major, who apparently did not know Robinson and who was lulled by his uninflected speech into thinking he was a fellow white, confided, "Well, let's be reasonable, Lieutenant Robinson. Let me put it this way: how would you like to have your wife sitting next to a nigger?"

Robinson exploded. He raged on the phone for several moments, drawing the attention of many who were within earshot. That was not the end of it. He took his grievance not only against the situation at the canteen but with the provost as well to the battalion commander, who led Robinson to believe he sympathized with him and who offered to write a letter on his behalf to a general—but who otherwise let matters stand where they were.

In fact, however, matters were not left to stand. Robinson was transferred out—attached rather than assigned (which meant he could be reassigned anywhere) from the relative security of Ft. Riley to Camp Hood, a particular hellhole for black soldiers, deep in the heart of Texas. There the lines between races could *never* be called into question. The next stop for GIs training there was nearly always a foreign battlefield.

It is at this point, in the beginning of 1944, that Robinson's service record indicates a hospital board at Brook Army Hospital in Texas declared that he was qualified for "temporary limited service" due to his ankle injury. This meant that combat service would be restricted unless a special waiver was granted upon request. The timing of the finding suggests that Robinson himself, fearing the future that was being designed for him, may have sought it. There is additional evidence to support this. At Camp Hood, a fellow lieutenant, attached with him from Ft. Riley, Harold B. Gary, was one of several officers present when Robinson sought the aid of the unit's doctor, Adamson, a black physician, asking him to submit a diagnosis concerning Robinson's ankle injury that might actually disqualify him from combat. In any case, it placed Robinson, at a time when he was having obvious difficulty within the system, in a position where he had a modicum of control over others' plans for him.

Robinson was transferred to the 761st Tank Battalion at Camp Hood in the beginning of April. The 761st was one of those battalions, like the Tuskeegee Airmen, that owed its existence and, ironically, its distinguished service record to the scorching insults of segregation. The all-black tank battalion, nicknamed the Black Panthers, was originally housed at Camp Claiborne in Louisiana. Its membership was largely drawn from northern and eastern states, which automatically put it up against the laws, customs, and attitudes of the deep South. Apart from the army's own policies of segregation, the soldiers faced even harsher conditions off base. In the town of Alexandria, closest to the base, black GIs were regularly roughed up by local authorities and by patrolling MPs. On one such occasion in early 1942, a black soldier was arrested and beaten by MPs in the Little Harlem area of town. The arrest provoked a confrontation that escalated to the point where groups of whites armed with pistols and shotguns confronted black crowds said to have gathered in the thousands. When word of this spread to Camp Claiborne, members of the 761st went into action: they took to their tanks, loaded their guns, and rolled off toward the front gates of the base under the glare of spotlights and the booming of voices over loudspeakers. Only a hastily improvised negotiation prevented a full-scale assault on white Alexandria.

Within a year, the 761st was moved to Camp Hood, a somewhat more remote area, and also one where the terrain for tank training was more varied. But for black soldiers, the change was hardly comforting. The small towns surrounding the sprawling base were no more friendly, and living conditions on the base were, if anything, even worse. David J. Williams, a white second lieutenant assigned to the command of one of the black tank units on base, recalled the look and feel of the quarters for these segregated soldiers:

"When I turned up on the base, I was driven through the gates and I saw all around me these gleaming white concrete buildings. Very impressive. I knew what kind of conditions Negro soldiers usually faced and I thought, 'This isn't bad.' Then the jeep kept going. Pretty soon, we came to the top of a hill. Way down on the other side, in a valley, was this muddy open tract—I don't know how else to describe it. The only buildings there were a string of tents—old, ragged, World War One tents. There was one big circus-type tent—that turned out to be the place where they showed movies, it was the rec hall, where you went to socialize. That is, where the black soldiers went to socialize. This muddy field was their living quarters. It was unbelievable. The heat and mosquitoes, which you had no protection from, were unbearable. Sometime along the way, they got around to taking down the tents, and in their place they put up cardboard and tar-paper shacks. At least they had screens to keep out the mosquitoes. But that was it.''

The 761st, as they had in Louisiana, used the very conditions they lived with to fuel and to direct their lives. Under siege, they came together, and as a fighting unit they developed a cohesiveness and a stature no one anticipated.

The commanding officer of the unit was Col. Paul L. Bates, a white officer from northern California and a former all-American football player from Western Maryland College. Until he was placed in charge of the 761st, Bates had had little contact with African-Americans.

"In eight years of playing football—through high school and college —I never encountered a single black player," he said. Bates saw from the outset what his men were up against and tried, in spite of his limited background and knowledge of black life, to provide leadership for the unit, particularly in the way it came to grips with white prejudice.

"I made it a big point," he said, "to teach these men things I knew they didn't know as a group. One of them is that whitey thinks you're sloppy, you're dirty, you smell bad. So everybody takes a bath and the sergeant supervises them that they use a washcloth and they scrub themselves. Your clothing; we set up tailor shops so we had the smartest-looking uniforms at parades and reviews when we were alongside other troops because everything was clean, pressed, and spotless. Our boots were shined like you couldn't imagine; our men would go out of their way to salute officers and to look them straight in the eye when they were doing it.''

But the way the unit came together as a group was only incidentally a matter of hygiene or parade formation imposed by white commanders. The deepest sources of unity came from the battlefield and from the ability to direct a collective sense of rage at a palpable, recognizable enemy: units of white soldiers.

The men of the 761st were designated "school troops." In training, that meant they served as "the enemy." Their tanks rolled into the field against mechanized units of tank destroyers. These units of white soldiers faced the school troops in field examinations to qualify for combat.

The tank destroyers, Colonel Bates said, "would go through the three principal maneuvers a military force would make—which is attack, defend, and retrograde, going backwards. They would be placed in situations, the tank destroyers, where they would do all of these. My tankers would be the enemy. . . . It gave my men this wonderful opportunity . . . to maneuver against these people. And we caused more of them to fail their tests than you could possibly imagine because my men could outthink and outmaneuver them."

The men of the 761st exulted in their triumphs, which went well beyond the boundaries of the training field. On one occasion, the soldiers gathered boisterously after routing a destroyer unit. "The logo of this destroyer unit was 'Seek, Strike, and Destroy.' Our guys were laughing their heads off," Colonel Bates remembered. "One of them said, 'Man, their motto should be 'Sneak, Peep, and Retreat'! Well, this attitude that they could outdo whitey gave them tremendous pride and confidence when we finally did go overseas."

The unit ultimately served under Gen. George S. Patton in Europe and distinguished itself there in the heaviest tank fighting of the war. There were instances, Colonel Bates recalled, where the ferocity and bravery of his men were almost beyond belief. "I believe they fought against Germans not as Germans so much as against the white man. I know of cases where one of our men would be shot out of a tank, and because he'd outrank somebody in a nearby tank, he'd say, 'Get out! I want it, I know where the motherfucker is, I'm gonna get him!' "

Robinson became a platoon leader of Company B of the 761st sometime in April 1944. As the story went, Robinson told his men to understand from the outset that he knew nothing about tanks and that they would have to teach him. The men, according to Rowan, responded with amazement and appreciation—officers were rarely so honest. But it was not quite that simple.

Robinson was a different sort of soldier. "He was kind of aloof, very straight, dressed really sharp, didn't swear much, was religious. He was a really good person, but he was never close to anyone," David Williams remembered. "I thought I was as close to him as anyone, but I didn't really have a sense of what went on with him. He was a very private person."

Another member of the 761st, Harold B. Gary, had a different view. Jackie, he said, was "primarily interested in Jackie. And I knew him fairly well. He was the kind of guy who tended to pick on people who were smaller than he was or who he felt were less important than he was."

E. G. McConnell, one of the unit's three youngest members—someone who had a history, in his own words, "of cutting up a bit"—remembered Robinson as something of an older brother, someone who "used to sit with us when we were goldbricking and just talk to us, listen to us. He understood what we had gone through because he had gone through it too." Later on, though, when the war ended and Robinson was a star with the Dodgers, McConnell said, "a couple of us who knew him very well went all the way out to a clothing store in Harlem to try to get him to come to a reunion of the 761st, but he wouldn't even look at us. He made out like he didn't even know who we were."

In his work, said David Williams, Robinson was a stickler for details. He carried out to the letter his charge as a platoon leader, which meant overseeing everything from the state of uniforms to the upkeep of weapons and the maintenance of vehicles. As a platoon leader, he rode in the second tank off the point in formation and was charged with making sure all commands were properly executed.

During these months, when work was so demanding and living conditions so bleak, Robinson, with the help of David Williams, organized a baseball team. "We chipped in whatever money we could, we put together patchwork uniforms, spent every cent we had on equipment —bats and balls. A single baseball got so incredibly beaten up, and yet they were precious to us. We held on to them for dear life," Williams said.

The officers had a softball team too. And, said Colonel Bates, "when Jackie came up, we just went back as far as we could go. When he hit a ball, it didn't come at you round, it came at you like a disk."

Robinson was a pitcher for his team. "He threw a lot of junk, but he was fast, too, he was amazing," Williams said. More than anything, his competitiveness took over.

"I'd remind him any number of times, 'Hey, it's only a game.' It wouldn't matter. It was like talking to a deaf man. He just wanted to win." Once, Williams remembered, the team lost on the last play when the catcher allowed a passed ball, permitting the winning run to score.

"Jackie was all over this guy, name was Ivory Fox—it was terrible. Poor bastard couldn't get away, apologize, anything—that was the way it was. The guy was an idiot, a jackass, I don't remember all the names Jack unloaded on him. Ivory just stood there shaking in his boots and took it."

But the athletic teams Robinson helped organize were very much bound up with the unit's larger success. "The teams we had were terrific," Colonel Bates said. "We had a boxing team that never lost a match even though we boxed against division, because some of the guys were professionals. We had the third-ranking light heavyweight, a guy named Reilly, and there was this great pride the guys developed with the help of these teams."

Making the most of a difficult situation, Robinson rose to a position of authority and respect he had not counted on when he joined the military. He learned something about leadership he had not fully known as a star athlete.

"Jackie Robinson gained pride and strength as a leader from our men," Colonel Bates said. "He got as much or more from them as he himself gave." Whether or not he was liked, however much he kept to himself, this brief membership in an all-black fighting unit that had answered prejudice with performance was one of the genuinely formative experiences he had just prior to his breaking baseball's color barrier. It is unfortunate that the way he finally separated from the military has almost completely obscured this period in his life.

On the evening of July 6, 1944, Robinson, with a weekend pass in hand, checked himself out of McCloskey General Hospital. He was undergoing examinations to determine whether or not he would have to sign a waiver exempting the military from responsibility if he chose to go overseas with his unit. The unit was shortly scheduled to ship out, and by now, Robinson was, by all accounts, undecided about whether or not he would consent to go.

He boarded a bus near McCloskey in Temple, Texas, and traveled thirty miles to a black officers' club at Camp Hood. He stayed there for several hours, then left, either alone or in the company of a young woman, identified later as the wife of another lieutenant in the 761st. He then got on a bus at station number 23 at 172nd Street, outside the officers' club, heading for the Central Bus Station at Camp Hood.

Fifteen minutes later, by the time the bus had finished its route around the broad perimeter of the base, Jackie Robinson's military career was in shambles and his whole future thrown into doubt.

CHAPTER NINE

Anyone who served in the 761st knew about bus transportation at Hood in the same way they knew about it at Claiborne and at scores of other military facilities. At Claiborne, when soldiers queued up to catch a bus, drivers permitted ten to fifteen black GIs on first. They were directed to the back of the bus, and then the remaining seats were filled by white soldiers. It did not matter how long anyone had been waiting; the division according to race was a given.

At Hood, there was a variation. Black soldiers were directed to the back of the bus, but because the base was so big and the bus circuit around it so long, drivers regularly forced black passengers off the bus whenever additional seats for whites was needed. It did not matter what time of day or night, it did not matter how far a soldier might have to walk; the policy, never openly acknowledged, was scrupulously executed.

When Jackie Robinson boarded the Southwestern Bus Company's shuttle service at station number 23, he knew all about the practices and habits of the bus company—and the military's willingness to tolerate them. In addition, Robinson was almost certainly aware that the problem of segregated transportation on military bases was coming to a head. In recent months, the killing of a black GI by a bus driver in North Carolina had made news in the black press. An even more publicized incident involved Robinson's friend Joe Louis and Sugar Ray Robinson near a military base in Alabama, where Louis was jostled by MPs after using a telephone in a white area of a bus station to call a cab. Additionally, it was known that a new Pentagon directive outlawing segregation on buses operating on military bases was shortly to go into effect.

In a statement to military authorities later that night, Robinson said he "entered at the front of the bus and moved towards the rear and saw a colored girl sitting in the middle of the bus. I sat down next to the girl." This was the wife of Lt. Gordon Jones of the 761st.

Mrs. Jones also gave a statement to authorities—many days later— in which she corroborated this preliminary sequence. The bus driver and passengers said that Robinson and Mrs. Jones got on together, not separately. Several years later, when Robinson recounted the story to Ed Reid of the *Washington Post,* he recalled that the incident began when "I ran into one of the Negro officers' wives . . . and offered to accompany her home on the bus."

The passengers and driver may have thought that Robinson's subsequent behavior was inspired by his being with a girlfriend. One passenger remembered overhearing the young woman saying to Robinson, "What are we going to do now, honey?"

The young woman was light-skinned and may initially have been mistaken for a white woman. A black man seated alongside a white woman on a bus in the South, no matter how innocent their relationship, would have touched off battle-station alarms from Baltimore to Biloxi.

In fact, Robinson and Jones might had been something more than a casual relationship. No one contacted in the 761st, from Colonel Bates down to those who served alongside Robinson, remembers a lieutenant named Gordon Jones in the unit. Robinson, at the time, according to Carl Rowan, had broken up with Rachel and was seeing "a pretty peach-skinned girl in a nearby town, hoping that she would be the magic balm needed by a heart on the rebound."

Whatever the actual circumstances, the bus driver, Milton N. Renegar, stopped his vehicle and ordered Robinson to move to the back of the bus. As surely as Rosa Parks, but with no movement waiting to back him up, he refused to budge. The driver insisted. Robinson stayed put. White passengers became offended, particularly when Robinson, far from sitting silently, let the bus driver and anyone else who chimed in know what they could do with their ruffled feelings.

The driver and several of the passengers made a point of telling authorities that Robinson upset them because he used vulgar and insulting language. Robinson denied it, but when he made a statement to MPs, his anger, barely containable, made denials useless:

"He [the driver] tells me that if I don't move to the rear, he will make trouble for me when we got to the bus station, and I told him that was up to him. When we got to the bus station, a lady got off the bus before I got off, and she tells me that she is going to prefer charges against me. That was a white lady. And I said that's all right too, I don't care if she prefers charges against me. The bus driver asked me for my identification card. I refused to give it to him. He then went to the dispatcher and told him something. What he told him I don't know. He then comes back and tells the people that this nigger is making trouble. I told the bus driver to stop fuckin' with me, so he gets the rest of the men around there and starts blowing his top and someone calls the MPs. Outside of telling this lady that I didn't care if she preferred charges against me or not . . . I was speaking direct to that bus driver, and just as I told the captain [indicating Captain Wiggington, camp officer of the day], if any one of you called me a nigger, I would do the same.''

In the driver's statement, he asserts that after Robinson declined two commands to move, he told him ''that I had a load of ladies to pick up and I was sure they wouldn't want to ride mixed up like that, and told him I'd rather he would either move back to the rear or get off the bus.'' A white passenger, Mrs. Elizabeth Poitevint, who made sure authorities understood that though ''I had to wait on them during the day, I didn't have to sit with them on the bus,'' recalled that the driver's last command to Robinson was ''to get off the bus or move to the back.''

Because Robinson neither got off the bus nor moved to the rear, the driver went for help as soon as he pulled into the depot. A crowd, sensing trouble, gathered, heightening tensions further. MPs were soon called to the scene, and Robinson was taken into custody and whisked off to a detention area for questioning.

A midnight investigation followed. The officer in charge, Capt. Gerald M. Bear, an assistant provost marshal on the base, completely ignored what had happened on the bus and accused Robinson of ''using vile and vulgar language,'' of constantly interrupting, and of showing no respect for authority. A Private Mucklerath, who had volunteered as a witness, complained that Robinson had physically threatened him for no reason. An MP who had also been at the depot, seeking to offer support for Mucklerath, testified, ''Mucklerath came over to the pickup and asked me if I got that nigger lieutenant. Right then the lieutenant said, 'Look here, you son of a bitch, don't you call me no nigger. I'm an officer and God damn you, you better address me as one,' or words to that effect. I again cautioned the lieutenant about his language, that there were ladies present.'' Another witness, a private, Lester Phillips, swore ''that I did not hear anyone call this colored lieutenant a nigger and did not hear anyone say anything at all to him. All the people there were trying to quiet him down, and there was such a crowd around there that I couldn't see very well.''

When the "investigation" was completed, Captain Bear had filed three separate charges against Robinson for a general court-martial.

The assumption made by Bear was that he had an open-and-shut case. All he had to prove was that Robinson had been insubordinate, disrespectful, and discourteous to the arresting and interrogating officers. Simple. Robinson had been ordered to wait in an adjoining room while Bear interviewed his witnesses. But Robinson kept interrupting, lounging in a half doorway, bowing "insolently" from the hips, offering mock salutes. Disrespectful? He gave his answers at one point in baby talk, pausing, Bear said, "for minutes . . . no, seconds" between each word. Discourteous? Check the MPs at the bus depot, the guards on duty.

But something happened on the way to the stockade. Between the time of the incident and the court-martial, almost a month later on August 2, Robinson made some calls and wrote some letters. Joe Louis was contacted, and members of the Negro press were alerted. Robinson wrote a letter to Truman Gibson, the civilian aide to the secretary of war, outlining what had happened, not so subtly reminding him—and the Pentagon—that because he was a prominent athlete, his case was almost certain to be well publicized. Then he wrote a letter to the NAACP asking for advice and legal help. A third-party "anonymous" letter to the NAACP pointed out that Robinson was being set up, that charges of drunkenness were being added to those of insubordination.

Colonel Bates, commander of the 761st, refused to sign the necessary papers to allow a court-martial. The army was forced to remove Robinson from the 761st altogether, placing him in another unit whose commander agreed to sign the court-martial papers.

Robinson's suggestion that his case would be publicized also registered. A memo documents a telephone conversation between Camp Hood brass, specifically Colonel Kimball of the Fifth Armored Group, and a chief of staff of the XXIII Corps, emphasizing the serious likelihood of embarrassment to the army through unwanted publicity if the case went forward.

The drunkenness charge was dropped. Of the original three charges and specifications actually filed, only two pertaining to Robinson's conduct *after* the incident on the bus were accepted. That third charge, a violation of the 95th Article of War, was set forth with two specifications. The first: "In that Second Lieutenant Jack R. Robinson, Cavalry, Company 'C,' 758th Tank Battalion, did, at Camp Hood, Texas, on or about 6 July 1944, wrongfully use the following abusive and vulgar language toward Milton N. Renegar, a civilian, Hood Village, Texas, in the presence of ladies, 'I'm not going to move a God damned bit,' or words to that effect, and 'I don't know why that Son-of-a-bitch wanted to give me all this trouble,' or words to that effect."

The second specification: "In that Second Lieutenant Jack R. Robinson . . . did . . . wrongfully use the following vile and obscene language toward Elizabeth Poitevint, a civilian, Killeen, Texas, 'You better quit fuckin' with me,' or words to that effect."

The dropping of the third charge and its specifications, it has been pointed out, was not an unmixed blessing for Robinson. By removing events in and around the bus trip itself, he could no longer provide a context for his behavior. He would be forced to defend himself only on the narrowest and most technical issues of insubordination and of showing disrespect to an officer.

Still, it is likely that the case had become too hot for the army to handle, and that some behind-the-scenes settlement might have been in the works before a word was spoken in court.

The prosecution presented a case, its best case, but it was easy to pick apart. Captain Bear's assertion that Robinson had been insubordinate rested on his being able to prove that Robinson disobeyed specific orders. But in Bear's original report, he wrote only that he "requested Lt. Robinson on several occasions to remain at ease and remain in the receiving room and that I would talk to him later." Additionally, he wrote, he ordered Robinson to be "seated in a chair, on the far side of the room."

The defense zeroed in on the obviously confusing nature of the commands. If Robinson was to be "at ease," how could his posture possibly be called into account? If the purpose of the command was to keep him out of earshot while the interrogation of others proceeded, why would it have been insubordinate for Robinson to have briefly stepped out of the waiting room altogether? And if, as Captain Bear testified under cross-examination, he ordered Robinson—not once but "about three times"—to "go out and remain at ease," how did that square with the command to be seated? No answers were provided.

A second issue was whether Robinson had been placed, in military terms, "in arrest" that night. "In arrest" allows an accused person to move freely about with the understanding that he has technically been arrested. In this case, because Bear demanded that Robinson involuntarily accept transportation back to Temple and the hospital where he was undergoing tests, the court wondered if the "in arrest" designation was being confused with confinement to quarters:

THE COURT: Do you know the difference between confinement and arrest in quarters?
BEAR: Yes, I do.
THE COURT: In arrest in quarters can carry no bodily restrictions?
BEAR: I considered him in arrest in quarters.
THE COURT: In arrest in quarters, yet you admit that you sent three MPs to see that he got back to where you decided to send him?
BEAR: Yes, I did.

Besides Captain Bear, the other witnesses—MPs, guardhouse officers, Pfc. Mucklerath—were equally ineffective. On the other hand, the defense presentation, consisting of brief appearances by Colonel Bates and other members of the 761st, testifying to Robinson's character and reputation, and then an appearance by Robinson himself, made it clear that any conviction would have exposed the army in just the way it was seeking to avoid. Robinson was acquitted of all charges. The entire hearing, deliberation, and decision consumed approximately four hours.

But that was not the end of it. Whatever was involved in the acquittal, the United States military was still a segregated institution, and because of that, those who challenged any of its laws, customs, and traditions—including segregation—were seen as hostile and undesirable. Jackie Robinson's case was only one of many, part of an increasing and uncomfortable pattern that confronted the army with a much larger question than any single black soldier's claim for justice. The war for democracy abroad had triggered another kind of war at home, also for democracy, one that called into question the very ideals the army and the nation said it stood for. From Camp Claiborne to Walla Walla, Washington; Mare Island, California; Camp Gordon Johnston, Florida; from Detroit to Harlem; the military was increasingly forced to defend its outmoded and authoritarian system of race privilege against what amounted to an unofficial insurrection. The military countered in the only manner it knew—by repression and punishment. Arrests, courts-martial, dishonorable discharges, and prison sentences were used with ever-increasing frequency as the one war wound down and the other picked up.

Robinson may have been innocent, but his days in the military were over. He was, from the moment he walked out of that courtroom, an ex-soldier as far as the army was concerned. He knew it and, in fact, may not have minded. The 761st had gone overseas, and if it had ever been his intention to go with them, he had no desire now to ship out with another unit. Behind him was not only an acquittal in a court-martial but a battery of tests that clearly indicated the extent of damage to his ankle from that old football injury. On July 21, 1944—fifteen days after the incident on the bus but before his case actually came to trial—an Army Retiring Board convened at McCloskey General Hospital recommended that Robinson be retained in the military only in "permanent limited duty capacity." Robinson now wrote a letter, which he sent airmail special delivery, to the adjutant general's office in Washington, asking to be discharged from the service. As Robinson himself told it, "my letter was timed to reach the adjutant general's desk about the same time my court-martial papers got to his desk. I was gambling that he would notice that I had been acquitted in an obvious attempt to frame me, that perhaps the top brass would view me as a potential troublemaker who would be better off in civilian life."

He did not have to wait for the adjutant's reply. Within weeks, he was transferred from the unit he had been assigned to for the court-martial. By late September he was transferred again, this time to an infantry unit at Camp Breckinridge, Kentucky, to await the formality of a discharge.

Robinson was, as the military puts it, "honorably relieved from active duty 28 November 1944 at Camp Breckinridge, Kentucky, by reason of physical disqualification. His temporary commission in the Army of the United States terminated 30 June 1948 by operation of law.''

Technically, this represented an honorable discharge. But it was subtly different from a full honorable discharge, and it rankled Robinson for years. For one thing, it was a discharge without any accompanying veteran's benefits. For another, the "physical disqualification" mentioned by the army was, in fact, peculiar in the sense that it related to a prior condition rather than one acquired in the army. Robinson himself pushed for a discharge on that basis. Military authorities, looking to be rid of a troublemaker, may have used that same basis.

In his early autobiography with Carl Rowan, Robinson makes reference to "a medical discharge." In Robinson's 1972 autobiography with Al Duckett, there is reference only to "my honorable discharge." In 1958, around the time he began work on the book with Rowan, Robinson requested—and received—a clarifying "official statement" on his military service and discharge.

Rachel Robinson, in an interview published in the book *Legends,* said that her husband was discharged "because he was not suitable material—whatever you want to call it. He was considered a troublemaker." In fact, the interviewer, Art Rust Jr., recalled that in a radio interview Mrs. Robinson said that her husband had been dishonorably discharged. "I thought I hadn't understood correctly, so I asked her again," Rust said, "and she repeated it—said he had been dishonorably discharged. Then another time, when I reminded her of what she had said, she vehemently denied ever saying that.''

Because the army was still a bastion of segregation and because mutinous behavior of any sort by blacks was viewed as a danger to order in the ranks, discharges became an important coercive tool. According to Harold Rosenthal, who covered the Dodgers for the *Herald Tribune* in Robinson's first years after Rosenthal himself had left the service, the army had several types of discharge, only one of which was honorable and one dishonorable. Some intermediate discharges, he said, not really honorable or dishonorable, took care of troublemakers while sparing the army administrative difficulty. "The intermediate one was where they wanted to get rid of you pretty bad but not enough to give you a dishonorable discharge, which could cause a big goddamn fuss." The different types of discharges, Rosenthal believed, were actually color-coded: "I don't know, but one was white, the dishonorable was yellow, and the other was maybe green. But the paper on which the orders were written were these different colors."

While the army denies that any such color coding took place, the U.S. Communist Party organ the *Daily Worker,* on August 25, 1945, carried a feature story: "Blue Discharge Is Job Bar to Negroes." GIs receiving this form of less-than-honorable-but-not-dishonorable discharge, said the *Worker,* found the already difficult problem of locating a job virtually impossible: "Louis Coleman, secretary of the International Labor Defense, says that a number of these discharges have been brought to his attention. 'Holders of such discharges have poor prospects of employment,' Mr. Coleman said, 'and especially if the holder is a Negro.' " The article goes on to say how the discharge worked, giving anecdotal evidence of numerous Jim Crow cases, informing veterans that a special bureau was being set up to help them through the office of Congressman Vito Marcantonio.

What color coding, if any, was used in Jackie Robinson's case is not known. Robinson did manage to find a job soon after he left the service, but he was all too aware that his time in the military had left him, like thousands of other returning black veterans, vulnerable and uncertain about the future.

Indisputable is that his army experience led him to make decisions that he would later regret, especially when he became famous and had a job where he was earning more money than he had ever imagined.

CHAPTER TEN

When Robinson emerged from the service, he thought about the future in terms of the past. He was a great athlete whose future was narrow and uncertain. He could coach somewhere, he could catch on as a player with a black professional team, maybe in baseball. Prior to the war, he had had some contact with a few Negro League players. Hilton Smith, the great Kansas City Monarchs pitcher, had met Jackie on the coast in 1942 when a team of black stars—including Robinson —played an exhibition game against a service team of white major leaguers led by Red Ruffing. Smith says that Robinson at the time asked for help in locating a job, and that he, Smith, contacted the Monarchs' owner, J. L. Wilkinson, who ultimately invited Robinson to join the Monarchs in the spring of 1945.

But Robinson said that he found his way to Negro professional baseball a little differently. In his final days at Camp Breckinridge, he says he encountered another Monarchs pitcher, whom he identified only as "a brother named Alexander" (probably Ted Alexander), who told him the Monarchs were searching for players. "I was looking for a decent postwar job. So I wrote the Monarchs. After checking me out," Robinson said, "they responded rather quickly and accepted me on a tryout basis for spring training."

The prospect of playing baseball in the Negro Leagues was never especially thrilling. In his one brief prior brush with Negro Leaguers —that exhibition game on the West Coast—promoters ducked out before Robinson and his teammates were ever paid. Salaries in the Negro Leagues, except for top stars, were low, and living conditions, mainly on the road, were harsh.

Robinson also had an offer to coach basketball at Sam Houston College, a tiny black college in Texas. The offer apparently came through his old friend and mentor, the Rev. Karl Downs, who had connections at the school. But as welcome as that offer was, it too was low paying, little more than a stopgap.

The reality was that Robinson was completely unsure about where to go and what to do. Because he had had such enormous success as a player in the past, the path ahead must have seemed doubly galling and unsettling. Sometime after his leaving UCLA but before his military service, his relationship with Rachel Isum had turned serious. He had given her a bracelet, a ring. They were engaged, though there had been no discussion of a wedding date. But during the war years, Robinson's hopes for marriage had seemed to wane. He and his would-be bride were heading in very different directions, with very different sets of prospects. Rachel was pursuing a promising career in nursing. Having transferred from UCLA to a nursing school near San Francisco, she planned to become a nursing cadet. Her interests and her ambitions were strong. She had a sense of the future. Robinson did not.

Though the official versions of Jackie's life stress that his broken engagement came close to breaking his heart, the facts seem less simple.

Robinson says that while at Ft. Riley, he "shook with youthful jealousy and rage" when Rachel informed him of her plans to become a cadet and, in response to his ultimatum for her to desist, she sent back his ring and bracelet, breaking off their engagement, something he says stunned him.

But if he was traumatized, he seemed fully prepared to get on with his life. He acknowledges finding another girlfriend and giving her the bracelet that he had given to Rachel. In addition, said fellow OCS candidate Harold Gary, who claims that he and Robinson were frequent companions at that time, "I was with him when he received all those trinkets from Rachel, and he didn't seem either surprised or all that broken up over it. Maybe he was, but if so, he really kept it to himself."

Though Robinson, and everyone who knows him, claims he never touched alcohol, he was not immune to other soldierly diversions. Though there is no information about the "other" woman, he, Gary, and other officers regularly visited Austin when they had time off. "There was a family there that put us up so we could all go out and have a blast," Gary remembered.

Sometime between his court-martial and his final transfer to Camp Breckinridge, Jackie looked up Rachel again. He saw her on a visit to the Bay Area where he was also visiting his brother Frank's widow and children. According to Rowan, the engagement ring was in the glove compartment of Robinson's car, and he casually mentioned that to Rachel, but "neither the technique nor the circumstances seemed satisfactory for a reengagement."

Later, after his discharge, Robinson saw Rachel in Los Angeles just before he assumed his job as a coach in Texas. Rachel then accepted his ring, but she was soon to be on her way to New York to find work as a nurse. Her family had given her a small amount of money as a graduation present, and her mother had found living accommodations for her with a family friend. Rachel asked her fiancée:

"Can't we postpone it for just a little while? You've accepted this job as a coach, but you're still talking about baseball with that Kansas City team?"

The engagement seemed about as solid as Robinson's future.

The coaching job with Sam Houston College carried him through the winter. His team, drawn from a student body of only thirty-five men, did well, but there was little reason, financial or professional, to consider staying on.

When Robinson wrote to the Monarchs asking about playing for them, his letter was quickly answered. He would, pending his performance on the field, be offered a job. The pay, probably the best he could have gotten from any Negro League team then, would be $100 a week, minus meal money and incidental expenses on the road. This was not bad, and more than comparable for seasonal work or even for everyday jobs in industry, though lacking any security or even the commitment of a contract (Negro League contracts then were mainly verbal). Still, the job was with the Kansas City Monarchs, perhaps the most prestigious of all black professional sports organizations.

The Monarchs had a proud and long baseball history. In the founding years of the Negro Leagues, the care and effort that went into building and maintaining the franchise created a winning tradition on and off the field.

Buck O'Neil, both a player and a manager for the Monarchs, was there at the beginning and at the end, and he knew Kansas City as few did:

"The Negro League was organized right here in Kansas City. Baseball had been played for years elsewhere, but Rube [Foster] organized the League right here in Kansas City and the city was always special.

Kansas City then was wide-open. Boss Pendergast ruled Kansas City and all the doors were open everywhere. All the great jazz musicians came through Kansas City, anybody who was anybody came here. You could always get a job playing here in Kansas City, and as far as baseball was concerned, the Monarchs were one of Kansas City's prime products, and because of that people would come from all over to see us play. They'd come from Omaha and even further away, they'd come in September to see us play, to be in Kansas City and see the town and maybe buy their winter clothing—and when they came all the hotels would be full, the restaurants, the streets, the stores—and the Monarchs had so much to do with that.''

The tradition meant that the Monarchs got the best baseball talent. They paid more and offered players better living and traveling conditions—the team had two buses, not one. There was always a winning atmosphere.

"The reason we had such good ball clubs," O'Neil said, "was like the Yankees. If you were a player and a scout came to your door from the Yankees and one came from another team, your eyes would light up for the Yankees. Same with the Monarchs. Everybody wanted to come and play with the Kansas City Monarchs.'' In recent years those players had included Satchel Paige, Othello Renfroe, Willard Brown, Bullet Joe Rogan, Hank Thompson, Hilton Smith—and now Jackie Robinson, who, it turned out, came to see playing in the Negro leagues generally and with the Monarchs specifically very differently.

Robinson clearly responded to the Monarch tradition. He had a great year on the field. Though no official stats were kept, Arthur Mann, the Dodger executive, calculated from his own sources that Robinson hit .350 through the season. He was adequate defensively; most agreed he did not have the arm for shortstop and had difficulty going to his right on ground balls. While he was not the fastest of runners, he was devastatingly quick and supremely alert, always a threat.

Robinson's combativeness and intelligence impressed teammates and opponents alike. "Jackie didn't have the ability at first," said teammate Newt Allen, "but he had the brains. We had a ballplayer here that was a much better ballplayer than he was—Willard Brown. He could hit, run, throw. But Jackie had one-third ability and two-thirds brains, and that made him a great ballplayer.'' Brains meant that Robinson did things a little differently, but always with the single focus of finding ways to win games. He was a great bunter, everyone agreed. "Tell him something once and you never had to tell him again, he'd pick your brains and you'd never even know it," said Frank Duncan Jr., a player with the Elite Giants then and the son of Robinson's manager with the Monarchs.

"He picked up a whole bunch of little things, like how pitchers give themselves away," Duncan said. "Pitchers fall behind two and oh, three and one, they very rarely throw curve balls. That's a little thing, but it matters a lot. Here's something else Jackie learned to do that nobody else did. He's on first, guy singles to left. Running from first, Jackie's running towards the left fielder. He can see him all the way. Nine out of ten guys stop at second. Jackie used to keep going, go about halfway. He'd make a little fake dash like he was gonna try to get back to second so he'd make the guy throw to second to get him. The minute he did that, he'd just walk on into third—and everybody'd be laughing."

There were great players to see and to learn from. Teammate Satchel Paige, already in his forties, was still baseball's greatest pitcher. And then there were veterans Willie Wells, Pee Wee Butts, Ray Dandridge, Quincy Trouppe, Double Duty Radcliffe, Gene Benson, and many, many others—younger players like Bonnie Serrell, Sam Jethroe, Larry Doby, pitchers like Leon Day and Hilton Smith, legends like Josh Gibson, Buck Leonard, Cool Papa Bell.

Robinson, whose baserunning became a signature of his game, inevitably learned from Cool Papa.

"You had to see Cool Papa to believe him," said Willie Grace of the Cleveland Buckeyes. "Cool would jump off the base a few times, get big leads—and he'd be telling you when he did that he wasn't going to steal. That wasn't the way he did it. He just wanted the pitcher to throw over so he could see his move. When he stole, it was all quickness. He'd walk off the base, that's all—just two or three feet, no more. But then when you looked up, he was on second base! He'd take that little walk—and forget it, he was gone."

On the bus to and from games, the Monarchs talked baseball incessantly. It was part of their tradition. In her book *The Kansas City Monarchs,* Janet Bruce recounted one of these team meetings on wheels:

" 'We went to school on a team,' Newt Allen asserted. 'When we were riding on the bus or when we used to ride on the train, we would sit up and talk about how we're going to pitch to this guy or how we're going to watch this man.' But the players were in agreement that the discussions *after* the game set them apart. 'That was one thing we did here . . . that the majors never did,' remembered pitcher Connie Johnson, who signed with the Chicago White Sox. 'They never did talk about the game. The game's over, that's it. Whether you win or lose, we were talking about the game—what happened, what we could have did, what we didn't do. We called it a skull session.' "

But for all that he might have picked up, Jackie Robinson had little use for Negro League baseball. Like the army, that other great but poisoned proving ground, life in the Negro leagues turned out to be more painful than educational.

For one thing, Robinson just did not comfortably fit in. One of the few college-educated players in the league, he was the only one who had attended a large, predominantly white university. He was, as he had been elsewhere, something of a loner. He not only refrained from drinking, smoking, and excessive partying, it disturbed him that so many other players would indulge themselves, thereby risking what small chance they had to advance their careers.

While Robinson was soft-spoken, to many "a perfect gentleman" away from the field (where he was always a furious and vociferous combatant), everyone soon came to learn how tightly wound he was. Practical joking, for example, was universally accepted in the league —but not by Robinson.

"All the ballplayers used to hang around in each other's dugouts," remembered Willie Grace, "and we had this thing where we'd try to make off with each other's bats and things like that. One night, we played the Monarchs a game in St. Louis, and I'm over in their dugout beforehand, laughing and kidding around with some of the guys, and, you know, I picked up this bat, handling it like it was mine, and then I walked away with it. Soon as I got to my dugout, I gave it to one of our mascots to hide real quick. Then when they started taking their batting practice, that's when Jackie noticed that his bat was missing. So he came over and started raising all kinds of sand. I mean it was bad. We had a big pitcher with us, guy named Bremmer, who stepped in front of Jackie and said, 'Hey, ain't no kids over here now.' Jackie's manager, Frank Duncan, had to come over and tell him, Hey, this has been going on as long as there's been baseball and always will go on. They won't steal your glove or anything like that, but they'll take a bat just for the fun of it'—and he talked him down. By the way, first time Jackie faced Bremmer after that in a game, he hit one into the left-field bleachers!''

But it was not just the horseplay that was off-putting. Almost every phase of life in the Negro Leagues bothered him, and from day one. In a scathing and (especially for Negro League players and fans) up-setting piece written in 1948, when Robinson might have been seeking to aid Branch Rickey in his quarrel with Negro League owners who had accused the Dodger owner of stealing players—including Rob-inson—Jackie blistered Negro League baseball as needing a "house-cleaning from top to bottom."

He criticized the failure of owners to furnish their players with contracts. He attacked low salaries, sloppy umpiring, and the misera-ble living conditions.

"During the actual season," he wrote, "players have to make the jump between cities in uncomfortable busses and then play in games while half asleep and very tired. Umpiring is unsupervised and quite prejudiced in many cases. The umpires are quite often untrained and favor certain teams.

"When players are able to get a night's rest, the hotels are usually of the cheapest kind. The rooms are dingy and dirty, and the rest rooms in such bad condition that the players are unable to use them."

What does not appear anywhere in the article is an attack on the prejudice that produced Negro League baseball in the first place and that lay behind its continued existence. The delicacy of Robinson's position in 1948 may account for that, but what is certain is that at the heart of his complaint was his continuing inability to stomach racism, as he felt other Negro Leaguers did. His attack on the indulgent life-style of some players, for example, did not come from his being either a puritan or a phony but because he saw it as playing into the hands of those who were all too willing to keep baseball segregated.

"We'd ride miles and miles on the bus," the late Othello Renfroe told Jules Tygiel, "and [Jackie's] whole talk was, 'Well, you guys better get ready because pretty soon baseball's going to sign one of us.' "

Renfroe was just one of many who remembered that Robinson's reaction to discrimination on the road could become downright scary. Frank Duncan Jr. recalled a story that he had obviously picked up from several teammates of Robinson's:

"They had left some place in Alabama and they were in the bus. Satchel was traveling on his own, and they stopped to get some gas. Jackie had to go to the bathroom so he asked the filling station attendant where the bathroom was. The guy said, yours is over there—and he pointed off in the distance or something. Jackie said, 'What do you mean "my bathroom"? There's a bathroom right here. The attendant tells him no, the colored bathroom's over there and the white one's over here. Jackie says, 'What the hell are you talkin' about?' and he goes to the first bathroom he sees, which was the white one. The guy comes at him, yelling and cursing and really worked up, and then Jackie, through instinct, hit him. Jackie hit him and the guy's head was hanging across that gas pump when they left there. Everyone was just scared to death. Four or five of them grabbed Jackie and pulled him back in the bus. The traveling secretary left the money, left the money right on the gas pump and they took off. And then they talked to Jackie, told him how he couldn't do those things, how risky that was and how lucky they were to get out of there alive that time."

Whatever Robinson thought changed nothing. Bus travel and southern towns, bad food and poor lodging, the daily round of insults and acquiescence continued—to the point where twice during the season Robinson thought seriously of quitting. The first time, Monarch management talked him out of it by offering him an additional $100 a month. The second time, in September, there was no dissuading him. Robinson, saying that he was too tired to continue, that he needed rest, jumped his team and headed back to Los Angeles.

But by then, his life and that of the nation had been irrevocably changed. On August 28, 1945, he had signed with the Brooklyn Dodgers, becoming the first African-American in this century to be placed under a playing contract to a major league team.

CHAPTER ELEVEN

While the ancient Greeks insisted that character was fate, and while our own mythmakers have so matched Jackie Robinson, history has always been messier than myth—and the story of how this pioneer became intertwined with the integration of baseball is no exception.

Long before Robinson was even a name in a scout's mind, the campaign to integrate baseball was under way. In 1931, Westbrook Pegler, then a reform-minded journalist, and Jimmy Powers of the *New York Daily News* both called for baseball to drop its ban on black players. But the real push began years later, in 1936, when the *Daily Worker* began a steady and unremitting campaign for integration that did not stop until the walls finally fell. The *Worker* effort, spearheaded by sports editor and writer Lester Rodney, was clearly part of an overall political assault by the Communist Party against racial discrimination—i.e., class warfare—in American capitalism. A year or so after the *Worker* began its push, the *Pittsburgh Courier,* the most widely circulated Negro weekly in the nation, initiated its own campaign. The *Courier* campaign was not so much the reflection of an organized effort as an ad hoc one, in this case by sportswriter Wendell Smith, who soon was joined by others in the black press, most notably Sam Lacy of the *Chicago Defender* and Joe Bostic of the *People's Voice,* a Harlem-based paper that eventually launched the political career of Congressman Adam Clayton Powell Jr. Over the years, the *Worker* and the *Courier* worked separately and, when it was convenient, in tandem. Rodney, who created a daily sports section for the *Worker* in 1937, noted, "I have a letter from Wendell Smith thanking us and offering to share interviews; you know, he would do one and I would do one, they were in Pittsburgh, we were in New York. We ran each other's articles, we helped each other out."

What was remarkable was the passion and the insistence of the campaign, which was generally lost on white America—though not on those in government who were always vigilant to the twin menaces of communist agitation and black unrest.

Rodney and the *Worker* from the start targeted the Dodgers, perhaps because Rodney, in his own words, was "both a communist and a Dodger fan," but also because the paper's base of operations was New York, and the Dodgers, more than the blue-blood Yankees or the characterless Giants, fit the mold. In early 1943, the *Worker* published an open letter to Branch Rickey, in splashy bold print, calling on him to sign three prominent Negro League stars—Josh Gibson, Sammy Bankhead, and a young catcher named Roy Campanella—as a way of dealing with a wartime shortage of players in the majors.

Wendell Smith of the *Courier* was a former high-school athlete who had been burned by racism in his youth. "Wendell was born in Detroit and he lived in a white neighborhood," said Smith's widow, Wyonella, "and he never really had any experience with segregation. He was an athlete and he grew up on the same block with Mike Tresh, who later became a catcher for the White Sox. They were friends and teammates. Mike was a catcher and Wendell was an outstanding pitcher. One year their team was in the American Legion championship game. Those games were covered by scouts. Wendell pitched and won this game, one to nothing and afterwards, this scout came to Wendell and said he wished he could sign him up but he was the wrong color. He signed Mike and the opposing pitcher. And that's when Wendell decided that if he did nothing else, he would see that blacks got an opportunity to play in the major leagues."

The war years, precisely because they depleted the majors of its talent pool, provided an unparalleled opportunity to pressure baseball for change. Robinson's Pasadena "tryout" with the White Sox in 1942, though it was a groundbreaker, was only a footnote to the campaign. The *Courier* and the *Worker* reported the results of a late 1930s poll of major league managers, showing a large number, including Reds manager Bill McKechnie and Dodgers manager Leo Durocher, favoring integration and implying that only the owners were blocking it. By 1940, under pressure from the *Courier,* Pittsburgh Pirates owner William Benswanger indicated that he would favor an end to the ban. In 1942, the *Worker,* between its regular calls for letter-writing and petition campaigns, publicized a series of spring-training games between the Dodgers and mixed teams of Cuban all-stars. Its March 4, 1942, sports pages carried the lead, "Dodgers Play Cuban-Negro Stars Today." The article went on to point out that the Dodgers had split four games the previous spring with the all-stars, reminding readers that Leo Durocher had publicly "spoken out against the jim crow ban."

But if 1942 seemed to be an important year in the struggle, it was only a prelude to what was coming in 1943. If readers of the *Worker* were really attentive, they came to understand that that was the year the color barrier fell—perhaps.

The year began with the *Worker* calling for fans to write New York teams asking them to end segregation, specifically to pressure the Dodgers to replace recently drafted shortstop Pee Wee Reese with the Negro League star Willie Wells. The Wells-for-Reese campaign was soon folded into coverage of a possible new West Coast tryout for Negro stars, including Nate Moreland, Biz Mackey, and Robinson's old UCLA teammate Kenny Washington. The tryout was called off at the last minute, but that failure segued into the possibility of success at an even higher level.

In mid-March, the *Worker* reported that "a brown-eyed, tan-faced rookie" outfielder, Luis Olmo, had greatly impressed the Dodgers and manager Durocher during spring camp. The article compared Olmo to Joe DiMaggio and went on to remind the Dodgers that their urgent catching needs might easily be filled by signing Josh Gibson.

A week and a half later, when it appeared certain that Olmo would actually make the club, the paper underscored the significance of the move. "An interesting and utterly important development is taking place here in the camp of the Dodgers," the story began. "The thing we have to report is the manner in which the Dodgers are accepting Luis Olmo, the only Puerto Rican ever to get into a Dodger uniform."

What was "utterly important" was not Olmo's DiMaggio-like skills, but the ease of his acceptance among his peers—teammates and rivals alike. In case *Worker* readers had a hard time understanding what that meant, the paper emphasized the point: "In fact, this dark-complexioned Puerto Rican kid is helping to break down whatever little prejudices some may have had towards colored people. . . . The Dodgers, much to their credit, have taken Olmo in as an equal without giving much thought to the fact that his skin is colored and that he is the first Puerto Rican ever to make the Dodgers." Never mind that the Washington Senators had carried Cuban ballplayers since the Thirties. This was Brooklyn, where social justice and baseball flowed together like mighty tributaries.

When Olmo did finally make the club, the comparisons to DiMaggio were expanded to include other Yankee greats Tony Lazerri and George Selkirk. The signing of Olmo, far from getting the Dodgers off the hook, only made them an even greater focus of attention. That spring, the Young Communist League opened what the *Worker* called "a nationwide campaign to end Hitler's shame in the major leagues." Petitions were being circulated everywhere, but most heavily in Brooklyn where "the campaign has picked up most steam and promises early and positive results."

Later that same spring, the Communist-dominated National Maritime Union joined the YCL's petition drive by urging Branch Rickey in particular to end "the continuance of the Hitlerite Jim Crow policy in the big leagues."

By the end of 1943, the *Worker* believed its campaign was paying off, that "new glorious vistas for the American pastime" were in the offing and that by the following spring there was "every hope that . . . such great Negro stars as Josh Gibson, Dave Barnhill, Jesse Williams, Hilton Smith, Buck Leonard, and many others will be in their rightful place in the big leagues." The *Worker,* in a separate article, featured thumbnail sketches of the players, thereby becoming the only paper outside the black press to give readers a sense of who these Negro League stars were.

The reasons for optimism went far beyond the acceptance of Luis Olmo (who hit reasonably well, .303, with little power, four homers, playing part-time). The drumbeat for change now began to come from official quarters. A committee of the New York City Council, whose new members included Adam Clayton Powell Jr., Mike Quill, and Communist Benjamin J. Davis Jr., was on record in support, as was Congressman Vito Marcantonio. Most importantly, baseball itself seemed to be stirring. For the first time, the question of integration was on the agenda of the winter meetings, scheduled that year for New York. A petition by members of the Negro Publishers Association to make a presentation on the subject had been granted, and the way seemed clear, so some believed, for decisive action.

The meetings at the Commodore and New Yorker hotels were given further weight when, at the last minute, the delegation of Negro Publishers was augmented by the inclusion of the great singer, actor, and activist Paul Robeson.

For the *Worker,* Robeson's appearance eclipsed even that of the

Negro publishers. Though no press was admitted to the ballroom where Robeson spoke, it was as though the *Worker* alone was eyewitness to history (actually, in a later article the paper explained that it came by its "exclusive" by listening at an opened transom):

"The Negro player question occupied first place on the agenda of this all-important meeting which was attended by the presidents, vice-presidents and general managers of all the 16 major league clubs," the paper reported.

"[Commissioner] Landis, in introducing Robeson, said, 'It is unnecessary to introduce Paul Robeson. Everybody knows him for what he has done as an athlete and an artist. I want to introduce him to you as a man of great common sense.' Then departing for a moment from the introduction to set the tone of the whole meeting, Landis firmly stated, 'I want to make it clear that there is not, never has been and, as long as I am connected with baseball, there never will be any agreement among the teams or between any two teams preventing Negroes from participating in organized baseball. Each manager is free to choose players regardless of race, color, or any other condition.'

"Then, 'Now, Paul Robeson will speak to us.' And the famed Negro artist rose to speak.

"For twenty minutes, Robeson spoke to the magnates and when he finished the assembled magnates broke into loud and sustained applause which amazed veteran baseball men who have been covering these annual meetings for many years.

"Robeson ended his impassioned plea for the immediate entrance of Negroes into baseball by declaring, 'I urge you to decide favorably on this request and that action be taken in this very season. I believe you can be assured they will reflect highest credit on the game and the American people will commend you for this action which reflects the best in the American spirit.' "

Needless to say, the significance of this moment was as exaggerated as the prose. By relegating the presentation of specific proposals by the publishers to a position of less importance than Robeson's appearance, the paper may have unwittingly given a boost to Landis and the owners, who were looking to shelve the matter. And as far as the publishers were concerned, the last-minute inclusion of Robeson turned out to be not quite the blessing the *Worker* assumed.

Sam Lacy, a writer for the *Chicago Defender* and a driving force, along with Wendell Smith, behind the campaign for integration, had been replaced in the delegation to make room for Robeson. He was furious.

"The publisher of the *Defender* and the head of the Publishers Association agreed that Robeson should have a stronger voice and so I was supplanted by him. And I was the one who actually set the thing up," he said.

But it wasn't personal pique that got to Lacy so much as the sense that a profound strategic mistake had been made. Robeson's appearance had the backing of the *Worker*. The *Worker* was a Communist paper, Robeson's political leanings were all too obvious, and the consequences of having him—and the *Worker*—as allies at that point were dubious to say the least. By then, Lacy said, he and Wendell Smith had joined forces among black writers, and together they had concluded that Robeson and communism could only spell defeat for what they wanted.

"Yes, Wendell and I both knew they were involved, but we didn't want their help. We wanted to be completely divorced from any communistic influence," Lacy said. "That's the reason I knew Paul Robeson was going to be rejected when he went out there—we knew it and didn't want it to happen."

Though Lacy then resigned from the *Defender* to protest its decision to include Robeson, the rift in the ranks was kept from public view. The campaign continued. A united front of uneasy allies, as in the larger political world, was for the time maintained, but the cracks were there.

By then, however, the campaign was larger than anyone's advocacy. The war had not only fractured nations, it had broken old structures and ways of thinking. Change was simply in the air, part of the rhythm of things. As the military itself had been shaken by racial confrontation, so had the rest of society. There had been riots in major American cities: Detroit, New York, Chicago. The labor scene especially was a constant source of friction.

In 1941, at the urging of A. Philip Randolph, a national Fair Employment Practices Committee had been established to investigate numerous complaints of discrimination in war production and government hiring. The FEPC was further strengthened by executive order in

1943. And then, with the ending of the war, the drive to end discrimination in employment had a momentum of its own. In New York State, legislation was passed establishing a statewide version of the FEPC, and in New York City, Mayor La Guardia, under constant pressure from leaders like Adam Clayton Powell Jr. and Benjamin Davis, created his own Anti-Discrimination Committee including, ultimately, a subcommittee especially designed to hasten the integration of professional baseball.

The highlight of the 1944 season was not anything that happened on the playing field, but the sudden death of Commissioner Kenesaw M. Landis, foe of integration despite his words to the contrary. For a time, until a new commissioner was named, Landis's administrative aide Lesley O'Connor, along with the presidents of the National and American Leagues, formed a Baseball Council to run the game. Sam Lacy wrote to various owners and to O'Connor urging that action toward ending the color ban be hastened. Lacy was then invited to appear at a special spring meeting of owners in Detroit. Out of that meeting, a committee was formed consisting of Lacy, Larry MacPhail of the Yankees, and Branch Rickey of the Dodgers to explore the ways in which baseball integration might take place.

Meanwhile, Wendell Smith's revolving searchlight had isolated Boston for action. There he discovered that a local liberal councilman, Isadore Muchnick, had been pressuring the city's two major league teams to integrate. When Smith suggested to him that he could provide players for a tryout, Muchnick's threat to join forces with a noisy group advocating the imposition of Sunday blue laws (which would have effectively wiped out Boston baseball's most profitable day) seemed to be just enough to jar the Red Sox, who claimed there had never been a club policy to bar qualified black players if only they could be found.

Smith found them: Marvin Williams of the Philadelphia Stars, Sam Jethroe of the Cleveland Buckeyes, and rookie Jackie Robinson of the Kansas City Monarchs.

On a weekend in mid-April 1945, the men turned up in Boston and there waited with Smith for what would soon be written off as just another shuffling of the deck—but was actually the opening round of a whole new game.

CHAPTER TWELVE

The Red Sox tryout was a farce. As much as Wendell Smith tried to put the best face on it, the players saw the jokers they had been dealt. First, when they arrived in Boston, the tryouts were put off for several days, ostensibly because of the death and funeral of President Roosevelt. The players laughed among themselves about it in their hotel room—except for Robinson. He was angry. He told Wendell Smith, "Listen, Smith, it burns me up to come fifteen hundred miles to have them give me the runaround."

When the tryout finally was held on April 16, nothing came of it. The *Pittsburgh Courier* ran a front-page story about it, dwarfing coverage of Roosevelt's funeral, but the players knew its insignificance better than anyone. When Sam Jethroe rejoined the Cleveland Buckeyes, he talked about it. "Sam told us what a joke that so-called tryout was," Willie Grace said. "He said you just knew it was a farce because when the guys were out there, Joe Cronin, who was managing the club, didn't even bother to look. He was up in the stands with his back turned most of the time. He just sent some of his men out there and told them to throw some balls, hit some balls to us, and then come back and say we had ability."

In fact, Cronin, days after the workout, broke a leg, was hospitalized, and never again pursued the question of signing the players. But Wendell Smith wasn't about to stop with the Red Sox.

On his way back from Boston to Pittsburgh, he stopped in New York to talk with Dodger general manager, Branch Rickey. Weeks earlier, Joe Bostic, a writer who worked for both the Negro weekly *People's Voice* and the *Worker,* created a stir at the Bear Mountain, New York, spring training home of the Dodgers. Bostic, without advance notice, simply turned up with two older Negro leagues players, John "Showboat" Thomas and Terris McDuffie, and demanded a tryout for them.

The tryout was held, with Branch Rickey personally in attendance. Rickey, though he made some bland, noncommittal statements to the press afterward, was actually enraged. According to one writer,

Rickey reacted to a "sickening red tinge" behind the effort. He told Bostic that he did not appreciate being confronted and that he was "more for your cause than anyone else you know, but you are making a mistake using force. You are defeating your own aims."

Though Bostic and others may have concluded that Rickey was the least likely to break the color barrier, Smith may have been one who knew otherwise. Rickey for some time had been developing a still-secret plan to integrate the game, and he had certainly been a principal target of pressure by protesters.

When Smith met Rickey in Brooklyn, he told him about the Boston tryout and, particularly, about Jackie Robinson, who, Smith felt, was the most likely candidate to make it. Rickey, according to several accounts, said that he was unfamiliar with Robinson; he had heard about him as a football player but not as a baseball player. In any event, from that moment on, he began to follow Robinson more closely.

Robinson was scouted by the Dodgers' three top scouts assigned to the Negro leagues: George Sisler, Wid Matthews, and Clyde Sukeforth. Later that summer, Rickey made a trip to Los Angeles to gather personal information about Robinson. What Smith knew that day in Brooklyn was what many in the white press then and afterward did not know: that Branch Rickey was perhaps the *most* likely major league executive to finally break the color barrier.

Smith, like Sam Lacy and others pressing for the integration of the sport, could not guess what was in Rickey's heart. Why he would have been more likely than anyone else to decide for integration had to be a puzzle. Rickey was an archconservative who had been prominent not only in baseball but in politics. When he was chief executive of the St. Louis Cardinals in the thirties, he was seriously talked about as a possible Republican Party candidate for governor. His archenemies were (in no particular order) Roosevelt, communism, and welfare.

When he came to New York in 1942, he quickly earned the reputation of being both a blowhard and skinflint. *Daily News* columnist Jimmy Powers dubbed Rickey "El Cheapo," and the name stuck to him like his bushy eyebrows. He had a reputation of recruiting talent at the lowest possible cost. He had done that in St. Louis, creating an innovative and extensive farm system, and he was doing that in

Brooklyn when the controversies about integration began to spread beyond the black press and the *Daily Worker*.

What Wendell Smith probably did not know was that Rickey, since the middle of the war, had been planning to introduce black talent as part of his scheme to revolutionize and revitalize the Dodger system.

Arthur Mann, Rickey's assistant, said Rickey had a "six-part plan" to introduce black players. The stages were:

1. The backing and sympathy of the Dodgers' directors and stock-holders, whose investment and civic standing had to be considered and protected.
2. Picking a Negro who would be the right man on the field.
3. Picking a Negro who would also be the right man off the field.
4. A good reaction from the press and public.
5. Backing and thorough understanding from the Negro race, to avoid misinterpretation and abuse of the project.
6. Acceptance of the player by his teammates.

As early as 1943, Rickey outlined his plans for an expanded farm system to the Dodgers' board of directors. At the same time, he approached a local citizen, the banker George McLaughlin, and sounded him out about the possibility of signing a black player. Rickey tried out his suggestion on McLaughlin because he was a heavy backer of the team and an influential member of the community.

"We are going to beat the bushes, and we will take whatever comes out," Rickey reportedly told McLaughlin, "and that might include a Negro player or two." McLaughlin supposedly answered that he could see no objection to that.

But whatever political, economic, or local pressures were driving him, Rickey was heading into uncharted waters, and who he was as a navigator mattered greatly.

One of the classic Rickey stories, one he told years later, went back to 1904 when he was a baseball coach for Ohio Wesleyan University. The team had a black catcher, Charley Thomas, and when they checked into a hotel in South Bend, Indiana, prior to a game with Notre Dame, Thomas was denied a room. Rickey says he persuaded management to let Thomas have a cot in his own room. Then, hours later, when Rickey returned to the room, he found Thomas sitting alone, weeping, pulling at his hands. As Arthur Mann tells it, Thomas kept saying, "Damned skin! Damned skin!"

What actually happened was in all likelihood less dramatic. When Mann sent Thomas a copy of a book containing that story, Thomas replied by sending Mann a Christmas card saying that he thought the book was "a masterpiece" but that the episode at the Oliver House "is exaggerated and I am quite sure that Mr. Rickey didn't say what the reporters enlarged upon."

One of Rickey's surviving daughters, Jane Jones, remembers that the story about Thomas was one of those things "we got at the table," but she too thought the business of Thomas trying to pull the skin off his hands was an exaggeration.

Jones, however, believes that her father had always been sensitive to discrimination. In St. Louis, she was once hauled into court on a traffic ticket, and her father, interceding on her behalf, became distracted by police interrogating a black suspect accused of murder.

"It was around 1932," Jones said. "I was sixteen then. This man was being grilled for murder, with a knife or something, and Dad walked right over and busted right in on the grilling. He just didn't want to see the guy mistreated; he was a lawyer and he knew people had rights and he wanted to see to it that this guy had someone there for him." Jones laughed. "He wound up giving the guy his card and then, after that, hired him as a chauffeur!"

Rickey, up close, was an autocrat. He came from a desperately poor but devout farm family, and because he had been an entirely self-made man, the principles he lived by he expected others to follow as well.

"There were fourteen of us at the table all the time and we had a lecture all the time. Sometimes there would be strangers at the table. The chicken man might come for two or three weeks, and you never knew who you would find sleeping in your bed," Jones said, "but Dad just carried on anyway."

Rickey's five daughters were called "the boys." His son, Branch Jr., known as "the Twig" to the press, was just "boy" within the family. "When Dad said, 'C'mon, boys, we're going to the movies,' " Jones said, "everybody went."

But within his system of autocracy was the secret heart of the large moral commitment he was so soon to make. "One of Dad's lectures was that sometimes in life you lose, but that when you find you have, you have to get into the canoe and paddle along,'' said Jones. She remembered an incident when her father couldn't paddle. "My sister Alice had gotten engaged to a wonderful man who happened to be Catholic—and Dad just didn't like Catholics. So he carried on and on about it. He was just terrible. It didn't matter. Alice brought her beau home—who Dad later came to adore—but I couldn't stand to be at dinner with them. I left and came back late at night. Dad was up reading and I said to him, 'You always told us to get in the canoe and paddle when we lost, but you weren't being honest when you said that.' Well, Dad just hit the roof. 'You're calling me a liar!' he said, and he stormed out of the house. He didn't come back for hours. But when he did, we made up. He told me he was wrong. He wouldn't wear a white carnation going into the chapel when Alice and Ed got married, but he changed and he loved Ed as though he was his own son.''

Rickey's commitment to fairness and justice in breaking baseball's color barrier was similarly on his terms—but it was just as powerful and just as enduring.

There is, by now, almost an air of folklore in the coming together of Rickey and Robinson. It has become a part of American legend. Because of that, what actually happened is harder to see.

The legend has the first meeting between the men occurring on August 28, 1945. Dodger scout Clyde Sukeforth had been dispatched to Chicago to see Robinson in a Negro League game, to test his arm, and then, if he thought it was adequate, to bring him in for a meeting with Mr. Rickey. Sukeforth and Robinson have both described their wariness in that Chicago contact. Robinson refused to throw for Sukeforth because he had injured his shoulder a few days previously. Sukeforth, a dour and fair-minded New Englander, shrugged and decided to ask Robinson to return with him to meet with Mr. Rickey anyway. "I met with him that night in the hotel; we talked for about an hour and a half I guess," Sukeforth said. "I asked him all the questions I thought Mr. Rickey would ask him, like [about] his troubles in the army, his physical problems, and so on. The more I talked to him the more impressed I was with him, with his determination and intelligence and aggressiveness. I asked him to meet me in Toledo, that I had to see a doubleheader there the next day.''

Robinson turned up between games of the doubleheader, took the train back to New York with Sukeforth, and the day following, on Monday morning, met Rickey at the Dodger offices at 215 Montague Street in Brooklyn.

Three eyewitnesses were at that meeting. Two of them are dead. But all have given their accounts of what took place, and each man's version, with variations, supports the others'. Robinson said Rickey's first words to him were, "Have you got a girl?"

Sukeforth remembers the question about having a mate coming a little later in the conversation. All of the men agree that Rickey play-acted through many of the likely situations that Robinson would face. "To show me what I'd be up against," Robinson said, "he acted out a series of one-man dramatic scenes. He was a room clerk in a southern hotel, an insulting waiter in a restaurant, and a sarcastic railroad conductor. Then he took off his coat and played the role of a hot-headed ballplayer and swung his fist at me."

Robinson remembered Rickey's face as it contorted, the sweat clinging to his clothes and skin, the words of vaudeville psychodrama tumbling out:

"You're playing shortstop and I come down from first, stealing with my spikes high, and I cut you in the leg. As the blood trickles down your shin, I grin at you and say, 'Now how do you like that, nigger boy?' " Then, in the World Series: "So we play for keeps there, Jackie; we play it there to win, and almost everything under the sun goes. I want to win in the most desperate way, so I'm coming into second with my spikes flying. But you don't give ground. You're tricky. You feint, and as I hurl myself, you ease out of the way and jam that ball hard into my ribs. As I lie there in the swirling dust, my rib aching, I hear that umpire crying, 'You're out,' and I jump up, and all I can see is that black face of yours shining in front of my eyes. So I yell, 'Don't hit me with a ball like that, you tar-baby son of a bitch.' So I haul off and sock you right in the cheek."

Robinson at one point asked, "Do you want someone who would not have the courage to fight back?"

Rickey thundered, "I am looking for someone with courage *not* to fight back."

Sukeforth, Robinson, and Rickey all agree that Rickey at that most timely moment then whipped out a copy of Papini's *Life of Christ* and handed it to Robinson. Turn the other cheek was the lecture of the day, the point of the play. It was all in Scripture.

The legendary meeting ends with Robinson signing with the Dodgers—in secret; word was to be withheld until the team chose to announce it—for a signing bonus of $3,500 and an agreement for a salary of $600 a month when Robinson began play with the Montreal Royals, the Dodgers' number one farm team.

All that is missing in this play script is what went before. Rickey's original six-point plan highlighted picking the right player on and off the field, getting good press coverage, winning the support of the black community. These component parts of the master plan were hardly the result of spontaneous combustion in a single meeting.

Contrary to legend, Rickey and Robinson had met before. Both men had had time to size each other up, to think, to ask questions of others, before anything like an official contract was placed on the table and Robinson, perfectly aware of why he had come to New York, signed it.

CHAPTER THIRTEEN

Wendell Smith became aware that Rickey was probably interested in Jackie Robinson about a week after the meeting they had following the Red Sox tryout in April. Rickey contacted Smith then to inform him that "more might be going on" than he had been able to talk about before. Smith said he specifically asked Rickey if he was thinking of signing Robinson for the Dodgers, and the answer—as recounted by Jerome Holtzman—was that Rickey was sending one of his scouts to follow Robinson on the Kansas City Monarchs.

Smith concluded at that early point that the Dodgers were interested in Robinson. "I was tempted to write it, that the Dodgers were talking to him," he said later, "but it would have killed it. I was sworn to secrecy. When Rickey and I talked on the phone, we never used Jackie Robinson's name. It was always 'the young man from the West.'"

Through the season, there was continuing contact between Rickey and Smith, particularly as Jackie's fiery temperament became known to Rickey. At one point, Rickey phoned Smith after learning that Jackie had threatened to punch an umpire during a game.

"Mr. Rickey called me and asked if Jackie was a belligerent type of individual," Smith said. "I didn't want to tell Mr. Rickey, 'Yes, he's tough to get along with.' A lot of us knew that. When he was aroused, he had a sizable temper. But to survive, he couldn't be a Mickey Mouse."

During that same '45 Negro League season, Ted "Double Duty" Radcliffe was briefly a member of the Monarchs. In that time he claims to have roomed with Robinson, and that Jackie had taken to him because "he had heard that because I could get the girls, he wanted to be where the action was." Radcliffe, who has had a reputation as something of a yarn-spinner, had his own skein for Robinson:

"On June the thirteenth, we went to Newark, New Jersey. Don Newcombe was there then and they had him to pitch against Satchel and the park was packed. The park couldn't hold but eighteen thousand, but they had to put in extra seats so they had about twenty-

109

three thousand and Satchel showed 'em up. We beat 'em thirteen to nothing. Jackie had two doubles, a single, and a home run that night —and stole three bases. That night Branch Rickey sent George Sisler and Clyde Sukeforth, his two top scouts, over there to get Jackie. I was sitting in the door of the clubhouse—it was hot that night when they came up—and I knew George pretty well because he had been following Birmingham for a while [Radcliffe's former team was the Birmingham Black Barons], and we talked about Jackie. And he thanked me and he went on in, and when Jackie got dressed, they took him over to the Knickerbocker Hotel, and so he came back around one o'clock that night. He said, 'Well, it's done. I signed to go to Montreal in '46.' ''

Radcliffe was adamant about the timing of the story, emphasizing that he was no longer with the Monarchs in August, when Jackie's signing in Brooklyn took place.

"In August, I was with the Globetrotters, not the Monarchs," he said, "so I know what I'm talking about."

The details of the game—the 13–0 Monarchs win, behind Satchel Paige; Don Newcombe pitching for Newark; Jackie Robinson's four hits, including a home run, and three stolen bases; the heat (the temperature had reached ninety degrees that day)—are specific. It was certainly true that George Sisler and Clyde Sukeforth, along with Wid Matthews, were Branch Rickey's top scouts assigned specifically to watch the Negro leagues, and it was true that Radcliffe and Sisler knew each other and would have recognized each other if their paths crossed at the ballpark. Still, it is worth noting that neither Clyde Sukeforth nor anyone else remembers the evening.

Radcliffe may have been mistaken or inventive about Robinson's signing a Montreal contract then, but he was not mistaken about a meeting.

Rickey's daughter Jane Jones, who frequently drove her father from place to place in those years, recalls that "one day he wanted to go to a game in New Jersey, Newark I think, I'm not sure, but Mother wouldn't go so I don't think he went."

What Jones does remember is that she drove her father to work around the same time, went upstairs to the Dodger offices with him, went into his office, and was sitting there with him when Jackie Robinson was announced. Jones could not date the meeting, but she knew from the way the men dealt with one another that it was a first meeting.

"I had no idea who Jackie Robinson was," she said, "or that Dad was going to see him or anything. . . . He said this won't take long, sit still, so I just pulled up a chair and sat by the side and it was just like I was not there."

Robinson, she says, stood in the doorway. She remembers how large and dark he was, and that her father did not look up from his desk. He was working on some papers and continued to work as Robinson stood there. "I remember the stories about the first meeting, that there was supposed to be an impressive handshake between them, but there was nothing," Jones said. "I don't recall Dad ever getting up. And while he was looking at his papers, he just started in telling [Robinson] about himself, about his mother, his brother, a brother who was killed, his war record. He got into a whole thing about the kind of binoculars they used on tanks in the unit Jackie was in—that was the unit that went to the Battle of the Bulge. Dad knew that, too."

Jones remembers that the men had "a nice repartee" and that her father then posed some situations that Robinson might face if he played in the major leagues. "I had never heard him use that kind of language before," she said. "I do remember driving with him once when he referred to someone as a bastard . . . no, no, he wasn't the man to swear."

Rickey asked Robinson if he had a sweetheart, Jones said, and when Robinson said that he did, Rickey wanted to know if he had known her long. "Jackie said she's a nurse, and Dad said, 'Do you have plans?' I don't remember what he said, only that later, in the fall, my husband and I went to a football game with Jackie and Rachel."

Jones specifically said Clyde Sukeforth was *not* in the room for this meeting. When Sukeforth was asked, he seemed certain that the meeting he witnessed was a first but, after talking to Jones, acknowledged that there might indeed have been an earlier meeting he knew nothing about.

The reality was that Rickey proceeded cautiously, carefully, making sure that nothing would be left to chance—even something like a meeting where a contract was expected to be signed.

111

Jones said there was no contract signed that day, no agreements reached, only that her father asked Robinson specifically to think over what they were talking about, to talk to friends and loved ones about the possibility of signing before he came to any decision.

Robinson, on two different occasions—once earlier in the summer, then after the August 28 signing—jumped the Kansas City Monarchs. The reason usually given for each of his AWOL trips was his unhappiness with life in the Negro leagues, but much more likely was his need to sort out what he had suddenly been confronted with.

When his first meeting with Rickey ended, he phoned his family—not Rachel, with whom the future was still pending. He tried to explain to his mother what had happened, but it was difficult.

"He didn't really know what it was all about," said his sister, Willa Mae. "The first thing he said was, 'I don't even know what the major leagues are, what are they talking about?' So none of us got really excited till he got back and explained it to us in more detail."

No one knew what he was talking about. Mack knew something about the major leagues, Mrs. Walker said: "He used to listen to the World Series on the radio, so he knew there were two teams that played each other and that it was a big deal, but he didn't know anything about what took place before the World Series."

Following his second interview with Rickey, when he signed a contract, he proposed to Rachel. She stalled him, wanting to wait until late fall or winter, when he would return from a barnstorming trip he was scheduled to make to South America. The door he was opening now had nothing to do with downtown ballrooms in Los Angeles; the life he was proposing, exciting and challenging as it might be, led to places as unknown to him as to her, requiring total effort and concentration—and inevitably a profound revision of her own plans. She also needed time to think.

If Rickey had had his way, public knowledge of Jackie's signing with the Dodger organization would have happened with as little fanfare and as close to spring training as possible. But from the start, the politics and pressures of the time demanded secrecy. No matter how masterful the master plan was, it turned out to have been more jerry-built than the architect intended.

Through late summer and into the fall, Mayor La Guardia's subcommittee on baseball integration was meeting and preparing a final report. Having resigned from the committee rather than compromise or reveal the fact that he had already been meeting with Robinson, Rickey was forced to stand back and take note of the discussion draft that the subcommittee produced in late September—one month after he had signed Robinson. Guided by Yankee owner Larry MacPhail, the draft report, citing a tangle of difficulties in reaching its goals, called for the establishment of black teams at different minor league levels with the understanding that "there should be no difficulty of promotion of Negroes within the system" up to any level.

Independent of the subcommittee, Communist Party candidate Ben Davis was pushing major league integration as a key plank in his reelection campaign for the City Council. A campaign flyer distributed on his behalf showed a split-page picture of a dead black soldier and a living black baseball player. The caption on the flyer read: "Good enough to die for his country, but not good enough for organized baseball."

Mayor La Guardia at the same time was also pushing baseball integration as election day neared. It became known to Rickey, through one of the subcommittee members, that La Guardia was going to use one of his popular Sunday radio broadcasts to make a pitch for baseball integration—so he could claim some credit for it when it happened. The subcommittee member, Dr. Dan Dodson, was quoted as telling Rickey, "I feel I must tell you, Branch. Our committee's an election football."

Rickey was more than aware of these pressures. They were forcing his hand in ways he had not calculated only months before. In the beginning of October, Arthur Mann had written Rickey, submitting to him a draft proposal for an article that would help publicize the Dodgers' signing of Robinson. Done with Rickey's approval, it was going to be a testament to the courage and vision it took to break the color barrier. Rickey, however, had a change of heart—and plan. He wrote Mann:

Dear Arthur:

We just can't go now with the article. The thing isn't dead—not at all. It is more alive than ever and that is the reason we can't go with any publicity at this time. There is more involved in the situation than I had contemplated. Other players are in it and

113

it may be that I can't clear these other players until after the December meetings, possibly not until after the first of the year. You must simply sit in the boat.

I am extremely hopeful that you will be willing to make some changes in the article. I don't mean to be a crusader. My purpose is to be fair to all people and my selfish objective is to win baseball games. . . .

There is a November 1st deadline on Robinson—you know that. I am undertaking to extend that date until January 1st so as to give me plenty of time to sign other players and make one break on the complete story. Also, quite obviously, it might not be so good to sign Robinson with other and possibly better players unsigned. . . .

> *Cordially yours,*
> *Branch Rickey, President*

But the politics of an electoral season forced Rickey's hand. The luxury of a package signing and announcement had become impossible. Within weeks of his letter to Mann, he was on the phone to La Guardia, asking him to hold off on his proposed Sunday broadcast. He contacted Robinson and told him to be prepared to fly to Montreal immediately to sign his minor-league contract.

Robinson at the time was in New York at the Woodside Hotel in Harlem, preparing to leave for his barnstorming tour. He was working out from day to day at the Harlem YMCA where two other ballplayers, Roy Campanella and Don Newcombe, occasionally joined him. They were among the other players Rickey was referring to in his letter to Mann. To this point, they believed that Rickey's interest in them was for a new team in the United States League—the Brooklyn Brown Dodgers. On the eve of his departure for Montreal, Robinson let slip to Campanella that his contract was going to be with organized baseball.

For Robinson to have revealed what was happening was understandable. He had been living with his secret all summer, bound to the extraordinary pressures that silence had exacerbated. Whom could he speak to, what could he say? On the eve of a truly historic moment, what certainly was a high point in his life, he was just one man alone among millions of people of color in America, a nation still unaware and still, as a collective entity, hostile to the very notion of equality between the races.

The following day, October 23, 1945, the whole world knew what Robinson had been living with. The news out of Montreal, much as Rickey and Robinson might have wished otherwise, was a bombshell, having little to do with favorable press or control of the reaction in the Negro community. From that day forward, neither Jackie Robinson nor Branch Rickey would ever enjoy the comfort of anything so solid as a "six-part plan."

CHAPTER FOURTEEN

The announcement was electrifying, so much so that it was easy to lose the tangled lines of its subtext. When the crowd of waiting reporters was ushered into the office of Montreal Royals president Hector Racine, Robinson looked calm and in control. He was anything but that.

"In the papers the next day, they reported that I had been cool and had handled myself well during the interview. I may have created that impression," he said, "but I was nervous as the devil. I had never faced such a huge battery of writers, and I knew that every word I said would be recorded and then interpreted. The stories would be printed in Canada and the United States. If I said the wrong thing or created the wrong impression, I would have the sportswriters and the fans down on me. And that would just about finish me before I ever started."

Rickey, all too aware that the focus was to be on a single man, had tried to warn Robinson about the storm that was whipping up. "Just be yourself," he cautioned. "Simply say that you are going to do the best you can and let it go at that." Instead, what Robinson had to say was a little different:

"Of course, I can't begin to tell you how happy I am that I am the first member of my race in organized ball. I realize how much it means to me, my race, and to baseball. I can only say I'll do my very best to come through in every manner."

By contrast, the company line specifically sought to downplay any interpretation of the signing in terms of race relations. The *New York Times* noted, "Signing of the player, according to Secretary Harold Parrott of the Dodgers, 'was not a sudden move to be interpreted merely as a gesture toward solution of a racial problem. Robinson was signed on his merits as a shortstop after he had been scouted for a long time.' "

Rickey and the Dodgers had been careful in their selection of Robinson; he had been selected not just because of his talents but because he had the kind of impressive personal qualities that fit the plan.

Therefore, at this critical juncture, it was important that the media get the story right. Under the circumstances, however, even with a coordinated public-relations effort, it was a crapshoot. Dodger officials tried to set the tone.

"Mr. Racine and my father," said Branch Rickey Jr., head of the Dodger farm system, "will undoubtedly be severely criticized in some sections of the United States where racial prejudice is rampant. They are not inviting trouble, but they won't avoid it if it comes. Jack Robinson is a fine type of young man, intelligent and college bred, and I think he can take it too."

The mainstream press, for the most part, followed suit, emphasizing Robinson's background, highlighting the fact that he was "college educated," that he had drawn numerous "all-America" and "all-star" notices as a four-letter athlete at UCLA. Tolerance, equality of opportunity, looking at skill, being blind to skin—all coincided with an optimistic mood in the country following a war in which the defeated enemy had been defined by its repulsive doctrines of racial superiority. Letting a black man play baseball didn't mean socialism was just around the corner.

"We don't agree with those who think that other major league ballplayers will resent Jackie Robinson and others of his race," wrote Dick McCann of the *Washington Times-Herald*, "if and when they make the grade. Your American athlete is, essentially, a good sport . . . far fairer than even the American fan."

"I guarantee if Jackie Robinson hits homers and plays a whale of a game for Montreal, the fans will lose sight of his color," commented W. N. Cox of the *Virginia Pilot*.

Some commentaries attempted to be thoughtful, but these too were within parameters hoped for by Rickey. Was Rickey's effort sincere or a publicity show? How would major league players—all of them white at this point—actually go about the business of getting along with a Negro player? How long would it be before other Negro players were part of the picture?

There was some opposition. Jimmy Powers of the *New York Daily News,* who fifteen years earlier had theoretically favored integrating the game, could barely hide what was on his mind behind his questioning of Branch Rickey's sincerity: "We question Branch Rickey's statements that he is another Abraham Lincoln and that he has a heart as big as a watermelon and that he loves all mankind."

W. G. Bramham, the commissioner of minor league baseball, warned, "Father Devine will have to look to his laurels, for we can expect Rickey Temple to be in course of construction in Harlem soon."

To praise, speculation, or viciousness, the answer given by Rickey and the Dodgers lay in Jackie Robinson's character, as reworked to fit the colors not of race but of the flag. Robinson's color was coal black but his character was spotless, like that of Joe Louis, a living testament to why this move should and could be made.

But nowhere in any press account or even in the private back-grounders offered to the press was there any mention of Robinson's troubles as a youth, his difficulties in the army, or stories about his explosive temper, especially where matters of race had been involved. In short, there was no real information on his life.

But it was hard to make what was happening conform to a script, because foul lines could never contain a social revolution. The black press understood this in ways that the mainstream press never could. Edgar T. Rouzeau wrote:

"The hopes and anxieties of the Negro race were placed squarely on the shoulders of Jack Roosevelt Robinson, the first of his clan to land a place in organized baseball. The announcement by the Brooklyn Dodgers . . . was received in Harlem with a mixture of joy and trepidation."

Ludlow Werner, the editor of the *New York Age,* also understood Robinson's elevation in collective terms, but with a very different emphasis. His main concern was Jackie Robinson:

"I'm happy over the event but I'm sorry for Jackie. He will be haunted by the expectations of his race. To 15,000,000 Negroes he will symbolize not only their prowess in baseball, but their ability to rise to an opportunity. Unlike white players, he can never afford an off-day or an off-night. His private life will be watched, too, because white America will judge the Negro race by everything he does. And Lord help him with his fellow Negroes if he should fail them."

Another quarter was heard from too—one that Rickey must surely have been expecting but that must still have sent special chills down his spine. Writing in the *Daily Worker,* columnist Mike Gold noted,

"That Branch Rickey of the Brooklyn Dodgers has just signed a Negro ballplayer for his team is a bit of news that gladdens many hearts made sick and sad by racial fascism growing rapidly today.

"Sometimes, when you hear these Bilbos and Rankins sounding off, you get the feeling that America must be heading for hell in a fascist rocket.

"On the other hand, however desperate, crazy, or extreme reaction becomes, the American people still keep on inching along. This baseball victory against Jimcrowism may not sound like much to a cloistered philosopher brooding over fascism in the library.

"But the signing of Jackie Robinson is a strong signal in the hurricane of history. . . . This victory should demonstrate to Communists something forgotten in recent years . . ."

Almost certainly, Rickey's greatest fear was that there would be, just over the horizon, an uprising, a riot, a local parliamentary rebellion, that could transform his still-evolving experiment into a social nightmare. The immediate needs were practical; Robinson and his wife would need housing, local people would have to be there for him from town to town to help steer him away from danger, temptation, exploitation. Put in a somewhat different light, Robinson would, for a time, have to be watched.

What is now abundantly clear is that from the start, the government was as interested as Rickey was in taking stock of this potentially explosive development. Though the cold war was not yet in full flower in late 1945, race relations and communism were still high on J. Edgar Hoover's agenda of subversive threats. The dramatic signing of Jackie Robinson was a *national* security problem before it was one for ballpark gendarmes.

The FBI's extensive clipping file on Robinson began in 1945, as did the receiving and sending of intelligence between itself, the Dodgers, and leaders of black organizations like the NAACP. Walter White, the NAACP's long-time chief, was an old friend of Hoover's and had willingly worked with him over the years to keep the organization purged of communist infiltration and influence. Rickey was not only grateful for these connections, he saw them as an aid in his current problem. Over time, he came to count on them.

Robinson, meanwhile, had all he could handle trying to make sense of what had literally changed his life overnight. When the announcement was made, he was immediately cast as a symbol, yet Robinson was plagued by both his celebrity and his obscurity. Some were genuinely surprised he was the player chosen by organized baseball.

Satchel Paige was still considered by many to be the best pitcher in the world. Paige, a legend for decades, was actually incensed that Robinson had been selected first. "Somehow I'd always figured it'd be me," he said some years later. "Anyway, those major league owners knew I wouldn't start out with any minor league team like Jackie was. . . . But signing Jackie like they did still hurt me deep down. I'd been the guy who started all that big talk about letting us in the big time. I'd been the one who opened the major league parks to the colored teams. I'd been the one who the white boys wanted to barnstorm against. I'd been the one who everybody said should be in the majors. But Jackie'd been the first one signed by the white boys and he'd probably be the first one in the majors."

"They picked [Jackie] for his intelligence," said Othello Renfroe, a Monarch teammate, "but we had a lot of ballplayers we thought were better ballplayers. Jackie had only played in our league one year."

The barnstorming tour to Venezuela, scheduled to begin around the time Robinson was signed, was delayed for a few weeks because of local political upheavals. The additional time only increased the pressure Robinson already felt, and the trip heightened the perception among his fellow Negro-league players that the wrong choice might have been made. The barnstorming team featured such stars as Buck Leonard, Gene Benson, Quincy Trouppe, Parnell Woods, Sam Jethroe, and Roy Campanella. The games, in Caracas against a team of Latin stars led by the father of future major leaguer Luis Aparicio, produced an explosion of offensive firepower from the Americans, with nearly everyone hitting well above .400. Jackie, with all eyes on him, hit .281 and was generally unimpressive.

"When we got down there, Robinson didn't look too good because he hadn't been playing as long as some of us," said Buck Leonard. "We didn't think he was too good—at that time. Of course now we see what he really did. You know, you can be wrong about a ballplayer. You can look at him and don't think much of him, and then he turns out to be one of the best ballplayers of all time."

Robinson was noticeably uncomfortable. He had been picked for the tour, he knew, not because he was a star but because others would be able to work with him, help him with skills they knew he would need if and when he became a big-leaguer. Ever since rumors had begun circulating in the summer that he would be the first chosen, different veterans had gone out of their way to pass along what they knew, knowing that if Robinson failed, they would all fail. At one point, Cool Papa Bell had worked with him on baserunning and handling middle-infield defense against base stealers. "Dizzy" Dismukes had had a session with him where he hit countless ground balls to him so he could better learn to move to his right.

In Venezuela, the team's manager, Carlton Snow, pulled Gene Benson of the Philadelphia Stars aside and asked him to room with Robinson and to work with him, because he had long experience playing against major league competition in many postseason barnstorming tours.

Benson remembered Robinson vividly from those days: "He was just a swell person. I had been told he was controversial and used to get involved in fisticuffs all the time. But when we started rooming together, I didn't see any of that."

What Benson saw was a player who did not hang out with others, who did not drink or smoke, who loved playing cards, who missed his girlfriend, but who seemed to be carrying the weight of the world on his shoulders. "He used to ask me all the time, 'Why did they pick me? Why did they pick me?' " Benson said. "He asked me that every other day."

Benson tried to work with Robinson in a variety of ways. Because they played different positions—Benson was an outfielder, Robinson an infielder—there were only limited technical skills to work on. Benson was a great curve-ball hitter; Robinson became perhaps the best curve-ball hitter of his generation. Benson believes that Jackie probably learned to hit the curve on his own, and anyone who knows the difference in their stances will have a hard time seeing what it was Benson helped him with. Robinson was a straight-up hitter, holding the bat high over his right shoulder. Benson, a left-handed hitter, had one of the oddest stances in the history of the game, turning his body almost a full ninety degrees so that he was standing laterally in the batter's box, facing the pitcher, holding the bat down near his waist rather than off his shoulder. The advantage Benson had, he said, was that it enabled him to keep his hands still as long as possible, moving them only at the last split second with as short a stride as possible.

Robinson, on the other hand, was a lunge hitter. But he was proficient at hitting the curveball because, even though his body would come jumping forward, he kept his hands back as long as possible—just as Gene Benson counseled.

Benson remembers that he and Robinson talked baseball—and life—constantly, moving from the field to the dugout to their room, where they often stayed up half the night, going over whatever was on their minds.

At first Benson, like so many other Negro leaguers, was not sure of Robinson's abilities. Benson remembers that much of their early "work" together really had to do with confidence building.

"He'd say, 'You're a better ballplayer than me.' I'd nod my head and I'd tell him, 'I'm old. And I wouldn't say I'm better than you—you don't know how good a ballplayer you are, because you haven't been proven, you haven't had the opportunity.' I said, 'You'll make it.' Whether I believed it or not, I would tell him this."

While Benson could not at first answer the question about Robinson's chances, he did believe that anyone who was good enough to play well in the Negro leagues should be good enough to play in the majors. It wasn't chauvinism but experience that made him believe it.

He emphasized to Robinson that he would be able to pick up specific skills he would need—like turning the double play—along the way, not to rush anything to a point where it made him tense or uncertain.

"I'd say to him, the big thing about playing baseball or any other sport is don't ever let yourself tighten up. You've got to let yourself be relaxed. I told him about different major league players who were fine during the season but then couldn't do anything in the World Series because pressure took over. Then I remember one night, about three o'clock in the morning, I said to him, 'Jackie, one thing I want you to know about playing in the major leagues. Where you're going is easier than where you're coming from.' Well, he sat straight up in bed. 'You mean that?' he said. 'You bet I do,' I said, and then I told him why."

Robinson couldn't believe that the majors would be easier than Negro-league ball, Benson said, because he really didn't know what he was going to face.

"He thought I was saying that as players we were better than major leaguers, and I wasn't saying that—although I believed quite a few of us would have been stars up there. I said to him, 'I'm gonna tell you why—it's not because we're better ballplayers, it's because it's easier.' He didn't know what I meant at first. I explained to him that everything that's outlawed in their league is allowed in ours. In our league, for example, throwing at you is just part of the game. If you're a good hitter, they're not gonna brush you back, they're gonna throw at you. If you say anything to the umpire, all the umpire is gonna do is say, 'Get in there and hit.' I told him about the spitball: it's outlawed in their league, not in ours. Yeah, there are guys who do it illegally in the major leagues, but it's against the law. In our league, *anybody* can throw the spitter anytime he wants. You gotta hit the spitball in our league. You gotta pick yourself up outta the dirt and hit the spitball in our league. And if you decide to dig a hole in the batter's box to get a good swing at that pitcher, that's liable to be the hole you'll never get out of again.''

The experience Benson had had hitting against pitchers like Bob Feller, Dizzy Dean, and other major league stars was balanced against having to hit regularly against the likes of Satchel Paige, Hilton Smith, and Bullet Rogan.

"I told him one day, if you can hit .200 in this league, you might be able to hit .300 in the other one. He always used to say, 'You mean that?' And I'd have to go into it with him. . . . I told him, 'I remember the first time I'd joined the Stars, I hadn't been there too long. I'd gotten away to a good start. And they were talking about me all over the league. We went to play the Homestead Grays, and I'll never forget it. Their whole pitching staff, all of 'em, walked over to our dugout and lined up in front of me. My teammates there and everything. They lined up in front of me and they said, 'You hit the ball here, you hit the ball there, you hit the ball all over all the time. We wanna see how good you can hit today lying down.' I told Jackie, 'I promise you, they don't do that in the other league.' ''

From these conversations, and from the day-to-day experience of games over a period of weeks, Benson slowly came to believe that Robinson had something about him that would indeed enable him to make it. Some of it had to do with education and just plain intelligence. "I saw pretty soon that you need to tell him something only once, he never forgot anything." But it was more than aptitude. Jackie held himself like an athlete. He not only had great natural ability, he respected that ability, Benson said, by the clean way he lived. It came from a deep place, from pride and determination. Above all, Benson found that Robinson was committed—not just to baseball, but to what he was being asked to do.

"We talked about everything, not just baseball, all the time," Benson said. "What I found that I didn't really know before I met him was that he was a great race man. Jackie Robinson was signed because of his personal self. But they didn't really know what they meant by that. He was high-strung, so much so that he paid with his life to go through what he had to. It caused him an early death because he just blew up inside. But Jackie was a man who would do anything to help one of his own. That was his secret, you understand? He went out and gave his life for black athletes."

CHAPTER FIFTEEN

When Robinson returned to the United States, the first order of business was marriage. He had almost forgotten; one of his assignments in South America was to return with a diamond wedding ring for Rachel. She had given him a design of just what she wanted and left it to him to do the rest, to search out the diamonds—which were known to be much cheaper in South America—and then to have the ring made.

Robinson remembered the ring but forgot the design. Instead, he returned with a ring that, Rowan reported, "was just the kind . . . she did not want." He brought other gifts. One was "a large alligator bag that was so out of style then that many women would have scorned it as a suitcase." One gift, a jewelry case, pleased Rachel—one out of three wasn't a bad batting average, Rowan surmised. Jackie's batting average for the wedding ceremony and the honeymoon, however, was considerably lower.

The wedding was held in Los Angeles on February 10, presided over by the Reverend Karl Downs. Rachel had spent months designing and putting together a flowing satin wedding gown; Jackie got himself into a rented tux. The end of the ceremony called for a recessional and a planned drive-away for the young couple. It did not quite come off. Robinson, spotting a group of invited friends from the old Pepper Street gang, broke away to spend a little time. The friends joked about the occasion, the loss of freedom in marriage, the coming wedding night—while Rachel waited sourly outside for Jackie and their car, which would finally get them on their way. Robinson eventually arrived—but their car did not. The Pepper Street stalwarts had confiscated the vehicle for their own purposes and returned it later, after Jackie and Rachel had repaired to the church and sat around till all the wedding guests had left.

A "Just Married" trip to an eastside hotel followed, but Robinson had forgotten to make reservations. That meant makeshift quarters— and, remembered Rachel, the bouquet of flowers she had been expecting was not in the room. Next was a trip to San Jose, to a house belonging to an aunt of Rachel's. The house had a wood-burning stove, which neither Rachel nor Jackie knew how to use. Rachel remembered opening cans of pork and beans that first night and then being unable to heat them. Then the Pepper Street gang turned up, looking for further adventures, and the next days, the remainder of the time in San Jose, were spent watching the Harlem Globetrotters, who were in town. Then, Rachel told Rowan, "we got bored with the small town of San Jose, so we went to Oakland and some friends of Jack invited us to stay with them. I had grown up with the romantic notion that on a honeymoon you don't stay with people; you stay by yourselves; but anyhow, we stayed with this family, and what do you know? The Globetrotters came to Oakland!"

But all this was an innocent and even good-natured prelude to a time of trial unforeseeable in anyone's social calendar.

Approximately two weeks after they were married, Robinson was scheduled to report to the Dodgers' spring training camp in Daytona Beach. He and Rachel would be met in Florida by the journalists Wendell Smith, Sam Lacy, and Billy Rowe. The newsmen, with connections to the black community Rickey did not have, would make all the necessary arrangements for the Robinsons to insure that these first days and months would go as smoothly as possible. Through the help of a local NAACP official, Mary McLeod Bethune, the journalists located a family who offered to house the Robinsons. Another house, close to the Royals' ballpark in nearby Sanford, was also selected, one that offered Robinson the advantage of being able to come and go, shower and change, without having to risk trouble among his white teammates.

But everyone was flying on automatic pilot, hoping for the best. The racial atmosphere in the nation and particularly the South was tense, volatile, and unpredictable. "In February 1946," noted historian Charles Hamilton, "a Negro war veteran, still in his uniform, was dragged from a bus in Batesburg, South Carolina, beaten, and blinded by local police. A local jury acquitted the attacker, the police chief." But that was only one of countless assaults, murders, lynchings. A Ku Klux Klan riot in Tennessee resulted in the arrest of twenty-eight blacks, with two being killed while in police hands. During the year, with lynchings still commonplace and the threat of increased violence ever greater, Eleanor Roosevelt, Walter White, and others formed the National Emergency Committee Against Mob Violence. They had an

arduous if not impossible task. Segregation was still the legal foundation for social life in the South and was the de facto reality of life in
the North. The landmark Supreme Court decision outlawing segregation in the schools was still years away, and the civil rights acts of the
Kennedy and Johnson years were as yet undreamed hopes.

The Robinsons' trip from Los Angeles to Florida was a slow descent into the netherworld; for Robinson it was a flashback to the hell
he had left behind in the military, and for Rachel it was an awakening.
While she was surely familiar with the boundaries within boundaries
of American bigotry, she had no firsthand experience with life in the
South until this spring-training trip.

The journey began routinely enough as the couple prepared to board
an American Airlines flight for the first leg of their journey to Daytona
Beach. Robinson's mother was there to see the couple off and to give
them shoeboxes full of fried chicken and boiled eggs to see them
through their flight. The food was something of an embarrassment to
Rachel, who was aware that one of the stereotypes of black people
was that they would "picnic" on public transportation. But the gift
was reluctantly accepted and the couple was off to their new world.

In New Orleans, there was a scheduled stopover. But when Rachel
and Jackie debarked, they were told that their places on board had to
be surrendered to military personnel flying on government passes. An
hour's delay for a new flight stretched from midday into the afternoon
and beyond. With an indeterminate delay on their hands, the couple
took a room in a downtown black hotel. "We entered this place and I
was almost nauseated," Rachel said. "It was a dirty, dreadful place,
and they had plastic mattress covers! Lying on the bed was like trying
to sleep on newspapers."

The day-long delay reached into evening, but they were finally
placed aboard a Florida-bound flight that made a stop in Pensacola—
where the Robinsons were paged and then removed from the flight
again, because, said airline officials, the plane was heading for stormy
weather and seats had to be emptied to allow for the weight of additional fuel. The additional weight turned out to be two white passengers. This time they were told no connecting flight would be available
until the next day—if then—and that they might better consider train
or bus connections. Whatever they chose to do, getting to Daytona
on time was out.

The airlines provided a car to take the couple into town. Black bellboys at one of the white hotels helped locate a private house with a room for rent. The house, Rachel said, was almost "overrun with children." That night the Robinsons boarded a bus for Jacksonville, sixteen hours away.

For the length of the trip, the couple was not only forced to sit in the back of the bus but to move to the very rear bench, which had no reclining backrest. Before they reached Jacksonville, when other black passengers—workingmen—crowded onto the bus, the Robinsons had to take turns standing even though some seats in the white section of the bus were empty. Rachel said, "I looked at my new going-away trousseau suit and the ermine coat that Jack had saved for years to buy me as a wedding gift, and I could see the stains from the overalls worn by the men going to work in the fields and the rock quarries. I felt like weeping."

And Jackie, largely because he perceived what his wife was going through, felt like quitting. Wendell Smith was on hand to greet the couple as they finally arrived a day late and definitely worse for wear at the bus station in Daytona. Billy Rowe, also on hand, remembered that at first it was hard to tell that anything had happened: "I said to Jackie, 'Hi, I'm your chauffeur.' He looked at me and he looked at my car and he cracked, 'I've had better chauffeurs and I've had better cars.' But Jackie was very angry about that bus business, but he didn't say anything to anybody." Until that night, Rowe recalled, when, after Rachel had gone to bed, Robinson, sitting around with the three writers, told them what had taken place. Come the next morning, he said, he was not reporting for spring training. He was leaving.

"He told Wendell and me, flat out, 'Get me out of here,' " Rowe said. "We told him, 'You can't do that.' But he was in no mood to listen. He wanted out and that was that. We told him if he did that, he'd blow the whole thing, and he said, 'Just get me out of here!' So, to appease him that night, I actually made a point of excusing myself to go get train tickets—and when I came back, I told him I had them. And then Wendell and I talked to him, talked to him for the rest of the night."

Rowe wasn't sure if Robinson was intending to quit or was just going to "leave" until better arrangements could be guaranteed. Robinson insisted, Rowe said, that while he could endure almost anything himself, he could not stand by and see his wife abused in the way she had been. Still, Rowe was not wholly convinced that the fury and the hurt were all on Rachel's behalf. At one point later on, after Rachel had described the moment when they were forced to get to the back of the bus, Rowe realized something else:

"When the driver said, 'Hey, the back of the bus!' they got to the back of the bus, and Jackie was furious, of course. But it was Rachel who really had the word for that. She said her man suddenly had to become a boy."

Sam Lacy was more matter-of-fact: "He was just sick of it, that's all. He didn't want to go through this sort of business. He had come from an integrated society, played at UCLA, went through all that stuff in the army, and he just wasn't prepared to put up with this type of treatment—although I think what really made him furious was the fact that Rachel was involved in it."

Sometime near dawn, Rowe recalled, Robinson finally gave in, changing his mind once more. Rowe was unsure what finally turned him, but the night's talk, if it did not simply wear him down, tapped another and deeper level of awareness, one that reached beneath personal feelings. "Finally, the next day . . . I don't know how to say this . . . it was not a problem of the airlines doing this or the bus company doing that, it was that the whole thing was bigger than him. He understood that, I think. That his being there meant something for sports . . . for the country," Rowe said.

Whatever may have been hanging in the balance after one fateful night was all but forgotten when crowds of reporters and photographers made history—and a story line—out of Robinson's appearance at the ballpark the next day. Within days, the word was out that the "experiment" was successful, that Robinson and another black player, pitcher Johnny Wright (signed mainly to provide Robinson with company on the team and a roommate on the road), had been absorbed without incident. The players were there to get a fair trial and a fair shake. As the *Sporting News* put it, weeks later:

"The white Montreal players have accepted Jackie Robinson, shortstop, and John Wright, pitcher, as their teammates. From the first workout at Kelly Field, hidden away in the Australian pines . . . there has been no friction. The colored boys go about their daily chores quietly.

" 'There are 48 players on my squad,' said Manager Clay Hopper, 'and Robinson and Wright are only two of 'em. They will get the same chance to make good as the rest of the players. No favoritism will be shown to anybody.'

"Robinson and Wright are highly pleased with their reception. 'Everybody here has been very helpful,' said Jackie."

The reality, however, was something else. From the first moment, just getting to the ballpark could be dangerous and uncertain.

"People would call out names at you, vile epithets, everything you could think of," Sam Lacy said. "And sometimes we'd be met by people outside the park who'd surround your car with sticks and bats and rocks. That first day, they were standing at the front gate. We couldn't go in that way. We had to back off. Jackie found a hole in a fence and we went in through that."

Robinson and Wright both felt like freaks. When they first crossed the field, heading toward the clubhouse, approximately two hundred minor leaguers were working out, and all of them seemed to be staring at them, Robinson remembered.

The clubhouse man, Babe Hamburger, doled out uniforms to them and urged the men to do their best and to "just be yourselves." But Robinson felt only that he and Wright were in hostile territory, "that anything could happen anytime to a Negro who thought he could play ball with white men on an equal basis."

Clyde Sukeforth shepherded Robinson and Wright to the field, introducing them to their manager, Clay Hopper, a Mississippian who had made a career of following Branch Rickey's orders, but who was personally, deeply opposed to the mixing of races on or off the field. He turned the players over to their first routines, urging them, in a lazy southern drawl, "to just throw the ball around and hit a few."

After their first day, Robinson and Wright were moved from the houses they had initially been placed in Daytona to one near the ballpark in Sanford. Everything seemed to be going according to plan when, the following night, Smith and Rowe met the players for dinner. The journalists were unusually quiet, Robinson remembered, until Rowe suddenly got up from the table and announced that he was going to gas up the car.

"You guys leaving us?" Robinson asked.

"No," Smith said, "we're all going to Daytona."

Within forty-eight hours of their arrival, it had been made clear to Dodger officials that the town of Sanford simply would not accept blacks and whites on the same playing field. Word had been passed that the very presence of the two black players in town posed a real and immediate danger—to them. Because the situation was so perilous, Smith postponed telling the players why they were returning to Daytona until they were safely out of town. Robinson, unaware as he was, could only suspect that he was involved in another phony major-league tryout and could barely control his fury at Rickey and the Dodgers for what they had done to him. He began talking again about heading back to California once and for all.

On the way out of town, Robinson noticed a group of men standing on a street corner in their shirtsleeves. "It looked like a typical small-town bull session," he told himself, thinking, ironically, that Sanford had turned out to be a reasonably nice place. That is, until Smith and Rowe finally got around to telling him what had happened.

In a strange way, Robinson, though miserable and on edge, inadvertently discovered in this episode that Rickey *was* committed to him. Far from canceling the experiment, the Dodger boss canceled the town of Sanford. He moved the Royals from their base there and brought them to Daytona, away from the Dodger camp—to the black community where city officials were not likely to raise objections. The move was not exactly received with gratitude by Robinson and Wright, because the white players were all moved into luxurious beachfront hotel accommodations while the two black players were segregated in whatever private accommodations could be found.

In the days following, Robinson remained tense, suspicious, and angry. Under enormous media pressure as well as that from the situation, Robinson pushed himself. He was assigned to play shortstop on a second-unit squad. The team's regular shortstop, Stan Breard, seemed to be a fixture, and Robinson, in all likelihood, did not believe he was going to replace him. Perhaps because he perceived the odds to be long, perhaps because he was all too aware of the scouting reports that questioned the strength of his arm, he made a point of throwing as hard as he could whenever he took infield practice. He would move to his right and then, from deep in the shortstop hole—though there were no base runners—peg the ball to first with as much on it as possible. Before the Royals had readied themselves for their first intrasquad game, Robinson's arm was so sore he could not lift it to the height of his shoulder to comb his hair.

With the eyes of the baseball world on Rickey and his great experiment, the thought of Robinson sitting out games or performing poorly was greatly disturbing. Robinson simply had to be in there to prove his value. Rickey convinced Robinson to take a turn at second, where the throw to first was easier. Robinson tried but could not even manage that. Rickey had him moved to first base, a position he had never played. Though not required to throw, he was unable to handle the footwork and other moves around the bag. Fortunately, Robinson's sore arm was just one of those common spring-training aches after a winter away and not a tearing of tissue.

Robinson improved rapidly over a period of days and, under the close and nervous eye of Rickey, began to show flashes of the skills the organization believed he possessed.

On one occasion, Rickey sat with Clay Hopper during an intrasquad game. Robinson made an especially brilliant play at second base, diving for a ball behind the bag and then making a backhand flip to the shortstop for a force-out. Rickey thundered something about their having just seen a superhuman play.

"Mr. Rickey," Hopper reportedly replied, "do you really think a nigger's a human being?"

Rickey responded by saying nothing, explaining years later that he kept silent because he knew that Hopper's prejudice had been nurtured since birth, and that as a consequence his beliefs were sincere. The real response, though, was that performance would be the answer to anyone's prejudice.

Rickey and Robinson, both speaking from the same hymnal, had a message for the outside world: people, no matter their background, were basically fair; American democracy, even in the South, perhaps especially there, would always respond with willingness to give others a chance; and performance, in the end, mattered more than prejudice.

In his early autobiography, done with Wendell Smith, Robinson described his first spring-training game—against the Dodgers in Daytona. He had come to the park on edge, expecting a hostile reception from white spectators. Instead, when his name was announced, there was cheering—not only from the jim crow section of the stands but from the white sections too. Robinson claims he heard voices of encouragement, someone drawling, "Come on, black boy! You can make the grade!" And another, "They're giving you a chance, now do something about it!"

If readers still needed the word, Robinson had it:

"I think I should say something here about Southerners. They have always been assigned the chief blame for keeping Negroes out of organized ball. . . . Well, I discovered that afternoon in Daytona—and many times thereafter—that most of the people below the Mason-Dixon Line accepted my presence on a baseball diamond along with white players. The American sports fan—North or South—is fundamentally the same. Above everything else, he admires and respects athletic prowess, guts and good sportsmanship. And he demands a fair chance and fair play."

The only problem with these sentiments is that they might as easily have come from the Dodger front office as from Robinson. They almost certainly did not reflect what Robinson was going through. The on-field pressures remained constant and complicated. Robinson, even when his arm healed, found himself at second base, a position he was largely unprepared to play.

He did not hit, and he looked awkward in the field. Some writers covering the team concluded that the experiment was over, that good sentiments had overwhelmed good sense on Rickey's part, and that the rest would only be a shabby ending to a dream that had never had substance.

The hostility and menace continued. At Jacksonville, the Royals showed up for a scheduled exhibition game against the Jersey City Giants only to find the ballpark padlocked and crowds milling around the gates. A city ordinance forbid blacks and whites from appearing on the same field together. At De Land, another game was canceled, supposedly because of a problem with stadium lights. The scheduled game, however, was a day game.

At Sanford, in a game against Indianapolis, there were threats and the possibility of official interference if Robinson or Wright took the field. Jackie was placed in the starting lineup anyway. He went through an inning, got a hit, stole a base, came sliding home on another hit, and as he raised himself from the dust, was confronted by a local sheriff. The sheriff announced to him and to everyone else that the game was over, that "nigras" and whites were not allowed on the same field, and then, when Robinson moved to the bench, that they were not allowed on the same bench, either.

If Robinson felt any goodwill coming his way from teammates and fans, his response, at a minimum, was suspicion. Black fans in particular, because they made a point of cheering anything he did, embarrassed and even angered him. He did not socialize with white players. In Daytona, he lived and spent much of his time in and around the home of the Harris family, where he and Rachel had been placed. He said that he and his wife wound up going to the same black movie theater so often that he began to worry that his eyes might be going bad.

On the road, he was nearly always in the company of Wendell Smith, Sam Lacy, and Billy Rowe, "the chauffeur." Because Jackie loved playing cards, poker players were found, mainly in the black districts of Miami—a favorite journey, Rowe said.

"Friends of Jackie would get in those games and the friends of colored people down in Miami," Rowe remembered. "There was a big Negro newspaper down there. People were friendly to us. We used to have to carry a lunch, though, because if you needed to eat outside, even if it was a hot-dog stand, they were just terrible to you. You went in the store and bought it but couldn't go inside and eat."

As spring training drew to an end, Robinson's nerves had been so wasted, Rachel said, that he could barely sleep, much less relax enough just to play the game. But when the team went north in the second week of April, Jackie—though not Wright—made the trip.

After the poor spring he had, that was perhaps more than he'd expected, and for a while it was enough. True, he would be alone, out of position, and uncertain that he would ever make it through the year. But because he had made it through that volatile southern spring, when it would have been easy to cast him aside entirely, he had renewed respect for Rickey and his plan.

CHAPTER SIXTEEN

If sportswriters had believed or even suspected that Jackie Robinson was a publicity stunt or a clever political maneuver by Branch Rickey, that vanished in a single game—Robinson's first as a member of the Montreal Royals.

The Royals' season opener that year was against the Jersey City Giants in Jersey City. The mayor of Jersey City, "Boss" Frank Hague, held a clambake for the party faithful, with fifty-one thousand admissions sold for the opener, though Roosevelt Stadium seated only twenty-five thousand. But as festive as the occasion was, with red, white, and blue bunting draped everywhere, the day belonged not to Boss Hague but to Jackie Robinson.

Robinson had one of the memorable debuts in baseball history, going four for five, hitting a homer, driving in four runs, stealing two bases, and leading his team to a 14–1 shellacking of the Jersey Giants. So spectacular was his effort that New York's tabloid writers, usually facile with superlatives, seemed not quite ready for Jackie in prime time. The *Daily News* botched his bio, referring to him as "the cool, colored lad who first rose to prominence as a football star at U.S.C." The *Daily Mirror,* searching for just the right word, noted that "Boss Hague's minions . . . and the packed park agreed that Robinson was faster than a black market sale."

Almost as if Rickey had had a free hand in designing the day, Robinson's special skills, even beyond numbers, were the day's attraction. He had power, yes—his third-inning home run, a line shot over the left-field fence, seemed to jump off his bat. He could steal a base—yes, he was fast. But another dimension made him a wholly new kind of offensive force. In the fifth inning, Robinson surprised everyone (though not anyone who knew his game) by dropping down a perfect bunt for a base hit. He then stole second base. On the next play, an infield groundout, he took third. By then, his baserunning had caught the eye of the opposition. Robinson, in what fans everywhere would soon recognize as a signature display of how much he was *in* a game, danced off third base, daring the pitcher to keep him from stealing home. He danced this way and that, faking a break for home, coming back to third—till the Giants' pitcher, Phil Oates, totally distracted, broke stride and balked, allowing Robinson to score.

Coming after the poor spring he had had, this one-day offensive show was a kind of necessary explosion. Robinson not only cleared his system of building tensions but also of any doubts about his ability that he might have been harboring. It turned out that he would have to call on all that and more.

The Royals were on the road for two weeks before arriving in Montreal for their home opener, and Robinson was reminded anew that what he had experienced in Florida was what he could expect anywhere at any time. In every town, the living accommodations were invariably segregated. The minimal professional acceptance Robinson found from teammates on the field and in the clubhouse was not matched by so much as a social word from them away from the field.

Opposition players were under no constraint to even get along professionally. In Syracuse, the usual racial epithets were embellished by the releasing of a black cat to cries of "nigger pussy" from the Syracuse dugout while Jackie was kneeling in the on-deck circle, waiting to hit.

With a trip to Baltimore on the schedule, the International League president, Frank Shaugnessy, phoned Rickey, pleading with him not to allow Robinson to play there for fear of "rioting and bloodshed" that might wreck organized baseball. Rickey would not yield, however, insisting that those who promoted such behavior would only be more emboldened if he held Robinson back—and so the games went on, bristling with vituperation from the Oriole dugout and with the ever-present threat of a riot that never developed.

When the Royals finally turned up in Montreal, the Robinsons' first task was finding living quarters. To their surprise, they found neither closed doors nor racial antagonism, locating an apartment in a French-speaking area of town. Residents there had little experience with black people, much less a black person who was already something of a celebrity. Not only did the Robinsons find that they were welcome, but they were shown the sort of deference that might have been reserved for visitors from outer space. Neighbors helped them with everyday tasks like shopping. When Robinson walked down the street, residents signaled one another from house to house in time to poke their heads out doors and windows to get an up-close peek at him as he passed.

The Robinsons later acknowledged how much they appreciated being accepted by their neighbors in Canada, but the very nature of that acceptance could only have deepened that sense of isolation that dogged them throughout the season.

The Royals, like most minor league teams, ate cafeteria-style when they traveled. While admission to dining rooms was not a problem in most northern cities—Baltimore, a southern city, was an exception—teammates for the most part avoided sitting at the same table with Robinson, as he did at their tables.

Al Campanis was a Royals utility player then, and he already had some sense that his baseball future might be tied to working with the talent of others. "There were a few of our guys who'd yell back if anyone got on Jackie," Campanis said. "They'd raise hell right back if it came to that—you know, 'You wanna pick on somebody, pick on me,' that sort of thing. Johnny Jorgenson, Dixie Howell, Herman Franks. But in the cafeterias, I'd see Jackie sitting mainly by himself, so I'd go over and sit down with him."

Campanis was also directed by the front office to help Robinson with his middle-infield play. As a second baseman, Robinson had two glaring weaknesses. He was simply too slow going to his right; that problem could only be addressed by moving him rightward, letting him play more toward the middle of the field than he might have, Campanis said. The other and more serious problem was turning the double play. Robinson did not really know how to pivot.

"There are at least five ways of making a double play as a second baseman, and I knew four of them. Jackie at first really didn't know any of them," Campanis said.

Robinson's instinct was to come directly across the bag and throw in the manner he had learned as a shortstop. But at second, this not only wasted time, it also exposed him to a blind-side hit. Campanis broke down the double-play moves into segments.

"Jackie became a good second baseman," Campanis said. "He had a good arm-snap and good body control. He was a real athlete, you see. He was easy to teach, and with his size—he was such a big man —you couldn't anticipate that. He learned that so quickly."

What Robinson really learned in spring training and the regular season was the ability to perform under acute pressure—not the pressure of big games, but of being the centerpiece of a social experiment whose outcome involved so much more than himself. He had to face the fact that he was not just a person but a symbol, a living entity asked to endure insult and injury, even the risk of death, all without complaint or aid, just to prove that any person who played by the rules was entitled to play the game.

But play the game Jackie Robinson did. Through April, Robinson hit .361, drove in seven runs, stole eight bases, and became the kind of baserunning threat not seen in the game since Ty Cobb. And Robinson's April was no fluke; that was his performing stride for the season. He wound up leading the International League in hitting with .349, was second in stolen bases, tied for first in runs scored, was the leading fielder among second basemen—and the league's Most Valuable Player.

Al Campanis, assigned to teach Robinson, says he wound up learning from him: "I don't know when I first understood this, but I learned with Jackie that there's something wherein I can learn from every man, and in that I am his pupil before I am his teacher. What he taught me specifically were things that were not in the book—like stealing third with two outs. Who ever thought of that? They always tell you not to do that, you can score on a hit, so why risk anything? But the fact that he got on third and then bothered the pitcher with his running up and down the line made things happen—plus the fact that you score on an error or a wild pitch or a topped single or a balk. So he changed a lot of thinking by doing that. Maybe he made a pitcher groove one, and then again it was easier to steal third base than second base, nobody keeps you tight on second."

Because he played in a far-northern city, in another country, one relatively free of racial tension, Robinson did not have to fight for acceptance among Montreal fans. That he was "different" even helped him, as hometown crowds adopted him as a favorite, responding to his daring style of play with shouted encouragement on the field and friendly calls to him wherever and whenever he was spotted in town. But no matter the size and scope of his success, danger stalked him all season long.

In Baltimore, Robinson was held out of the lineup on one road trip because of a hamstring injury. In the ninth inning of a game with

Montreal leading by a run, the Orioles got the tying run on with two out. At a conference on the mound, the Royals players decided that if any ball was hit to the outfield on the right side, the team's right fielder, Johnny "Spider" Jorgensen, would make the play because he had the strongest outfield arm.

"It was three and two on the hitter, and yeah, he hits this gapper to right," Jorgensen said. "So I went and cut the ball off like we decided. I look up and as I wheeled, I saw the runner rounding third base. I could throw then, I really could throw. I said, 'Shit, fuck this, it's duck soup.' I didn't even go for the cutoff man, I went straight to [catcher Herman] Franks. I laid it right in there. He had plenty of time. I heard our second baseman say, 'Uh-oh', and there it was: the whole scene exploded. The guy slid in, Herman rode him across the plate and buried the goddamn ball in his ribs, and the lid came off the whole stadium. I mean, it went sky-high."

The teams in that era had their clubhouses in center field, and the Royals had to exit the field on the run for fear of the fans. But after the crowd's initial explosion of anger over the play, the target of their wrath became Jackie Robinson, who had been neither on the field nor in the dugout when the game ended. Robinson was in the clubhouse being treated for his injured leg. Even more alarming was the absence of security in and around the clubhouse. For reasons neither Jorgensen nor any of the other players understood, the threats of violent disruption in Baltimore had not resulted in any kind of police protection. A baseball crowd had virtually become an officially sanctioned lynch mob. To make matters even more alarming, the Royals' manager, Clay Hopper, vanished almost as soon as the commotion began. A handful of players, including Jorgensen, remained behind with Robinson, waiting and waiting.

Vigilantes were still lurking around outside the clubhouse in the early hours of the morning, Jorgensen said: "They were yelling, 'Come out of there, Robinson, you nigger son of a bitch, we'll getcha! We'll getcha!' There were three of us who stayed with him—Marv Rackley, who was my roommate and a southerner, and Tommy Tatum, who had been filling in at second for Jackie. Finally the clubhouse boy came back and said the coast was clear and we could go. There was just us, no one else. You would have thought that Hopper, who is the fucking manager of the ball club, would have gotten protection for us by then, but no, we were out there on our own. And there were no buses then, we had to get back and forth any way we could. So we went looking for cabs and finally wound up getting on a street-car that went back into town and we dropped Jackie off about a block from the house he was staying in.''

True to his word to Rickey—or because he knew how alone he was —Robinson kept whatever he was feeling to himself. ''When we came into the clubhouse after the game, we saw him just sit there and never say a word. He was nonchalant like nothing was going on,'' Jorgensen said. ''Was he scared? I don't think so, but I don't know, you couldn't tell. We all tried to be as nonchalant as he was, but none of us wanted him to go out there alone.''

But if Robinson was able to show others that he could take it, privately it was all he could do to hold himself together. Robinson seethed at the separate treatment he got. When he stayed in private homes or Negro hotels, he always knew why. Black players who knew him at all knew that his fuse was short, his feelings of rage ever in jeopardy of exploding. Joe Black, later a teammate on the Dodgers, met Robinson for the first time in 1946 at the York Hotel in Baltimore. The York was the principal African-American hotel in town, and Black remembers that when Edgar Snow, the manager of the Balti-more Elite Giants, said he was going to introduce him to Robinson, Black inwardly readied himself for the impact.

''Snow called Jackie over and introduced him to me—and I can remember his voice. You'd thought he'd be 'brr-rrrr-rrr,' but he was a very quiet, polite person. I wasn't prepared for that. I remembered he had nice black, wavy hair.''

At home, the pressures he was living with were more noticeable. Rachel, his major support, had become pregnant, and then her preg-nancy became complicated, a fact she withheld from Robinson until she was treated and sure she would not miscarry.

She could not avoid noticing what her husband's teammates, coaches, and front-office handlers had been blind to—that far from maintaining his equilibrium, he was coming apart at the seams. He began to have trouble eating and sleeping, going for days at a time unable to hold down a meal or to pass a night asleep. For much of the time he was nauseated. At the end of July, Rachel finally forced him to see a physician, who told him that he was suffering from ''nervous exhaustion''—which called for immediate rest and recuperation. A ten-day respite from his team was arranged, with the approval of Clay Hopper, but in less than half that time Robinson was back, fearful that any extended break would be seen as goldbricking.

The Royals swept to the International League flag, winning by nineteen and a half games, sweeping the play-offs, and entering the Junior World Series as one of the strongest minor league teams in history. Their opponent, winner of the American Association pennant, was Louisville, a team and a town hostile to racial mixing.

At the Series opener in Louisville, just by taking the field Robinson marked another first: no black player had ever been on the field in an American Association game in this century. Black fans turned out in record numbers to find seats in segregated Parkway Field. To many white fans, however, the mere presence of Robinson was a provocation beyond endurance. From the moment he set foot on the field, he was jeered and taunted.

Frank Rickey, Branch's brother and a Dodger troubleshooter, had been following Robinson all season and reporting his findings to his brother. The front office knew what Jackie was up against, perhaps in ways that he himself did not know. Frank Rickey reported that "an International League manager who refused to be quoted said, 'I doubt whether Jackie can take it when he is dusted off every day in the NL. I offered to buy a suit of clothes for any pitcher on our club who knocks him down—I don't mean to hit him. I haven't had to pay off yet. One pitcher told me, 'We have a tough enough time with the colored boy to get him out, without wasting pitches.' "

Frank Rickey measured the response to Jackie in Louisville, noting that the taunting he received surely affected his play, a fact that would have to be taken into account before any decision was made to bring Robinson up to the majors and to larger hostile cities like St. Louis and Cincinnati.

"Appearance of JR in the opening game at Louisville evoked a chorus of Bronx cheers," Frank Rickey told Branch, "but the Royals' star took the jeering in stride. With the demand for seats by his Negro followers greater than the supply, members of his race crowded the roofs of buildings adjacent to Parkway Field to watch R perform. A slight disturbance occurred in the stands, reportedly resulting in the arrest of one Negro patron. Although JR made only one hit in three games in Louisville, he performed sensationally afield."

But when the team got back to Montreal, the script changed. Canadian fans, knowing the insults and threats endured by Robinson, turned their wrath on the entire Louisville team. It was impossible for a Louisville player to step to the plate without receiving the sort of welcome that might have reminded him of what Robinson had had to take in the opening games of the series. The Royals, able to win only one of three games in Louisville, swept the Colonels in Montreal, and Robinson, inspired by the support he got from hometown fans, went on a tear, getting seven hits, leading his team at bat and in the field, ultimately scoring the winning run in the final game.

His performance was matched by the spontaneous outburst of the fans following the final out. They poured onto the field, chanting Jackie's name, seizing him and hoisting him to their shoulders along with manager Clay Hopper, then snake-dancing around the park, singing the "Marseillaise" and other songs. When Robinson was finally able to reach the locker room and dress, the crowds were still not done with him. They waited for him to emerge, and when he did, they burst through police barriers, chasing him down the street. *Pittsburgh Courier* writer Sam Maltin described the scene for readers back home:

"It was a demonstration seldom seen here. Again the crowd started hugging and kissing him. He tried to explain that he had to catch a plane. They wouldn't listen, refused to hear him.

"They held on to him but—as he had done in his football days at UCLA—Robbie gently fought off his admirers and pushed his way through until he found an opening. Then he started running.

"The mob was running after him. Down the street he went, chased by five hundred fans. People opened windows and came pouring out of their houses to see what the commotion was about. For three blocks they chased him until a car drew up and someone shouted: 'Jump in, Jackie!' That he did—plunk in a lady's lap. They brought him safely to the hotel.

"Men three times the age of Robinson, old-timers in the local sports scene, men who had seen some of the greatest Canadian athletes in action, failed to recall an ovation that matched that given to Robinson."

Maltin said that the spectacle of Robinson being pursued through the streets marked perhaps the only time in history that a white mob chased a Negro "not because of hate but because of love."

But for Branch Rickey, there was another and even more telling meaning. Robinson's success was a triumph of skill. Jackie Robinson's ability on a baseball field made it possible finally to look at the whole question of the color line in baseball not as a political or social divide but as one having exclusively to do with winning or losing.

CHAPTER SEVENTEEN

In retrospect, it is hard to imagine that Jackie Robinson did not know where he was headed as the 1946 season unfolded. He was not only the best player on the best minor league team in baseball, but the "experiment" had been broadened so that now other black players were in the minors to assure him that he was part of a program. Roy Campanella and Don Newcombe were at the Dodgers' double-A farm team in Nashua, New Hampshire; Roy Partlow and Johnny Wright had been assigned to the class-A Three Rivers team. Today, it seems reasonable to suppose that Jackie Robinson might have been able to conclude, sometime during his stay in Montreal, that he was headed for the major leagues. But that was not the case.

Robinson knew better than anyone that he was having a great season, but he was also keenly aware that that guaranteed him nothing. Twenty-seven years of life had put him on his guard. He had been an "all-American" and gone nowhere with it; he was just two years past the nightmare of his endgame with the U.S. military. As much as he was now in the headlines, in his own mind he was still just another black GI returning to civilian life looking for a steady job.

At no time during the season was Robinson led to believe that he was going to be promoted to the majors. In its last months, when the Royals had made a runaway of the race in the International League, there was considerable speculation that he would be brought up—but it didn't happen. Rickey, in fact, went out of his way to explain why Robinson was going to stay put. It would have been unfair to Jackie, the move was too important, better to think of him starting the year with the parent team when there would be less pressure and he would have a better chance, etc., etc.

For Robinson, that meant continued uncertainty—and a salary of just $600 a month, barely more than he had made with the Monarchs and not enough to support a family. He was not yet ready to think of himself as a professional athlete, much less a racial pioneer. The "opportunity" that had suddenly come his way made him doubly determined not to allow himself or Rachel to live in a dream world.

In March of '46, before Robinson's spectacular debut with the Royals in Jersey City, a predominantly black veterans group, the Veterans Committee Against Discrimination, held a mass picket in front of the offices of the *New York Daily News,* protesting an article by *News* sports editor Jimmy Powers that belittled Rickey's efforts to sign Robinson and other black players and that predicted (though Powers had never seen him play) that Robinson would never make the majors.

Robinson, a vet like those marching, was aware of the demonstration on his behalf. Harlem celebrities, including the actors Lloyd Gough and Earl Jones, had turned out for this demonstration, and reports of it were prominent in the black press and in the *Daily Worker,* though it did not make the mainstream papers.

At the beginning of June, the *People's Voice* carried an article—with a photograph of Robinson—announcing that he had accepted chairmanship of the New York State Organizing Committee of a group called United Negro and Allied Veterans of America. Robinson's participation was largely symbolic, but he was committed enough to later speak at an organizing conference for the group. Following that, he was named honorary New York State commander of UNAVA, a position that, though it did not commit him to campaign actively, was an honor he accepted and apparently took seriously. The organization sought to help black vets deal with postwar problems of readjustment.

In November 1946, the publication *Fraternal Outlook* published an article on the opening of the Solidarity Center in Harlem of the International Workers Order. Robinson was listed as a member of the Center's advisory board.

In December, another little-known publication, the *Michigan Chronicle,* reported that the Detroit Committee to Fight Racial Injustice and Terrorism was sponsoring a mobilization in Washington, D.C., the following month, and that in conjunction with the mobilization it was holding two fund-raisers in Detroit. The principal speaker at those fund-raisers was to be Jackie Robinson.

All of Robinson's early and tentative political alliances were with organizations soon to be labeled subversive by various government agencies. The United Negro and Allied Veterans was named in December 1947 as a communist front by the Internal Security Subcommittee of the U.S. Senate. The International Workers Order was cited pursuant to Executive Order 10450. The newspaper *People's Voice* was named by the California Committee on Un-American Activities as being "communist initiated and controlled."

At the very last moment, Robinson backed out of his scheduled Detroit appearances. The suddenness of his withdrawal left group sponsors with no time to find a replacement speaker, thus forcing them to cancel the fund-raisers entirely. So far as anyone knows, this was the last time Robinson's name was ever linked with any group the FBI took seriously—save for the different civil rights groups Robinson associated himself with in the fifties and sixties.

But what brought about his seemingly sudden decision to dissociate himself from the Detroit group and any others of a similar nature? While Robinson's Freedom of Information Act (FOIA) record provides no answers, clearly events by now had their own dynamic, one dictated largely by his great season at Montreal. Whatever Rickey's timetable had been, whatever ambiguity was left in his commitment, Robinson's year with the Royals had changed everything. While Rickey had been able to resist the pressure to bring him up for the last part of the '46 season, he was under much more pressure to bring him to the Dodgers in '47.

Nonetheless, Rickey was still wary of the other owners, who, no matter what they said publicly, remained, in private, adamantly opposed to Robinson's elevation—though there is some confusion about how that opposition was expressed.

In a speech given in February 1948 at Wilberforce College in Ohio, Rickey mentioned that at the winter meetings of 1946, the baseball owners had colluded against him to keep him from breaking the color barrier. Rickey said a secret report had been circulated by the owners, "after I had signed Robinson and before he had ever played a game," which condemned what he was trying to do. After the report was circulated, it was then collected, and to date no copy of it has ever surfaced.

The owners, of course, have denied that any such report existed. But those close to Rickey heard the story from him many times. Arthur Mann quoted from the report in his 1950 book on Jackie Robinson. "However well-intentioned, the use of Negro players [in the big leagues] would hazard all the physical properties of baseball," Mann says the report read.

Red Barber, in his account of the '47 season, subtitled *When All*

Hell Broke Loose, said the quarrel at the winter meetings then resulted in a secret vote, 15–1, against black players, but that a policy committee consisting of Larry MacPhail, Phil Wrigley of the Cubs, Sam Breadon of the Cardinals, and Tom Yawkey of the Red Sox was formed to "study" the issue.

A. B. "Happy" Chandler, then the commissioner of baseball, also acknowledged a 15–1 vote in several interviews he gave in the years before his death. But he placed it at the beginning of 1947, *after* Robinson had been at Montreal but before he came up to the Dodgers.

"This is the part I don't think anybody knows about," he told the *Washington Star and News* in 1972. "The owners had a meeting in New York in 1947. The Robinson case wasn't on the agenda, but one of 'em brought it up anyhow. They kinda felt Branch Rickey was going to try to bring a colored boy in.

"They voted it down fifteen to one. I don't remember whether they voted specifically against Robinson or blacks in general, but I do remember that Mr. Rickey, of course, was the one dissenting vote. . . .

"You wouldn't believe some of the things those owners said at that meeting. One of 'em flat out said if we let Robinson play, they'd burn down the Polo Grounds the first time the Dodgers came in there for a series."

Chandler may have had a stake in promoting his own importance in baseball's integration, because he also said that Rickey afterward came to him to ask for support in the face of the 15–1 vote and that Chandler said, "Bring him in. He'll play if he's got the capacity to play." He may also have been mistaken on the question of timing; the winter meetings following Robinson's year in Montreal took place in California, not New York, and no stories link the vote to the West Coast meeting.

What is unarguable is that Rickey, at the end of 1946, felt pressured in ways that went far beyond any "six-part plan." He was now flying on his own. He may or may not have had the support of the baseball commissioner (as events in the next months would highlight), but the time was now past when he could hold back. Whether it was the owners' continued and insulting opposition, the increased heat he felt from civic groups demanding that Robinson be brought up immediately, or just his own sound baseball judgment, Rickey concluded sometime during that winter to take the step. But precisely because he had no backing, he proceeded with utmost caution.

Rickey almost certainly met with Robinson when he was at the California winter meetings. Robinson was home with Rachel and their newborn son, Jackie Jr. Though Rickey could have told Robinson that he was thinking of bringing him up to the Dodgers, he didn't; instead, the discussions, according to Arthur Mann, were about money. After the '46 season, Robinson put together a barnstorming team, scheduled to play games between October and November. Robinson was guaranteed $5,000 by the promoters, but when the players went to cash their checks, they bounced. Robinson had to lay out $3,500 of his own money—what he had saved from his signing bonus—and he wanted Rickey to help him. There was little Rickey could do, and Robinson turned to the NAACP; Thurgood Marshall interceded on Robinson's behalf, but the money was never recovered.

Rickey was thinking farther ahead. Within a month, he sent out invitations through Herbert Miller, the head of the Brooklyn YMCA, to several black community leaders to attend a meeting at the Brooklyn Y in early February. The purpose of the get-together was secret, but the language of the invitation implied that Rickey had something important to say: "Come prepared to hear Mr. Rickey and discuss with him the things which are on his mind as well as ours in connection with projection of what seems to be inevitable," the note said.

The meeting was held at the Y on the evening of February 5, and more than any other action taken by Rickey since the close of the season, it indicated to the public that he was going to promote Robinson. The meeting underscored Rickey's extreme sensitivity to the volatile social and political implications of his decision. His speech to the selected audience of black leaders reflected his determination, at all costs, to control rather than be dominated by events.

Rickey discarded a prepared speech he had brought along, launching into an extemporaneous harangue meant to dramatize his concerns to the thirty community leaders. He reminded them that what he was about to say was to be held in strict secrecy. Then he referred directly to Robinson, saying that he had not yet made the decision to bring him up or have him spend another year in the minors. *If* he did bring him up, he warned, "the biggest threat to his success—the *one* enemy most likely to ruin that success—is the Negro people themselves!"

If Rickey's audience was taken aback by this, he had barely warmed up. "Every step of racial progress you have made has been won by suffering and often bloodshed. This step in baseball is being taken for you by a single person whose wounds you cannot see or share. But he is first a ballplayer and has proved himself that. He has the ability and the aptitude to succeed in the big league. History shows that you use each of your steps of progress as signal victories, as you have a right to, because you have fought for them. But you haven't fought a single lick for this victory, if it is one.

"And yet, on the day that Robinson enters the big league—*if* he does—every one of you will go out and form parades and welcoming committees. You'll strut. You'll wear badges. You'll hold Jackie Robinson Days . . . and Jackie Robinson Nights. You'll get drunk. You'll fight. You'll be arrested. You'll wine and dine the player until he is fat and futile. You'll symbolize his importance into a national comedy . . . and an ultimate tragedy—yes, tragedy!"

Rickey's politics were as obvious as his language.

"For let me tell you this!" he continued. "If any individual, group, or segment of Negro society sees the advancement of Jackie Robinson in baseball as a symbol of social 'ism' or schism, a triumph of race over race, I will curse the day I ever signed him to a contract, and I will personally see that baseball is never so abused and misrepresented again!"

Who knows what his audience thought about Branch Rickey that night? They surely came away with the sense that *something* was about to happen; the question was, what really was in Rickey's heart at that moment? Had he finally gotten into the canoe and decided to paddle along? Had he come to the point where it was time to end the midnight rambling, to go home and say, finally, that the time had come, that the simple rightness of what had to be done could no longer be postponed?

Rickey almost certainly knew that his man would become a symbol of a social "ism," and that those looking for symbolism would not relent, even if the press was more favorable than he could hope for. He was faced with having to gamble in an area where what he wanted, more than anything, was certainty.

He could not even be sure of his man. He knew enough about him, through his extensive intelligence network, to understand that

Robinson's makeup was more complicated than the ideal he had in mind. An even more interesting question is whether Rickey knew at this point about Robinson's political activities. He might have: Robinson's sudden cancellation of the Detroit appearances has the fingerprints of official meddling all over it.

What is certain is that by the spring of 1947, Branch Rickey was determined to risk what he had to bring Jackie Robinson to the majors. And almost as certain was his sense that Robinson would provide him with the same cover off the field that he had pledged to give him onfield: a three-year period where he would turn the other cheek and keep silent in the face of any and all provocation.

CHAPTER EIGHTEEN

Jane Jones said that her father had an uncanny ability to make people believe that he was confiding in them. "Dad would say to someone, 'You're the only person I've told this to, and I don't want you to repeat it to another soul,' and then he'd proceed to say the same thing three different times on the same day to three different people—and they'd all wind up thinking that they were the only one."

Red Barber, the Dodger announcer then, was one person Rickey confided in. He took Barber aside in March 1945 at Joe's Restaurant in Brooklyn and told him that he was going to bring a black player to the Dodgers. Barber, a southerner, said he was stunned and later thought of quitting. He did not, he says, because he heard a voice from the grave—that of Judge Landis—telling him the most important thing any reporter could do is report. "I heard that word *report* and peace came," Barber said. He became instrumental, as Rickey hoped he would, in winning over public opinion—because he was able to "just report."

Another person Rickey took aside prior to the 1947 season was the rookie pitcher Clyde King. Like Red Barber and so many others, King was won over by this willingness to confide in him.

"He told me before Jackie actually came," said King. "This was in '47, before spring training. He was like a father to me. He knew I was a southerner and I guess he wanted to sound me out. He told me straight he was going to break the color line. He didn't mention any other names than Jackie—though I guess he had others in mind as well."

Tygiel and others have said that Rickey went into that spring campaign with a careful strategic plan to bring up Robinson. The planning was evident in several ways.

First, Rickey took the unusual step of switching the Dodgers' and Royals' spring-training sites from Florida to Cuba, away from trouble and publicity. This also meant that while Robinson would be working out with the minor league team, much of his time on field would be spent in head-to-head play with his future Dodger teammates.

In addition, the Dodgers were booked to play a number of exhibition games in Panama against different Latin American all-star squads. Though the Dodgers had in the past played exhibitions in Latin America, there was now added significance to the fact that the team would be on the field, every day, against integrated competition.

But from the start, Rickey's plans unraveled like yarn from an old baseball.

By the time the Dodgers reached Panama, a revolt was gathering among players, most of them born in the South, over the prospect of Robinson's joining them. The team's road secretary, Harold Parrott, went out drinking one night with the garrulous pitcher Kirby Higbe, who had conflicted feelings about what was coming. He suggested to Parrott that a petition against Jackie might be in the works. Parrott was horrified. He immediately informed the team's manager, Leo Durocher who in turn, rang an all-quarters alarm, and even though it was after midnight, he hauled his players before him in a barracks mess hall.

Durocher, whom Rickey was counting on for support when he elevated Robinson, "wouldn't have been able to spell *equality* much less preach it," Parrott said. "He would have been the first to tell you that all men were *not* created equal." His single, abiding reason for supporting Robinson was that a player of his caliber meant money—for everyone in the organization, Durocher included. Swaddled in a yellow dressing gown, with Parrott at his side, Durocher lit into his bleary-eyed troops. "I don't care if the guy is yellow or black or if he has stripes like a fuckin' zebra, I'm the manager of this team, and I say he plays. What's more, I say he can make all of us rich . . . an' if any of you can't use the money, I'll see that you're traded."

When Parrott informed Rickey, who was still in the United States, the owner immediately set out for Panama, where he summoned the different troublemakers before him one by one.

"There were about four of us," said Bobby Bragan, then a third-string rookie catcher with the team. "There was Ed Head from Bascomb, Louisiana, and Dixie Walker and I from Birmingham, Alabama, and Eddie Stanky's home was Mobile. Carl Furillo was part of this too, even though he was from Pennsylvania. He was just a very emotional guy and he went around telling anyone who'd listen, 'I won't play with that black sonuvabitch.' "

With Furillo, Rickey's approach was as blunt as Durocher's. "Mr. Rickey was innovative," Bobby Bragan said. "He had a tremendous vocabulary and he could mesmerize you. He could sit Carl Furillo down in front of him and tell him, 'You are the dumbest athlete I have ever been associated with,' and then put a contract in front of him and he'd sign it." It took even less than that to turn Furillo around on Robinson. Accept Jackie as a teammate or find himself out of a job, Rickey told him. Furillo was no longer a rebel.

With Eddie Stanky, nicknamed the Brat and referred to, somewhat cynically by beat writers covering the team, as "a devil on the field and a priest off it," Rickey needed neither blunderbuss nor stiletto. Much as Clay Hopper had, Stanky replaced Dodger blue for the Confederate flag. Having recently been given a raise, he volunteered to help out in the clubhouse, on the field, any way he could.

Bragan, the third-string catcher, was not so easy to impress. "He took the worst tongue-lashing of all," said Arthur Mann, Rickey's assistant, who was present. But Bragan held firm.

" 'Would you play any differently with someone like that on the team?' Mr. Rickey asked me," said Bragan. "I told him, no, sir. So then he asked me if I'd rather stay here or be traded, and I told him I'd rather be traded."

Bragan's resistance, according to Mann, far from incurring Rickey's wrath, earned him his respect; it took courage and a strong sense of worth to risk so much by standing up for what he believed. These were values much admired by Rickey, values he had seen, in a different way, in Robinson. Ultimately, Bragan, who regarded Rickey with much the same kind of feeling as Clyde King, yielded. Being another kind of Missouri politician, Rickey realized that Bragan had little future as a player, and so he opened the way for him to have a career in the organization—just as he did for Clyde King.

But Rickey had his hands full with Dixie Walker, "The People's Cherce," whose popularity among fans was, if anything, surpassed by his standing among teammates.

"Dixie was soft-spoken, a real laid-back guy," Bragan said, adding impishly, "He always knew where the bargains were and the guys looked to him for that. You know, in Cincinnati, he somehow would know that the Palm Beach Company was letting ballplayers have suits and sport coats at a discount. If there was a haberdashery in Brooklyn or New York or a place that had ladies' garments, Dixie knew about it—he knew about all the discounts everywhere. He was a guy who had clout among us.''

Rickey first heard rumors of Walker's unhappiness during the winter. By the beginning of spring training, Walker let Rickey know exactly where he stood: like Bobby Bragan, he wanted out if he had to play alongside a black player, and nothing would change his mind.

Later that spring—toward the end of March—Walker became the only player on the team to put his feelings in writing, leading some to believe that he was responsible for a petition against Robinson signed by a number of players. Like the ''15–1'' vote, no copy of the petition has ever surfaced, but Walker's letter did:

March 26, 1947

Dear Mr. Rickey:

Recently the thought occurred to me that a change of Ball clubs would benefit both the Brooklyn Baseball Club and myself. Therefore I would like to be traded as soon as a deal can be arranged.

My association with you, the people of Brooklyn, the press and Radio has been very pleasant and one I can truthfully say I am sorry has to end. For reasons I don't care to go into I feel my decision is best for all concerned.

Very sincerely yours,
Dixie Walker

Though Walker remained with the Dodgers through the season, he continued to be adamant about wanting a trade, which Rickey obligingly pursued, nearly landing a little-known minor leaguer named Ralph Kiner as part of an exchange package with the Pirates, winding up instead, at year's end, with Preacher Roe, Billy Cox, and Gene Mauch.

As ''laid-back'' and as easygoing as Walker was, there was nothing genteel in his unapologetic attachment to segregation. A couple of years later, when he believed Rickey and Arthur Mann were contemplating magazine pieces naming him as the ringleader of the move to block Robinson's entrance to the big leagues, he warned them he would sue if they said anything to damage his reputation.

Rickey's plan to have Robinson show his skills on the field against the Dodgers worked brilliantly in Panama. In a dozen games against the Dodgers and local teams, Robinson hit over .500 and was a terror on the base paths. But the groundswell to bring him up to the big club that Rickey expected never materialized, and back in Cuba Robinson's performance dropped off. By then, doubt and mistrust were once again awakening Jackie's suspicions. Too many things were pointing away rather than toward Brooklyn.

For one thing, there was the way Rickey chose to house the players. The Dodger and Royal squads were put up in separate parts of Havana, with the Dodgers staying in the downtown, posh Hotel National, while the Royals were billeted in comfortable quarters at the National Military Academy, the site of their training ground. But for reasons never believably explained (it was important to duplicate U.S. living conditions, integration was still a sensitive issue on the team, the Dodger hotel was owned by Americans, etc.), Jackie and the other black players on the Royals' roster—Roy Campanella, Don Newcombe, and Roy Partlow—were housed in a shabby hotel many miles from the training camp. The move infuriated all four players, who couldn't understand why segregated housing in a country that was already integrated had even been contemplated.

The living conditions were atrocious. The Dodgers gave the players meal money and a rented car, but left them to fend for themselves even though none of them spoke or understood Spanish. The hotel, to Don Newcombe, was "cockroach heaven"; to Sam Lacy, who along with Wendell Smith accompanied the players to Cuba, it was "a little sleazebag place, second-class, maybe third-class."

Newcombe and Robinson at different times came down with bouts of dysentery. Newcombe recalled sitting in a restaurant one night "eating a bowl of soup and a big cockroach floated to the top and I almost threw my guts up. That was the way we had to live." What kept him, Robinson, and Campanella going, he said, was that "we had the audacity to want to play baseball."

Also not quite worked out was the specific position Robinson would play. Pee Wee Reese was set at shortstop, just as Eddie Stanky was at second. The Dodger weaknesses were at third and first. Third was ruled out because of Robinson's arm—which left first base.

In Panama, Robinson was unceremoniously handed an old mitt,

given a lecture by Rickey on going out and being a dervish on the field, and then faced the reality he had faced the year before when he took a brief try at the position—his feet got hopelessly tangled, and the effort of learning only got in the way of his being able to play.

So, if it was in Rickey's mind that his moves would incite an irresistible demand to promote Robinson, he was sorely mistaken. The press, which had been behind the move, spent more time wondering whether Robinson could play first. Robinson had come to believe that he was once more about to be betrayed. One night, Wendell Smith excitedly came to him with the news that Rickey had just said he was going to bring Robinson up on April 10.

Robinson laughed in Smith's face.

It was easy to see why Robinson might doubt Rickey. He did not know him well enough to trust him. A year in the minors at minimum pay hadn't persuaded him. Neither had the presence of other black players now in the organization—first-rate players such as Newcombe and Campanella. Robinson was unsure about who they were.

Campanella in particular rubbed him the wrong way. To every insult, real or imagined, he seemed to take a directly opposite tack from Robinson. He was in camp to play ball, and glad to be there. That was all. Years later, Campanella publicly told a story on himself relating to that Havana camp that simply had to have set Robinson's teeth on edge.

According to Campanella, a TV broadcaster, Bob Edge, was sitting in a box with Branch Rickey and Ernest Hemingway. Edge, said Campanella, was flabbergasted when he saw Campanella come out of the dugout for the first time. Without a trace of embarrassment, Campanella said Edge laughed and told him, "I thought you were carrying a watermelon on each hip." Edge reported that Rickey "chuckled." Then the announcer told Campanella, "Anyhow, you hit a line-drive single. The way you went down to first, I knew that no matter how fat you looked, you could run. . . . Well, Campy, I've got to say you impressed Hemingway and me."

But Jackie Robinson continued to wonder what kind of games were going on under the sun. Rickey might be a white man playing Abraham Lincoln; he might also be just another carnival operator, looking to pick people's pockets. Robinson certainly did not know Rickey well enough yet to know that both those characters were part of his makeup, and that his intentions and actions might actually invite a genuine and welcome partnership in a venture that went far beyond the signing of a professional baseball contract at minimum pay.

The Dodgers and Royals left Cuba for New York on April 6, with still no public hint of the decision that would be made. The *New York Post* in early April declared that Robinson had not gotten a fair trial by being shifted to first base, the implication clearly being that Rickey had engineered a fast one to keep him off the team. A number of columnists concluded that he would either not make the squad or would wind up as a reserve.

The last and final blow to his careful plan awaited Rickey when the team returned to the mainland. The Dodger president had been counting heavily on Leo Durocher's leadership to facilitate Robinson's acceptance on the team. Rickey had even let it be rumored in the press that he would let Durocher make the final decision on Robinson. But on April 9, just days before the opening of the season—and one day prior to the date Rickey had given Smith—Commissioner Chandler shocked the Dodgers and the baseball world by announcing that he had suspended Durocher for the coming year for "conduct detrimental to baseball." The decision was made following hearings Chandler held to investigate charges by Durocher, in a ghostwritten newspaper column, that known gamblers had been spotted at a spring-training game in seats set aside by Yankee owner Larry MacPhail. MacPhail, in turn, charged that Durocher regularly permitted and took part in gambling in the Dodger clubhouse. The real feud, though, was between MacPahil, a foe of integration, and his old partner and rival, Branch Rickey. Durocher, in all likelihood, was a nice guy who finished last in a situation not of his own making—this time, anyway.

In any case, this last and greatest challenge left the "six-part plan" in tatters. Chandler's decision robbed Rickey of his manager and of any time to make other arrangements. Whether or not Chandler intended it, his action seemed to have the incidental effect of blocking Robinson's promotion.

But Rickey's response could not have been more decisive. The following day, Clyde Sukeforth, who had scouted Robinson, was named interim manager of the team. And then, in the sixth inning of the Dodgers' game with the Royals at Ebbets Field, a team official strode into the press box and tacked an announcement to the bulletin board:

> *The Brooklyn Dodgers today purchased the contract of Jackie Roosevelt Robinson from the Montreal Royals. He will report immediately.*
>
> *Branch Rickey*

Down on the field, even as the announcement was being pinned to the wall, Robinson was at bat, bunting into a double play. But Royal players and their manager, Clay Hopper, who had just gotten the word, were flashing broad grins and thumbs-up signs to him as he came back to the dugout.

What Robinson realized in that moment on April 10 was that for all his doubts about him, Branch Rickey had kept the faith. Robinson also knew that this moment would be a test of his own faith—not in Branch Rickey, but in his ability to survive.

Part 2
Manchild in the Promised Land

CHAPTER NINETEEN

Postwar America was a country of profound contradictions, and nowhere more so than in the area of race relations. Gunnar Myrdal's *An American Dilemma,* published in 1944, laid out a fundamental contradiction in American life. On the one hand, the Constitution, the Bill of Rights, the Declaration of Independence, spell out in painstaking detail ideals of individual liberty, equality, freedom, and justice. These ideals Myrdal named the Creed, and the reality they sustained was democracy.

On the other hand, Myrdal wrote, "the American Creed represents the national conscience. The Negro is a 'problem' to the average American partly because of a palpable conflict between the status actually awarded him and those ideals."

But the peculiar confluence of a worldwide economic depression followed by a world war presented America with an opportunity to deal with that contradiction as never before. All the nation's history leading up to the postwar period had been merely a static interim in which the Creed and "the problem" had existed side by side. But now America was out in the world, and what it did affected people everywhere. A new day, a new chance, was at hand.

Underlying Myrdal's analysis—widely shared by social scientists and leading intellectuals of the day—was optimism. He believed, with almost prophetic certainty, that the Creed itself would be the engine to bring about the long-awaited and genuine settlement of the dilemma. "Behind all outward dissimilarities, behind their contradictory valuations, rationalizations, vested interests, group allegiances and animosities, behind fears and defense constructions, behind the role they play in life and the mask they wear, people are all much alike on a fundamental level. And they are all good people. They want to be rational and just. They all plead to their conscience that they meant well even when things went wrong."

One cannot begin to understand the impact of Jackie Robinson's breaking of baseball's color barrier without seeing it in the optimistic context described by Myrdal. That optimism, in large part, shaped the thinking and planning of those who were standing uncertainly before history. In the minds of Branch Rickey, Jackie and Rachel Robinson, and millions of other postwar Americans, integration was only a dim possibility. But it meant that the opportunity for one black man to play professional baseball alongside a field full of white men had significance far beyond the ballpark.

From day one, every step Robinson took seemed tuned to the national imagination, to the dreams—and nightmares—of millions of people. The real burden Robinson bore was that he knew this. The day he set out for spring training that year, Robinson said he was so nervous and upset he did not want to go. But something else was driving him.

From the moment he emerged from the first-base dugout at Ebbets Field, he knew that every at bat, every hit, every stolen base, every play in the field, mattered more than games. But at the same time, all that mattered was to stay focused upon the game—not upon anything so grandiose as history. In this strange moment it seemed that history could be shaped to the contours of a baseball field. But that only amplified to the point of relentlessness Robinson's determination to go all out, to make winning the final proof of the experiment.

Robinson was caught up in the usual concerns of a rookie—playing time, making a good impression on his teammates, manager, and coaches—but he was always forced to contend with more. And then circumstance intervened as well. The Dodgers did not have a permanent replacement for Leo Durocher until the second game of the season, when they brought in sixty-two-year-old Burt Shotton, a quiet Rickey loyalist who, after Connie Mack retired in 1950, became the last manager in the majors to wear street clothes in the dugout. His inert presence was a blank rather than a support.

The day Robinson donned his Dodger uniform for the first time, the team began a set of three exhibition games with the crosstown New York Yankees. Robinson did not distinguish himself in the games— normally a turn of no consequence. In his case, however, it counted enough for several Yankee players to remark to the *Sporting News* that he was "too clumsy" at first and would soon find himself out of the starting lineup.

Robinson was alone in the clubhouse at this point. Because the Dodgers' spring roster had not yet been fully pared from 40 to 25 players, he did not even have a regular locker. His first day, he was assigned a hook on the wall. With the hook went an aloofness if not hostility from his teammates. Al Gionfriddo, joining the club later in the spring, remembered that Robinson used to wait to shower until all the other players on the team had finished theirs.

Robinson's debut at Ebbets Field was not up to the history of the moment. The crowd was relatively small—26,623—for the opener against the Braves, a game won by the Dodgers, 5–3. Robinson went hitless but distinguished himself in the field, said Red Barber, playing first base flawlessly "as though he had never played any other position."

Robinson was right in the middle of his team's late-inning rally that decided the game. In his first three appearances at the plate, he had grounded to third, flied to left, and hit into a double play. But with the score tied and a runner on first, Robinson came up and laid down a perfect sacrifice bunt. In fact, the bunt was so good, the Braves' first baseman, Earl Torgeson, fielded the ball and threw it away, off Robinson's body, allowing both runners to advance to scoring position, where they were then driven in on a game-winning double by Pete Reiser. Robinson's first major league hit came in the next game, a 12–6 rout of the Braves. It was also a bunt—but a clean bunt single rather than a sacrifice.

Robinson, however, through the first month of the season, remained in a slump, that ate at his confidence daily. In the second series of the year—against the hated Giants at the Polo Grounds—he hit his first home run. But soon after, he got caught in an 0-for-20 streak and was, according to Arthur Mann, "within a single day of being benched."

His slump and his isolation from his teammates weighed on him, but no more so than when he was exposed to the racial taunts and provocations that were directed at him by opponents with the clear intention of driving him out of baseball.

The first test came early, in the Dodgers' third series of the season, against the Philadelphia Phillies. The Phillies manager was Alabama native Ben Chapman, whose racist views were known even during his playing days with the Yankees. From the moment Robinson set foot on the field, Chapman, joined by a number of his players, directed an almost unprintable barrage of verbal abuse at him that continued for the rest of the series. A full quarter of a century later, Robinson still seemed gun-shy in reporting what he heard:

"Almost as if it had been synchronized by some master conductor, hate poured forth from the Phillies dugout," he said.

" 'Hey, nigger, why don't you go back to the cotton field where you belong?'

" 'They're waiting for you in the jungles, black boy!'

" 'Hey, snowflake, which one of those white boys' wives are you dating tonight?'

" 'We don't want you here, nigger!'

" 'Go back to the bushes!' "

Every time Robinson was within eye contact, the Phillies waved and hooted, gestured obscenely, picked up bats and pointed them at Jackie, imitating sounds of machine-gun fire.

The unrelenting viciousness was also directed at Robinson's team-mates, warning them about all the diseases they would catch if they shared combs and other personal items with him. Unable to answer because of his pledge of silence, Robinson acknowledged the incident brought him closer "to cracking up than I ever had been. . . . For one wild and rage-crazed minute I thought, to hell with Mr. Rickey's noble experiment." The only saving moment came during the third game when, finally, a lone teammate, Eddie Stanky, screamed at Chapman and his cohorts, "You yellow-bellied cowards, why don't you pick on somebody who can answer back!"

Chapman's behavior was so egregious it drew press notice and then a reprimand from Commissioner Chandler and National League president Ford Frick. Chapman, caught off guard by anyone taking Robinson's side, explained that his race-baiting was only hard bench-jockeying. White rookies, he said, were referred to as wops, dagos, Polacks, and they never complained. Taunting Robinson was no different.

The Phils' management—sensitive to the bad publicity it was getting, but actually committed to the same jim crow view of big-league baseball, suggested to Dodger officials that it would be helpful if a photo could be arranged showing Jackie and Chapman shaking hands. Rickey agreed and persuaded Robinson, who, though humiliated at even the thought of it, went along because his boss had asked him.

When the session was arranged on a subsequent road trip to Shibe

Park, Chapman, fearing for his job but as adamant as ever, refused to actually shake Robinson's hand. Instead, he held a bat—with two hands. He was willing, he said, to have Robinson grip the bat—with one hand.

Within that first month, the incidents mounted. The first time the Dodgers went into Pittsburgh, the Pirates refused to take the field until they were given five minutes to play or forfeit. At home, crowd mikes that were placed near the backstop had to be removed because radio listeners were picking up the foul language that was being directed at Robinson.

In early May, Stanley Woodward, the sports editor of the *Herald Tribune* reported that members of the St. Louis Cardinals tried to instigate a player strike against Robinson. The story claimed that National League president Ford Frick found out about it and issued a warning to the players that they would be banned for life if they went ahead. The ultimatum was delivered, the story said, through the Cards' owner, Sam Breadon. The players, but not Frick, denied that such a warning was ever issued. The players also categorically denied that they had ever planned to strike.

The story of the threatened strike has never quite been pinned down. Tygiel, for example, says that "the St. Louis Cardinal strike, although generally accepted as an integral part of the Robinson legend, remains an extremely elusive topic."

But other teams were also involved. The Chicago Cubs, according to pitcher Hank Wyse, actually took a strike vote before their first game of the season at Ebbets Field. "We voted not to play. I'm not sure, but I think the vote was unanimous," Wyse said. News of the vote was apparently relayed to the league office because, thirty minutes later, Wyse said, "a telegram came saying that anybody that didn't play would be barred for life."

It was Wyse's understanding that the strike vote the Cubs took was being taken by every other club. The veteran Cubs first baseman and outfielder Phil Cavaretta "had got a letter from the other clubs, and so we held a meeting without the manager or any of the coaches so we could take the vote," Wyse said.

Wyse also said that Cub starting pitchers had standing orders to knock Robinson down: "Paul Erickson knocked him down four times before he came up to hit, and then we put in another pitcher so they couldn't get back at him. But in the beginning, no one retaliated. "No one even said a word," Wyse said. "Jackie didn't say anything, their bench never said anything, even the umpire said not one word."

The Cubs first-base coach, Roy Johnson, taunted Robinson with a charge that Branch Rickey had covered up for him by concealing a collegiate rape incident. "Ole Hard Rock said, 'There's other guys should be in here instead of you, you ought to be hung for raping that white girl in college.' Jackie got so mad he blowed his top, but he didn't charge Roy, and after the game when Roy was waiting for him, Jackie just went up in the clubhouse," Wyse said.

Most serious of all were the threats made against Robinson's life. Every day, mail would come pouring into the Dodger offices for Robinson, and invariably it would include death threats and threats to kidnap or harm Robinson's wife and infant son. The threats became so frequent—and so unnerving—that the club finally decided to screen Robinson's mail for him, informing him only of those that were considered authentic.

One such threat—actually three of them—surfaced on the Dodgers' first visit of the season to Cincinnati, just when Robinson was coming out of his slump. Directly across the river from Kentucky, where there was a known Ku Klux Klan cell, Cincinnati was especially loud in its opposition to Robinson. He was taunted and reviled as he was in Philadelphia, only this time from the stands as well as from the dugout. Rex Barney, a Dodger rookie then, recalled, "I was warming up on the mound, and I could hear the Cincinnati players screaming at Jackie, 'You nigger son of a bitch, you shoeshine boy,' and all the rest."

But few knew how serious the occasion really was. Harold Parrott, the Dodgers' road secretary, was one. He was the team official who culled Robinson's mail.

"Usually I didn't show Robbie the hate mail," he said, "most of which was scrawled and scribbled like the smut you see on toilet walls. But this time I had to warn him, and I could see that he was frightened."

The FBI searched the rooftops and upper stories of every building overlooking the ballpark, Parrott said, and then when the national anthem was played, with its background sound effects of exploding bombs, he realized—as Robinson might have—"that that precise moment would have been the ideal cover for gunfire, if someone were indeed going to take a shot."

Beyond the ballpark, life was just as burdensome. When the Dodgers traveled, Robinson kept to himself, ate by himself, pretended —for the sake of his teammates—to be staring out train windows or engrossed in a book so that he might spare anyone the embarrassment of having to socialize with him.

Living accommodations were a constant insult. In Philadelphia, the Dodgers turned up at the hotel they normally stayed in, the Benjamin Franklin, only to be told that all the rooms had been taken. Players and baggage were directed to the sidewalk. One Dodger player, Kirby Higbe, loudly asked Robinson "if some of your people could take us in?"

In St. Louis, the Dodgers were booked in the swanky Chase Hotel —except for Jackie Robinson, who stayed sometimes in private homes, sometimes in a hotel patronized only by blacks. In Cincinnati, Robinson was allowed to stay with the team at the Netherlands Plaza —provided he took his meals in his room or away from the hotel and stayed out of the swimming pool.

Whenever the team arrived in a new town, all the other players had their baggage taken care of and had cabs ready and waiting—only Robinson and Wendell Smith, his companion through those early days, were left to fend for themselves.

At home the situation was exacting in another way. Robinson and his family were strapped for a place to live. At first, when it was unclear whether their address for the year would be Montreal or Brooklyn, they stayed at the Hotel McAlpin in midtown Manhattan. The crush of interest brought reporters and the curious to their door at all hours of the day and night. Rachel Robinson remembers having to push pots and pans under beds and into closets anytime she heard someone knock. Taking meals and baby-sitting were constant problems. In the early days, the Robinsons took turns going to the hotel cafeteria to eat, the other staying behind with the baby.

After a while, the Robinsons moved in with a family in a residential section of Brooklyn—and that, said Rachel, was hardly an improvement. They had one small bedroom and part of a hallway where they could install a crib. Getting upstairs and down with a carriage, she said, was an everyday challenge. They couldn't use the living room because "the woman with whom we shared the apartment seemed to entertain friends constantly, day and night. . . . Jackie and I took bus rides or we pushed the baby carriage up and down the street late at night for recreation, because we had no car, no baby-sitter, and virtually no friends."

But in the beginning of May, despite all these obstacles, Robinson began to hit. In a series at the end of April in Philadelphia he flashed the first signs of coming out of his slump, and then through the first half of the May, when he hit in fourteen straight games at a .395 clip and was a terror on the base paths, it was as though everyone—teammates, opponents, fans, sportswriters—collectively woke up to what kind of player he might be. Suddenly Branch Rickey's experiment no longer seemed so experimental.

Press coverage of Robinson through the initial weeks of the season, when his tenure with the team seemed most shaky, was highly favorable. The run-ins with Chapman and the peculiarities of being the lone black player in the majors were sympathetically conveyed to readers. With the report in the *Herald Tribune* of the threatened Cardinal player strike during the second week in May, however, there seemed to be a turn.

In a study of New York newspaper coverage of Robinson's first year, researcher Pat Washburn found that "May 10 was a critical point in the newspaper coverage of Robinson. . . . Until that date all three [major] papers avidly supported his entry into the major leagues. But following May 10, both the *Times* and the *Herald Tribune* altered their coverage of Robinson, virtually eliminating race identification [or] terms and reports of incidents with a racial connotation." Washburn never clearly explained why the coverage changed, but it undeniably did—and most likely because, from the start, the actual story of race was too hot to handle.

It was far easlier to report what Robinson did from day to day on the field. And that, it turned out, spoke volumes.

As his play became eye-catching, huge crowds turned out to see him wherever he went. Attendance records were set in Philadelphia, Chicago, St. Louis. Rain and weekday dates did not slow the flow. Around the time the Dodgers reached Chicago during third week of the month, Robinson was labeled by one columnist as "the most lucrative draw in baseball since Babe Ruth."

The hate mail, the threats, the incidents never stopped—only they were not part of the developing story. The story that was being conveyed was that Jackie Robinson belonged in the major leagues. "At the start of the road trip," said Jules Tygiel, "many still questioned whether Robinson belonged in the big leagues. . . . In city after city, Robinson showed skeptical sportswriters and fans that the Dodgers had not erred."

Whatever Robinson was going through he kept largely to himself. Neither teammates, team officials, nor even his wife seemed to know for sure. "I tried again and again to get him to talk about the problems he was meeting," Rachel said, "but he didn't want to burden me. He would never talk about those things at home. But I knew they were eating at his mind, for he would jerk and twitch and even talk in his troubled sleep, which was not like him."

Robinson's sister, Willa Mae, remembers getting a phone call from Jackie "in the early days in Brooklyn" in which "he just blurted out, 'I can't take it anymore. I'm quitting' "—but she wasn't precisely sure when the call was made. Roger Kahn, who covered the Dodgers a few years later, says that Robinson specifically told him the talk about quitting came after the Chapman episode. As Kahn tells it, Robinson said, "All of a sudden I thought, the hell with this. This isn't me. They're making me be some crazy pacifist black freak. Hell, no. I'm going back to being myself. Right now. I'm going into the Phillie dugout and grab one of those white sons of bitches and smash his fucking teeth and walk away. Walk away from this ballpark. Walk away from baseball."

Only Wendell Smith, Robinson's constant companion in that time, might have known for sure what he was thinking and went through that decisive month. But Smith, like Robinson, was aware that the story of baseball's first Negro player was larger than any individual, and so his commentary remained selective till the end. What Smith and everyone else understood was that at the beginning of the month, Robinson's tenure in the game was uncertain—and at month's end, he was a national hero.

CHAPTER TWENTY

Bigotry, like competition, enters new and different phases. Those —and there were many then—who say that opposition to Robinson melted within a month or so were believers in the results of games. But the nature of the competition then was such that it was possible, for a time, to believe that something so intractable as the American Dilemma could resolve itself within the perfectly lined dimensions of a baseball field.

Robinson's pact with Rickey was to play ball. His pact with himself was to prove beyond any measure that he could not only play with white men, he could play so well that the doors would have to open for others. He was never content merely to fit in; to integrate, he knew that he would always have to be one step ahead.

The Dodgers had a pennant to win that year and everyone knew it would not be easy. They had gone to a play-off the year before, losing to the Cardinals, and experts again favored them—but for the unknown quantity represented by this lone black player.

Robinson complemented his fourteen-game hitting streak in May with an even longer one—twenty-one games—in June, as the Dodgers moved up through the pack, returning home from a long western road trip in which they pulled to within a half game of the lead, then held by the Boston Braves. Two out of three wins over the Braves at Ebbets Field moved the Dodgers into first, and thereafter they and the Cardinals battled through the summer.

To everyone who saw him, Robinson was simply a new and different kind of player. If sociologists were trying to figure out who he was and how exactly he fit in, fans, whether they wanted him there or not, were being daily exposed to that infrequent but familiar gift of the baseball gods—a true star.

From the moment he stepped from the dugout, something was different about him. True, the look of him, coal black in his cream and blue Dodger flannels, was a shock in that year. But he *walked* differently. He had broad shoulders and spindly legs, and when he moved from the bench to batter's box, from point A to point B, his pigeon-

170

toed gait looked more arthritic than athletic. But when he was in full flight, the pigeon toes, arms, legs, elbows, everything seemed to be flying off at different angles. It made no sense for anyone so large to move with such speed and power, with such grace. Or call it graceless elegance; there was and is no oxymoron for the way Jackie Robinson ran.

When he took his stance at the plate, he held his bat cocked high over his shoulder—too high some said for the kind of bat speed needed to get around on major league pitching. But that pose, too, was another signature of his, because from it he had unbelievable agility and control. When a pitch was released, his bat instantly dropped into the launch position, and he turned his hips in such a manner that even the most casual fan could feel the massive shift of weight coming forward onto his front foot. "Lunge hitter," said many, including the great Johnny Sain, who believed Robinson would never be able to handle the curve ball.

He was one of the best curve-ball hitters ever.

His quickness enabled him to do things with a bat others could not. He could bring his hands through a ball with the unflinching commitment of a power hitter. But he could also touch bat to ball with the precision of a surgeon. He bunted forty-two times, nineteen for hits, in 1947.

What roused the baseball world more than anything were his antics on the base paths. Though his high-water mark in steals was thirty-seven (in 1949), he was the father of modern base-stealing. He opened the way for another kind of game in which Maury Wills, Lou Brock, and Rickey Henderson flourished. As with everything else, Robinson did not steal to pile up numbers; he stole to win games, to dismantle the opposition. One Dodger fan, a surrogate for all, remembered:

"I was out at Ebbets Field one day. Meyer was pitching for Phila-delphia, and he walked Robinson. Now this annoyed Meyer no end. The next batter, Campy, got decked immediately. Right at the head. Robinson danced off first. Meyer looked at him, threw to first, and Robinson got back. He danced off first. Meyer looked at him, threw to first, and Robinson went to second. Stole it clean.

"Now Meyer was really furious. He walked off the mound behind the rubber, talking to himself, his hands on his hips. He got back on the mound, peered in for a signal, and on the next pitch Robinson stole third. Now Meyer is frothing at the mouth. He's hysterical. The catcher comes out, the first baseman comes out, the manager comes out. Everyone is around him, and he's screaming, frothing, jumping up and down like a madman.

"The game resumes. Robinson starts to dance off the third-base line. Everyone in the ballpark senses that he's going to go. Meyer looks over at Robinson, and he makes a wild pitch, and Robinson trots home. Two guys had to come to the mound and physically drag Meyer into the dugout.''

Robinson won fans over because he could rouse them, but he also won over his team, his league—and the nation—not only by being a lion but by having to be a lamb. Everyone knew—from day one, when a Confederate teammate could no longer stand the abuse and screamed back for tormentors to pick on someone who was *allowed* to fight back, that this dismantler of opponents had to do it with one hand tied behind his back.

In Chicago, in June, in the ninth inning of a tied game, Robinson reached base, the potential game-breaking run. He began his dance, drew two throws, then stole second. He got up, dusted himself off, and started in all over again.

The pitcher, Bill Lee, fired back to second, this time nearly picking Jackie off. Robinson slid safely back to the bag, becoming entangled in the legs of the Cubs shortstop, Len Merullo. Merullo, in disengaging himself, in plain view of everyone in the house, kicked Jackie—and Robinson, in just as plain view, raised an arm in fury to retaliate, and then, as if wired to Rickey's Bible, amazingly stopped his fist in midflight.

In the first thirty-seven games the Dodgers played that season, Robinson was hit by pitches six times and made to eat dirt in almost every game he played. But his answer, invariably, was to get back up, hold his peace, and only play that much harder.

Sportswriters noted the almost surreal stoicism he seemed to project. Opponents slowly began to acknowledge his courage. In a game at Pittsburgh, Robinson collided on a play at first with Hank Greenberg, the aging slugger who had endured his own trials becoming a major leaguer. In the following inning, when Greenberg walked and was standing at first, Robinson apologized for bumping him the inning before. Greenberg shrugged it off and told him to hang in there, and that when the teams got together again, he'd like to sit down with him and share some war stories. Later in the season, in a game between the Dodgers and Cards, Enos Slaughter, on a routine ground-out, crossed the first-base bag and deliberately spiked Jackie. It was all Robinson could do to check his desire to retaliate. His pitcher, Ralph Branca, had a no-hitter at that time, and that helped. Robinson spent his fury barking at Branca to stay focused. The next inning, though, when Robinson reached first base, he let Stan Musial know that he would like to take Slaughter and some of his cohorts apart. "I don't blame you," the Cardinal star quietly replied.

More importantly, Robinson saw that his teammates began to accept him. But the first, hesitant gestures of acceptance were magnified in the reporting—either for the sake of the experiment or for those doing the reporting. Robinson being taken into the fold as just another Dodger with a number on his back was proof, after all, that America worked.

Some stories acquired the status of myth. Pee Wee Reese, depending on the witness, walked over to Robinson early in the season when cascades of abuse were pouring on him from opposing dugouts and wrapped an arm around him as if to tell the abusers he was on Jackie's team, not theirs. Different observers, including Harold Parrott, remember the moment taking place in that first series against the Phils. Rex Barney and others place it weeks later in Crosley Field. But Robinson said the incident took place in Braves Field at the beginning of the following season.

Social acceptance was another thing entirely. Meals together, nights out on the road, these were nearly always excluded. No Dodger in those early years ever raised a whisper of objection when Robinson was forced to use segregated facilities or had privileges restricted. Al Gionfriddo, who came to the team in a June trade that sent Kirby Higbe to the Pirates, recalled that Robinson never showered till everyone else finished. "One day I hit him on the butt," he said. " 'You're part of this team,' I said . . . 'Just because in some states Negroes can't shower with whites, that doesn't mean it had to apply here in our clubhouse.' And he just looked at me and laughed. And we both got up and took a shower."

Card playing was an icebreaker—for Robinson and his mates. He was an avid gin, poker, and bridge player, and in the six-guns-and-cigar-smoke atmosphere of jocks at the table, he relished the challenge. He held off initially, but over time he let himself join in. His wariness never let down, however. In one game, Hugh Casey, a hard-drinking southerner who had been another of the original petitioners against him in the spring, hit a losing streak playing poker. "Tell you what I used to do down in Georgia when my poker luck got bad," Casey said, turning to Robinson in drunken friendliness, "I'd just get up and go out and I'd rub me the teat of the biggest, blackest nigger woman I could find." Casey then reached over and rubbed Robinson's head. Robinson said that he was nearly overcome with rage, but that he did not respond because his "teammates were more embarrassed, more pained" than he was.

In the end, he was accepted not because the Dodgers were more democratic than the rest of America but because they needed him.

In the beginning, Pee Wee Reese was important. During the spring, when Dixie Walker, a friend, came to him with the petition, Reese turned him down. Pee Wee was a linchpin: if he had signed, others were sure to follow.

"I wouldn't sign it," he said. "I wasn't trying to think of myself as being the Great White Father, really, I just wanted to play the game, especially after being in the Navy for three years and needing the money, and it didn't matter to me whether he was black or green, he had a right to be there too."

Ralph Branca has generally been given less credit for helping Robinson than Reese, but he was probably more responsible than anyone else for initially rallying his mates.

The usual Branca-Robinson story of that year involves a game in St. Louis in late August. On this one play, Robinson pursued a pop-up toward the Dodger bench. He stumbled, pitched toward the dugout, and would likely have mangled himself but for Branca—who rose from the bench and bear-hugged him. Like the arm-on-the-shoulder story, this one has also been used to illustrate Democracy on the Dodgers.

Branca says, "I didn't do it because he was black, I did it because he was my teammate, and I probably would have done it if it was the opposition. It was an instinct thing."

Branca, from Mt. Vernon, New York, says the presence of a black player on the team never bothered him because he had played with and against blacks all his life. But he had a cold-eyed view of the great experiment. "Only my opinion, but I think Rickey did it for money," he said. "Rickey knew we were going to draw a lot of people. And we did. Remember what the minimum salary was then? It was five thousand dollars. I gave a speech once and I asked the audience to guess what Jackie made that year, with Rickey knowing what he was going to have to go through. People guessed ten thousand, eight thousand. Nope, I said. I was making six thousand five hundred dollars. He gave him five thousand dollars, the minimum."

Branca's steely view gave him a clearer sense of Robinson's real value to the team—and also what the team needed to do to make full use of his talent. In June, following the Merullo incident in Chicago, Branca, without Robinson's knowledge, called a team meeting. Joe Black, a later teammate, learned about it. "Branca called a meeting in Chicago, but they didn't let Jack know. It was all the white players. And the essence of the meeting was, Branca told them, 'Look, this guy Robinson is gonna lead us to a pennant. And we all want that money that we can get playing in the World Series. But you know these other teams are trying to get him to start a fight so he can be kicked outta baseball, so we have to protect him.' So they made a rule that if anything happened, the first guy closest to Robinson was supposed to knock him down and lay on top of him so that when pictures and stories came out, they couldn't say Jack was right in the middle."

Plan A never had to be executed, but it was in the minds of Robinson's teammates from June till the end of the season—whatever they thought about him personally.

More than anyone, Robinson *made* acceptance happen. He was bound by his pact with Rickey and by a more important one with himself. He kept quiet, turned the other cheek, avoided interviews, and even—as Rickey demanded—declined all offers for commercial endorsements through the first half of the season. The one exception he insisted upon was accepting an invitation to appear on the radio show *Information Please*. He turned over the fee he got to the United Negro College Fund.

As the Dodgers moved into the lead in July, Robinson continued to lead his team. He was among the league's top hitters, run scorers, and base stealers. He was his team's top home-run hitter (eventually finishing in a tie with Pee Wee Reese). But it was *how* he played that was unforgettable. In one game in Chicago, he scored all the way from first on a bunted ball; in Pittsburgh, he stole home—for the first time in his career. In New York, he sparked a ninth-inning, come-from-behind rally to beat the Giants before a sold-out crowd of over fifty thousand. He fanned delirious images of the first world championship in Dodger history.

At one home game, when the public address announcer pointed out that Rachel and Jackie Jr. were in the crowd, the fans got to their feet and cheered.

On the road, the taunts, the insults, the pitches at his head, the spikings, continued but were less frequent—not because civics lessons were being held in the clubhouses, but because the league was learning about Jackie Robinson's competitive drive. Characteristically, Leo Durocher would one day phrase it, "He doesn't just want to beat you, he wants to shove the bat up your ass."

When Ewell Blackwell, the Reds pitcher, was trying for a second straight no-hitter, he had one into the ninth inning in a game against the Dodgers in Cincinnati. With one out, Eddie Stanky broke up his bid, hitting a ground-hugger straight at him. Blackwell couldn't bend over far enough to get it, and the ball skipped into center field. After the next batter flied out, Blackwell, still obviously upset, began screaming racial obscenities at Robinson as he stepped into the batter's box. He aimed the first pitch squarely at his head. Blackwell was a tall (six foot five inches), skinny man with long, snakelike arms. His nickname was the Whip.

Robinson picked himself up and lined Blackwell's first hittable pitch into right center field for a solid base hit.

In late August, the Cardinals' Harry "the Cat" Brecheen had the Dodgers 7–0 in the eighth inning of a game at Sportsman's Park. With no one on, Robinson topped a pitch down the first-base line. Brecheen, a great fielder, quickly scooped up the ball, but instead of flipping on to first for the easy out, he stood in the baseline with the ball in his hand. Robinson looked up, saw him, jammed on the brakes, and let Brecheen make a show of tagging him out—to the delighted howls of the crowd. But August was not April. And by this time, Jackie Robinson knew who he was and where he was going.

"You play your position like you're supposed to," he said sharply under his breath. "Next time you do that, I'll knock you on your ass."

Robinson finished the season hitting .292, leading the league in steals (twenty-nine), and ranking second in runs scored (to Johnny Mize of the Giants, who hit fifty-one homers). September was a blaze of glory for him. In a pennant-deciding series against the Cards at Ebbets Field, Robinson went six for thirteen, with a homer, double, and four singles. With a pennant in hand, the borough went mad.

In late September, the team was feted at Borough Hall in downtown Brooklyn. The high point of the celebration was the announcement that Robinson had been named Rookie of the Year by the *Sporting News*. Only that spring the paper had confidently assured its readers that if Jackie had been white and six years younger, the best he could have hoped for from professional baseball was a workout with a class-B team.

And following the parade, on September 27 there was Jackie Robinson Day. Family members from California were there, along with 26,123 fans at Ebbets Field. Robinson received gifts and heard speeches praising him. Leaders of the black community in Brooklyn, including the principal organizer of the Day, the Reverend Sandy Ray—who would later become an important and influential figure in Robinson's life—joined white teammates and civic leaders in what surely must have seemed like the dawning of a new age.

Days later, Robinson became the first black player in World Series history. The Dodgers lost in seven games to the hated New York Yankees, and though Robinson did not hit especially well (.259), it hardly mattered; he was, triumphantly, just another Dodger.

There were other, smaller triumphs too. Dixie Walker publicly credited Robinson—along with Bruce Edwards—for the great year the team had. He also asked to have his request for a trade torn up—which Rickey refused to do.

But of all the triumphs, large and small, none were more significant than two separate personnel moves made during the second half of the season. On August 27, the Dodgers brought up a second black player, twenty-seven-year-old pitcher Dan Bankhead, a strikeout pitcher from the Memphis Red Sox, personally scouted by Rickey.

On July 5, the Cleveland Indians announced the signing of twenty-two-year-old outfielder Larry Doby of the Newark Eagles, effective immediately.

As a result of the year Robinson had had, the doors were now open. Major league baseball, a cornerstone of American culture, would never again be an exclusive preserve limited to whites. On Jackie Robinson Day, Bill "Bojangles" Robinson referred to Jackie Robinson as a "Ty Cobb in Technicolor." But what Robinson had accomplished in this single season made him seem to the world more like a rainbow version of Hercules or Henry V.

CHAPTER TWENTY-ONE

How could there have been success so sweet? From one end of the country to the other, what he had done was on people's lips. He was the rage of talk shows, promotions, commercials. He was on the cover of *Time* magazine, he had offers from book and movie companies for the story of his life. It was estimated that when all the extra revenues were totaled, he made more money in that first season than any other major league ballplayer, with the exception of a few top stars.

He was on the road, first with a barnstorming team, then on the rubber-chicken circuit that stretched out everywhere.

People wrote to him, confided in him, reached out to him not as a mere athlete but as though he had somehow combined in his person the unique qualities of a movie star and a political leader. They projected onto him hopes and dreams that were barely imaginable prior to his meteoric rise.

The letters he got (even, in a backward way, including the threats) emphasized the very special niche he had carved out for himself.

One fan had been aware that cheering sections of black fans might have been an embarrassment (all too true) because they cheered *everything* he did. The fan wrote:

> *I'm writing this for two reasons. One, is to let you know that there are plenty of people, black and white, rooting for you that aren't the type that will hurt you by yelling their heads off every time you catch a simple pop fly.*
>
> *The other reason is I know how much guts it takes to go out on that field and play the kind of ball you're playing under so much pressure. . . .*
>
> *If your batting average never gets any higher than .100 and if you make an error every inning, if I can raise my boy to be half the man that you are I'll be a happy father."*

A hotel bellboy wrote:

Mr. Robinson

Saw you play in Wichita and also in St. Louis . . . and decided I wanted to name my expected child for the first Negro in league baseball. And above that a good sport and a gentleman, something our race needs as bad as they do a square deal. Little Jackie Lee was born the 8-15-47- 2pm (a girl) at St. France Hospital.

> *Yours for many years*
> *Big league baseball*
> *to a fine, fine sportsmanship*
> *T.S. Washington. Bell boy at Eaton Hotel*

And then, of course, he got propositioned. The winner of a beauty contest wrote:

I'm a working girl and I don't have much money, nothing like you do but I manage. I live with my mother and younger sister and brother. Mr. Robinson, you can't possibly know how I feel every time I hear your name. Its like a thrill going all through me. I want you to love me just once. Just once and then I might be satisfied. I know that you're a married man and have a son but you don't have to be an angel. . . . Oh Jackie (if I may call you that), if you're ever near Akron, I want you to just look at me, just touch me. Someday, sometime you will be taking a vacation and you might be near Akron. You must answer this letter, you have to."

(Actually Robinson *did* answer this one—he told the young woman that she was suffering "from some kind of mental delusion," and that "when I married Mrs. Robinson, I exchanged vows to love, honor and cherish her for the rest of my life.")

His impact was felt everywhere, and touched people of every conceivable type.

A young black woman, editing an autobiographical book for a Harlem pastor, told Robinson that the pastor had once, in childhood, been "the only Negro on a white team." Opponents, she said, taunted him with the chant:

God made a nigger and he made him in the night.
God made a nigger and he forgot to paint him white!

The woman wanted to know if Robinson had also been subject to the same chant. "It would give added point," she wrote, "to Jim's tale if we could point the parallel between his case and yours, some 25 years later. Will you help us?"

Across the country, in every black community from the cities of the North to dusty rural outposts of the South, people huddled around radios, much as they did to catch the fights of Joe Louis, to take in the doings of this new and very different hero.

"I live in a small negro town," a storeowner wrote. "We go to Memphis for all our amusements but there is no greater thrill than a broadcast of the Dodgers ball game. . . . We are so proud of you, and want you to know we southerners think you are tops."

Percy Sutton, a former Tuskeegee Airman who then was a young law student, said, "God, I was working two jobs at that time. I worked four till midnight in the post office, and from twelve-thirty to eight-thirty I was a conductor on the D train. I was working sixteen hours a day and going to Brooklyn Law School. . . . I took a day off I remember to listen to the radio when Jackie began playing . . . his first game. We were in Sheepshead Bay, gathered around the radio, and we were betting our heads off over everything, what would Jackie do, even what side of the plate he'd hit from . . . it was such an exciting thing, it sent chills up and down your spine."

This electronic communion was mysterious, transforming. The actress Ruby Dee, who would eventually play Robinson's wife in the 1950 film *The Jackie Robinson Story,* said she met Robinson for the first time "on the radio when he first joined the Dodgers. Oh, I was never interested in baseball at all before then, but I found myself listening to games . . . and I began to pay attention. . . . I mean I had heard about the Negro leagues, but I had never seen a game or heard one till Jackie came to the Dodgers. . . . I don't remember the times and places I actually met him, but the first time I began *seeing* him was on the radio."

As Rickey was aware that the experiment was not just about one player, Robinson took the same position, but from a very different perspective. As far as he was concerned, there was no comfort in

181

knowing other players were in the pipeline. As far as he was concerned, it all hinged on what he did.

When Dan Bankhead came up to the Dodgers, Robinson roomed with him. The two were very different. The Dodger publicist Irving Rudd recalled that Bankhead might have been "one of the greatest pitchers in baseball history if he were white." But Bankhead, he said, was "a frightened black man from Tennessee who [was] emotionally scarred by racism." Bankhead, a talented hitter as well as pitcher, had little of Robinson's intense focus or ability to handle pressure. In his first game he surrendered eight runs and eight hits in just three innings, though he homered in his first major-league at bat. He was shipped back to the minors at the end of that same season, came up again in 1950, and was finished by 1951.

When Larry Doby joined the Cleveland Indians, the move was sudden. Cleveland owner Bill Veeck, unlike Branch Rickey, did not believe that a long preparation would be useful. Doby was literally on the field the day he was hired. But Doby said Veeck knew exactly who he was when he signed: "The first time I met him, there was a big, fat notebook on his desk that contained everything there was about me from the time I was born till the time I caught the train in Newark to come and join the ball club."

Unlike Robinson, Doby was not a regular in that first season, and his tenure from the start was shaky. Contrary to popular belief, his manager, Lou Boudreau, far from helping him, actually made things tougher.

"The first day I took the field in Chicago, I stood on the sidelines for five minutes and no one would warm up with me," Doby said. "You'd think the manager would take it on himself to see that I was warmed up, but I guess he had other things on his mind." One player, Joe Gordon, eventually came over and thereafter warmed up with him regularly for the remainder of the season. There is a story—part of the legend—that Gordon, after seeing Doby with his head in his hands after a strikeout, made a point of sitting next to him and putting his head in his hands after following him to the plate and striking out. "Never happened," Doby said with a laugh. "That was for the movie —but that man, may his soul rest in peace, was one of those who helped me from day one—and so did Bob Lemon and Jim Hegan. The rest of it was something else."

When the season ended, Doby barnstormed with Robinson. The two men did not share war stories, Doby said, "because we knew all too well that what we had been through was the same. To talk about it would only have made us angry, made things worse."

Doby was, if anything, a more gifted player than Robinson. But he was younger, quieter, seemingly more tentative. There was no way to read his future chances. The pressure on Robinson remained unabating.

In that early period, Robinson turned his attention to the Harlem community, which was just a subway ride from Ebbets Field. Robinson never needed anyone to tell him what conditions were like anywhere black people lived. Harlem was just larger, its problems more inescapable than any other community's. Every day, black newspapers and the few black political leaders on the scene, such as Congressman Adam Clayton Powell Jr. and City Councilman Ben Davis, pointed out the daily, grinding reality of injustice affecting the lives of millions of ordinary citizens.

From the time Robinson joined the Dodgers, an informal group of prominent Harlem figures got together to exchange ideas with him. The group included Rudolph Thomas, the director of the Harlem YMCA; Dr. Arthur Logan, an activist physician; the local heads of the Urban League and the NAACP; Percy Sutton and other young community activists. On at least one occasion, one of those who dropped in to break bread was Paul Robeson.

The actual substance of the meetings, according to Percy Sutton, "was basically feel-good talk. He [Robinson] wanted to know about Harlem, wanted to learn about the things that were happening in Harlem. . . . It wasn't a regular meeting; we came together, talked, listened to Jackie tell his experiences. He'd tease us. 'I'm not going to give you enough to write a book.' "

The group was touched and surprised by Robinson, who, after all, was a celebrity athlete, not a social activist.

"From day one he never wavered in his passionate opposition to racism," Percy Sutton said. "You've got to appreciate that Jackie Robinson was a class athlete before he ever played baseball. He was an aggressive officer in the military at a time when those of us who became officers knew the indignities you had to be submitted to. . . . Yes, he had to overcome a hot temper and learn to prevail in spite of that. . . . He knew better than anyone that it was one thing on the ball field and another the minute you left it. America wasn't ready to bring down those barriers in '47, '48, '49, '50. It was one thing to be called a nigger on the field or when they hollered it out from the stands. You're out there, the juices are flowing, you're ready. . . . But when you leave and you're winding down and you go to your hotel to sleep, and you can't go to that hotel and you go to one where you can't sleep at all, you've got all night to think about it. And the better qualified you are, the harder all of that becomes. Jackie said this: it's not the field of play, it's what happened off the field."

Robinson's special qualities, his celebrity, were of interest not only to those who respected and admired him, but also to those who wished him ill and who feared everything he seemed to stand for. Ardent segregationists, who still made up a sizable portion of the population, were unmoved by what he had achieved.

But the enmity and ignorance of these people mattered far less than what was being imagined and conceived in places of power—in government, where the emergence of a popular, black hero was viewed, somehow, as a threat to the Republic.

The FBI, as early as 1946—and possibly before—opened a file on Robinson. Their initial interest in him seemed to stem from his being the first black player in professional baseball. But as his FOIA file shows, they had clearly noted his involvement in the Negro and Allied Veterans group. What more they knew about him, his army career, his thinking, his personality, and his desire to extend himself beyond baseball, is not yet clear.

At the same time, the House Un-American Activities Committee, waving its broadsword of anticommunism to stifle all forms of leftist dissent in the country, was particularly interested in getting prominent people with a past before it to "name names" or otherwise to profess their loyalty in full and humiliating public view. Jackie Robinson was one of the early targets of HUAC.

On December 31, 1947, just seven months after the committee's "appearance" program had been initiated, a committee investigator named Alvin Stokes contacted Branch Rickey expressing an interest in Jackie Robinson.

Rickey, through his ample political connections, conducted his own informal check on Stokes and determined that he had the appropriate

FBI and congressional credentials. He then authorized Arthur Mann to meet with him.

Mann first met Stokes at a Harlem restaurant on January 2, 1948. Mann was surprised to discover that Stokes was black. Indeed, Stokes was an anomaly as a witch-hunter and as a political figure in the white political establishment of the day. In an ironic way, Stokes, like Jackie Robinson, was a barrier breaker.

A native of Westwood, New Jersey, Stokes attended both NYU and Columbia, taking a degree in 1922. According to his son, Alvin Jr., he became involved in real estate—because "he wanted to be his own boss"—and then became active in local politics. His dream, his son said, was to run for office. It was an impossible dream back then. In 1940, he became a secretary to the sheriff of Bergen County.

He was the only black Republican of note in Bergen County, perhaps in the state of New Jersey. "He was a secretary in an administrative sense," his son said, "sort of in the way Khrushchev and Stalin were secretaries in the Communist parties." His father, in other words, saw to it that things got done.

He was ultimately rewarded with a job in Washington, working for Republican congressman J. Parnell Thomas, chairman of the House Un-American Activities Committee. (Thomas was eventually tried, convicted, and jailed for tax evasion.)

But Stokes's background as a Republican was interesting in still another way as far as Robinson and other possible black witnesses were concerned. Stokes understood as no white politician did what daily life with black skin was like in America.

"My father convinced himself that what he was doing was totally in the black interest," Stokes's son said, "because he understood the double curse of being branded a communist. Black people had enough trouble as it was to have to then have to deal with that—that was his point of view. He wanted black people growing up to have it easier than their parents, so they wouldn't have to operate under the hands of this scourge."

According to his son, long before any official reason was concocted for Robinson's appearance, Stokes had targeted him for the committee. "He could have had Lena Horne and Joe Louis, but Jackie was the number one target—and I think Louis was the fallback. . . . My dad did his homework. And these people were very eager to have the cloud lifted from them. He told me Lena Horne even fixed dinner for him.''

The negotiations to get Robinson before the committee, however, were protracted. Mann says he and Stokes agreed on two points: that if Robinson appeared it would have to be voluntary, and that there could be ''no political identification'' attaching to Robinson or to the Dodgers in letting him testify.

The idea was to have him before the committee immediately—in the spring of 1948. The Dodgers were then training in the Dominican Republic—again to avoid the complications of segregation in Florida —and Robinson, at the time, had his hands full. He had turned up in camp thirty pounds overweight, and Leo Durocher, back from his year's suspension, took one look at the roll around his middle and decided that it was an affront to his authority as a manager.

He had Robinson out daily in the broiling Caribbean sun performing a peculiarly fiendish routine called ''high and low.'' Robinson, in a rubber suit, had bucketfuls of balls tossed to him, one after the other, one baseball high, the other low, until the game (or the player) was finished. The urgency of his getting into shape seemed to supercede everything. Camp stories were full of Robinson's heft and the slimness of his contribution. The effort of shedding weight appeared to tire him. He did not hit well. His play appeared listless. To many, he seemed not the player he was the year before.

Yet that was not all of it by any means. Rickey and the Dodgers were moving on. The experiment, hard fought and still questionable, had succeeded. Two more players, Campanella and Newcombe, were now ready—almost. Others were in the pipeline. But much more re-mained. Larry Doby had so far not lived up to expectations. Another team, the St. Louis Browns, had signed two black players—Hank Thompson and Willard Brown—only to cut them by season's end. Resistance to integration around the majors and minors was still al-most as strong as ever. Plus, the agitation for change from radical groups continued unabated.

Before camp ended, Rickey took Campanella aside and told him he was the best catcher the Dodgers had—but that Rickey was going to pull a fast one with him. He was going to bring him up as an *outfielder*, not a catcher. He could not possibly make it as an outfielder, so, said Rickey, he would have to cut him after a month, send him to triple-A

St. Paul, and bring him back later in the year. That way, Rickey said, Campenella would be a pioneer in breaking the color barrier in the American Association. Campanella argued that he was a ballplayer not a pioneer—but he was not about to buck orders. He opened the year with the Dodgers and was gone by May 15.

On the other hand, the plan to get Jackie Robinson to Washington did not yield to any similar sleight of hand. Before a date could be arranged for Robinson to testify, the committee chairman, Parnell Thomas, took ill. The hearing had to be postponed.

Arthur Mann said that Robinson had already agreed to testify and had simply "left the matter with the schedule makers." But there was more to it than that. Mann also noted that for the next eighteen months, Alvin Stokes maintained contact with the Dodgers because of the communist threat that appeared to surround the Dodgers. "He was particularly helpful," Mann said, "in conferences relating to the proximity of subversive influences to Negroes in the Dodger organization."

The threat was made to seem real enough. The eagerness with which Rickey and Bill Veeck had embraced integration seemed to pale. "Both Rickey and Veeck reinforced the opinion that few blacks were ready for the majors with statements that few qualified players remained in the Negro leagues," wrote Jules Tygiel. "The rationale for these statements [remained] unclear. Both the Dodgers and Indians had scouting reports that indicated otherwise."

If Stokes's son, Alvin, is correct, Robinson's appearance was a problem because there was, as yet, no agreement on what he would say. Jackie Robinson could not simply walk into a committee room and turn against everything he knew to be true, to renounce his own experience that had included a particularly bitter and scarring encounter with the United States government. Robinson, in the beginning of 1948, needed time and attention—something, Alvin Stokes Jr. said, his father was prepared to give.

CHAPTER TWENTY-TWO

Nineteen forty-eight was a forgettable year for the Dodgers. Though favored to win the pennant, from the start they seemed caught in reverse. The thrill of the previous season clung to them more like a hangover than a halo. It was hard to imagine that this was essentially the same team that overcame all obstacles, including the most significant one of racial prejudice, on the way to carrying the mighty New York Yankees to seven games in the World Series.

Of course, there were differences—important ones. For one, there was a new manager, the one they might have had all along. Leo Durocher, with his rasp and brass, his ladies and his Las Vegas lifestyle, seemed suddenly to fit the team like an overdose of amphetamines compared to the season-long tranquilizer offered by Burt Shotton.

Durocher's boot-camp approach to Jackie Robinson's weight problem not only left him wilted going into the season but resentful as well. Robinson did not get along with Durocher. He resented both the way he had been dealt with in the spring and Durocher's willingness to talk about it to the press. "Robinson will shag flies till his tongue hangs out," Leo told reporters. "Jake Pitler will see to it that Jackie chases every fungo up a palm tree for the remainder of the Dodgers' stay here in Ciudad Trujillo."

Durocher was also having his problems with Rickey. At the outset of the campaign Durocher had argued with him over Roy Campanella, wanting Campy on the team from the start because he was the best catcher the Dodgers had. Without him, the team had to go with Bruce Edwards, overrated and injured, or Gil Hodges, who Durocher believed was not a catcher at all but a first baseman. Under Rickey's cloak-and-dagger arrangements, Campanella, though he was on the squad through April into May, was not allowed under any circumstances to catch.

The Dodgers went nowhere through the first month. Eddie Stanky had been traded to Boston to make room for Robinson at second base, but now Robinson, because he wasn't hitting, moving well in the field, or doing anything, was on the bench and Gene Mauch, a utility infielder, was the Dodger second baseman.

Durocher believed Robinson and another player, Pete Reiser, were still out of shape, and so extra workouts were ordered for them—in season. Prior to games, a coach took a bucket of balls and hit endless grounders to them in the infield.

Through much of the summer there was no real pickup, and the air between the front office and the bench, and between Robinson and Durocher, was probably irreversibly poisoned. In the beginning of July the Dodgers lost six games in a row and fell into the cellar, a skid that almost certainly sealed Durocher's fate.

When the Dodgers turned up for a sold-out series at the Polo Grounds in early July, last place leered at them from every corner of the ballpark. Durocher was on his way to the guillotine—and Robinson was still in a funk. He arrived late for one of the games at the Polo Grounds and made a dramatic entrance onto the field from the center-field clubhouse, coming down the steps, making the long walk across the outfield to the Dodger dugout. The crowd, spotting him, roared. He was as popular as ever, especially among the ever-increasing number of black fans who now were regular patrons of major league—rather than Negro league—games.

Durocher was infuriated by the reception.

"Well, Showboat, you sure know how to be late!" he croaked.

It was something of a last hurrah in a Dodger uniform for the Lip. In a little more than a week, on July 16, the Dodgers and Giants shocked the baseball world by simultaneously firing their managers. Technically, Durocher was not fired but, in another one of those elaborate Rickey wand-wavers, *resigned*—and then signed on with the Giants! In New York baseball circles, it was akin to Napoleon taking command of the Russian army. In reality, it was only front-office politics—Rickey resisting a move by co-owner Walter O'Malley to fire Durocher outright by working out this more elaborate scheme with the Giants.

It brought Robinson a reprieve, however. With Durocher off his back and Burt Shotton back in charge, he managed to turn his season around. The Dodgers struggled out of the basement, even contending for a while in the early part of September before falling to a third-place finish. Robinson wound up the season hitting .296, a point less than the previous year. His base-stealing totals were off—down to twenty-two from a league-leading twenty-nine—but his second half left no doubt that he was the same player who had earned Rookie of the Year honors the season before.

He was secure in his job, as much as a black baseball player in the majors could be. But when he looked around, the only other black player in the National League was his teammate, Roy Campanella. In the American League, Larry Doby had posted a solid year, and the Indians had added a second black player, the indefatigable Satchel Paige, who, even though he carried as many years as stories on his long, lean frame, helped his team to a world championship. But that was it. The two black players who had appeared with the Browns in '47 were gone, and no other team in the majors seemed close to opening their rosters.

In '49, the Dodgers added Don Newcombe, but still no other teams moved. Satchel Paige was a year older and slower, and Bill Veeck, who along with Rickey had been willing to stick his neck out to sign (and profit from) black talent, sold his interest in the Indians by the end of '49. There was no guarantee yet that the experiment would endure beyond what Robinson and those few others produced on the field.

Robinson felt a more-than-special need to make sure it all worked. He had put too much into it, been through too much, to see it all go for naught. He had been changed by what had happened and, to an extent he could never have imagined, had been boxed in by it as well.

In every way he could, he sought to lend his good name to a fight he knew was larger than his Dodger career. During the course of the '48 season, the newly named director of the Harlem YMCA, Rudolph Thomas, traveled to Pittsburgh, home of the *Courier,* the most prestigious black newspaper in the country, and also home of the Pirates.

On one of the Dodger road trips through Pittsburgh, Thomas met with Jackie Robinson and specifically asked him to sign on as a coach and youth director at the Y that fall. Robinson, perhaps to Thomas's surprise, immediately accepted and was probably instrumental in securing Roy Campanella's later willingness to help. On the surface, it was just the kind of the "good" work that an athlete, looking for a kindly word or two from the media, might seek, but Thomas and the Harlem Y represented something a little different.

Thomas had been named acting executive director of the Y in 1946. At the time he was forty-two years old, having served the Y for twenty-five years in various capacities. He was a college graduate with a degree in business administration, but more importantly, his years at the Y had earned him the most advanced degree possible—in the streets of Harlem and in the corridors of New York politics.

The Y was, in an impoverished community, a multimillion-dollar institution that served as employer, innkeeper, soup kitchen, counseling office, recreation center, springboard, and stopgap for literally tens of thousands of people. "The Harlem YMCA was the principal gathering place for black Americans in the country," said Gardner Taylor, the longtime pastor of Brooklyn's Concord Baptist Church, the largest Baptist congregation in the nation. "Hotels were closed to blacks. And there was a saying back then that if you sat in the lobby of the Harlem YMCA long enough, you would very likely see every prominent black person in America."

As a past business manager of the Y, Thomas was thoroughly familiar with the way money flowed in and out of the organization. When he was employment director, he personally saw to it that when a new eleven-story main building for the Y was constructed in the 1930s, 50 percent of those employed would be black. This was a particularly difficult and sensitive undertaking because it meant taking on closed construction unions during the height of the Depression when unemployment was rampant among white as well as black workers.

For years, Thomas had the informal nickname "Mayor of Harlem." He was the person anyone went to anytime with problems large or small. He was the one who knew how to deal with the white establishment, whether it was in matters of fund-raising, contract-framing, or relationships with unions. Eventually, his friends included men such as the Rockefellers, the president of Columbia University, Dwight Eisenhower, governors, and mayors. Thomas knew how to deal, in Gardner Taylor's words, "with downtown New York."

Thomas knew better than anyone else how thin the ground was under Robinson's feet. It could break and swallow him up at any time. He knew as well as anyone that because Jackie Robinson was an inspiration and a hero to millions of other downtrodden people, he was a natural target for those who wanted to make sure the downtrodden would never get much traction under their feet. Thomas saw not only that Robinson was a role model, but a vulnerable one too. He hoped the Y would give Robinson cover even as he gave it additional prestige.

Robinson, from his occasional uptown meetings, knew about Thomas and was receptive to him from the start. He agreed to work as a youth director, which meant that he would be available as an adviser, coach, and organizer for young people in the Y. This became part of Robinson's off-season routine once his barnstorming commitments were finished—and remained part of what he did through the following decade.

But, more importantly, Thomas became a crucial figure to Robinson, someone he found he could turn to in almost any kind of situation. According to Gardner Taylor, Thomas became something of a surrogate father to Jackie.

Anyone viewing 1949 from the vantage point of the grandstands saw nothing more complicated than a great player enjoying his greatest year. That year Robinson dismantled the National League and in doing so probably guaranteed that the experiment could never be rolled back.

He was the league's leading hitter, finishing with an average of .342. He led the league in stolen bases with 37; he led all second basemen in turning double plays with 119. He was third in the league in runs scored, doubles, and triples, and to top it off, the Dodgers won the pennant, went to the World Series (though they lost to the Yankees again), and Robinson was named the league's MVP.

But throughout this period of almost total triumph, the unfinished negotiation with Alvin Stokes and HUAC continued. Stokes met with Robinson and Rachel secretly; the results of the meetings have never been divulged. Stokes's son, Alvin Jr., guessed that Robinson's past associations "probably caused him some trouble," and that he was under pressure to come forward and clear himself.

"I do know," Alvin Jr. said, "that—more than once—my father told me that he remarked to Robinson, 'You know, Jackie, there's life after baseball.' And this was something I think Rachel appreciated from my father."

Nothing on or off the record indicates what the nature of this surely anguished "negotiation" was for the Robinsons; in fact, they both, in all their later comments, writings, and public utterances, never even acknowledged that a "negotiation" took place. But according to Alvin Stokes Jr., one did. And according to him, what transpired can never be understood in the Manichaean terms in which the Red scare is usually presented.

To be sure, the stakes were high. The committee's goals were part of a government-wide strategy to smash the American Communist Party and all its satellites and support mechanisms by almost any means necessary, including those that infringed on individual rights and liberties. In conjunction with the committee's "program," there were high-profile show trials of Communists, such as that of the "Communist 11" (one of whom was Robinson's old supporter New York City councilman Ben Davis), espionage investigations, and a general purging of the ranks throughout private industry for "security" reasons.

"Robinson was concerned that he couldn't walk the black community, where people might say, 'Who the hell appointed you—you know, we have enough political spokesmen,' " Alvin Stokes Jr. said. Clearly, Robinson feared that he would be seen as a turncoat. Stokes Sr. argued that communism was an issue that played into the hands of the most racist politicians in the country, "the Bilbos and the Rankins." It was possible, even necessary, for blacks to resist communism with the same fervor with which they fought racism and segregation. *That* was the goal, defeating racism; the fight was obscured and confused when it became attached to the support of communist-sponsored causes.

It is not clear that Robinson ever accepted that argument. Stokes, however, had another. If Robinson played by the rules, the rules would *help* him, not hurt him. The connections he made as a celebrity could be used not only for personal benefit but to aid in the very struggle he cared about most. Stokes used himself as an example; *he* had made it through the gauntlet. He had connections now—including, Alvin Jr. said, with a powerful black attorney in New York State, a Republican named Grant Reynolds. "It would not be far-fetched to assume that my father was a bridge between Robinson and Grant Reynolds," Stokes said. "Reynolds had good connections with the Rockefeller wing of the Republican Party in New York State."

Above all, Stokes Sr. had history on his side—or at least the history that was happening out there in plain view. In his meetings with a very receptive Branch Rickey—who hated communism with a fervor equal to that of any conservative politician in the country—Stokes enlisted his support in obtaining Robinson's cooperation. What Stokes was able to tell Rickey—and perhaps what Rickey most feared—was that communist pressure on baseball threatened the experiment.

Jules Tygiel noted, "The failure of organized baseball to follow Rickey's lead more actively sparked protests by radical groups in several cities. When Larry Doby appeared in Washington, representatives of 'American Youth for Democracy' picketed the ballpark and urged the Senators to hire blacks. In California the local Communist Party applied pressure on Pacific Coast League clubs to recruit blacks. . . . In San Francisco where the Seals had entered 'preliminary negotiations' to sign Sam Jethroe, the National Maritime Union passed a resolution in favor of this action."

Rickey argued often that breaking the color barrier was not about challenging anyone's politics, it was about fair play—allowing qualified players to play baseball. Pure and simple. Those who wanted to exploit the situation and build it into a political cause were as much the enemy as those who were determined to keep the game lily-white. According to Arthur Mann—and everyone who knew Rickey well—Rickey's hatred of communism was absolute and unshakable. He felt Robinson was not in a vise at all, but rather had an unusual opportunity to finally shed the restraints that had been imposed on him for the past three seasons and to speak out—for himself, for democracy, and for America.

"The first contribution of Jackie Robinson—so well known to Rachel and a few others," Rickey wrote in *The American Diamond,* "was the self-imposed restraint to preserve and advance healthy race relations under terrifically trying circumstances."

But next in importance in Rickey's mind would be Robinson's stepping up to the mikes before Congress and denouncing communism.

The pressures on Robinson were unrelieved. They came from every quarter—including from his employers and his spouse. He was no longer an independent agent. Even if, on his own, he had been prepared to walk away from his major league career rather than testify, he was unable to do that; he had others to think about—and, as Alvin Stokes (and Branch Rickey) underscored, there was everything to fight for.

Robinson wanted to make sure that whatever he said would include as strong a denunciation of racial injustice as he could make. Stokes concurred; that was no problem. The committee was indeed worried about turmoil in the black community—but its focus was on stopping communism. Still, there was the question of how his appearance could be arranged; it had to have a plausible context and no appearance of duress could be attached to it.

The answer came in the spring of 1949. That April, in Paris, at a gathering called the Congress of the World Partisans of Peace, Paul Robeson was quoted in an AP dispatch as saying that it was unthinkable for "American Negroes to go to war on behalf of those who have oppressed us . . . against a country [the Soviet Union] which in one generation has raised our people to the full dignity of mankind."

The statement was just what the committee was waiting for. Robeson had all along been a prime target of the committee and of the government.

Robeson's position in the African-American community was extraordinary—and to the government, dangerous. He had been an all-American football player at Rutgers prior to the First World War, graduating with Phi Beta Kappa honors, then going on to earn a law degree from Columbia University. He had a distinguished career as a singer and stage actor, breaking barriers and precedents almost everywhere he went. The unwritten but formidable restrictions against blacks in major parts on Broadway were shattered when he appeared in leading roles in *Othello* and in Eugene O'Neill's *The Emperor Jones*. His magnificent bass-baritone singing voice thrilled audiences the world over. A large and imposing man with tremendous personal magnetism, Robeson became a special hero to African-Americans, who saw in him a measure of accomplishment and pride that could not be ignored. From the start, Robeson was never someone who coveted success for himself alone; throughout his long and illustrious career, he was a passionate fighter for racial justice. Over the years, he had increasingly aligned himself with communist causes—though never joining the Communist Party itself—because he believed the Party was consistent and unequivocal in its opposition to racism.

In his book *Naming Names,* Victor Navasky noted that, for witnesses appearing before the committee, "there was, although it was not remarked at the time, a *de facto* double standard when it came to blacks. Unlike whites, blacks interested in getting back to work were not automatically required or expected to name names. Instead, they had a number of options, among which the most effective was to denounce Paul Robeson.'' Black witnesses were not required to name names for fear that they would be turned into martyrs and elicit too much unwanted sympathy.

When Jackie Robinson finally did appear before the committee on the morning of July 18, after a year and a half of ''negotiation,'' as traumatic as it must have been to think of betraying one of his earliest allies, he was prepared to denounce Paul Robeson.

CHAPTER TWENTY-THREE

From the vantage point of a half century later, it seems puzzling that the Hearings Regarding Communist Infiltration of Minority Groups by the Committee on Un-American Activities of the House of Representatives could have been taken seriously, but they were.

The goal of these hearings was to see if America's minorities—principally blacks—were loyal to the country. Though none of the congressmen on the panel, which included a little-known Californian named Richard M. Nixon, would quite come out and say it, the real question was whether or not 15 million black Americans constituted a fifth column inside the United States.

The hearings produced several kinds of testimony. For example, Dwight D. Eisenhower, whose words were unusually heated for him, testified that Negroes were loyal Americans:

"Throughout the almost four years that I was commanding in Europe and in Africa, I daily encountered soldiers of the Negro race. It no more occurred to me to question their mass patriotism and loyalty than it would have occurred to me to entertain such doubts about the entire force. . . . Moreover, I should like gratuitously to add to this testimony that I have seen or experienced nothing since the close of hostilities that leads me to believe that our Negro population is not fully as worthy of its American citizenship as it proved itself to be on the battlefields of Europe and Africa."

But the main body of testimony had a far more narrow purpose and was drawn almost exclusively from black witnesses, the most notable being Jackie Robinson.

The witnesses individually and collectively went out of their way to denounce communism and Paul Robeson. Alvin Stokes, the committee's investigator, sounded the direst of warnings that the threat facing the country was real and the enemy insidious: "The Communist Party has for the time being camouflaged its program for the setting up of an independent Negro Soviet Republic in the so-called Black Belt of the South. This proposal was and is cunningly calculated to promote civil war in which the Negro people would be sacrificed to the machinations of Moscow." How did Stokes know this? "To cite a case in point, I attended a welcome-home rally for Paul Robeson held on June nineteenth, 1949, at Rockland Palace, One Hundred and Fifty-fifth Street and Eighth Avenue, New York City. The speakers at this meeting, by inference, deplored the lack of rebellious spirit on the part of the Negro people."

Stokes, though he may have been wired to his own alarm system, nevertheless provided a lead other witnesses had to follow. Referring to Robeson's recent Paris statement, Stokes said, "With that voice, [Robeson] managed successfully to identify Negroes with communism in many politically illiterate minds. . . . A report of a survey of the reaction of white persons to Robeson's statement made by competent white reporters revealed that more than fifty percent of nearly one thousand persons questioned in the seven cities believed that, one, the Negro population of the United States is communistically inclined. Two, that Negroes would be disloyal to the United States in the event of war, providing they had the opportunity to commit disloyal acts. Three, that Negroes and Jews contributed little to victory in the last war."

The parade of witnesses did their best to dissociate Robeson and communism from the collective character of African-Americans. Distinguished sociologist Charles S. Johnson, after his ritual disavowal of ever having been a party member, pointed out that African-Americans had a long history of loyalty to the country in the face of awful oppression and that too often "shortsighted and perhaps emotionally disturbed persons" equated the legitimate expression of grievances with "communism."

Lester Granger, the national director of the Urban League, noted that Paul Robeson's Paris statement to a "Communist-sponsored conference" had raised a furor "that would have been ludicrous if it had not been so tragic." No one could seriously believe that blacks, so unquestionably loyal to begin with, could be swayed to sedition by Robeson's remarks. Robeson was a fool—someone who had just a year before predicted that Henry Wallace, the third-party candidate of the Progressive Party, would carry the presidential election. "Racial common sense," Granger said, kept most Negro spokesmen "from the error" of even having to respond to demands that blacks disavow him.

There was one more point to be made: as Granger and other moderate leaders saw it, battling racism could not succeed without the willing and active support of whites. "Even under the best of present conditions," he said, "it is hard for the so-called average person of color to retain faith that in some predictable future his racial disabilities will be removed. That such faith is generally maintained is entirely due to the courageous and often self-sacrificing support which the Negro group has received from white Americans of democratic conviction and liberal impulse."

Against this backdrop, Robinson came before the committee with his own thirty years of history to guide him. He was not a "political" person, but he had been deeply seared by experience. He didn't need anyone to tell him that things were better or worse than he knew himself. But when he finally spoke, his words were not his own.

Prior to Robinson's appearance in Washington, he consulted Branch Rickey on what to say. Rickey prepared a speech for him. According to Dan Dodson, "Mr. Rickey gave Jackie a speech draft which was very rough and contained words in it like 'a person could not be horsewhipped.' I tried to change the pattern of it to use a slightly different approach."

For a time, it was believed that a committee drafted the statement Robinson ultimately gave. But almost a year later, Rickey received a letter from Granger that said, in part: "I confess that I was miffed when I read in Bill Roeder's story of Jackie Robinson that 'a group of Negro leaders' had helped him to prepare the Washington testimony. How small can a group be—or am I stouter than I think!"

Actually, Granger may have had some help—at least according to Alvin Stokes Jr.: "Granger wrote the speech—but my dad had a hand in it too."

And lest there be any lingering doubt about the quid-pro-quo nature of the testimony, two other witnesses—one of them Alvin Stokes, the other the professional informer Manning Johnson—specifically cited the group Negro and Allied Veterans, to which Robinson had belonged, as a Communist front. Manning Johnson noted that the group "is a current Negro veterans organization. Immediately after the war the Communists made desperate efforts to win over Negro veterans, and this organization was one of the Communist fronts set up to get the Negro veterans into the Communist Party."

On the morning of July 18, 1949, Jackie Robinson made his long-delayed appearance before the House Un-American Activities Committee. With flashbulbs popping and an army of reporters scribbling down his every word, Robinson began by saying that as a professional ballplayer he was as far removed from politics as anyone could imagine.

But he acknowledged that politics—the politics of Communists and even of the committee itself—were issues he could not avoid. A lot of people had urged him not to testify, and "not all of this urging came from Communist sympathizers," he said. It wasn't pleasant to be in the midst of all this when it "had nothing to do with the standing of the Brooklyn Dodgers in the pennant race—or even of the pay raise I am going to ask Mr. Branch Rickey for next year."

Robinson then launched into a long and eloquent denunciation of racism, cataloguing the humiliations, injustices, and outrages that ordinary black people faced every day in America. It is not possible to say what Robinson had demanded be included in this portion of his remarks, or what he may have contributed himself—though its careful tailoring to the needs of the committee remained unmistakable.

"As I see it," Robinson said, "there has been a terrific lot of misunderstanding on this subject of communism among the Negroes in this country, and it's bound to hurt my people's cause unless it's cleared up.

"The white public should start toward real understanding by appreciating that every single Negro who is worth his salt is going to resent any kind of slurs and discrimination because of his race, and he is going to use every bit of intelligence such as he has to stop it. This has got absolutely nothing to do with what Communists may or may not be trying to do. And white people must realize that the more a Negro hates communism because it opposes democracy, the more he is going to hate any other influence that kills off democracy in this country—and that goes for racial discrimination in the army, and segregation on trains and buses, and job discrimination. . . .

"And one other thing the American public ought to understand, if we are to make progress in this matter: the fact that it is a Communist who denounces injustice in the courts, police brutality, and lynching when it happens doesn't change the truth of his charges." The committee was told that "Negroes were stirred up long before there was a Communist Party, and they'll stay stirred up long after the Party has disappeared—unless jim crow has disappeared by then as well.''

And then it was time to pay the piper.

''I've been asked to express my views on Paul Robeson's statement in Paris to the effect that American Negroes would refuse to fight in any war against Russia because we love Russia so much,'' Robinson said, in his clear, high-pitched voice. ''I haven't any comment to make on that statement except that if Mr. Robeson actually made it, it sounds very silly to me. But he has a right to his personal views, and if he wants to sound silly when he expresses them in public, that is his business and not mine. He's still a famous ex-athlete and a great singer and actor.''

What Robinson was trying to get across, he said, was that the American public ''was off on the wrong foot when it begins to think of radicalism in terms of any special minority group.'' Negroes, in particular, had ''too much invested in our country's welfare for any of us to throw it away because of a siren song sung in bass.''

Almost five decades later, Robinson's denunciation of Robeson seems mild. But the effect at the time was as dramatic and as powerful as anyone on the committee (or in the Dodger front office) could have hoped for. Robinson's appearance created a sensation in papers all across the country: page one in the *New York Times* with the complete text of his remarks printed within, even an editorial the next day saying he had gone ''4 for 4'' in hitting out against discrimination.

The Urban League printed a pamphlet (half paid for by Rickey) containing the text of the speech, to be distributed in black communities everywhere.

In the soon to be filmed *Jackie Robinson Story*, the concluding scenes would show Robinson playing himself, appearing before the committee with montages of the Statue of Liberty and cutaways to Branch Rickey answering Robinson's doubts about whether or not he should testify by letting him and the world know that the restraints of the past three years had been lifted and he was, at long last, free to ''fight back.''

This was a special touch, fact inflated for political effect. Nineteen forty-nine was the year Robinson's well-known vow of silence officially ended. On the field, he was free to more openly express himself —and he did, challenging umpires, answering opposing players who continued to taunt him, letting his aggressive personality emerge around teammates and reporters who badgered him or who rubbed him the wrong way.

But what an irony this unshackling was! Jackie Robinson freed from his restraints was compelled to testify against a man who, beyond being a personal supporter and friend, had, as much as anyone, paved the way for Robinson's own remarkable breakthrough. Though Robinson argued he was "just a ballplayer," he knew well enough what effect this public dismantling of Robeson would have.

Robeson's career in the United States was already well on the way to being destroyed. Concert engagements, stage and movie contracts, were drying up. Record stores refused to carry his recordings. His only possibile livelihood came from abroad, but within the year following Robinson's testimony the government took his passport from him. In the space of just three years, his income dropped from $104,000 a year—a staggering sum for that time—to $2,000. And whenever "progressive groups" tried to offer Robeson a concert appearance in this country, he and those who came to hear him were placed in peril. Rock-throwing mobs shouting patriotic and anticommunist slogans broke up a 1949 Robeson concert in Peekskill, New York, forcing the singer to flee and leaving behind scores of injured and terrified patrons.

As far as the government was concerned, the most important effect of HUAC's hearings was that Robeson had finally been isolated as a "Communist," and his prestige and influence in the black community was smashed.

Robinson returned from Washington the same day he testified— some said because he did not want to chance having to put up with segregated accommodations in the nation's capital. But more likely the reason was that the Dodgers had a game that night in Brooklyn, and the less fuss the better. He was a ballplayer, first and last. The press corps following the team had been surprised to find out that his name was on a witness list published on July 8, just before the All-Star game, in which Robinson was scheduled to appear for the National League team. They had virtually no advance warning when, following a postponement, he turned up at the Capitol on the morning of the eighteenth. On his return to Brooklyn, they were unsuccessful in prying from him any more than what he had said into the committee's microphones. The big story of the game that night turned out to be Robinson's booming triple to center field in another Dodger victory.

The press praised Jackie Robinson for standing tall and striking a blow for democracy. As the *Daily News* put it, "We imagine Monday, July 18, 1949, will go down in Jackie Robinson's memory book, if he keeps such a thing, as a red-letter day." Robinson might also have thought of it as a white-letter day.

CHAPTER TWENTY-FOUR

Robinson's testimony passed like summer lightning.

"Never even paid attention to it, didn't bother about it," said Harold Rosenthal, the sharp-eyed veteran beat writer for the *Herald Tribune*.

The extent to which Robinson had been compromised, never fully disclosed then or later, remains an open question. Was there more required of him then or after his playing career? Did he, for example, agree to inform officials either in government or in the front office if "communist influences," already a sensitive matter to the Dodgers and to investigator Alvin Stokes, were hanging around? Robinson's FOIA files to this day remain heavily censored and unusually hard to open.

Robinson's testimony could so quickly be forgotten because of something peculiar to the times. It was the beginning of a new decade, a decade in which the idea of racial equality, even of actual integration, was gaining currency beyond "progressive" circles. The phenomenon called Dodger culture fit the new time perfectly.

Those Dodger days have since passed from the streets and quirky old angles of Ebbets Field into folklore. The Dodgers of the fifties will be the Boys of Summer for as long as there are Grecian urns. There will always be bouquets of sentiment for the ballpark originals who surrounded Jackie, Pee Wee, Gillie, the Duke, Newk, and Campy. Red Barber and Connie Desmond will forever be behind the mike celebrating Old Goldies, rhubarbs in the pea patch, and high cans of corn to center field. The Dodger Sym-Phony band will forever pipe strikeout victims back to the bench or brass up its version of "Three Blind Mice" to greet the evening's umpires. Gladys Goodding will be there to bring a tear to the eye grinding out the national anthem. Hilda Chester, "Senator" John Griffin, Happy Felton's Knothole Gang, and an army of boozing, wisecracking, backslapping press wags—authors of nasty private off-color skits along with a ton of inside firsts and enough scoops to fill a Good Humor truck—still wander the streets of the old borough like ghosts who never made the trip west.

"Characters" were always a part of Brooklyn lore. What was new and different was that the characters were now black and white and together. The team was no longer a collection of beloved misfits usually headed for the second division and near bankruptcy at the box office, but a new inscription on the Statue of Liberty. The Dodgers, even though they didn't have the pitching, had the pitch: they were the melting pot.

Unlike the blue-blooded Yankees or the bloodless Giants, the Dodgers—some of them—rode the subways to and from the ballpark, and lived in real neighborhoods among real people. Pee Wee lived in Bay Ridge, Gil in Flatbush, Jackie and Campy in Queens.

When the Robinsons and Campanellas lived in St. Albans, they were among a handful of black families that resided in this very middle-class neighborhood. Count Basie, Illinois Jacquet, and Herbert Mills of the Mills Brothers also lived there.

The Robinsons, completely unfamiliar with middle-class New York life, tried as best they could simply to be a part of the scene. During Christmas that first year, they became friendly with their next-door neighbors, the Satlows. Rachel would visit with Sarah Satlow, who, like Rachel, was a professional nurse. Rachel came home from a visit to the Satlows one day having noticed they had no Christmas decorations. She and her husband concluded the Satlows must have been too poor to spend anything extra for the holidays, and so they went out and bought them a tree—which they presented to them. The Satlows, who were Jewish, were embarrassed but touched. They could not refuse a gift of friendship. They set up their tree, decorated it, and invited the Robinsons over to make sure they saw it, never revealing their secret until years later. And, added Mrs. Satlow, "we've had a tree every year since."

In the neighborhood, Robinson was seen as just another father—and then some.

Stephen Satlow, a friend of Jackie Jr.'s, remembers that the neighborhood kids used to throw a football around on the street, and that on one weekend afternoon Jackie Sr. came out. "We used to have this thing where we'd measure how far we could throw a ball," Satlow said. "If you could reach one sewer length, you really had an arm. Well, this one day, I remember Jackie told me to go out for a pass and I ran and ran. I reached one sewer and was waiting for him to throw me the ball. But he said, 'Go out! Go out!' So I kept going. I went two whole sewers before he threw the ball. It was this high spiral that was almost like a pinpoint speck in the sky and it came crashing down in my chest!''

Satlow also remembered that Robinson visited him once when he was hospitalized with a ruptured appendix: ''He brought me a training mitt [a much smaller than average-sized glove]. I put my little fingers in it and they got lost in the big fingers.''

That was part of it too. Robinson visited hospitals—with no hoopla, no publicity. Tommy Villante, a publicist for the beer company that sponsored Dodger broadcasts and who sometimes played golf with Robinson, said the press was never tipped off before, never told afterward; it was strictly person to person, ''that was just the kind of guy Jack was.''

But the drama Robinson was caught in made him larger than just another sports hero. Depending on who they were, people were moved, frightened, or impervious to who he was, but all were now caught up in the changes he represented.

At the opening of the 1949 season, the members of the Dodgers and the press corps surrounding the team had been living with the ''experiment'' for two years.

When the Dodgers arrived in Georgia that spring for three exhibition games against the Atlanta Crackers, the black players faced death threats and more excitement than anyone could remember. The games were all sold-out—two in Atlanta, one in Macon. Blacks from all over the state made plans to come to the games. The grand kleagle of the Ku Klux Klan, Dr. Samuel Green, vowed that the games, which violated state laws against mixed athletic competition, would never take place.

But it was now 1949, not 1947. Whereas a couple of years earlier, establishment figures from President Truman to the leadership of the NAACP had found it convenient to resist efforts to push for a federal antilynching bill, the pressure for action on civil rights had now intensified to the point where President Truman had in 1948 issued an executive order desegregating the nation's armed forces. At the Democratic National Convention in 1948, a ''strong'' civil rights plank in the party platform, eloquently advocated by little-known Minneapolis mayor Hubert H. Humphrey, prompted a walkout by delegates from the South—"Dixiecrats"—who ran a third-party candidate against Truman in the general election. The Dixiecrat candidate, J. Strom Thurmond, did no better than Henry Wallace at the polls.

When the team arrived at the Atlanta airport, Pee Wee Reese, the Dodger captain, strode over to a large rock on the ground immediately adjoining the airstrip, turned it over, and laughingly joked to the players and the accompanying members of the media, "I don't see no grand kleagle coming out from under here."

"Yeah, we were afraid when we got to Atlanta," said Harold Rosenthal of the *Tribune*. "We didn't know who the hell was in the Ku Klux Klan, including the chief of police. All we knew was there was this big story about Dr. Samuel Green, the grand kleagle or whatever they called him. You know, the games will never take place, boycott Coca-Cola because they own the Crackers. So we get to the hotel and Dick Young [of the *Daily News*] comes to my room, says, 'Lemme use your phone.' He calls this guy, Dr. Samuel Green. The kleagle. He's a doctor, a pediatrician. And [Young] gets into a conversation. He starts to taunt the sonuvabitch. He says, 'You're a doctor?' Guy says, 'Yes.' Dick says, 'You take the oath?' Guy says, 'Yes.' Dick says, 'Okay, what would happen if they brought you a Negro child and he was strangling to death. What would you do?' Well, Jesus Christ, I hear the guy choking on the other end of the line and they both start shouting at each other and then Young hangs up. He turns to me and says, 'You better lock your door, we're gonna be here three nights.' "

On the field, the black players may have been frightened, but they were also emboldened. Roy Campanella remembered that he approached Robinson and talked to him about the death threats, and that Robinson had kidded with him. He nodded toward the sections in right center field reserved for blacks and said that when the shooting started, "it'll take less time for me to get to our people from second base."

Death threats and trips through the South were now part of what the *team* went through. In Cincinnati, in 1950, another serious death threat was made against Robinson. Once more the FBI was called in. The death note, signed by someone or a group named The Three Travellers, said that Robinson would be shot on the field if he played.

Because of the proximity of rooftops that overlooked the ballpark, the threat was brought to the attention of the team. The players listened somberly as the note was read to them, along with assurances that police units would be out in force that day. After a moment, Gene Hermanski, the outfielder, wisecracked:

"Why don't we all go out wearing number forty-two today? That way they won't know who to shoot!"

In Birmingham, during one spring-training swing, black fans burst from their roped-off portion of the field and came swarming toward Robinson. Tommy Villante remembers, "That was the only time I ever saw him that way. He was genuinely frightened—I mean out-of-control frightened. He took a bat and started swinging at the people as they surged towards him. He hollered at them, 'Get away! Get away!' "

Players kidded him about that incident, too—because, said those traveling with the team, it was clear Robinson was no longer a social experiment or a lone-wolf activist but just another teammate, a guy from Brooklyn who happened to be a star; his color, like that of any white player, bled into the common hue of a uniform.

Harold Rosenthal remembers a road trip through the Midwest. The Dodger train, wherever it went, was regularly met by crowds of people, mainly wanting to see Robinson. It was a phenomenon of the time prior to 1952, when teams switched exclusively to air travel.

"It was the St. Louis to Chicago run," Rosenthal said. "Oh, God, that was important. It was when they had the Twentieth Century and the Commodore Vanderbilt and that train they named for a Polish opera star. Anyway, they held the train up in St. Louis after a day game even though it was against the law to do that, you know, you can't hold up the mails. But here come the heroes, the Brooklyn Dodgers, the Bums. So off we go and soon we get to Moline, Illinois."

Robinson by then was a regular at the Dodger card table. On long train rides like this one, the game ran with the train.

"I remember coming down the aisle," Rosenthal said. "They played cards in the dining car; they would pull the tablecloths off and you had the bare tables and you would face each other, see? And as I came by, Jackie was reaching over. The train had stopped. It was at a station, but you could see there were a lot of people out there . . . and Jackie just reached over and pulled down the shade. Gee, I never saw people lined up at a train like that since Babe Ruth. You know,

Ruth would go out there, light up a cigar and all of that. Jackie? No way. He just kept the game going.''

All of the reporters traveling with the team saw what Rosenthal saw: beyond the card tables and the pulled shades, the death threats and the overflow crowds, was black and white together: the team, not the cause. And nowhere was that more apparent than in the relationship of Robinson and Pee Wee Reese.

The pairing was genuine but not intimate. In the best sense, it was professional: the two men formed one of the finest double-play combinations of the day. That meant that from early on, beginning in Robinson's sophomore season when he switched to second base until 1953 when he was shifted to the outfield, the two men had to work together —and did.

Reese and Robinson learned each other's moves around the bag, how each liked to have the baseball delivered, how each man's positioning could help the other. With a runner on, for example, the two had worked out a set of signals that allowed each to know what the other was going to do. Writer John Lardner recalled that in a game against the Reds once, with a runner on first, Reese edged toward the second-base bag. It was a decoy, which only Robinson knew. The Reds' first-base coach, watching Reese, cautioned his runner to watch out. The runner was taking an unusually large lead, threatening to go because the Dodgers' first baseman, Gil Hodges, was making little effort to hold him close. With the runner eyeing only Reese and Hodges, Robinson was able to suddenly sneak in behind him, take a pickoff throw, and tag him out.

Reese was a media darling and a player especially cherished by teammates because he was a true captain, tough and fair. An intense competitor, he originally won his Dodger shortstop job by supplanting Leo Durocher. In his competition with Leo, he was never daunted; as a rookie, it was said the only real question he had of the older player was where he got his clothes.

Reese was an unlikely man to be at the center of a team. He was always deceptively boyish-looking, with fair hair and a small, puckish mouth. He was not a large man, five feet ten, though his nickname had nothing to do with size (he had won a marbles championship at the age of twelve, and the love of marbles and the nickname stuck with him into adulthood.)

Growing up in the South, Reese acknowledged that many of his friends and family members were intensely prejudiced. Friends, he said, regularly taunted Negro children and threw rocks at them when they passed by. Later on, some of his relatives taunted him for being willing to play on the same field with a black man.

Reese says he could never bring himself to call people names or throw rocks, although he never went out of his way to stop it. He did not feel the prompting of a cause when Robinson broke in; it was just that Robinson, as a teammate, deserved a shot like any other player —as Reese himself had. For the first two or three years Jackie played, Reese said, "he'd been a big black guy who came into a white man's game." But then, "I started to appreciate him when I put myself into his shoes—a white player trying to break into a black league. No way I could have done it. . . . Jackie Robinson helped me more than I helped him."

Over the seasons, these professional partners became genuine friends who, in a larger sense, symbolized the possibilities of amity across racial lines.

In *The Boys of Summer,* Roger Kahn said that several themes sounded "through the years of Harold Henry Reese, the son of a southern railroad detective and catalyst of baseball integration. The first was his drive to win, no less fierce because it was cloaked in civility. A second theme was that civility itself. Reese sought endlessly to understand other points of view as with Robinson. . . .

"He was Jackie Robinson's friend. They played hit-and-run together and cards and horses. Anyone who resented Robinson for his color or—more common—for the combination of color and aggressiveness found himself contending not only with Jack, but with the captain. Aware, but unself-conscious, Reese and Robinson came to personify integration."

Robinson personified integration because he fit a heroic and somewhat unreal role, having passed through the hellfire of prejudice to baseball stardom and, ultimately, to a level of national prominence where members of the U.S. Congress could cast him, for their own purposes, as a spokesman for black Americans everywhere.

What was missing in this picture, of course, was the Jackie Robinson who had so far been kept under wraps. Nineteen forty-nine was such a crucial year for him not because he won the MVP or even had the "opportunity" to appear before a congressional committee—but because, beginning in that year, he began to assert himself in a new way, one that was not dependent on anyone's idea of who he was and what he should be doing.

CHAPTER TWENTY-FIVE

During spring training in 1949, Robinson got into a troubling incident with a youthful teammate, a little-used pitcher named Chris Van Cuyk.

In an intrasquad game, Van Cuyk and another player on the team opposing Robinson's began taunting him. Van Cuyk was a large man, six foot five, with a penchant for wildness, on and off the mound. For Robinson, the racial insults and demeaning obscenities were nothing new. But suddenly he answered back, shouting at Van Cuyk as he stood in to hit against him. His first time up, he lined a single to center and then, leading off first base, began deliberately to unnerve the young pitcher—who was already shaky because of his uncertain spot on the roster. Robinson danced and feinted, broke and stopped, until Van Cuyk, in a panic, tried to pick him off, only to throw the ball away, allowing Robinson to advance to second.

The next time Robinson hit, Van Cuyk aimed a ball at his head. And then another. The second time Robinson picked himself out of the dirt, he challenged the hulking young pitcher to a fight on the spot. The two players had to be restrained.

The press, of course, was aware that Robinson's three-year "pact" with Rickey had expired and that he was now "free" to be himself. The man they saw on the field that day was the one they had already decided was the "real" Jackie Robinson.

Bill Roeder of the *New York World Telegram* noted that this new Robinson was "in no way a Milquetoast." He was not implying praise.

"In the future," he wrote, "those who step on him, or on his feelings, are likely to hear about it just as young Chris Van Cuyk did yesterday. What began as a barbering session, a once-over-lightly from one bench to another, grew into a genuinely nasty name-calling, beanballing spat brought on because Robinson decided he was being ridden too hard."

Within days, the episode drew the attention of baseball commissioner Happy Chandler, who then reminded Robinson that his conduct till then had been exemplary. Chandler cautioned him against being too pushy: "I think you would be smarter to continue acting in the same manner you did during your first year in baseball."

The "new" Jackie Robinson, even as he wound up having his best season ever, was acquiring a reputation for being thin-skinned, out of line when he answered back with more than a ballplayer's skills.

Any number of "incidents" involved him. Robinson began protesting calls, arguing loudly and visibly when he thought umpires made mistakes. Writers picked up on his taunting of opponents and umpires—and also his seeming ease in showing either indifference or contempt for them.

Dick Young epitomized the growing friction between the press and Robinson. Robinson, from the start, had been wary of the press—and especially of Dick Young.

"The sportswriter who seemed to be doing his best to make me revert to the old cheek-turning, humble Robinson was Dick Young of the *New York Daily News*. I used to think he was a nice guy personally, and I knew he was a good sportswriter. As time went by, Young became, in my book, a racial bigot," Robinson said.

Others in the media who were aware of Robinson's feelings strongly disagreed. "Dick Young did more in his own way to break the doors down for this guy than eight other newspapermen combined," said Harold Rosenthal. But over time, it did seem as if Young became more interested in breaking Robinson than in breaking down doors.

In 1952, Robinson appeared on a television program, *Youth Wants to Know,* and in answer to a question from a youthful member of the audience said that he thought the New York Yankees, still without a black player, were prejudiced in their hiring practices.

Dick Young bore in on Robinson because he knew that Robinson had, in private, accused Yankees manager Casey Stengel, who was known to sprinkle his media-pleasing monologues with epithets like "nigger" and "jungle bunny," of being racist. Young argued that Stengel was not a racist and that Robinson was wrong in his judgment.

"If there was one flaw in Jackie, it was the common one," Young said. "He believed that everything unpleasant that happened to him happened because of his blackness."

Robinson's relationship with the press increasingly set off sparks, even over trivial matters. One time Robinson sat out a game because

213

of a sore shoulder, Harold Rosenthal remembered. "I heard it on the radio—Robinson's gonna take a day off. So I say to myself, 'What the hell is this, we're getting our news off the radio?' I said to Robinson, one of the few times I spoke to him, 'Hey, Jackie, that isn't quite fair. We follow this goddamn club day in day out, we live with you guys, and all of a sudden I hear this on the radio?' He says, 'You can't tell me what to do.' I said, 'I'm not telling you what to do, I'm just telling you my opinion.' He said something else and walked away and that was it—but anything he did then was suspect to me."

Robinson's teammates and his employers were aware of his relationship with the press and may also have been influenced by it. Carl Erskine, who counted himself a friend then and afterward, believed Jackie came on too strong:

"When [Rickey] lifted the ban, I think Jackie just gushed with these responses that he'd been trying to control. I think it was overkill on Jackie's part. Well, he took exception to so many things at that time." Erskine added that he used to talk privately with Robinson, urging him to be more restrained. Branch Rickey, Erskine added, wound up "thinking it was a mistake to lift the ban" when he did.

Ironically, at the same time that this new, more assertive Robinson was emerging, another "new" Robinson emerged, just as easily judged—the one who had been brought into line by the government. If the fear had been that Robinson, left on his own, would become a dangerous champion of "radical" civil rights causes, Citizen Robinson, carefully draped in hues of the flag, soon acquired the appearance of a mainstream character, a "safe" celebrity.

This Jackie Robinson was someone with commercial possibilities that seemed unlimited—proof of the openness of the American dream. Following the '49 season, Jackie Robinson endorsed products, did a well-publicized stint as a salesman in a department store, and had contracts for personal services, radio appearances, and a movie based on his life.

The Jackie Robinson Story starred Robinson himself. No actor was better suited than he was to play the part. Indeed, to his costar, Ruby Dee, he was a perfect movie star: "He had the most gorgeous smile you ever saw. It just lit up a room."

Robinson had an entourage around him all the while the film was being made—just the way stars do. He imported family, friends, even

214

old rivals. Jack Gordon was there through the shooting. Old UCLA teammate Kenny Washington had a bit part as a Negro league manager.

Robinson was told by the film's director, Alfred Green, not to act, "to just be himself," Ruby Dee said. He seemed pleasant to work with, a man at ease with his fame and with his performance. There was a single moment, though, when she saw something else.

"There was one scene where I was supposed to be in the gym or something, massaging his shoulders," she said. "I still have the picture of it in my head. . . . Right before that moment, in rehearsal, I put my hands on his shoulders but my hands were cold, and he snatched himself around and he just glared at me. I apologized . . . and for the rest of the time, I kept trying to warm up my hands."

Dee, who eventually suffered from the blacklist herself, believed that Robinson had had a gun put to his head for his HUAC appearance; that it was part of the "horror" of the period. But part of the payoff was being allowed to make the movie and to continue as a prominent person. "People get caught in the dilemma in different ways," she said with no trace of rancor. "Because being black, you just don't know what a challenge that is. You had to do many things in order simply to survive. . . . He who pays the piper calls the tune. We know how devastating white vengeance can be and we know how divide-and-conquer works. . . . Anyway, I think my husband and I felt more sympathy than anger."

For Robinson, the difficulties of being a black celebrity were nowhere felt with more acuity than his relationship with Dodger management. At the end of the 1950 season, Branch Rickey sold his 25 percent interest in the team. Rickey's departure, the result of years of internecine warfare with his chief rival, Walter O'Malley, was a severe blow to Robinson, and a clear indication that the way ahead was anything but guaranteed.

Robinson despised O'Malley—and the feelings were almost certainly mutual. O'Malley, who had made a name for himself processing bank foreclosures during the Depression, was never committed one way or the other to the experiment, although he was a dedicated financial warrior in wresting control of the lucrative Dodger franchise from Branch Rickey. He was probably involved in any number of machinations over the years to compromise Rickey's standing with the press and public. His squeeze play to force his partner to sell out was superbly Machiavellian, confounded only by Rickey's equally devious ability to protect himself. O'Malley, aware that Rickey had lost heavily in the stock market and was in desperate need of cash, offered to buy him out for $350,000—exactly what Rickey had originally paid for his share of the club in 1942, but far under the actual value of the share. Rickey hedged for a while, until he found an "outside buyer," William Zeckendorf, who claimed he was willing to pay more than a million for the share. O'Malley, not knowing if the offer was bogus, was forced to up his own bid to that level, which Rickey then accepted. O'Malley's control of the club meant trouble for Robinson.

O'Malley demanded absolute allegiance—and a purging of all those who had been loyal to Branch Rickey. "The two Rickeyphiles O'Malley detested but couldn't get rid of right away were Red Barber and Jackie Robinson," said *Bums* author Peter Golenbock. Robinson in particular seemed to nettle O'Malley. "At the time I didn't know whether O'Malley was jealous of [Rickey] or was down on him because he had brought integration into the game," Robinson said. In any case, O'Malley made life hard.

Early in his stewardship, O'Malley accused Robinson during spring training of deliberately missing exhibition games, and of complaining about segregated accommodations. Robinson bitterly resented O'Malley's charges—and the way he chose to express them. He had summoned Robinson and Rachel to his office for the dressing-down. Both Robinsons responded with indignation; Robinson informed O'Malley that he had missed some exhibition play because he had been injured and to check out his injury with the trainer. As for complaining about segregated housing, Robinson suggested that if O'Malley and other owners had more guts, black players wouldn't have to put up with such indignities in the first place. Mrs. Robinson was just as pointed: "Bringing Jack into organized baseball was not the greatest thing Mr. Rickey did for him. Having brought Jack in, he stuck by him to the very end. He understood Jack. He never listened to the ugly little rumors like those you have mentioned today."

In reality, the new Jackie Robinson really fit no one's mold. No other athlete or celebrity of his time had been placed in his position— and he understood that even better than those who typecast him. He was far more aware than any sportswriter, fan, owner, or congressional investigator that the change he represented remained very much on his shoulders.

While writers of the period did not make much of it, Robinson saw clearly that the pace of change was slow. The floodgates were made of iron but had not opened. While different teams had signed black players to minor league contracts, few had made it through to the majors. The New York Giants, no doubt uncomfortable with the Dodgers' success, had brought up two black players—Monte Irvin and Hank Thompson—in 1949. The Braves promoted Sam Jethroe in 1950, but the Cleveland Indians, after the departure of Bill Veeck, released Satchel Paige at the end of the '49 season. By the end of the '51 season, there were still only three teams with black players aside from the Dodgers.

In practical terms, what that meant was that even after his pact with Rickey had expired, Robinson remained unusually cautious and restrained as a ballplayer. However, he did give himself license to be like any other player when it came to gametime disputes. Because he had a quick trigger, that often made him seem "outspoken" and even, as some writers suggested, a bit of a showboat.

Early in 1954, Walter Alston's initial season as the team's manager, in a game at Wrigley Field, Duke Snider hit what seemed like a certain home run, but because the ball bounced back onto the field, it was ruled a double. Robinson was out of the dugout like a shot, arguing the call, but when he paused to take a breath, he suddenly saw he was alone. Neither Snider, the coaches, nor any other players were at his side. More galling than that, Robinson saw his manager sitting silently and stoically in the dugout. Jackie was out on a limb—and the limb had been sawed off in front of thirty-five thousand people and a full press box. He came back to the dugout and nearly came to blows with Alston, who was perhaps his least favorite manager.

But the incident, like so many other on-field eruptions, was misleading. Despite a temper he was never able to quell, despite a competitive aggressiveness that put him nose to nose, insult to insult, with anyone at any time, he watched himself as carefully after he was "freed" as before.

"In all the years I knew and played with him," said Carl Erskine, "I never saw him in any kind of fisticuffs that I was present for. There was never any kind of open confrontation that got in the way of any kind of game circumstance—and believe me, he had to have some tremendous restraint to bring that off. I never saw him in a heated, yelling argument in the clubhouse with a player. Yeah, he had some strong things to say to some writers, but not ever in a confrontational way, like 'Here I am, egging you on.' Oh, yeah, later on he was a holler guy—but that was something else, part of his being a Dodger.''

Robinson ''watched himself'' in any number of ways. Harold Rosenthal remembers that in all the years he covered the team, neither he nor anyone else ever saw Robinson ''fooling around.'' Where many ballplayers openly bragged about their sexual conquests on the road, Robinson moved from town to town with the restraint of a monk. Harold Rosenthal remembers one night when he and Dick Young had been out on the town in Cincinnati: ''It was about eleven o'clock, and Jackie was coming out of the Netherland Plaza where we stayed. He was all by himself, and Young—you know his brashness—he says, 'Jeez, he's gotta have something going to be out this late'—but I never saw him fool around and nobody else did either.''

When Joe Black turned up as a spring-training rookie in 1952, he was assigned to room with Robinson. Dodger management had told him they hoped some of Robinson's ''competitiveness'' would rub off on him. Black was both nervous and thrilled; Robinson was a hero to him, as he was to nearly all younger black players then, and Black was worried about how to comport himself. He had met Robinson briefly years before (in 1946, when the Montreal Royals had come through Baltimore), but so much had changed since then.

Black put his bags down in the middle of the room and then sat by a window looking out, waiting for Robinson. Then the door opened and Robinson was there.

Robinson said simply, ''Hi, I'm Jackie.''

''I said, 'Hi, I'm Joe Black.' ''

Black then reminded Robinson of their earlier meeting, which Jackie acknowledged without particularly seeming to recall it. What was uppermost in Black's mind was really not their past meeting, but which bed to take. He asked Robinson.

'' 'Take whichever one you want,' Robinson said. I said, 'No, you're the star.' '' Robinson waved him off, and Black then asked him which bed he had slept in the night before. Robinson pointed to

218

one of the beds, so Black took the other. Robinson made sure Black knew where towels, sheets, and other household items were kept. Then, said Black, "He says, 'Hey, you're big. How much do you weigh?' I said, 'Two twenty.' He said, 'You can fight too, can't you?' I said, 'I sure can.' He looked at me—and I'll always remember that look—and he says, 'But we're not gonna fight.' I didn't know what he meant, so I asked him. He tells me that they're gonna be calling us names wherever we go, whatever we do. I was surprised by that, because it was like five years after, right, and everybody said the bad stuff was in the past. No, Jackie said, 'They're gonna call you names and they're gonna do something, you won't know what exactly, but it will be something—and we're not gonna fight.' He said it just like that. He said, 'That's what they want us to do. And we're going to ignore them.' I'll never forget his talking to me like that."

At that point, Robinson was speaking as both pioneer and as team leader, for despite what anyone said, for good or ill, everyone understood without a beat of hesitation that he and the Dodgers were synonymous. This team, years in the making, rocked by palace intrigue and even social revolution, was emerging as one of the best ever, the careful result of a system built by Branch Rickey with innovation, penny-pinching, piety, and passion. At the end of all that, Jackie Robinson knew that as this team flourished, so went that very fragile flower of opportunity that had been inching up from the ground. No matter how he had been crowded, compromised, and limited, the struggle was on the field—exactly where Jackie Robinson was surest about what he could give.

CHAPTER TWENTY-SIX

The Dodgers struggled through 1950, favored to win the pennant, but lagging through most of the season. For a good part of the summer the Philadelphia Phillies—the "Whiz Kids," led by Robin Roberts and Richie Ashburn—seemed to have the race in hand. But the Dodgers narrowed a huge gap to a handful of games in early September. On September 6, Don Newcombe pitched both ends of a double-header against the Phils, shutting them out in the opener and pitching into the eighth inning of the second game, trailing 2–0, when he was removed for a pinch hitter (a game eventually won by the Dodgers 3–2 after Newcombe left). But in that same game, a foul tip fractured the thumb of catcher Roy Campanella, who then missed eleven games. Still, the Dodgers pulled to within two games of the Phils with just two games left—both at Ebbets Field.

The Dodgers took the first of the two, bringing the entire season down to a single game. Newcombe and Robin Roberts exchanged five shutout innings. The Phils scored in the sixth, but the Dodgers tied the game in their half of the inning when Pee Wee Reese hoisted a short fly into the screen in right field. The ball should have been in play, but instead of bouncing back onto the field, the ball trickled down the screen and lodged in a crack at the base of the wall. Reese circled the bases, laughing all the way.

The Dodgers had a chance to take the game in the ninth, but a crossup on the base paths wiped out a potential winning run, and then, in the tenth, the Phils won the game—and the pennant—on a three-run homer by Dick Sisler.

Robinson had another strong year—not up to his MVP numbers of the year before (he hit .328 with fourteen homers), but enough to reinforce his presence as an all-star and team leader.

It was the end of the Rickey era in Brooklyn, and also the end for Rickey's man Burt Shotton as manager of the team. But significantly, Robinson's performance was augmented by those of the team's other black stars. Roy Campanella had an all-star season with thirty-one homers, while Don Newcombe won nineteen games and Dan Bankhead added a respectable nine wins as a spot starter and reliever. Other, younger Dodger stars also came into their own: Gil Hodges, in his third full season, hit a career-high thirty-two homers; Duke Snider, in his second full season, hit thirty-one. It was springtime for the Boys of Summer.

In '51, the Dodgers finally seemed to gel. By midsummer they had thundered their way through the National League, leaving the Phillies far back in the standings, with only the New York Giants putting up any kind of resistance. As late as August 11, the Dodgers held a thirteen-game lead. On that day, the Giants were shut out at home by Robin Roberts, while the Dodgers split a doubleheader with the Braves. Dodger manager Charley Dressen (whose nickname among the players was "I"—as in ego) was loudly on record, having said Durocher's team "won't bother us anymore."

But 1951 was a strange year. Later lovers of hard-luck teams would record it as the year of Bucky Dent's birth. But for that generation of Dodger fans, it was simply the End of the World. The Giants struggled back from the impossible deficit, winning thirty-seven of forty-four games down the stretch to force the Dodgers into having to beat Robin Roberts and the Phillies on the season's final day just to gain a tie for the pennant.

This finale in Philadelphia, despite all that followed it, was one of the memorable games in Dodger history. The Phils, in the early innings, moved out to a 6–1 lead. But the Dodgers fought back to an 8–8 tie and extra innings.

In the bottom of the twelfth, the Phils had the bases loaded with two out and one of the league's toughest contact hitters, left-handed Eddie Waitkus, at the plate. The infield shaded to the right, with Robinson pulled over toward the first-base hole. Waitkus hit a sharp, seemingly uncatchable shot up the middle. The ball whistled just to the right of the second-base bag, heading into center field. Somehow, swung around as he was, having to move to his right—the scouting reports still said he was too slow that way—Robinson sprawled, tumbled, dove in a heap toward center field. His right hand jammed into the ground, forcing his elbow up into his ribs and abdomen like a pile driver, nearly knocking him unconscious. But somehow he snared the ball in the tip of his mitt, preserving the game.

To teammates, fans, and writers alike, it was one of the great defensive plays ever made, even more so because the game was on the line. It was all Robinson could do to get himself back to the bench afterward. He was in such excruciating pain from the fall that it appeared for a time that he might pass out. Rachel, in the stands, wept to see him in such obvious agony.

Though Jackie had given his team a life, it was not clear that he could continue. His teammates needled him, tried to make light of his injury—but all the while they held their breaths, hoping he would be able to go on. Robinson elected to remain in the game.

In the fourteenth inning, in his next at bat, Robinson drove one over the left-field wall to provide the winning run that sent the Dodgers back to New York still tied for first place. Never mind that lurking there at the end of that upcoming three-game play-off was a specter named Thomson; Jackie Robinson had rewritten the script on heroic finishes.

Robinson's surge was part of a magnificent season. He finished the year hitting .338 with a career-high 19 homers, stealing 25 bases, scoring 106 runs, and leading all National League second basemen in putouts, assists, double plays, and fielding percentage. The MVP award went to teammate Roy Campanella. The call was close enough to suggest Robinson's poor relations with the press might have affected the voting, but there was absolutely no question about his leadership role on the team.

He was at his best through the three-game play-off, as though his passion, as in Philadelphia, could will his team to victory in New York. The Giants took the opener at Ebbets Field, 3–1, but the following day Jackie got his team on the board immediately, homering in the first, driving hits in his next two appearances, accounting for the Dodgers' first three runs in a 10–0 rout.

In the deciding game between these ancient crosstown rivals, Robinson's single drove in the first run of the game; in the eighth inning, he scored his team's third run—enough, with Don Newcombe pitching, to all but guarantee victory. The score was 3–1 with three little outs to go. But fate, in its twin guises of Branca and Thomson, had another ending in mind. A fatal pitching change, a memorable three-run homer, and a chaotic trip around the bases followed, and the Miracle of Coogan's Bluff joined Babe Ruth's called shot at the pinnacle of baseball's greatest moments.

In a curious way, nothing showed Robinson's mettle more than his actions in following this epic defeat. When Thomson hit his homer, films show that Robinson followed after him, making sure he touched each base. When both teams had finally threaded their way through the mad dash of fans on the field, Robinson walked over from the Dodgers clubhouse to the Giants dressing room to offer congratulations to the winners. He was the only Dodger to do so.

Because the team was such a great one, filled with stars from top to bottom, Robinson's role was open to a wide array of interpretations. Some writers who had a difficult time with him, said Harold Rosenthal, chose to report only what he did specifically in games. His role on the team was thereby underreported. Other writers, because they did not share his background or experience, were prone to see him as either a savior or an epic troublemaker. Even an enormously sympathetic writer such as Roger Kahn, on the other side of the veil, tended to see Jackie in outsized proportions. He described meeting Robinson once, years after his retirement: "Under the broad brow, the fine features were set in a well-proportioned face. What was most remarkable was the skin. It shone, unsullied ebony. I should expect that Shaka, the chieftain who built the Zulu warrior nation, had that coloring, imperial black."

Kahn reported that when he asked Branch Rickey "if he was surprised by the full measure of Robinson's success, [he] heard him laugh deep in his chest. 'Adventure. Adventure. The man is all adventure,' " Rickey replied.

Robinson's role on the team in these years was complex, especially because his job was so delicate, the team was so good, and the management so fraught.

Joe Black believed Robinson's leadership was monumental, but came in a context that was four-sided rather than monolithic.

"In my opinion, what made the Dodger team so great in the fifties was [that] Jackie Robinson brought an attitude of competitiveness. You could not fake out," Black said. "If you went out there and didn't give one hundred percent, Jackie would let you know. But then there was Pee Wee. Pee Wee was like a mother hen. If anybody had problems, Pee Wee would sit and listen and he'd give his opinion. And Hodges was a silent, quiet guy, and he'd say things that were so funny—he was just a tower of strength for us. And then Campanella:

you just looked at him, I mean, he had the knack of making everything light, of getting everybody to laugh. To me, I always thought the Dodgers were put together by four different type leaders that made a team a team. . . . and Jackie was the focal point.''

Carl Erskine had a clear sense of what made Robinson the man in the middle: ''We drew big crowds wherever we went, and of course we had a really good team. But Jackie's presence, you'd almost have to say that the personality of this team centered around Jackie. Not that anybody tried to put him in that position, but he was the central focus. In St. Louis, for example, blacks used to sit in the pavilion and the whites in the regular stands. Well, the whole game seemed to take on the feeling of what Jackie did. In other words, the score was almost beside the point, because if Jackie made a good play, got a base hit, stole a base, boy, the blacks were up like you couldn't believe. If Jackie made an error or struck out, the white crowd would erupt.''

As a ''holler guy,'' there was no one like Jackie. Rachel Robinson said she never heard her husband curse, but on the field, teammates' and opponents' ears caught fire.

No one went after Leo Durocher the way Jackie Robinson did—and vice versa. Robinson would come to the top step of the Dodger dugout, screaming obscenities at Durocher, asking him about Laraine Day's perfume and whether or not his movie-star wife was keeping him happy; Durocher, in turn, insulted Robinson venomously for his weight, his loud mouth, his thin—but not his black—skin.

From his position at second base, Robinson was all over his pitchers. It did not matter if they were black or white, though he surely kept an eagle eye out for the kinds of racial pressures that might get in the way of winning games.

Joe Black remembers that in his first weeks with the team in 1952, the insults, supposedly a thing of the past, that were coming from the dugouts and the stands were startling in their intensity—just as Jackie Robinson had warned.

''Philadelphia was the place where I was most surprised,'' he said. ''I wasn't looking for it there. But they had this big fat guy there who used to holler at the top of his lungs, 'Robinson, King of the Niggers.' I came out of the dugout four steps behind Jackie one night, and this guy yells, 'Hey, Robinson, there's your little baboon behind you.' And the people would just hoot and holler. Man, it was something.''

At Pasadena Junior College, Jackie Robinson starred in four sports. He starred on offense and defense in football; nearly led his league in scoring in basketball; broke his brother's national J.C. broad jump mark; and batted .417 on the baseball team, while leading the league in stolen bases and being voted most valuable J.C. player in southern California. PASADENA CITY COLLEGE ARCHIVES

At UCLA, Robinson's greatest fame came on the gridiron, though he lettered in baseball, basketball, and track as well. ASUCLA PHOTO DEPARTMENT

Robinson's military career was marked by his fighting an unfair court martial (he won) and by his receiving a qualified honorable discharge.

Perhaps the most important step in major-league baseball history: Robinson's step into the Brooklyn Dodgers' clubhouse in April 1947.

Robinson's first African-American Dodger teammate was not Roy Campanella or Don Newcombe but pitcher Dan Bankhead, who joined Robinson on the Dodgers in August 1947.

Jackie Robinson and Roy Campanella instruct a group of kids from a social center that proved important in Robinson's life, the Harlem Y.

At home with Rachel and Jackie Jr., in April 1947.

Uneasy allies: Leo Durocher and Walter O'Malley.

A happy group of Dodgers celebrate the 1949 National League pennant.

Ruby Dee poses adoringly on Robinson's shoulder in a publicity still for *The Jackie Robinson Story.*
BROOKLYN PUBLIC LIBRARY—BROOKLYN COLLECTION

Sugar Ray Robinson mugs for the camera, flanked by Don Newcombe and Jackie Robinson on the eve of the 1951 playoff with the Giants.
BROOKLYN PUBLIC LIBRARY—BROOKLYN COLLECTION

Branch Rickey was a tireless orator, a brilliant innovator, a notorious skinflint—and by bringing Robinson to the major leagues, Rickey forged a revolution that was long overdue.
COURTESY OF DONALD HONIG

Pee Wee Reese kneels over a fallen Jackie Robinson, and then a host of Dodgers
and Phillies crowd around, following Robinson's miraculous stab of a line drive
in the twelfth inning of the Dodgers' final scheduled regular-season game in '51.
Robinson won the game with a homer in the fourteenth, forcing the playoff.

The Dodgers (from left, in front: Rocky Bridges, Robinson, Reese, manager Chuck Dressen, Carl Erskine) celebrate the '51 pennant-tying victory over Philadelphia, not suspecting what fate has in store for them in the Polo Grounds.
BROOKLYN PUBLIC LIBRARY—BROOKLYN COLLECTION

The Dodgers greet Robinson after his first-inning home run in game two of the '51 playoff. BROOKLYN PUBLIC LIBRARY—BROOKLYN COLLECTION

Robinson with Jackie Jr. in 1949. BROOKLYN PUBLIC LIBRARY—BROOKLYN COLLECTION

Robinson demonstrates his old four-sport form with this spectacular leaping catch at second base, his most familiar position with the Dodgers.

Robinson before the House Un-American Activities Committee in 1949, giving testimony in which he denounced Paul Robeson.

Robinson receives a citation for outstanding "Christian citizenship" and a Bible at the annual dinner of the Brooklyn Division of the Protestant Council. At far right is the Rev. Dr. Gardner C. Taylor, who played an important role in Robinson's aligning himself with the Republican party.

Robinson stands at third base in Ebbets Field, shortly after the announcement of his retirement from baseball.

Robinson with the Reverend Dr. Martin Luther King, Jr., in September 1962, at a press conference aimed at raising funds to help James Meredith's struggle to integrate the University of Mississippi.

In this 1957 photo, Robinson presents a check on behalf of William Black, president of Chock Full O' Nuts Corporation, to Arthur Spingarn, president of the NAACP, for their "Fight for Freedom Fund." Looking on are Dr. Channing H. Tobias (at left) and Thurgood Marshall (second from right).
UPI/BETTMANN NEWSPHOTOS

Two old Olympic teammates, many years after Berlin: Marty Glickman and Mack Robinson. COURTESY OF MARTY GLICKMAN

New York governor Nelson Rockefeller campaigns for the presidency in Ohio in July 1968. Robinson, who allied himself closely with Rockefeller throughout the 1960s, is at right center, back to the camera.

The welcome to Birmingham was ironic for Robinson, Wyatt Walker, and Floyd Patterson, who had flown down to view the bombed wreckage of the Gaston Motel, where Martin Luther King, Jr., and other members of the Southern Christian Leadership Conference were staying. Robinson's immediate activism in this and other matters belies the prevailing impression from the '60s that he had forsaken his role as a civil rights pioneer. UPI/BETTMANN NEWSPHOTOS

David Robinson, third from left, and Jesse Jackson (at his left) join other family members, friends, and mourners in paying final respects to Jackie Robinson at Cypress Gardens Cemetary. AP/WIDE WORLD PHOTO

In St. Louis, the theme had a variation. The first time he pitched there, Black was called on to relieve. Warming up in the bullpen, he remembered that he was hoping that when the call came, the first hitter would be a journeyman like Solly Hemus. Instead, it was Stan Musial. When Black got to the mound, a warm-up toss nearly got away from him. He heard a loud voice from the Cardinal dugout: " 'Hey, Stan, you shouldn't have any trouble hitting that white ball with that big black background.' I put my glove over my face because I thought it was funny and I didn't want them to see me laughing. They didn't intend for it to be funny, but I couldn't help laughing. And then Jackie came running in from second base. He saw what had happened. He says to me, 'That was sorta funny wasn't it?' I said, 'Yeah.' Then he tells me, 'Now get the bastards out. Don't let 'em get under your skin. Shit, get their asses out. You've got the ball, shut 'em up.' "

Teams regularly used to sing "Old Black Joe" to taunt Black when he came in to pitch. Robinson was always there to bargain with him, calm him down, keep him focused on his job—which was to get batters out.

With Don Newcombe, Robinson was more of a provocateur than an older brother, wheedling and needling the large pitcher whenever he felt he needed "motivation." There was one time, Newcombe remembered, unsure of the year, when the Dodgers were playing the Phillies. Robinson was playing third that day—which meant, again, that the time was supposedly well past the point where the racial taunting had ended. Newcombe recalled that ordinary bench-jockeying then, from the Phils' dugout and others, zeroed in on Robinson. " 'Hey, Jackie, here's some black pussy for you,' stuff like that— they'd call you knotty head, black boy, anything derogatory they could think of." In this particular game, Newcombe said, one of the dugout coaches was getting on him. "He was calling nigger this and nigger that and all kinds of things, so Jackie called time and came over to the mound. 'Newk, did you hear what that man's saying in the dugout,' he said to me, 'the guy over there, hiding behind the watercooler?' I said, 'I hear that sonuvabitch, Jack.' He said, 'Well, what are you gonna do about it?' I said, 'Okay, wait till [Del] Ennis comes up.' He was the next hitter, so when he came up, I undressed his ass with a fastball. Ennis called time. I thought he was gonna come out to the mound and start a fight, but he turned around and went back to the dugout. And he said something to that guy—whoever he was—in the dugout. I played with Del years later in Cincinnati and I got around to asking him about that. He told me that when he went back into the dugout, he went right up to this guy. [He told me,] 'Newk, I said to that SOB that if he didn't leave you alone, I was gonna pull his tongue out of his head. I told him that he didn't have to hit off you, I did'—and we didn't hear any more from him.''

Newcombe recalled another incident, in Chicago (probably in 1956). Again, the agent provocateur was Robinson. A Dodger player, Rocky Nelson, had been thrown at after a Duke Snider home run. Robinson cornered Newcombe in the dugout. "Jackie said, 'Okay, Newk, what are you gonna do about it? They just threw at our guy. What are you gonna do about it?' I said to him, 'I'll get every SOB who comes up with a Cub uniform on.' So the next inning, three came up and three went down. Ernie Banks was one of them. Ernie asked Campy, 'What's he throwing at me for?' Campy said, 'Get in and hit, you've got a Cub uniform on.' I got seven of 'em before Alston came out to the mound to take me out of the game. I told Alston, 'If you take me out of the game before I get the other two, you've got no more guts than they have.' The umpire came to the mound and said he was going to have me and Alston fined. Pee Wee came to the mound and said, 'You are insane.' I said, 'That's right. If I get the other two, I'll still be crazy, so leave me alone.' Of course, they took me out of the game.''

Carl Erskine recalled that in Jackie's final year as a player, 1956, the team was coming back from Chicago for a big series against the Giants. Erskine had had arm trouble that year, a muscle tear so serious he found it hard to lift his arm to the level of his shoulder. In Chicago, he was in such pain that he telephoned the Cubs' trainer, someone he trusted, and asked for help. The trainer, Al Schuman, examined Erskine's arm. A bulging knot on the back of his shoulder had caused his entire upper arm to go into spasm. Schuman took Erskine to the Cubs' team doctor—never mind regulations—and the doctor administered a cortisone shot and told Erskine he was going to be "real sore" for a couple of days. On the way back to New York that same day, however, Erskine was informed by Walt Alston that he was going to pitch the next afternoon against the Giants. "I never asked out of a game in my life," Erskine said, "but I didn't see how I'd be able to do it."

The following morning, on his way to the park, Erskine picked up a newspaper and read an article about the Dodgers by the Giants' chief scout, Tom Sheehan. The article analyzed the Dodgers player by player, concluding that the Dodgers had become too old, too slow, "unable to cut it anymore." Specifically, the article singled out Erskine. " 'Erskine can't win with the garbage he throws up there these days,' it said. Man, I read that, I was so down, I couldn't believe it."

And then Alston came up to Erskine at his locker and handed him the game ball. "I couldn't hand it back to him, so I just kept it. I went out to the bench and I was really down. I remember I said a little prayer to myself."

Robinson yelled and chirped at him from his position at third base, Erskine remembered, and somehow, he says, he got through the first inning in order. "Then the second, the third inning. Dizzy Dean was broadcasting—it was the Game of the Week—so I knew people back home were watching."

Robinson made a great play in the field to turn a hit into an out, and then the Dodgers scored three in the last of the seventh off Giants' starter Al Worthington. When Erskine came off the mound in the eighth inning, he was unaware of what was happening until, he says, "this leather-lunged fan sitting back there who was yelling at me all day bellows out, 'Oiskine, Oiskine, ya got a no-hitter!' I had a no-hitter against the Giants through eight innings! I went out and pitched the ninth and got them out one, two, three. Al Dark grounded to me for the last out."

And then, Erskine said, the strangest thing happened. Instead of coming to the mound, Robinson made a beeline for the box seats near the Giants dugout. The celebrants at the mound saw him jawing with someone in the stands. It was the Giants' chief scout, Tom Sheehan. "They say Jackie was reputed to have read everything that was ever written in the newspapers, and here's Jackie over at the railing along third base, he's found Tom Sheehan sitting there. Jackie reaches into his pocket. He had that article in his hip pocket. He was carrying it around with him the whole game! He handed it to Tom Sheehan and said, 'How do you like that garbage now!' True story. I swear!''

When Jackie Robinson joined the Dodgers in 1947, he was 28, very old for a rookie. He had no learning time, no period of seasoning to perfect his skills. He had to make his impact immediately—which was exactly what he did.

For a period of five years, beginning in 1949, he was not just a star player but an incandescent one, at the very top of his game, among the two or three of the game's greatest players. Robinson not only revolutionized what fans saw on the base paths, he was a reminder, even a herald, of everything that baseball could be. He was not a good hitter but a great one. His lifetime batting average was a very respectable .311, but in the years between '49 and '53, he hit .329, drove in 463 runs, scored 540, stole 115 bases, averaged over 500 plate appearances, and was a perennial league leader in several fielding categories.

Robinson's spark as a performer matched his competitive intensity. Over the last seventy years, he is the major league leader in career steals of home. In 1955, the Dodgers won their lone championship after nearly three-quarters of a century in Brooklyn, beating the arch-rival Yankees after four unsuccessful tries during the Robinson years. There is no Brooklyn fan alive who does not cherish Johnny Podres's seventh-game 2–0 shutout—or the play, in a losing opening game, that set the tone for the Series. In the eighth inning, with the Dodgers trailing 6–4, Carl Furillo opened with a single to center. One out later, Jackie bounced a grounder off the knee of Yankee third-baseman Gil McDougald. Furillo advanced to third on the play as the ball caromed into left field—and Robinson, never breaking stride, went all the way to second. A sacrifice fly scored Furillo. Robinson, even though there were two out, defied conventional wisdom by moving up to third.

From there, he danced and bluffed, broke and stopped, trying to distract the Yankees' ace left-hander, Whitey Ford. Ford tried to ignore Robinson. Robinson was old and heavy then, no longer the baserunning threat he was as a younger player. Still, the crowd of almost seventy thousand was into it. On Ford's second pitch, taken with a full windup, Robinson broke for the plate and kept on coming. For one implausible instant, the streaking baseball and the runner seemed to converge in perfect balance—the harmony of mayhem. Robinson swept across the plate with a hook slide, going away from the Yanks' catcher, Yogi Berra—who went straight up in the air in protest when Robinson was called safe.

By '55, everyone in baseball understood that Robinson's skills had peaked and begun to fade. His legs were gone. His body had clearly gone to fat. Many assumed that this player had seen his best days, that in place of skills there was spirit. But Robinson, obviously, still had enough left. That was the message he brought thundering with him down the third-base line.

What nobody knew, not even Jackie's teammates, was that he was suffering from something far more complicated and threatening than bad legs or too much weight.

In 1951, Robinson, making the first of several attempts to establish himself as a businessman, opened the Jackie Robinson Clothing Store in central Harlem. The idea was to sell a line of inexpensive men's apparel. But a nearby chain store easily undersold him, and his store did not outlast his playing career.

Robinson had contacted his old Pasadena friend Jack Gordon and offered him a job at the store, an offer Gordon accepted, even though it meant moving east and going through what he described as a difficult period in his marriage. But he was eager to join Robinson, happy to get a job "where the action was," and eventually was surprised by what he discovered about his old friend.

One day (Gordon was unsure of the year, except that it was while Jackie was a player), Robinson appeared at the store and said he had a doctor's appointment, that he would be back later.

"He said if anyone called, take a message," Gordon said. "I asked him if he wanted me to drive him. He said, 'Naw, there's a place to park.' He was gone for a few hours, I guess, and then he came back. Came into the store and showed me his wrist. He had a diabetic bracelet on. Said the doctor told him that for a person who had competed in athletics for as long as he had, he had never seen a body that was as deteriorated."

For as long as he played, Robinson's teammates—Newcombe, Campanella, Pee Wee Reese, Joe Black—never learned about his condition. Robinson also kept his secret from the team's managers, coaches, and owners. His intent was not to mislead, but to continue playing as long as he could. This was not because he loved the game that much, but because baseball, for the time he was in it, was his livelihood and his pulpit. And even as his body began to break down, there was more for him to do.

CHAPTER TWENTY-SEVEN

In the period surrounding Robinson's testimony before HUAC in 1949, the floor of the U.S. Congress resounded with ugly racial debate, inflamed by the "communist" issue. On the day after Paul Robeson testified in New York on behalf of "The Communist Eleven," Mississippi congressman John Rankin denounced liberal New York Republican Jacob Javits for criticizing the Peekskill violence against Robeson. The debate hung interminably on whether or not Rankin used the word *nigger* in referring to Robeson and, therefore, whether or not the word should be stricken from the *Congressional Record*. The chair ruled that Rankin used the word *Negro*, a term that that "race should not be ashamed of." Rankin insisted, though, that he had not used *Negro* but *nigra*—as he had from the time he had been able to talk. The *Record* splits the difference by coming up with a political blank cartridge: "If that N— Robeson does not like this country, let him go to Russia and take that alien gang of Communists with him," Rankin says—in print.

In '50 and '51, anticommunist fervor, racial violence, and new openings to integration all seemed to become entwined with each other, as though they were part of a single, peculiarly American original.

In '50, the McCarran Act, with its provisions for forced registration of all communist and communist-front groups, was passed. Puerto Rican nationalists attempted to assassinate President Truman. Espionage cases against Judith Coplon and then the Rosenbergs tracked across the headlines from the end of '50 through the middle of '51. The number of lynchings accelerated. Rioting over a black family's moving into Cicero, Illinois, then an all-white city, precipitated a call for the National Guard by Gov. Adlai Stevenson. Harry T. Moore, a top NAACP official in Florida, was killed and his wife gravely injured by a bomb blast in their home in Miami in December 1951.

All the while, the walls seemed to be coming down—or at least beginning to crumble. In '50, the Supreme Court ruled against segregated facilities in three different cases, while the case that would eventually change the landscape of the country, *Brown v. Board of*

Education, was being heard locally in Kansas. In '51, the University of North Carolina admitted a black student for the first time in its history. President Truman, more sympathetic to civil rights issues than previous presidents, named a committee to supervise compliance with provisions against discrimination in the handling of all U.S. government contracts and subcontracts—though he seemed startled, even disbelieving, when confronted by detailed accounts of racial violence in the country.

According to Robinson's teammates Carl Erskine and Don Newcombe, Robinson followed all this avidly and had clubhouse opinions that he was never shy about expressing.

Invariably, whatever involved Jackie Robinson on or off the field acquired an extra dimension of racial politics. At the beginning of '53, Dodger manager Charley Dressen decided to move Robinson to third base to make room for a young, smooth—and black—infielder, Jim Gilliam. To do this, he had to bench Billy Cox, arguably the best third baseman in the game. The move could not have been more controversial and more likely to land Robinson in hot water.

Cox, regardless of his abilities, had always been suspect to Dodger management. He was originally acquired as part of the trade of Dixie Walker, which was designed to relieve racial tension on the team. An an internal report on Cox, prepared after the '49 season, suggested he was limited both physically and mentally. The confidential memo suggested Cox might be suffering from cretinism. "A 100% cretin is definitely a moron and some are even idiots," the report read, adding the proviso that "any doctor would have a right to laugh aloud at this suggestion" in relation to Cox, but that the player was nevertheless suspect and probably needed testing.

At the time Dressen benched him, Cox was thirty-four, angry—and white. Roger Kahn, in his second year covering the team, recounted that he ran into Cox and Preacher Roe in a coffee shop during spring training shortly after the decision to bench Cox had been made. Roe told Kahn that "Billuh's real upset." Then Cox asked Kahn what he thought of Gilliam. Kahn said he complimented Gilliam. Then, according to Kahn, Cox said:

"How would you like a nigger to take your job?"

Kahn did not realize that the target of the slur (as Cox later made clear) was Gilliam, not Robinson, but to Kahn it didn't matter. It raised for him the "infinitely barren" prospect of the "Robinson experience" ending with "Dodgers [calling] other Dodgers niggers."

Cox was soon restored to third, with Robinson moving to left field. But for the duration of the trial, the Dodger team, the melting pot in miniature, threatened to break along racial lines. And most curiously, it was Robinson—who surely was unhappy at being uprooted from a position at which he was an all-star—who was blamed for the trouble.

"Robinson didn't want to play third," said pitcher Russ Meyer. "He wanted to stay at second. True, Cox didn't want to get bumped out of his job, but the one doing the undercurrenting was Jackie. You know how Jackie was. Jackie could get something in his craw, and he'd agitate until he more or less got what he wanted. You know what I mean? He more or less said, 'Hey, I paid my dues. Now you guys dance to the fiddler.' "

In this same period, Robinson and his growing family moved from St. Albans, Queens, to Connecticut. But even something as simple as a change of residence could not take place without its becoming controversial—and public.

The Robinsons wanted to move because they, like any other expanding middle-class family, needed space. A second child, Sharon, was born in 1950, and in 1952 a son, David, was added. But because they were black and famous, the Robinsons' reasons for wanting to move and the trials they eventually went through in finding a new home received unusual attention.

Rachel Robinson had always insisted that she wanted a place "with a lawn and all the things that go to make for good family living." For years, she had a "dream house" in mind and architectural plans for it in the drawer. But her needs could never be quite so simple with race involved. The changing pattern of the Robinsons' old neighborhood bothered Rachel. What had been a predominantly white but integrated neighborhood was becoming predominantly black. The complexion of the schools changed—and that was not acceptable.

"As the community grew in Negro population," she said, "we saw that young families with several children were replacing older families with few or no children, with the result that not only was the school becoming overcrowded, but it was becoming virtually an all-Negro school." An all or predominantly Negro school meant that the Robinson children would not get the same advantages as white children.

In a predominantly white society it was important for black children to have access and contact, to have those "benefits that accrue from going to school with the people against whom one eventually must compete," she said. Her thinking—and her husband's—coincided exactly with then current ideas supporting the developing legal assault on school segregation in the country, which made the runaround they got searching for a new house more than the usual, anonymous drift through the labyrinth of excuses and dodges.

The Robinsons looked for a year before they finally found a property in North Stamford, Connecticut. Because of Robinson's fame, word of the family's difficulties in buying a house got out. The NAACP became involved. A long article in the *Bridgeport Herald* precipitated the formation of a committee of ministers and other property owners in Stamford, including Andrea Simon (mother of Carly and the wife of publisher Richard Simon), who eventually located a property the Robinsons could buy. The struggle to buy a home, however, was just part of a larger struggle that Robinson had been involved in from the day he signed his first professional contract.

As a leader and a pioneer, Robinson took an active interest in the progress of integration in baseball. Though the number of black players in the big leagues was by now dramatically increasing (by 1954, twelve of sixteen teams fielded black players), the most significant development was the even larger number of players entering the minors. Especially in the South, where segregation laws were still in force, any number of players had to endure everything Jackie Robinson went through—with no media watching.

Nat Peeples, the first black player in the double-A Southern Association in 1954, recalled that Robinson phoned him during spring training that year, shortly after he had been signed by the Atlanta Crackers.

"He told me my job would be harder than his," Peeples said. "We talked for a while. He told me what he had been through and what I could expect. Most important, he said, was to keep a level head. They'll call me anything and everything and I had to turn a deaf ear to it."

Robinson's personal bearing and courage remained an example to other ballplayers, especially when it came to dealing with the South and segregation.

The tours of the Jackie Robinson All-Stars through the early and mid fifties were lucrative and nearly always resulted in incidents pitting Robinson against someone. At one stop (somewhere in Georgia or Alabama, remembered Jack Gordon) a sold-out stadium saw police try to stop one of the games because a white pitcher was allegedly being used in violation of a ban on mixed athletic competition. The "white" pitcher was actually high-schooler Maury Wills, but Robinson did not inform the policemen that Wills was actually black. Instead, he took up the challenge of playing a game in violation of segregation laws.

"Wills was pitching a no-hitter and the crowd was really into it," Gordon said, "so Jackie says to these two big cops, in plain view of everybody, 'You wanna stop the game, you go out there and get that white boy yourself.' Nobody moved. Nothin' happened. The game went on."

Another time, the All-Stars pulled into Birmingham one night for a game the following day. Word had gone out that the game would be an integrated competition. After Robinson and the players had settled into a rooming house for the night, Luke Easter, the gigantic Cleveland first baseman, answered a loud pounding on the front door. Robinson, upstairs playing cards, asked Jack Gordon, sitting in on the game, to go and check out the commotion below.

"It must have been about two in the morning," Gordon said. "I went to the head of the stairs, and Luke is standing there with these two big troopers who said they were from Bull Connor's office and they wanted to see that boy Jackie Robinson.

"I went to Jack and told him. He said, 'You tell Bull Connor or whoever's down there that they can kiss my black ass.' Jack just dealt the cards and these guys finally turned around and went home—and the game took place, as scheduled, the next day."

Jackie never lost an opportunity to use his influence to make a difference on the major league circuit. The last big-league city to drop its racial restrictions on accommodations and ballpark seating was St. Louis.

For years, whenever the Dodgers traveled through St. Louis, the black players were housed at the all-black Adams Hotel while the white players enjoyed the comforts of the Chase Hotel. The luxuries of the Chase included air-conditioning, essential in the brutal southern summer heat. There was neither air-conditioning nor much real quiet at the Adams.

In '53, Joe Black recalled, the management of the Chase decided to accept the Dodgers' black players, but with restrictions. The players were not to appear in any public areas like the dining room, the posh upstairs nightclub, or the swimming pool. They were welcome so long as they remained invisible.

The players, Robinson excepted, declined the offer, choosing to go back to the Adams. "All of us said we were gonna go back there," Black said, "but Jackie said he was staying. We got out on the sidewalk where our bags were, we start picking them up, and Jackie says, 'I'm not gonna let them chase me out of here, that's what they want. I'm staying right here.' " Robinson checked into the Chase, then spent his time socializing at the Adams.

A year later, when Don Newcombe returned from military service, the Chase still demanded invisibility from black patrons. One day, Newcombe asked Robinson how long they were expected to put up with that. Robinson immediately took up Newcombe's challenge, and the pair then confronted the Chase's manager.

Newcombe says they were steered into the dining room and seated at a table. "I'll never forget it. Dean Martin and Jerry Lewis were sitting at another table. We shook hands with them. Then Jackie asked the manager of the hotel, straight out, what was the problem about our being regular guests at the hotel like anybody else. He says to the guy, 'It's seven years now, and my friend Don just came back from the Korean War, and I want you to give us an answer.' The guy said, and I swear it, 'The big reason is we just don't want you to use the swimming pool.' Jackie almost fell off the goddamned chair. 'I don't even know how to swim,' Jackie said. I told him something else: 'I don't swim during the baseball season because I'll hurt my arm.' "

But no matter what the hotel management said, their intent was clear. Black players were assigned rooms in remote corners of the hotel, usually with little light and unsightly views; they were either not served or tardily served in the dining room or nightclub. "And when they finally did bring you a plate of food," Newcombe said, "you were never sure what they put in it." But Robinson kept returning until the hotel's policies actually changed.

Robinson's reputation as a fighter—and a firebrand—followed him down through his final playing years. Given the volatility of his nature and his relations with the press, it remained easy to characterize him —to the point of caricature.

On a rainy night in Milwaukee in June 1954, Robinson and his teammates had been grousing about having to play a game that should have been called off. As the game proceeded, the Dodgers, caught in a tight pennant race, fell behind. Then, during a Milwaukee at bat, home-plate umpire Lee Ballanfant inadvertently made one of those nightmare calls that usually turn up in the late innings of company softball games when everyone has had one beer too many: he awarded a walk to a Braves batter on a 3-and-2 count. The Dodgers went wild, but their protest went for naught. An inning later, when Robinson came to bat, he was still steaming. He told Ballanfant, "That's the worst call I've seen in baseball." An epithet or two later, Ballanfant thumbed him from the game.

Robinson, in a rage, swung his bat as he headed back toward the bench. But because of the rain the bat slipped from his hands and sailed high over the dugout into the stands, striking a female patron in the head. Robinson was appalled and immediately rushed to the fan's aid. Even though no great damage had been done, he offered profuse apologies. But, as far as the press was concerned, the incident was further proof that Robinson was a player "out of control." (Later, Robinson was sued, and when he suggested a possible racial motivation for the action, the press slammed him for being oversensitive.)

The ease with which Robinson was labeled a popoff obscured his slowly emerging role as a spokesman for integration, the core of which was not fire but tolerance.

Joe Black recalled that Robinson in his last years in baseball was constantly being asked during the season to make public appearances at schools, luncheons, and other functions. "Jackie gave of himself, but when it came to schools especially, he always seemed to have time."

Black recalled an invitation to a school assembly in St. Louis in '54 or '55. "I remember he gets me up and tells me to get dressed. I say, 'Hey, it's eight o'clock in the morning and we don't play until tomorrow.' Didn't matter."

Black said that at the assembly, "a white girl, a senior, raised her hand and said that she and her family had been there for two years, that they were from New York originally, and that her parents were more prejudiced than anybody she knew in town. Jackie told her that was understandable, that was probably one of the reasons why they moved—they couldn't handle a colored person being their equal on the subway, in Saks Fifth Avenue. Then he made a point of commending this girl for standing up and saying what she did, because she was still willing to accept a person for who they were. Maybe life would change her, he said, but—I'll never forget this—he thanked her for being herself."

Over the winter, prior to his penultimate season, Robinson made a cross-country speaking tour for the National Conference of Christians and Jews. His theme was racial amity and mutual cooperation. His stature reached far beyond stadiums and dugouts. He was on friendly terms with political and business leaders. He had been introduced to President Eisenhower—at Eisenhower's request. At the Harlem Y's annual Century Club dinner at the end of 1955, New York governor Averell Harriman, trying to fend off pressure from civil rights groups on a controversial case involving the extradition of a civil rights activist to South Carolina, tried to reassure his listeners that he was a Dodger fan, thanks to Jackie Robinson.

Robinson counted Thurgood Marshall and Kenneth B. Clark—instrumental in crafting the winning Supreme Court arguments against school segregation—as friends. He had also been introduced to a young, heretofore unknown black minister named Martin Luther King Jr., who had suddenly burst upon the scene as the leader of a bus boycott in Montgomery, Alabama.

King, in those days, very much like Jackie Robinson years before, was heading through unnavigated waters. Though he was surrounded by a supporting movement—unlike Robinson in 1947—he was, like Robinson, facing long odds, physical danger, and demands on his conscience and behavior that were seemingly inhuman.

King, as the world found out, had his Golgotha where he wanted to turn back. He prayed for the strength to continue and—he later told one of his closest aides, Wyatt Tee Walker—he took Jackie Robinson as an inspiration.

"Jackie Robinson made it possible for me in the first place," King told Walker. "Without him, I would never have been able to do what I did."

As Jackie neared the end of his playing days, his skills may have eroded, but his effect on the country was growing.

CHAPTER TWENTY-EIGHT

No sports rivalry has ever equaled that between the Dodgers and Giants in their last years in New York. For the people of the boroughs, the teams were as bound to one another as Paolo and Francesca, the classical lovers doomed to an eternal embrace in hell.

Dodgers-Giants games were nearly always linescores on the margins of madness. One year it might be Bobby Thomson, another year, a beanball war. The games were nearly always played to sold-out houses in Brooklyn and upper Manhattan, before throngs of beery partisans, wilting in the rancid city heat and under unmoving clouds of vituperation, cigar smoke, and braggadocio. The rivalry was as inevitable for the players as for the fans.

In 1951, Leo Durocher was in his third year as manager of the Giants. He was as clear an inspiration for one side as Jackie Robinson was for the other. In a game at the Polo Grounds that year, the Giants pitcher was Sal Maglie, "the Barber," who claimed to have learned both nerve and precision in the Mexican League from a manager named Dolph Luque, who would fire a six-gun at his feet when he missed the plate in warm-ups. Maglie had long since learned to fire baseballs close to opponents' heads. In this game, he went after Jackie Robinson. Maglie, spurred on by Leo Durocher, regarded Robinson as a special target, and Robinson, in his fury, saw double when he looked at Maglie.

Following a pitch where he was sprawled in the dirt, Robinson, the game's great bunter, carefully tapped a little roller up the first-base line. Maglie was forced to come over and field it. Robinson left him printed in the earth like a cartoon Road Runner.

Four years later, at Ebbets Field, Maglie and Robinson were involved again, only Robinson was older now—thirty-six—and his days as a player were clearly winding down. He was no longer the offensive force he once was. Though he had hit .311 the previous season, he had stolen only seven bases, the lowest number in his career. Now his hitting was off too, and more than likely he was limited by the effects of the major illness he had to keep hidden in order to preserve his career. Beginning in '54, he had begun to think of retirement, though his plans were by no means clear and were obviously subject to revision.

In this particular game, Maglie was at his sharpest. The Giants had the game in hand, and Maglie, to keep the Dodgers off stride, buzzed different hitters when they least expected it. When Robinson came up one time, Maglie threw a pitch not at his head, where he would be able to duck, but behind him, freezing him in his tracks.

Robinson's mates, most notably Pee Wee Reese, goaded him to retaliate—not just for his own sake, but for the team's. Next time up Robinson pushed a bunt toward first. The Giants first baseman, Whitey Lockman, came in, fielded the ball, and turned, looking to shovel the ball to Maglie, who was supposed to be covering first. But Maglie had been there before; he did not budge from the mound. The second baseman, Davey Williams, came over to cover first—and Robinson hit him like a freight train. "A knee crashed into Williams's lower spine and Williams spun into the air, twisting grotesquely," wrote Roger Kahn, "and when he fell, he lay in an awkward sprawl, as people do when they are seriously injured."

Later in the game, Alvin Dark, the Giants' captain, tried to retaliate by capsizing Robinson at third on a hard slide. Jackie saw the play coming and tagged Dark in the mouth—only the ball bounced free, to Robinson's dismay. Afterward, Robinson's fiery play earned a special postgame citation from Dark: the great Dodger leader, he said, was "a Hitler."

For anyone who appreciated the intensity of this rivalry, there could have been no greater shock than hearing the first-breaking news on the morning of December 13, 1956, that Jackie Robinson had been traded to the New York Giants. The tabloids were plastered with banner headlines, and radio and television stations carried the story at the top of their newscasts. If the trade wasn't Hitler for Churchill, it was only because the Giants were being asked to give up just Dick Littlefield and cash.

The most painful aspect of the trade was its unsparing lack of sentiment. In the past, owners had been known for a certain clinical detachment in dealing popular but declining players, but this seemed exceptionally mean.

The trade of Robinson, in fact, was not about the coldness of cash but the heat of resentment. The antipathy between Robinson and Dodger owner Walter O'Malley had never slackened from that spring training in 1952 when O'Malley accused Robinson of goldbricking and Robinson lit into O'Malley for doing nothing about segregated housing in Miami.

The sense Robinson had of ill will from the front office, perhaps as much as his illness, was the sandstone that wore him down through his final seasons. If there had been no bad-faith dealings between them in the past, Robinson would have resented O'Malley anyway for having forced Rickey to sell his share in the club. But mistrust infiltrated *anything* that happened between them. Robinson's salary had been cut slightly from a high of $39,000 over each of his final three seasons. The cuts were always personal as well as financial. The naming of a manager likewise carried an almost paranoid weight for Jackie. Walter Alston, who Robinson believed was mediocre, seemed, because he was O'Malley's man, to be an enemy.

Alston cut Robinson's playing time over his final seasons. In 1954, he appeared in only 124 games; in '55, the number dropped to 105; in '56, he appeared in 117 games. He was also moved from position to position like a utility player.

At the beginning of the '55 season, after their near brawl in Chicago the season before, Robinson and Alston nearly had at it again. The team had finished the Florida portion of its spring-training games, and it was working its way home through the South. Robinson was getting little playing time, seeing action once in every three or four games. At one stop in Tennessee, when he found himself out of the lineup for the fourth or fifth straight day, Robinson complained—not to Alston but to Dick Young, who was sure to make ink. Young not only made ink but went directly to Alston with Robinson's remarks.

Alston, normally mild-mannered to the point of sometimes appearing comatose, was furious. A number of players who had worked for him over years were unanimous in saying they had never before or afterward seen him so ready for physical combat.

In Louisville, Alston called a team meeting. In it he complained about players who were criticizing him to the media, never once mentioning names. But the more he talked, the angrier he got. Robinson *knew* Alston was trying to goad him, but he kept quiet—that is, until Alston became more direct, bringing up the Chicago incident from the previous season.

"That did it," Robinson said. "Reason flew out the window. Soon Alston and I were shouting at each other almost at the top of our voices, and it seemed we might come to blows."

"There were other players who had the same feeling that Jackie did, that an inexperienced manager was telling vets how and when to play," Don Newcombe recalled, "but Jackie was outspoken about it. He didn't have to denigrate himself or lower himself to a white man. Jackie was always going to say what was on his mind—and he did. So in the clubhouse Jackie and Alston almost came to blows that day. And both those men knew how to use their hands, believe me. Thank God, there were two other guys who knew how to use their hands, too. Gil Hodges and Pee Wee broke it up before it could happen."

Newcombe knew that Robinson saw O'Malley's hand in Alston's treatment of him—though Newcombe did not agree with Jackie about this. While Robinson's troubles with O'Malley often seemed more petty than substantial, the core of the problem, Jackie continued to believe, was O'Malley's racial attitudes. During this period, following the Supreme Court decision outlawing segregation in schools, a series of churches had been bombed in the Miami area. Robinson and Roy Campanella were among a number of black players asked for their reaction to the violence. Campanella suggested that such incidents could be prevented if Negroes "stopped pressing to get too far too fast."

Robinson said that he was "irked that Campy, a Negro with children, should blame the bombings on Negroes who were asking only for their constitutional rights." O'Malley weighed in on Campanella's side, criticizing Robinson for making "ill-timed and intemperate" remarks.

"What it all boiled down to," Robinson said, "was that I was not O'Malley's kind of Negro." Increasingly, because of what was happening in the country, and because of his eagerness to be part of the change, Robinson refused to remain silent—especially on the job.

One of the great occasions in the Dodgers' final years in Brooklyn was Pee Wee Reese Night on July 18, 1955. Reese was perhaps the most popular player in Dodger history, and everyone associated with the team, certainly including Robinson, was determined to make the night special. But for Robinson, it did not turn out as expected.

The plan was to make the night a surprise. It wasn't advertised; fans coming to the park were given candles at the gate and then told that Reese would be given a surprise party in the last of the fifth inning, that the lights would be turned off and the candles lit. The subways around the ballpark were closed. Pedestrians walking outside the park had to have tickets in hand. Dodger publicist Irving Rudd called the evening "one of the great, glorious nights of Dodger history."

Merchants were asked to contribute gifts. They did, in abundance. The highlight was the presentation of a car to Reese. When the lights went out, and thirty-five thousand candles were lit, a fleet of cars, different makes from different dealers, entered the park from the center-field gate, circled the field, and then Reese's daughter stepped forward, fished into a bowl, and pulled out a set of keys for the car that was to be given away. She picked a Chevy—to howls of delight and cries of frustration. Publicist Rudd remembers that Roy Campanella, "a lovely, expressive man, [had] his cheek bulging with chew, and he says to me afterwards, 'Irvin, how come you didn't see that Pee Wee win that Imperial? . . . We're in the clubhouse in front of the whole gang. I said, 'Gee, the kid picked the key to the Chevrolet.' He said, 'Sheet, man, I'm talkin' about arrangin' things.' "

For Robinson, the evening soured because of another surprise in the surprise party. "When the lights went out and the candles were lit," Carl Erskine recalled, "everybody sang 'Happy Birthday' to Pee Wee. Then the lights came back up, and when they did, there was only one person in that whole park who was bothered by what he saw. The ground crew, in honor of Pee Wee, had gone to the top of the stadium where there were pennants on the roof flying for each of the National League teams. They had lowered those pennants, and in their place they had a raised a big Confederate flag in honor of Pee Wee's heritage."

Robinson was not only upset, he let everyone know it. "He was adamant," Erskine said. "He went berserk after the game. He was just making a real scene about the inappropriateness of that. That's one of the only times I said to Jackie, 'Doggone, this is not the time for that, this is uncalled for.' But there was a lot pent up in him, and even though he had a lot of respect for Pee Wee, he was just infuriated."

Robinson's anger and frustration clearly extended beyond his relations with any individual. Whatever he felt for Walter O'Malley, Walter Alston, the front office, or the ground crew, his day-to-day life as his career wound down was increasingly complicated.

He was a celebrity in the sports world in a way that no one had been before him. The great players of his era—DiMaggio, Williams, Musial—were heroes solely on the basis of their extraordinary athletic achievements. Robinson was now recognized as much for what he gave to society as for what he gave to baseball. His moral standing counted for as much as his stats.

Nearing the end of his playing career, it had been less than ten years since Robinson first set foot on a major league diamond, less than ten years from the time major league baseball was lily-white. While the game was obviously still infected by old attitudes toward race, black stars were now everywhere. Hank Aaron was making headlines for the Milwaukee Braves, Frank Robinson for the Reds. The Pirates had Roberto Clemente, the Cubs had Ernie Banks, and just a few subway stops from Ebbets Field, Willie Mays played stickball with kids and center field for the Giants.

All Robinson's training, his pride, his preparation, his past accomplishments, came from and centered on athletic stardom. The vigor and competitiveness of sport drove his sense of everyday relations and his sense of fair play. His passion for racial justice came as much from a desire to win as from a commitment to right thinking.

In these final seasons, Robinson became once again a man searching for his place. He let it be known—to Branch Rickey and to others close to him—that for the barriers to fall completely, those to the coaching lines, the dugout, and the front office must fall as well. Robinson did not seriously consider whether he wanted to stay in the game, because he knew those doors were still tightly closed. He was given no encouragement.

But Robinson carried himself proudly, enjoying his status as a veteran. He found solace and enjoyment in the camaraderie of the clubhouse. His friendships were built at the card table, in side trips to racetracks and golf courses.

Among his teammates, he was close to players who seemed to have no more in common with him than that they battled him in poker or bridge and wore Dodger uniforms. One such player was Billy Loes, the eccentric right-handed pitcher, a street kid from New York, also a card wizard, who once seriously explained that he had lost a ground ball in the sun. The explanation, universally ridiculed, was never ridiculous to Robinson or to anyone who realized that the sun setting behind Ebbets Field poked blindingly through the girders of the grandstand at an angle that certainly *could* interfere with a pitcher's attempt to field a ground ball.

Loes's friendship with Robinson was neither odd nor mysterious. Robinson was relieved of the burden of having to be anyone special with him, and Loes was disarmingly honest even as he seemed largely unaware of and indifferent to anyone's expectations of him.

Tommy Villante, the publicist, who knew both men well, says that Loes was one of the very few people who had the capacity to make Robinson laugh. Villante recalled an episode from late in Robinson's career. Loes had been hit with a paternity suit, filed in New Jersey. The Dodgers had contracted to play a number of home games each year at Roosevelt Stadium in Jersey City—part of O'Malley's pressure campaign to gain a new home for his team. That meant that every time the team went to New Jersey or passed through Newark by train on the way to Philadelphia, Loes had to go into hiding to keep from being served with a subpoena.

"Billy used to hide in the bathroom on the train, the whole bit—it was hysterical. Jackie, like everybody else, saw the headlines, so he asked him in spring training, 'What did you tell your mother and father?' Billy said, 'I just told them it was a publicity stunt.' "

Walter O'Malley also asked Loes about the problem. "For the first time in his life, Billy may have lied," Tommy Villante said. "He said there was nothing to it." The front office, wanting to make sure Loes attended all the Jersey City games, let him know that they would stand behind him all the way, pay legal fees, go to bat with the press. "The only thing O'Malley asked Loes for was to tell him the truth," Villante said. " 'Hah,' Billy told him, 'I don't even know the girl.' So Walter gets a lawyer, the trial date is set, everybody shows up in the courtroom, in walks this gal in a wonderful tight-fitting outfit—so Billy turns to the lawyer and says loudly enough for everybody to hear, 'Boy, I'd like to bang her all over again!' It's hard to explain it, I know, but Jackie just really enjoyed Billy."

Inevitably, what was uppermost in Robinson's mind then was what he was going to do after baseball. He had no answers. With mortgage payments to make on an expensive new house under construction in North Stamford, and a lifestyle that included exclusive private schools for three children, making money after baseball was a special problem. The only immediate answer was the old one—how he played the game.

In his last two seasons, particularly in 1956, his final year, he took advantage of whatever playing time he was given. In '56 with the Dodgers floundering and about to drop out of the pennant race at the end of July, Alston decided to install Robinson at third base. The move paid immediate dividends.

The day before the change, the Braves had moved five games ahead of the Dodgers by beating them 1–0 at Ebbets Field. In the second game of the series, at Jersey City, the Braves led 1–0 when Robinson connected for a two-run homer to give the Dodgers a lead. The Braves tied the game in the ninth and, had the bases loaded with one out, threatening to win it, when Robinson started an inning-ending double play. In the last of the ninth, with two men on and one out, he hit one over center fielder Billy Bruton's head to win the game.

It was just the beginning.

Robinson, injured and ill, played furiously down the stretch, leading his team to its sixth pennant since his arrival in 1947. He finished the year hitting a respectable .275, with ten homers, sixty-one runs scored, twelve stolen bases. In the series that followed, the Dodgers fell to the Yankees in seven games, but even there Robinson managed a signature statement.

With the Yankees leading three games to two, looking to close out the series at Ebbets Field, the two teams battled into the tenth inning in a scoreless tie. It was Robinson who won the game by spiking a line-drive single over the head of Enos Slaughter to set up a showdown seventh game.

However, with the end of the '56 season, Robinson was more aware than ever that his answers could not indefinitely come from the playing field. Thought of retirement had grown more acute when he picked up rumors from the front office that he might be traded over the winter. For the better part of three years a friend of his, Martin Stone, had been looking around on his behalf, checking out possibilities after baseball. Broadcasting was one. Robinson had done some work for NBC, even had an office in the RCA building. After making other inquiries on Jackie's behalf, Stone that fall finally located what he thought was a legitimate opportunity.

Sometime after the season ended, Robinson was put in touch with businessman and philanthropist William Black, chairman of the board of Chock Full o'Nuts, a fast-food chain, 80 percent of whose one hundred employees were black. After a number of preliminary meetings with Stone, Black agreed to offer Robinson a high position in the company. According to Martin Slater, a vice president with Chock at the time, Robinson represented a "tremendous feather in [Black's] cap. Jackie was such a celebrity."

Under normal circumstances, this development might have allowed Jackie Robinson to make a graceful exit from the game. Instead, it led to bitter controversy—like everything else in his career. The trade to the Giants obliterated another, perhaps more significant story: that Jackie Robinson, in leaving baseball to become a ranking executive in a white-owned corporation, would once again be consciously playing the role of a trailblazer.

Part 3

Invisible Man

CHAPTER TWENTY-NINE

Robinson's retirement was controversial because it was shrouded in secrecy and politics—just like his signing in 1945. Only this time, he was more in control.

Robinson first met William Black on December 10, two days before the Dodgers and Giants concluded their epic deal. Robinson entered the December 10 meeting not only with retirement in mind but with an exclusive contract for $50,000 from *Look* magazine for the details of his quitting when and if it occurred. Though Robinson had been briefed by Martin Stone, William Black was still a surprise for him.

Black was not a typical businessman, and his company, because of its racial hiring practices, was atypical as well. Black was a shy man; his quiet exterior masked an intense and nervous sense of perfection. A workaholic, he kept late hours and shunned the limelight, though he aggressively promoted his business. His most private pleasure seemed to be playing chess.

Black had originally wanted to be an engineer, but unable to find a job, he started selling shelled nuts at a staircase stand in the old Times Building on Forty-second Street in the 1920s. By the 1930s, he had built something of a nut empire, running a chain of exclusive shops in New York that did not survive the Depression. In place of his nut parlors, Black built a chain of fast-food restaurants, beginning again in the Times Square area. This time, he catered to people with little money to spend. His selling point was a health-food sandwich on whole-wheat nut bread—along with a nickel cup of coffee.

During the war years, a large number of Black's white employees left for military service. In their place, and only after what one aide described as careful screening, Black filled the positions with black employees. The balance between black and white in the company was such that hiring Jackie Robinson not only represented a public relations coup but good business sense too. Robinson, as vice president in charge of personnel, would handle issues like employee complaints, hiring, and firing.

Black was liberal, a Democrat, an admirer of Hubert Humphrey,

249

the most visible establishment advocate of civil rights on the scene then. Black appreciated Robinson's contributions and made sure he understood there would be no difficulty when and if he needed time off for activities outside the office, something Robinson very much appreciated.

If Black had been expecting Robinson to be angry and aggressive, as he had often been depicted in the press, he was pleasantly surprised. Instead, he found a soft-spoken, highly articulate, and intelligent man with little or no airs of self-importance. He *liked* Robinson —and Robinson, in turn, liked Black, or at least liked what he was being offered.

Robinson's annual salary, covering two years, would be in the neighborhood of $50,000, plus benefits—all of Black's employees, though nonunion, were given health and pension benefits.

For his part, Robinson was pleased that he had a real job, not a ceremonial one or one with just an office and a nameplate. As a director of employee relations, his duties would matter; he could make a difference among people too easily fired, not easily hired. A company flyer, distributed to all employees after Robinson signed on, emphasized the point. It read, in part: "AS TO JOB SECURITY: No employee will be dismissed without the right to present his or her case to Mr. Jackie Robinson, our Vice-President in Charge of Personnel." The flyer also informed workers that company loans at no interest were available to them, and that the person to see to secure them was Robinson.

Though his annual salary would be higher than any he had earned as a ballplayer, Robinson also understood the limitations of his job. It was not open-ended. Advancement was lateral, not vertical, since Chock Full o'Nuts was a one-man corporation. Power was not delegated, and rank was never confused with the basic reality that even presidents and vice presidents of the company served at the pleasure of William Black.

For all that, Robinson knew that this was the right move at the right time. He thought he might possibly squeeze out another season or two from his old man's body, but the challenge now seemed more demanding than rewarding. One unsubstantiated story says that he asked Rickey then about becoming a coach or manager, and that Rickey urged Robinson to return to school and finish his degree.

More immediately, Robinson worried about his family—particularly about his ten-year-old son, Jackie Jr., who was old enough to worship his father but too young to understand that he would no longer be a baseball star.

And then there was a more immediate and more complicated problem: how to tell his team and the public. When he talked with his wife, his closest adviser, he determined that while he owed O'Malley nothing, he did want to offer an explanation to E. J. "Buzzy" Bavasi, the general manager, who, Robinson said, "was always a decent guy."

Robinson said that before his meeting with Black, he had discussed with Rachel whether or not he should telephone Bavasi, and that she had cautioned him against saying anything until he knew for sure what was going to happen. He says he put in a call to Bavasi anyway—just to let him know that he was thinking about retirement. He was told the Dodger VP was in Chicago and not available.

The day following his meeting with Black, Robinson got a call from Red Patterson, a Dodger executive, asking him to come in the day after that to meet with Bavasi for an important discussion. Robinson put Patterson (and Bavasi) off, saying he would phone in later. He did —after he met with Black in New York to sign his contract with Chock Full o'Nuts.

Bavasi insisted on a meeting with Robinson. Robinson now did not want to meet with Bavasi; whatever Robinson felt about wanting to let Bavasi in on his thinking, the terms of the *Look* deal had now been triggered. He was contractually bound to withhold word of his retirement until it was revealed in the magazine. What Robinson did not know—and what he found out when he prodded Bavasi into disclosing over the phone what was so important—was that he had been traded to the Giants.

Then and afterward, there was a hue and cry about Robinson's values, his character, because he kept quiet about quitting. Bavasi blasted him to the media, saying that he was a person able to tell one story to the newspapers "while writing another for money." Those remarks, in turn, ignited Robinson, who said, "I thought Bavasi was a better friend than that. I've been as decent to him and the Brooklyn ball club as I could possibly be. For years I've agreed to go along with him in our salary talks, even though I knew I was underpaid. Now

251

that's my reward.'' Bavasi's response was to sarcastically point out that Robinson had a reputation for saying just what he wanted, but apparently did not look with favor on that right for others. In any case, Bavasi said, he was not about to lose any sleep over it.

In his *Look* article, Robinson was absolutely frank about why he kept everyone—including Giants owner Horace Stoneham, an innocent party to any Dodger family quarrels—on the hook:

"Horace Stoneham, the president of the Giants, phoned to ask me how I felt about [the trade]. I had to tell him I'd be glad to play with the Giants—*if* I decided to play at all. I said I had some thinking to do and would give him a definite answer in a few weeks. I couldn't tell him that I was through with baseball forever because I'd agreed long ago to write this story—when the time came—exclusively for *Look*.''

The hullabaloo over Robinson's retirement obscured a couple of salient developments. One was that Robinson *might* have changed his mind and played for the Giants. He had apparently secured the permission of William Black to do that if he wanted to—although nothing indicates that he came close to reversing himself. The blast from Bavasi about Robinson's character, most observers have agreed, doomed any possibility that he might actually have accepted the trade.

But another, far more consequential development may have sealed his decision to retire. On December 8, 1956, two days before he first sat down with William Black, five days before the trade to the Giants was announced, he became the forty-first African-American to accept the NAACP's prestigious Spingarn medal, named after literary critic and past NAACP board chairman Joel E. Spingarn.

The naming of Robinson for the Spingarn medal placed him in elevated company indeed. Past winners included A. Philip Randolph, Mary McLeod Bethune, James Weldon Johnson, and George Washington Carver. Robinson was the first athlete awarded the medal. His public standing had been far more consequential than that of past athletes like Joe Louis and Jesse Owens, or of prominent people in all other fields. At that moment, whatever his popularity among white Americans, Robinson was simply the most widely admired figure among African-Americans in memory. A national dream of liberation had first been projected upon him—as it soon was to be upon a more prepared political leader, Martin Luther King Jr.

In accepting the honor, Robinson paid particular tribute to Rudolph Thomas, the director of the Harlem YMCA, and to Lester Granger of the Urban League—thanking him, in particular, for his help in preparing for his 1949 HUAC appearance—and to Rachel and Branch Rickey.

The speech was unremarkable, hardly that of a political leader. There was no talk about strategy or goals. Instead Robinson underlined a passionate belief in the importance of principle. It was principle, he said, that enabled him to endure those first years when the urge to quit was strong. It was principle that made him speak out rather than keep silent.

"I was so often advised not to press issues," he said, "not to speak up every time I thought there was an injustice. I was often advised to look after the Robinson family and not worry about other people, and sometimes the biting criticism I got. . . . [made me wonder] if my course was the proper one."

The principles Robinson referred to included standing up for "human dignity, brotherhood, fair play," and he specifically saluted the unfolding struggle for civil rights in the country.

He praised his hosts: "The NAACP has stood out as the tireless champion of the rights and well-being of the Negroes in America."

Never mind that the NAACP's leaders and membership were generally considered "safe" by the FBI; that as an advocacy group it was often slow to act—as in the case of Lt. Jackie Robinson, who asked for but did not receive help from the organization at the time of his court-martial. Robinson, along with most other civil rights activists in 1956, believed a promising change had occurred at the top of the NAACP. The new executive secretary was Roy Wilkins, younger and more in touch with the rising mood of expectation in black communities around the country. Leaders of local chapters and area leaders were increasingly prone to be activists rather than decorous petitioners.

For Robinson the Spingarn medal was more than an award; it was a new challenge, and particularly after the bitter taste he had from how he left baseball, it was one he particularly welcomed.

Later in that same month, while baseball fans were arguing over the rights and wrongs of the trade, Robinson accepted the chairmanship of the NAACP's 1957 Freedom Fund drive, an expanded nationwide effort to raise large contributions and to solicit lifetime memberships to bolster the organization for a much broader, if still undefined, assault on the remaining pillars of legal segregation.

Robinson did not want to be a figurehead, though he suspected he had been chosen as chairman for just that reason. "Mr. Wilkins asked me to head the drive; he did so in the same spirit that many organization heads ask public personalities to participate in their work," Robinson said. "Get these personalities to agree to the use of their names on the letterheads, attend press conferences and a couple of ceremonial events, take a few publicity pictures, but let the real work be done by others."

Robinson wanted a taste of the real thing. He told that to Wilkins, who was surprised, but agreed to let Robinson travel and speak as much as he wanted—and Robinson specifically told that to his new employer, William Black, who had promised to give him time for outside activities. Just weeks after Robinson had accepted the job offer, this was being put to the test. Black, said Robinson, did more than honor his word: he also "gave me a check made out to the NAACP that was in five figures."

The announcement of Robinson's chairmanship created an immediate wave of enthusiasm in local chapters around the country. Requests poured in to national headquarters for personal appearances, raising expectations for the tour's success even further.

Although accustomed to being a celebrity, Robinson was the first to admit that he was a novice when it came to political organizing. He knew little about the history and character of the NAACP or other civil rights groups—other than what he had picked up by anecdote or had read in the papers. He was not familiar with the largely suppressed story of black-American organizations and individuals who had waged the struggle not for years but for generations. Robinson told Roy Wilkins he was not only determined to work at his position but that he wanted to learn. He asked Wilkins to put an experienced aide at his disposal. Wilkins agreed and asked Franklin Williams, a West Coast NAACP official (and later U.S. Ambassador to Ghana), to travel with Robinson for a couple of weeks.

Robinson's itinerary was nationwide, with the bulk of his appearances scheduled for January. In a one-week period, he was committed to speaking in Pittsburgh, Cleveland, Detroit, Cincinnati, St. Louis, San Francisco, and Los Angeles.

It was not remotely possible to fulfill all the requests for Robinson to appear. One such request came from a chapter in Clarksdale, Mississippi: "As we all know, Mississippi needs more help than most people in America. We are requesting therefore that our town branch be placed on [Robinson's] tour if possible." It was signed by Aaron Henry, then an unknown organizer, but later a founder of the Mississippi Freedom Democratic Party.

Another letter requesting an appearance by Robinson came from the young Alabama minister Martin Luther King Jr. King had recently led the victorious bus boycott in Montgomery and was now forming his own group, the Southern Christian Leadership Conference. Robinson personally replied to Dr. King:

My dear Reverend King:

It is with sincere regret that I find it impossible to come to Montgomery during the month of May. I have read with mounting concern of the attacks upon our churches in your city. There is no cause more deserving of support than the campaign for funds to rebuild these structures.

As you know, I have just recently undertaken a new job with the Chock Full O'Nuts chain in this city. . . .

I know you will understand my inability to be with you. If the campaign continues during the summer and into the fall, perhaps we may be able to arrive at a mutually convenient date for me to visit Montgomery.

Be assured of my desire to be of service. I remain

Sincerely yours,
Jackie Robinson

In his last autobiography, *I Never Had It Made,* Robinson says that as a neophyte, he leaned heavily on Franklin Williams, who became a close personal friend.

The two men met for the first time in Pennsylvania Station in New York, as they were about to board a train for Pittsburgh at the beginning of the tour. They shared a large sleeping compartment, and after initially settling into upper and lower berths for the evening, Robinson said a long, awkward silence followed. Robinson learned later that Williams believed he was withdrawn and uncommunicative. In turn, Robinson discovered that Williams was feeling overwhelmed. He was a Jackie Robinson fan and, Robinson said, "[Williams] says he kept asking himself, 'How am I going to prepare this famous baseball star to become a civil rights spokesman?' " Finally, Robinson broke the ice by asking Williams to tell him all he knew about the NAACP. Williams obliged with a lengthy history of the organization in the twentieth century, filling Robinson in on the great cases and all the great personalities who had belonged to the NAACP over the years, including Walter White, W. E. B. Du Bois, the Spingarn brothers, Thurgood Marshall (whom Jackie knew well enough as the lawyer in *Brown v. Board of Education,* and also as the NAACP lawyer who had personally handled a money dispute Robinson had had with some Negro all-star promoters on the West Coast early in his career).

The tour proved to Robinson, he said, that "it is not true that black people are not willing to pay for their own freedom." Wherever they went, there were not only crowds but people willing to contribute time and money. For the first time ever, the annual Freedom Fund drive netted over a million dollars. Robinson says he learned to be a pitch-man, at first basking in the adulation he received, speaking for only five or ten minutes, then gradually expanding his remarks to a half hour or more. "[Frank] shuddered when he thought about how I could have blown the whole deal," but instead the two men became a team, Robinson said. When they ran out of gimmicks to work the crowds, Williams shamelessly took to "selling kisses," coaxing "ladies to come down the aisle" for a buss from Jackie Robinson—in exchange for cash contributions, of course.

Williams's view of Robinson was somewhat at odds with Jackie's tendency to see himself as an accommodating innocent when it came to political leadership.

In a confidential memo to Roy Wilkins, Williams spelled out the importance of Robinson's role in the NAACP. He began with a detailed account of the tour:

"The Baltimore meeting, held in a church, was packed. Over 1,000 persons sat in a basement listening to the program over a loudspeaker system. At the conclusion of his remarks, Jackie Robinson went downstairs and talked informally with the people there." If there was a problem, Williams said, it came from chapter officials, one of whom insisted on "a lengthy and boring reading of letters."

In Pittsburgh, the two men began a full day of activities at 10 A.M., not returning to their hotel until the early morning hours the following day. Williams noted that "Branch Rickey attended the luncheon and spoke in addition to Jackie and the National Office representative."

In Cleveland, bad weather held down the size of the crowds, but in Detroit the problem was an oversubscribed luncheon. Highly enthusiastic and well-attended meetings took place in St. Louis and Cincinnati. In Oakland, the ten-thousand-seat arena was sold-out and "had standing room only with 100 persons sitting on the platform."

Jackie Robinson, said Williams, "proved extremely easy to work and travel with. It was clear that once having agreed to make this trip, there was no assignment or requirement which he considered burdensome. On one or two occasions we had no opportunity to shave or bathe between our morning arrival and late retirement. This did not seem to irritate or worry Mr. Robinson."

Williams noted that Robinson was not only eager and willing to learn, but that at times he seemed disappointed when instruction was not forthcoming. If cards outlining ideas for inclusion in speeches were given to him, he did not hesitate to turn to them.

Robinson was not an unambiguous plus for the organization, however. He was frank, Williams said, "almost to the point of naïveté." It was imperative, Williams recognized, that "in discussing matters with him that it be made extremely clear as to which matters are confidential and which are for publication." This problem, identified in his baseball career as "outspokenness," would later haunt him in the political world. But at that moment, it was just one additional hue on a bold and intriguing new canvas.

Franklin Williams saw what Roy Wilkins apparently did not see or was not interested in seeing: Jackie Robinson, in his first season as a civil rights campaigner, even without a background in politics, had every bit as much purpose as he did in his initial season as a big-league ballplayer.

"Jackie strikes me as being extremely confident of his ability," Williams wrote, "to 'open doors' for the NAACP." Whatever the NAACP had been in the past, it could be far more vigorous in the present. Robinson, said Williams to Wilkins, "is convinced that our problem flows primarily from a lack of communication or, as he puts it, our inability to get our story told."

Robinson, fully settled upon his new life, was determined to do everything he could to change that.

257

CHAPTER THIRTY

The baseball world that had been so central to Robinson's life and words over the previous ten years remained largely unaware of what he was doing and saying in this signal year of his life outside the game —except for one brief and overblown back-page contre-temps.

During the spring of 1957, *Daily News* columnist Dick Young interviewed Roy Campanella and asked him about a remark Robinson had allegedly made that Campy was washed up. Campanella—according to Young—said, "Jackie has made quite a few remarks and cracks since retiring, and I'm not surprised he said something like that about me. He's been shooting off his mouth about everybody, and most of the time he doesn't know what he's talking about." Campanella, said Young, blasted Jackie for being a clubhouse loudmouth, for stirring up trouble on the team, for leaving the game with more enemies than friends. If he talked to those he worked with in private industry "the way he talked in baseball, they'll wrap something around his neck and walk out."

The column in the *News* upset Robinson—enough so that NAACP officials fired off memos to one another, trying to figure out a response. As furious as he was, Robinson eventually stepped before microphones and said he had no quarrel with his former teammate, that he was too busy with NAACP work to be lured into arguments of this type—which was true. No matter what anyone in the baseball world was saying, no matter how painful, he was following a very different path. In this new world, events were moving with incredible speed.

It is hard, at a remove of nearly forty years, to appreciate the peculiar quality of the time. The Eisenhower presidency was at its midpoint. For most white Americans old enough to remember, the period was one of almost somnolent tranquillity. Elvis was gearing up and Johnnie Ray had teens swooning in the aisles. Robert Lowell, meditating on the peculiarity of the era, likened the rise of Eisenhower to an almost surreal summoning from "the mausoleum" of the Republic's heart.

No such ambiguity existed in the civil rights movement. Nineteen fifty-seven was brimming with hope and ideas for the future. For those who had actually been through it, the victory of the Montgomery bus boycott the year before, however limited, was an inspiration and a challenge.

The target of the movement was becoming clearer by the day: legal segregation in all its forms. No single strategy yet existed for ending the apartheid system in the country, but the resolve to do it had been awakened.

Jackie Robinson's person and achievement was incontestible proof that such change was possible. His fame, and the inspiration he provided, was based on his dramatic and successful single combat against an institution that was a symbol of American culture. How much more could be done when a whole people rose up?

Though Robinson was not involved in the Montgomery bus boycott, links can be seen between the strategy he followed during his first three years in baseball and Martin Luther King's strategy of nonviolent but active resistance.

In December 1956, as Robinson was retiring from the game and signing on to head the Freedom Fund drive, Dr. King was delivering a speech to a packed house of followers at the Holt Street Baptist Church in Montgomery. In the speech, King declared that what had happened was part of a "revolutionary change in the Negro's evaluation of himself." The aim of the movement was not confrontation, not to defeat the white man, but "to awaken a sense of shame within the oppressor and challenge his false sense of superiority. . . . The end is reconciliation."

Shaming whites until they understood their need for reconciliation was a moral and practical imperative with real goals: overturning segregation and establishing a working relationship with whites—in other words, playing on the same team. Use of such tactics as boycotts or arrests provoked by deliberate violation of segregation laws might be in dispute, but not the determination to see the struggle through. Specifically, the most immediate goal of all civil rights leaders then was to engage government and its leaders in a partnership for fundamental change.

Following his experience in Montgomery, Dr. King traveled to Africa along with several other prominent black Americans, including

Adam Clayton Powell Jr., A. Philip Randolph, and Ralph Bunche, to help celebrate the national independence of Ghana. At one embassy reception, King was introduced to Vice President Nixon. Nixon's presence was not only noted but taken as a sign of encouragement. King asked Nixon directly to encourage the Eisenhower administration to become more involved in the fight against segregation. Nixon in turn invited King to visit him in Washington. King, however, along with most other civil rights leaders, did not know Nixon and did not know what to expect.

Jackie Robinson, on the other hand, did know Nixon—not well, but well enough to follow up King's chance meeting with him with a lengthy letter. He too was intrigued that the vice president of the United States had turned up at a celebration for the independence of a black nation, and that he seemed sympathetic. In his letter, Robinson praised Nixon for going to Africa and appealed to him to use his good offices on behalf of the civil rights struggle at home.

Robinson took note of Nixon's reputation as an anticommunist, duly lauding "your telling refutation of anti-American charges made by the Communists." But then he offered praise of a different kind:

"It was most reassuring to have you speak out in the heart of Africa so the peoples of that Continent and of the world should know that," he wrote, quoting Nixon himself, " 'we will never be satisfied with the progress we have been making in recent years until the problem is solved and equal opportunity becomes a reality for all Americans.' "

Robinson knew he could count on something King and other leaders could not yet take for granted—that he would be heard.

"I am sure that in this statement you express the sentiment of the vast majority of the American people who wish to see an end to racial discrimination and segregation. As you indicated, much remains to be done but progress has been made, especially in recent years, and we are confident that this progress will continue at an accelerated pace until this evil is entirely eliminated from American life."

Robinson's goal was to get Nixon to believe that he could be the one, the new and different American leader—as unlikely as Lincoln had been in the last century, or at least as Branch Rickey had been in professional baseball. If a white politician like Richard Nixon stood in any proximity to the civil rights movement, the chances for change were so much greater.

Robinson was not being simply wishful. Unlike other civil rights leaders, he did have a certain cachet with white politicians who knew him as a star athlete. Nixon was definitely in that category.

Nixon responded to Robinson's letter immediately—the day he got back from his African journey. He praised Robinson even more effusively than Robinson had praised him. "Dear Jackie," he began, "As you can imagine, there were a number of letters on my desk when I returned to the office today after an absence of three weeks. I can assure you, however, that there were none which meant more to me than your thoughtful letter of March 19.

"It is a privilege to be working along with someone like yourself to achieve the important objective of guaranteeing equal opportunity for all Americans, and your expression of approval will be a constant source of strength and encouragement to me."

Though a member of HUAC when Robinson appeared before it in 1949, Nixon was not present for the hearing. The two men apparently met for the first time when Robinson was introduced to him (or vice versa) at the 1952 Republican National Convention in Chicago. A Republican delegate to the convention, Harrison McCall, remembered the meeting—in the lobby of the hotel where the California delegation was staying. McCall spotted Robinson standing in another part of the lobby and asked Nixon if he would like to meet him.

"Nixon replied," McCall said, "that he would very much like to meet Robinson. . . . After the introduction, Nixon remarked to Robinson, 'I notice you got a home run again today.' Robinson replied with his eyes sparkling, 'Yes, I had pretty good luck.' Then Nixon commented, 'Jackie, I remember very well the first time I ever saw you.' Robinson inquired as to when that was. Nixon replied, 'When you were playing football for UCLA in a game against Oregon.' Nixon then proceeded to describe an unusual play which occurred in that game, and Jackie Robinson recalled immediately the play Nixon referred to, even though it had occurred several years before, and proceeded to explain to Nixon the reason back of the play. I said to Nixon as we walked away that, while Robinson had undoubtedly met a lot of notables during his career, nevertheless I was sure there was one person he would never forget."

When Robinson wrote to Nixon after his African trip, he was counting on Nixon's not forgetting him, either. Robinson saw his task then as a balancing act, using his prestige and the example of his career to "open doors" for the NAACP and other civil rights groups, while at the same time building bridges to the white establishment—to politicians like Richard Nixon—who would be so necessary for success.

In this, he was not terribly different in what he thought than Martin Luther King in 1957—only he was in a better position to bring it off.

Because the Freedom Fund tour was so successful, it was extended into the summer and the fall. Wherever he went, Robinson's impassioned plea was for action and cooperation. Before a crowd of NAACP chapter members in Chicago in July, he stirred his followers with a rousing call for involvement and activism:

"Recently we have heard from many quarters expressions of concern that the NAACP, and the Negro generally, are going too fast," he said, citing the violence that had erupted around the attempt of a black woman to enroll at an all-white Alabama university the year before. "Apparently this frightened many Americans for, from many quarters, we heard the cry: 'You are going too fast—slow down—moderate—be more gradual.' I am sure, from Authorine Lucy's viewpoint, waiting four years . . . was a sufficiently long time to wait.

"Since the Reconstruction period almost one hundred years ago, not one single piece of civil rights legislation has been enacted by our congress. Now we have a bill pending before the Senate. All it does, in effect, is to ensure that Negro citizens shall be protected in exercising the rights and privileges guaranteed by the Constitution.

"We have waited almost one hundred years for these rights. . . . In my view, now is the time for Negroes to ask for all of the rights which are theirs. . . . It seems to me that all my life I have heard these cries for patience."

At the same time that he seemed to be calling for a charge to the barricades, he carefully pointed the way back to the center. And, specifically, he appealed to the establishment figure he knew, and the one he believed had shown more sensitivity to civil rights issues than other white politicians of his time—Richard Nixon.

He called on Nixon and others in high office to "state boldly their condemnation of violence and their belief in equality of opportunity. . . . Vice President Nixon, [White House adviser] Sherman Adams, and other leading American statesmen have recently made statements that are encouraging. . . . But I say, now is the time for them to speak out even more strongly. . . . Now is the time for those white Americans who are sensitive to discrimination and prejudice to take their stand side by side with the National Association for the Advancement of Colored People.''

Robinson's belief that he could pursue an opening with a politician like Nixon, an archenemy of liberals, may seem hopelessly naive today. But in the absence of perfect twenty-twenty hindsight, it is fair to ask if it was really so simpleminded for Robinson to draw on what he had already learned from experience. In that same Chicago speech, Robinson directly referred to that other anticommunist, conservative wheeler-dealer he had done business with—Branch Rickey.

''We can make progress,'' Robinson said, ''if our national leadership, of both major political parties, once decides that it should and must be made. When Mr. Branch Rickey decided that now was the time for organized baseball to admit Negro players, the change was so rapid that few of us today can even name all the Negro players in organized baseball. Certainly if such revolutionary change can be brought about in baseball, it can also be brought about in education, in transportation, and any other area of our American life.''

In August, only weeks after that Chicago speech, Congress passed the first piece of civil rights legislation in almost one hundred years. A weak bill, it provided for a civil rights commission and gave the Justice Department the right to file voter-discrimination suits, but it was a bill. Robinson and Nixon exchanged letters over the watering down of the bill in the Senate, with Nixon promising Robinson in early August ''that I shall continue to do everything I can to see that a more effective bill . . . is eventually passed.'' Weeks after that, in a more significant development, President Eisenhower ordered federal troops to Little Rock, Arkansas, to prevent interference with the integration of Central High School. For days the news was dominated by stories and images of federal troops, on orders from the president, defending the constitutional right to an integrated education. The partnership that Robinson believed in seemed, however hesitantly, to be emerging.

Robinson meanwhile kept up the pressure from his end through his contact with Vice President Nixon.

When Attorney General William P. Rogers, late in the year, declared that the administration would press for no further action on civil rights, Robinson fired off another letter to Nixon, acknowledging that though he had been impressed with the positions Nixon had taken in the past, the present was what counted. Robinson carefully reminded Nixon that he was "neither a Republican or a Democrat" and that, for a time, he had thought "the Republicans were doing the things that would enable me in good conscience to say they are for me." Rogers's remarks, Robinson stressed, put all that into jeopardy. Nixon replied at length, pointing out that Rogers's position did not represent an abandonment of the government's commitment to civil rights, only a realistic assessment of Congress. "All great movements of reform started slowly and encountered bitter opposition," Nixon wrote, but "they soon gathered an irresistible momentum and gained rapid acceptance. I fervently believe this will be the case in the battle for equal rights."

While it would be a mistake to either downplay or inflate Robinson's early relationship with Nixon, it would be just as mistaken to interpret the relationship as signaling some failure of understanding or commitment on Robinson's part. While he clearly believed in the importance of locating the governmental equivalent of a Branch Rickey, Robinson was unwavering in his belief in fighting at the grassroots level.

At the annual convention of the NAACP in Detroit, Robinson gave an eloquent closing address on the need for sacrifice. Everyone needed to give up something if the struggle was to succeed. Sacrifice was as old as history; sometimes it was grain, sometimes animals, sometimes even human life—but only by a willingness to surrender something of great value could results of great value be brought about.

The NAACP was at that time engaged in an internal struggle over how to spread its resources, particularly whether to fund the most volatile and uncertain civil rights projects—voter registration drives in the South. The newly formed Southern Christian Leadership Conference was winning converts and contributors with its fledgling efforts. The NAACP, on the other hand, refused to ally itself with the SCLC, saying that it did not have the resources to spend on questionable projects. Robinson stepped into the middle of this battle, suggesting that sacrifice also applied to his own organization.

"There are literally dozens of vital projects which the NAACP needs to be engaged in, to speed up the progress we are so proud of," he told the delegates, "but they have to shake their heads regretfully and say: 'Maybe we can do something along that line next year if we get the money for it.'

"It took more money to fight the school desegregation cases. . . . More money was needed, more money was sought, and somehow more money was gotten. You know what that money bought—nothing but the deathblow to legal jim crow in the United States of America. It was worth it, wasn't it? Anyone who sacrificed to help bring it about will tell you it was worth it a thousand times over! But you haven't sacrificed unless you've parted with something you will miss."

In December of that year, Robinson appeared on a Sunday religious talk show on the Mutual Broadcasting System. He knew that the larger audience listening to him—as well as the person interviewing him—wanted to hear something about his baseball past, so he talked briefly about the way his career was an example of how people of different faiths and backgrounds could learn to work together. But he revealed far more in this interview than people may have been listening for. He talked openly about his relationship with Vice President Nixon and what he hoped might come of it. Nixon was a man of power, a person in position to do something—and he had taken the pains, as other white politicians had not, to see how others lived.

"I have talked with the vice president about this very same thing," Robinson said, "and the thing that impressed me was when he said to me that people believe his change came about when he visited Ghana, but he said that he had the opportunity of going to India a few years ago. He was the only white man visiting there at that time, and he observed the attitudes of these colored people. He observed the way that they handled all types of situations. And he said he then went to Ghana and had this very same reaction and relationship being the only white man there. . . . He said that the thing that would really solve our problems would be that if each [senator and congressman] had the same opportunity of visiting these countries and seeing how colored people throughout the world worked and developed."

Never mind that Nixon (and apparently Jackie Robinson) was unaware that a white man was never a lonely Caucasian in India, or that Nixon might have had more than brotherhood in mind in pushing good relations in the third world; the sentiment was clear and its import significant. Times really were changing. The incredible years of Rob-

265

inson's own life were evidence that the most unlikely people could help bring about change.

Sitting there in that radio studio, Robinson said something even more revealing than his remarks about Nixon. He talked about his relationship with Karl Downs, the late minister, who had been so important to him in his youth. And then his mother. These two people had been the central influences in his life. His mother remained as close to him as anyone. Recently, he said, he had written her a letter.

"I wrote her," he said, "that I just have a feeling that there's something that I have to do—and I don't know what it is."

He might have felt the same way when he signed his first baseball contract, only now he was talking about his role in the most important social movement of the twentieth century.

CHAPTER THIRTY-ONE

Robinson's commitment to the NAACP led to his being voted onto its National Board of Directors at the end of 1957. In early January 1958, Roy Wilkins notified Robinson of his election, informing him of the seasonal nature of the board's policy meetings (four times a year, three of which the organization would provide rail fare for if the meeting was farther than one hundred miles from home). For Robinson's "guidance and benefit," he also enclosed a copy of the board's constitution, which said, in effect, that the executive secretary (Roy Wilkins) ran the ship.

Robinson was honored but not taken in by the election. Until the mid-sixties, he attended most meetings, absorbing as much as he could about NAACP policy and programs. But from the start, his sympathies and ultimately his commitments were not really to the organization but to the fight—as he saw it.

At almost the same time Robinson was being named to the NAACP board, he received another letter from Mississippi, from Medgar Evers, the field secretary in Jackson. Evers was hoping that Robinson could help with fund-raising by personally contacting different people whose names he enclosed. He also informed Robinson that February 16, 1958, was going to be designated "Jackie Robinson Day" by state NAACP chapters. Evers hoped that Robinson would attend a state meeting then as their honored guest.

But, Evers warned, whatever Robinson did, even if he chose only to write letters, there were dangers to take into account. "In corresponding with any of the individuals [named in the letter]," Evers said, "do not have N.A.A.C.P. on any part of the envelope. It is all right to be contained in the letter."

Robinson wrote the fund-raising letters, and he also turned up in Jackson. On February 16, he spoke for some length at the Masonic temple, which was ringed outside by hostile whites and state and local police.

"We wish the hearts of all men were filled with goodwill for their fellow human beings, but this goal is beyond our reach and we cannot wait until men's hearts are changed to enjoy our constitutional rights,'' he said, as much to those outside the hall as inside.

"The other night *Monitor,* a network radio program, broadcast an interview with a Klan spokesman who claimed to be a minister. This Klan spokesman said that he had two children and would not permit them to go to an integrated school. When asked what he would do about it, he said he had two guns, ammunition, and enough money to buy more guns. When asked if he was threatening violence, he said he hoped not, but many white southerners would die to protect their southern way of life.''

Robinson's message to this all-encompassing figure of regional terror was to stand aside. He exhorted his listeners to action, before action was popular in Mississippi. But the call was carefully modulated, in keeping with NAACP policy and with Robinson's own sense of what people living in the area were up against.

"I sincerely hope none of us stoops to the level of this type of person,'' he said. ''We may not be able to enjoy our full constitutional rights, but certainly our pride in our country is so great we will not get into the mud with this kind of an American whose violent expressions are reported around the world. We must press for our rights, but we must do it with legal pressures and by showing everyone we believe the Constitution was written for all of us and we do not intend to stop until we secure our . . . rights. This is all we ask for.''

Though Robinson skirted the issue entirely, his words highlighted a yet-to-be-defined difference between the NAACP and the SCLC. The NAACP, under Wilkins's leadership, was committed to working within the legal system. Dr. King's leadership of the victorious Montgomery bus boycott had opened the possibility of success through extralegal, nonviolent resistance.

Even though Robinson was delivering the party line, he still carried his own message. For those risking life and limb in Mississippi, he again reached for his ace in the hole. The vice president of the United States, he pointed out, was now on record supporting "necessary steps which will assure orderly progress toward elimination of discrimination" in the country.

People must not be discouraged, he said. The big question then was not a division over tactics within the movement, but a willingness to stand and be counted under the direst pressure. He finished his speech by recalling a story Branch Rickey had told him when he first signed. Rickey had received an avalanche of hate mail, but instead of succumbing to pessimism, the Dodger owner said he was reminded of an old couple on a train going up the side of a mountain. For a while the view from their seat was that beyond the mountaintop there was nothing—and the couple was frightened. "It appeared as if the train would go right over the precipice to their death," Robinson said, retelling Rickey's story, "[but] instead of going over . . . the train followed the curve of the track around the mountain and down the other side."

From the time he had volunteered to work with the Harlem YMCA, Robinson had a particular interest in young people. They were the ones most capable of change, most likely to be influenced by who he was and what he had to say.

During the fall of 1958, after President Eisenhower had turned down a request by civil rights leaders to convene a conference on the problems associated with integrating schools, Robinson was one of the principal participants in a "Youth March for Integrated Schools" in Washington, sponsored by a coalition of civil rights groups, including the NAACP and the SCLC. The march had an additional sense of urgency because a month earlier, a deranged woman had made an attempt on the life of Dr. King, stabbing him in the chest while he was autographing books at Blumstein's, a Harlem department store. King's condition, which seemed to change from week to week, was a a brooding reminder of how vulnerable anyone was who was willing to stand up and be counted in the fight for equal rights.

All through 1958 and into 1959, Robinson was at the zenith of his power. He had made the transition from the playing field to civilian life as adroitly as turning a double play. He was simultaneously a fighter for civil rights and a man in a gray flannel suit, as much a symbol of opportunity as he had been in baseball. His highly visible job still left him with time for other interests. He might have wondered why William Black found it so easy to have him take time off, whether it was on an extended speaking tour or, occasionally, for personal reasons—for an afternoon at a golf course or a day at the track. But he did not. It all seemed to fit Robinson's unique public aura. Wherever he went, he stood for something, whether it was for equal rights or just Chock Full o'Nuts.

Nineteen fifty-nine undoubtedly was a pivotal year for Robinson.

Because his public standing was so high, he was, whether he saw himself that way or not, a *leader* or at least a potential leader. In that year, Robinson not only continued speaking on behalf of the NAACP, he also became a newspaper columnist for the *New York Post,* then the most influential liberal daily in the United States. Robinson now had a forum in print three times a week to go along with a weekly radio show he had on WRCA. And though his column was placed in the sports pages, it was always intended to be about whatever was on Jackie Robinson's mind—which, invariably, was about the fight for equal rights.

The column provided an opportunity to speak to the top, to go right over the heads of those who blocked progress to those who could make a difference. "I intend to talk about everything that interests me," Robinson said, introducing his column. "Like politicians, for instance, who do things simply because it is expedient for them, but not helpful to the people of the country.

"Take two of the Presidential hopefuls, as an example." Robinson especially targeted Nelson Rockefeller and John F. Kennedy, the hottest presidential prospects in the two major political parties. He knew they would be looking for minority support, which, in turn, meant they would be paying special attention to what Robinson had to say.

He was wary of both candidates. He had heard Winthrop Rockefeller give a speech that made him doubt that Nelson could be seriously committed to civil rights. His criticism of Rockefeller, then governor of New York, was ironic—because of the relationship the men later developed.

"Rockefeller spoke up in Harlem and he promised to do everything he could for the Metcalf-Baker [fair housing] Bill," Robinson wrote. "But once he got elected he said he had to wait and see how the Brown-Sharkey-Isaacs Law worked out in New York City."

Kennedy seemed even less trustworthy. "I wonder what is [Kennedy's] real position on civil rights. He said one thing in New York and another thing to the Southern Governors when he addressed them in Jackson, Mississippi."

The focus of Robinson's column was unmistakable. Late in April, a mob of hooded men had broken into a jailhouse in Mississippi and dragged off a prisoner named Mack Charles Parker. Parker had been accused of raping a white woman, and in Mississippi that was a prelude to summary execution without the inconvenience of a trial. Parker's mutilated body was found floating in a local river days later—after Martin Luther King had fired off a telegram to Attorney General Rogers, demanding immediate federal involvement in the case.

Robinson used his column not to ask for help so much as to remind readers that politicians as well as mobs were responsible, and that what justice demanded, above all, was a political response from those in power.

"The lynching of Mack Parker is but the end result of all the shouts of defiance by Southern legislatures," Robinson said, "all the open incitement to disobey the law by Southern governors, and all the weak-kneed gradualism of those entrusted with enforcing and protecting civil rights."

Robinson was once again aligning himself with Martin Luther King and the Southern Christian Leadership Conference. This column, like most others he wrote, was not cleared in advance with the leadership of the NAACP. In addition, Robinson's ghostwriter for all his columns (though anything written was scrupulously reviewed and corrected by Robinson) was Al Duckett, who was also the ghostwriter for Dr. King's first autobiography and later helped draft the "I Have a Dream" speech.

Robinson went after local as well as national politicians. He stressed the importance of issues like housing and education. In a number of columns he emphasized the problems of drugs and youth violence, which he saw as threats that went beyond the inner cities.

But Robinson's position, as prominent as it was, was not an ideal one for leadership. His background and training left him, even with all his strong opinions, doubtful about his ability to lead others. He didn't try to do that; he didn't jockey for political position within the NAACP or any other organization. But politics intrigued him—to the point of his admitting to a friend, Jack Gordon, that the notion of running for office was appealing. Yet he was always mindful of constraints.

Instead, as a businessman and a famous person, he placed his celebrity at the disposal of a cause he believed in. As much as William Black had seemed content to have Robinson in his employ for public relations purposes (and to keep a buffer between him and his employees), Robinson was committed to making a go of it in the business world. His lifestyle and his financial obligations demanded much from him. Private school tuition for his children continued to be costly. His wife had returned to college, taking classes toward a master's degree at NYU in psychiatric nursing. Hefty mortgage payments had to be met on the home in North Stamford.

And then there was Robinson's diabetes, which, since his playing days, had never been brought under control. His weight and the tiring pace of his life both contributed to a general worsening of his condition.

When he retired from baseball in 1957, Robinson's right knee had become so badly swollen that on at least one day he was unable to get out of bed. His chronic knee problem, which he had always assumed was related to a football injury, was far more complicated.

Robinson's sister, Willa Mae, reported that "in the first week or two after he got out of baseball, he had to go having shots and all. He went into a diabetic coma and was in it for two weeks and more."

Jack Gordon remembers visiting Robinson in a hospital in New Rochelle once in these early years after his retirement. The problem, ostensibly, was his knee, but that was significantly related to a general circulatory disorder caused by his diabetes.

"We went up to see him this one time and we stayed awhile till Rachel came, and she asked how long we'd been there and I told her, then we left," Gordon said. "The next day, I spoke to her to find out how Jack was doing, and she said, 'You know, he lay there in bed after you left and wanted to know why Jack and Rudi [Gordon's wife] hadn't been by to visit him.' So all the time we were there, he was out of it."

Wyatt Tee Walker, the principal aide to Dr. King and also a friend of Robinson's, understood the balance of forces in Robinson's emerging life after baseball in a most pointed way. Jackie Robinson was, he said, for all the tremendous appeal he had for so many people, a person who for one or many reasons was not able to step up and be a leader. "There's a difference between being a spokesman and being a leader—and Jackie Robinson, for all that he had accomplished, was a spokesman."

But in 1960, with a presidential election looming, Jackie Robinson had a role to play, health permitting, that went far beyond words.

CHAPTER THIRTY-TWO

Nineteen sixty saw a spate of lunch-counter demonstrations and other sit-ins all across the South. At the beginning of February, four students from North Carolina A&T College were arrested in Greensboro, North Carolina for sitting in at a dime store. Within two weeks, thousands of others were involved. The movement spread to fifteen southern cities in five states, launching the decade of protest that was to follow. Civil rights leaders were, at the time, as astonished and perplexed as the rest of the country.

The students proceeded without leadership or organizations. They dramatized the evils of segregation as forcefully as they could, using nonviolent means. Not only were they prepared to be arrested, they intended to use jail as an organizing tool. They denied that they were violating the law when the law was segregation. When they were imprisoned, they refused to accept bail; to do so would be to acknowledge the legitimacy of the charges against them.

Instead, the jailed students secretly sent out a delegation asking for support—not to Martin Luther King or Roy Wilkins, who were too cautious and "political," but to Jackie Robinson. The late Marian Logan, a longtime supporter of civil rights causes and an eventual board member of the SCLC, remembers the students arriving at her house, asking for Jackie Robinson.

"That was really how Jack and I got together," she said, "because he started out trying to support those sit-in kids. This was before Martin was in it, you see. SNCC got very mad because Martin was slow to involve himself. These kids who were in jail, refusing bail, finally agreed to get one guy out and sent him up north with some of them on the outside. So they came to New York. They said, let's go to New York and we'll see Jackie Robinson. He was a hero of theirs, and they called him up—and then Jack called me. He told me the North Carolina sit-in kids were in town and that they wanted to get together—and I said, 'Oh, that's lovely, where are they?' He said, 'Can I tell them to come over to your house?' I said sure."

By the time the students arrived, Logan had contacted her husband,

Dr. Arthur Logan, and had him bring home sandwiches and soft drinks from a local deli.

"We sat around on the floor and ate and drank, and then they started singing songs they had made up in jail, about anything and everything that had happened to them. It was so charming . . . so Jack says, 'What can we do to help you?' That's how it started."

Robinson improvised a fund-raising campaign for the students. "We each contacted ten people for ten dollars and had them contact ten people for ten dollars or books and chocolates and cigarettes or whatever," recalled Logan. "And it worked. Before the day was over we had so many people you wouldn't believe it. We had people calling up mad, saying, 'How come you didn't call me?' Within a couple of days, we had over twenty thousand dollars. Jack laughed at me when I said, 'What do we do with all that?' He said, 'You'll know what to do with it!' "

Robinson and Logan weren't finished. "Arthur and Rachel said Jack and I committed sins together," Logan said with a laugh. In this case, the sin was contacting as many celebrity musicians as they knew —Ella Fitzgerald, Duke Ellington, Joe Williams, Sarah Vaughan, Carmen McRae—and persuading them "to do something for nothing."

They gave a benefit concert for the students on the lawn of Robinson's home in North Stamford. The concert marked the birth of the now well-established, annual Afternoon of Jazz, which years ago outgrew the boundaries of anyone's private lawn but still has as its purpose the raising of funds for designated causes.

But 1960 was also a presidential election year, and Robinson's interest in who would eventually reach the White House was as intense as his interest in the unfolding protest movement.

Toward the end of March, as the student protests in the South became a national story, former president Truman heatedly condemned the sit-in students and the civil rights groups, including the NAACP, that supported or condoned them. Truman said that no one had a right to interfere with a legitimate business, that if anyone sat in at a lunch counter he owned, he'd "throw them out."

Robinson blasted Truman in his March 25 *New York Post* column. He pointed out that it was management that chose to close down business rather than serve Negroes, and that Truman was "pathetic" in taking the stand he did.

"This corner can only point out that progress will not wait upon Harry Truman or anyone else. Our young people refuse to be contented with even Truman's patronizing gradualism. And it is exceedingly pathetic to hear a former President declare that he would resort to violence to oppose children peacefully asking to buy ice cream at a soda fountain."

At the same time, in the same column, Robinson released to his readers one of a number of letters in his possession written by jailed North Carolina students, to show the world the obvious sense of justice behind the movement. The letter he chose, which described details of everyday life in detention, included a specific reference to Martin Luther King.

"We are all very happy that we are able to do this to help our city, state and nation," wrote Patricia Stephens. "We strongly believe that Martin Luther King was right when he said, 'We've got to fill the jails in order to win our equal rights.' "

Days later, Dr. King appeared on the NBC television program *Meet the Press*. King too singled out Harry Truman for special condemnation as he carefully made the argument for the students' right to protest nonviolently to change an unjust system.

Robinson, in turn, devoted one of his next columns to Dr. King, still a controversial figure to much of white America. Robinson had known King personally for some time and had been a supporter all along. In the column, he praised King's tremendous personal dignity and the clarity he demonstrated in explaining why segregation was destructive for *both* whites and blacks.

In these early spring months, the presidential candidates were uneasy over whom the various civil rights leaders would support in the primaries and general election. The candidates all collected thick clipping files on the leaders—especially on King and Robinson.

On the surface, King and Robinson followed very different paths through the campaign. History has seemingly divided these men by party, ideology, and temperament. But history, in this case, is more a maze with teasing dead ends than a set of well-marked entrances and exits.

Robinson's path, featuring a breathtaking hairpin curve, is, oddly, an easier one to follow. Robinson began by coming out for Hubert Humphrey, the choice of many liberals, in the Democratic primaries.

Robinson's support for Humphrey coincided with the outbreak of student sit-ins in North Carolina—and with his own prior commitment to the protesters.

In the second week of February, he let Humprey know through a mutual acquaintance that he was willing to work for him. On February 16, Humphrey wrote Robinson, "I am honored with your willingness to work with us and pleased with your approval of my work." Humphrey added that he had personally contacted William Black, a long-time supporter, to make sure that Robinson could have time off to campaign—a request gladly granted, along with a $5,000 campaign contribution.

Robinson labored extensively for Humphrey. The Minnesota Democrat faced long odds against the better-financed John F. Kennedy, but Humphrey's strategy was to make maximum use of his labor and civil rights support. In Wisconsin, Robinson made numerous appearances, campaigning heavily in black areas of Milwaukee and other cities. The managers of the Kennedy campaign regarded Robinson as a distinct threat, but their thinking about him demonstrated either cynicism or a patronizing attitude toward minority voters.

Joseph Timilty, a key Kennedy aide, in a letter to Lawrence F. O'Brien (later White House chief of staff), recalled how the campaign decided to counter any impact Robinson might have in black districts:

> *You will recall that during the Wisconsin Primary Campaign we needed the services of some colored ball players to offset Jackie Robinson who appeared for Humphries [sic]. At the suggestion of the Ambassador [Joseph P. Kennedy], I consulted Duffy Lewis and obtained the services of the following players, who made personal appearances and speeches for us:*
>
> > *Lou [sic] Burdette*
> > *Hank Aaron*
> > *Bill Bruton*
>
> *I received a letter from Duffy asking if I could have autographed photos of the President, for each of the players . . . [in] Florida.*

Kennedy's victory over Humphrey in Wisconsin and then, most decisively, in West Virginia, sealed the Democratic nomination, but it also made Robinson's position in the upcoming campaign more intriguing. With Humphrey out of the race, his support might have been expected to go to Kennedy—or even to Adlai Stevenson, the other favorite of most white supporters of civil rights causes.

But even before Robinson publicly disclosed his preference, the Kennedy campaign knew that he was likely to throw his support to Richard Nixon, the conservative Republican.

Robinson's feeling for Kennedy was cool from the start. At an NAACP dinner late that winter, he refused to be photographed with JFK. There was consternation among the Kennedy people, who told the candidate that Robinson was really a Republican, although that didn't explain Robinson's enthusiasm for Humphrey. One Kennedy aide, Belford Lawson, patronizingly explained that Robinson's opposition to Kennedy was on the basis of philosophy, "which philosophy he didn't understand. You see, Kennedy was a reading man," Lawson said, "and you'd had to read to keep up with Kennedy. This was true of all people. If you didn't read, you didn't know what he was talking about and what he believed."

Nevertheless, Kennedy courted Robinson as if losing him might cost him the election. In a May 16 column in the *Post,* Robinson reiterated his support for Humphrey, but suggested that if the Democrats wound up with a candidate weak on civil rights, he might switch his support to Nixon—someone whose sensitivities on matters of race he had noted in the past.

Kennedy became so disturbed over the prospect of Robinson supporting Nixon that he paid a secret, late-night visit to the singer and activist Harry Belafonte in New York, to see what could be done to turn things around. He hoped that Belafonte, though a Stevenson supporter, might eventually be willing to help organize an offsetting group of prominent blacks for Kennedy to counter any move to the Republicans by Robinson.

Belafonte ultimately told Kennedy that he would do anything he could to see that Nixon was defeated, but when Kennedy pressed him to explain why someone like Jackie Robinson might back Nixon, Belafonte had no answer. He suggested to Kennedy that he forget prominent people like Jackie Robinson or Harry Belafonte and instead try to win the support of Martin Luther King. According to Taylor Branch, Kennedy then asked, "Why do you see him as so important? What can he do?"

David Falkner

Kennedy apparently did not perceive that King, little known outside civil rights circles and facing trumped-up state income tax evasion charges, might ultimately mean more to black voters than any celebrity. Kennedy (and perhaps Belafonte too) might have missed the real reason for Robinson's threatened switch to Nixon.

In the first place, the Kennedy camp was wrong in assuming Robinson was simply a Republican. True, he had ties to some black Republicans including Sandy Ray—the influential Brooklyn minister who had provided counsel and comfort during the time of Robinson's HUAC appearance—and more distantly to Alvin Stokes, who was still on the scene, actively campaigning for and in communication with Richard Nixon, his old friend from the committee. But Robinson's looming switch to the Republicans had a much simpler explanation.

He was asked to do it.

During the primary campaign, as the conventions approached, correspondence flew back and forth between Robinson and the Nixon and Kennedy camps. Kennedy wrote Robinson a long, defensive open letter, saying that he was not a weak but a strong supporter of civil rights and that his vote to dilute a section of the 1957 civil rights bill was on the advice of constitutional "experts" who urged him to uphold fundamental commitments to civil liberties. Robinson eventually sat down with Kennedy, but came away from the encounter more mistrustful than ever because he felt Kennedy "couldn't or wouldn't look me straight in the eye."

Nixon's courtship was more like a full-court press. Since their first exchange of letters in early 1957, Nixon had massaged Robinson with every civil-rights-related stroke in his repertoire. Surrogates like Senate Majority Leader Hugh Scott also paid court. Robinson's meeting in Washington with Nixon after the primaries was generally more friendly than his get-together with Kennedy, but he came away with the sense that Nixon was something of an operator who could resort to "cheap tricks" to get what he wanted, and that he had a tendency to be equally enthusiastic about any subject—including civil rights.

At the same time, Robinson was having a series of conversations with Rudolph Thomas, the director of the Harlem Y. Robinson confided in Thomas, as he had on so many other occasions, this time expressing his uncertainty about what role he should play in the upcoming election.

278

Thomas, who was surely not a Republican, contacted a mutual friend, Gardner Taylor, the Brooklyn minister of the huge Concord Baptist Church. Taylor was a lifelong Democrat and, more importantly, closely connected with Martin Luther King Jr. In that fall's other election, for leadership of the National Baptist Convention, Gardner Taylor stood for election and was seen by everyone as a stand-in for King, who was desperately seeking to build a national power base in the black church.

King's choice for president of the United States was a closely guarded secret. In 1956, he had voted Republican. He had met with Nixon following the Ghana trip in 1957 and had been both impressed and wary. He was leery of Kennedy as well. But his position was as pragmatic as either of the presidential candidates; he would not endorse either man, since he was more interested in seeing what both of them might do on behalf of civil rights.

Gardner Taylor understood the dimensions and subtleties of the situation perfectly. In his discussions with Rudolph Thomas, all of the different options were reviewed—and finally, when a decision was made, Taylor made a luncheon date with Robinson.

"I was on the Board of Education then, so I even had a city car at my disposal. We met at the Brass Rail in Manhattan. I remember it so well because Mr. Thomas never let me forget it," Taylor said. "I urged Robinson to support the Republican candidate, Mr. Nixon, in the election. Oh, he knew and I knew very well how he was being put upon by all kinds of people who wanted to use his name. The Kennedy people were after him, the Nixon people were. He was very cagey about that sort of thing. I told Robinson we needed black people on both sides of the contest, in both parties, to insure that progress would be made."

While Taylor nowhere mentioned King as a party to this, he did acknowledge that on at least one occasion he met with Kennedy on King's behalf—to let the senator know that disparaging remarks by Robert Kennedy about Robinson's working to break up unionizing at Chock Full o'Nuts were not welcome. "King shifted the matter over to me to protect his political purity," Taylor said. "I met with Kennedy and we sat in his car near the East River Drive and we talked. I told him that black people did not appreciate the slighting comment that Robert Kennedy made about Jack. Senator Kennedy said this was made in the heat of a political campaign and should not be taken too seriously.''

In any event, in early September, following the Democratic National Convention, Robinson announced his decision to support Nixon in the upcoming election and to campaign actively for him. The decision, without question, proved a watershed in Jackie Robinson's life.

CHAPTER THIRTY-THREE

The endorsement of Nixon had two immediate consequences. The first was that he was given leave, this time without pay, by William Black from his job at Chock Full o'Nuts. The second and more chilling consequence was that he was given "leave" from his duties as a columnist for the *New York Post*. The paper announced both moves on September 8, in a small throwaway story buried on an inside page:

"Jackie Robinson today was on leave of absence without pay from his job as vice president in charge of personnel of the Chock Full o'Nuts Corp. while he campaigns for Vice President Nixon.

"In announcing the leave yesterday, company president William Black said:

" 'It is my belief that a publically-owned company has no right to take sides in a political campaign. An employee of a company, however, has the right to speak out as he sees fit.'

"Robinson said he'd be back at his desk 'when the campaign is over.' He has had the job since 1957.

"Robinson, whose column has appeared in this newspaper three times a week for the past year, is also on leave from the *Post* while working with the Nixon drive."

Robinson rejoined Chock after the election, but never resumed his column for the *Post*. It was not his choice; the day before the election, he received a note from management informing him that he had been fired. The ostensible reason for letting him go, Robinson said, was that management felt his column had been "weak." Robinson was outraged, convinced that the real reason was that his politics were independent, just what the paper had claimed they wanted when they hired him in the first place. "There is a peculiar parallel between some of our great Northern 'liberals' and some of our outstanding Southern liberals," he noted. "Some of the people in both classes share the deep-seated conviction that only their convictions can possibly be the right ones. They both inevitably say the same thing: 'We know the Negro and what is best for him.' " What especially irked Robinson was that a short while before getting his pink slip, he had been the luncheon guest of the paper's editor, Dorothy Schiff, and its executive editor, James Wechsler, and both indicated how pleased they were with the column and with its reception from readers.

The loss of his column, which appeared alongside those of other liberal stalwarts such as Eleanor Roosevelt, deprived Robinson of the opportunity to explain why he had sided with the Republicans and their candidate. The chances are, of course, that no explanation would have sufficed, but the paper's editors were possibly thinking beyond their own readership to the black community—just as Robinson had in making his choice—where support for one candidate or another in a tight election might be crucial.

Robinson's position with Chock Full o'Nuts, though it was there waiting for him after the election, turned out to be another casualty of his decision. William Black, though a businessman, was also an important Democrat. Robinson's support of Nixon obviously did not please him. When Robinson had needed time off to campaign for Humphrey or for the NAACP Freedom Fund, there was no problem; he remained on the payroll, and Black backed him with publicly announced contributions as well. But when Nixon was the beneficiary, Robinson's time off came out at his own expense and with the disingenuous assertion that "publically-owned companies [had] no right to take sides."

Robinson's relationship with Black remained cordial, but it was hardly close. From time to time, Robinson visited Black at his spacious country home in Westchester, playing tennis on the executive's private court. But now Robinson's value to Chock Full o'Nuts was more of a question. The feather in Black's cap was not quite what it had been when Robinson was, in the public mind, simply the Man Who Broke Baseball's Color Barrier.

More than anything, Robinson's decision to support Nixon cost him prestige with the public—and did so without gaining a place for him in the Republican Party or the movement. In liberal political circles, the sense of disenchantment with Robinson was inevitable. But in the black community, the loss was anything but automatic.

For a long while it was not at all clear which candidate black voters would support. Kennedy had been the least liberal of the major Democratic candidates for the nomination, and his commitment to civil rights was anything but convincing. He had had trouble explaining his vote to weaken civil rights legislation not only to Jackie Robinson but to the black community in general. His public meetings with southern governors, an obvious attempt to shore up white support, were widely criticized. Over the years, Richard Nixon had seemed far more sensitive to issues surrounding race. Martin Luther King had praised Nixon in the past while saying little about Kennedy. It was widely known that King's father, "Daddy" King, the powerful Atlanta minister, backed Nixon and, over the years, Republican candidates in general. It was not unusual, even in 1960, for black voters to look more toward the party of Lincoln than to the party of the "solid South."

Robinson himself was there to make sure Nixon came through as advertised. As late as June, he received a letter from the vice president that seemed reassuring:

"I think we agree that henceforth no political party or special interest group can take the American Negro vote 'for granted.' The growing assurance and political sophistication of this group now goes far beyond economic gain; they want and are entitled to the basic freedoms and opportunities to which you referred. . . .

"As I attempted to indicate to you at lunch, I have consistently taken what has been called a strong position on civil rights, not only for the clear-cut moral considerations involved, but for other reasons which reach beyond our nation's borders."

Nixon's pitch was as practical as it could be. The cold war was on, and the United States could not afford to alienate the third world no less to squander the abilities and energies of 17 million American citizens. For Robinson and others in the black community, the risk in supporting Nixon seemed worth taking.

But 1960 was a revolutionary year, and old allegiances dissolved as quickly as patronage at stores hit by sit-ins. The presidential candidates, though they debated the great issues such as America's readiness for war, were well aware of what was taking place in the streets at home. The question was what, if anything, they would say about it.

For much of the campaign, Kennedy and Nixon both contented themselves with generalities about equal rights and support for civil rights legislation. But in October, after tumultuous months of riots, demonstrations, bombings, and shootings throughout the South, Martin Luther King Jr. was arrested as part of a group trying to picket a downtown-Atlanta department store.

The arrest of King touched off concern through political circles at both the local and presidential levels. Concern was converted to near-panic when King, when he was about to be released from jail, was detained by order of a judge in a neighboring county on an old, trumped-up traffic violation. King was transferred to a rural jail and then, in the middle of the night, to a maximum-security prison. Many of his supporters, including Jackie Robinson, feared for his life and tried to intercede with the presidential candidates.

One aide to Senator Kennedy, his brother-in-law Sargent Shriver, managed to persuade him to place a phone call to King's wife, Coretta. Just that. Kennedy called Mrs. King, who was pregnant at the time, and expressed sympathy. When word of that call got out, fear of losing the solid South swept the Kennedy campaign, while backers of Dr. King took heart. Amidst a fury of fence-mending and backdoor negotiating, Robert Kennedy, not wanting a "lynch-law judge" wrecking his brother's campaign, called the local judge who had imprisoned King and persuaded him to reverse himself and have King immediately released.

The intercession of the Kennedy campaign in this case is generally credited with turning the black vote decisively toward the Democrats. Though King himself did not formally endorse Kennedy afterward, his father did, in a well-publicized sermon at the Ebenezer Baptist Church. Kennedy campaign aides correctly reported a "sea change" within the black electorate in the closing days of the campaign.

What is not fully appreciated is that an internal struggle to support King took place in the Republican camp as well. Jackie Robinson led a small group of Nixon advisers who urged but failed to get the candidate to act. Robinson, according to Wyatt Walker, actually placed a call to Nixon on King's behalf, only to be rebuffed.

Nixon's failure to speak out was as calculated as Kennedy's willingness to. Nixon believed he could pick up votes, white votes, in the South, while his past support of civil rights legislation and his trip to Africa would preserve enough black support. Indeed, after Kennedy acted, a number of key black ministers in Atlanta announced their "reendorsement" of Nixon for president.

Robinson, however, was devastated and left politically unprotected. "I was in the behind-the-scenes struggle to persuade Dick Nixon to express his concern for Dr. King," Robinson acknowledged years later, "but apparently his most trusted advisers were counseling him not to rock the racial boat."

Robinson said that "several times during the Nixon campaign, I was on the verge of quitting and denouncing the vice president." He did not—at great cost to his reputation. More than that, because he was committed to the principle of building a base in both political parties, Robinson's efforts did not end with the election. Richard Nixon, in Robinson's mind, was just one flawed individual; he was not the party and he was not the cause.

Almost from the day the last votes in the election were counted, Robinson was looking to build bridges to other candidates. The most logical choice was Nelson Rockefeller, all but a next-door neighbor.

Rockefeller, the liberal governor of New York, was a man with obvious presidential ambitions and the means to pursue them. Robinson, in his 1972 autobiography, says he first met Rockefeller in 1962, "at a public event at which we were both speakers."

But in reality he had known Rockefeller for some time. The two had corresponded occasionally over the years and had met following Nixon's defeat in 1960. Rockefeller's official correspondence suggests that their coming together in the month after the election was at Robinson's behest, looking to get Rockefeller moving as a candidate for 1964.

A December 29, 1960, memo from Rockefeller aide Doris Thompson to the governor reminds him of his meeting two weeks previously with Jackie Robinson on the subject, apparently, of wresting political control of New York City and its huge base of votes from the Democratic machine:

"Mr. Robinson has been contacting people, has a number of them interested—and 'would like to get moving on it' and hopes you won't let it ride. He knows you 'can break this city machine' if you will only do a number of things.

"He says he would like to get moving on it, but can't do anything until he hears from you as to contacts you have made.

"This all sounds very vague to me, but I assume you know what he is talking about in view of your previous discussion."

Robinson's interest in Rockefeller at that point was preliminary and may have been limited to the problem of working locally to break the Democratic Party's stranglehold—and hence its ability to take the black vote for granted—in New York City. But one can speculate about the national dimensions involved—particularly since Robinson soon sought to initiate contacts between Rockefeller, Harlem leaders, and Roy Wilkins.

In a letter dated March 29, 1961, Robinson, joined by others, asked Wilkins to attend a specifically arranged meeting with Rockefeller. The purpose of the meeting, Robinson told Wilkins, was not local. "We believe that from time to time the presence of high governmental officials in the Harlem community for the purpose of engaging in informal discussions concerning matters of mutual interest will hasten the day when the complete equality of all citizens, regardless of race, color or religion, will become a reality."

Wilkins was not about to have Jackie Robinson draw him or the NAACP into a political position easily open to misinterpretation and attack from its principal base of support on the liberal left. Like many others, Wilkins had been appalled by Robinson's backing of Nixon and by his apparent hostility to Kennedy. On one occasion during the 1960 primary campaign, Wilkins had rebuked Robinson for attacking the likely Democratic Party nominee. Robinson had no business placing the NAACP in a position so open to compromise, Wilkins said. Robinson had testily defended himself:

"I have never spoken for the NAACP in regard to Kennedy," he wrote Wilkins. "As an individual I will continue to oppose him as long as he is willing to accept Governor Patterson's [of Alabama] support and will entertain the White Citizens Council."

This time Wilkins handled Robinson differently. His reply to the request to meet with Rockefeller was short, sweet, and subtle. The polite tone could not disguise the message that the leader of the NAACP had more important things to do than meet with an organizing committee of black Republicans for Rockefeller:

Dear Jackie:

I have your note of March 29 about the meeting scheduled with Governor Rockefeller for the afternoon of April 7.

I wish it were possible for me to attend but we are setting up a conference for all day Friday April 7 with some of our leaders from Mississippi in order to plan for intensified activity in that state.

> *Cordially,*
> *Roy*

No one had planned it, intended for it to happen, wished for it, or even believed that it was in anyone's best interest, but Jackie Robinson had become identified with the political rear guard, even though, heart and soul, he was as much a "race man," committed out front to breaking down walls, as he had ever been.

In all the reverses he suffered as a result of that calamitous election campaign, none was more grievous, more ironic, or more misunderstood.

CHAPTER THIRTY-FOUR

Jackie Robinson had caught a wave of history and rode its crest. But as the sixties progressed, he found himself left in the shallows at the time of a tidal wave.

Robinson's decision to back Nixon in 1960 was only one of several reasons for his subsequent slip from favor.

To begin with, the grassroots surge of civil rights activity in the country had a momentum of its own, and it required a very different kind of leadership than had been known in the past. Organizations like the NAACP and the Urban League, which had for years been out front on equal rights, suddenly seemed comatose compared to newer groups like SNCC, CORE, and later the Black Panther Party, and to more radical leaders like Malcolm X, Stokely Carmichael, H. Rap Brown, and Huey Newton. The veil was not so much lifted as torn to shreds, revealing faces and voices unfamiliar to most white Americans. The daily spectacle of sit-ins, demonstrations, and freedom rides, punctuated by mass meetings, freedom songs, and soaring oratory, were unimaginable in the South that Jackie Robinson knew in his years as a ballplayer.

In the North too there were new voices. The struggle for integration, James Baldwin said in a letter to his young nephew James, was not just about equal rights:

"The black man has functioned in the white world as a fixed star, as an immovable pillar: and as he moves out of his place, heaven and earth are shaken to their foundations. You, don't be afraid. I said that it was intended that you should perish in the ghetto, perish by never being allowed to go behind the white man's definitions, by never being allowed to spell your proper name. You have, and many of us have, defeated this intention; and, by a terrible law, a terrible paradox, those innocents who believed that your imprisonment made them safe are losing their grasp of reality."

In reality, Jackie Robinson simply continued, never breaking stride, never looking back. His move from Nixon to Rockefeller was not so much about his being a shifty Republican as about his fulfilling a goal eminently charged with common sense: building a permanent home at the top of both political parties, so that progressive and intelligent decision-making could occur with respect to civil rights. Robinson felt he was marching shoulder to shoulder with Martin Luther King, out front in the demand for real change.

All through 1961, King and the SCLC were engaged in an arduous and largely unsuccessful campaign to desegregate public facilities in Albany, Georgia, and nearby Terrell County. The resistance in Albany was shrewder, harder, and more organized than it had been in Montgomery. Violence was also more widespread. Bombings and shootings resulted. Black churches used for mass rallies or for voter registration efforts were burned to the ground. Robinson, all the while in touch with King, was handpicked by him to head a fund-raising effort to have three of the churches in Terrell County rebuilt. Robinson's efforts were successful, and enough money was raised that King was able to lead a triumphant caravan out of Albany to present one of the ministers with a check for enough to cover the entire cost of rebuilding.

But this engagement in the Albany campaign also cost Robinson with his own organization, which still regarded the SCLC and King with suspicion. All through the Albany campaign, the NAACP stood on the sidelines and carped at King's efforts—even though the consequences of failure there could jeopardize the entire movement.

"Reviews of King's performance in Albany were harsh," wrote Taylor Branch. ". . . The NAACP's Ruby Hurley observed tartly that 'Albany was successful only if the objective was to go to jail.' Slater King concluded that the Albany Movement had spread its demands too broadly, and movement critics compiled a catalog of King's tactical mistakes. The NAACP's *Crisis* magazine was preparing an article by two movement professors at Spelman College, Staughton Lynd and Vincent Harding, which encompassed nearly all of the conflicting criticisms: King's shortcomings as an absentee media star, his failure to rely more heavily on the courts, his insensitivity to local whites, his reluctance to go to jail more frequently, errors in handling the bus strike, and so on."

When it came to Jackie Robinson, Roy Wilkins resented his support for both Richard Nixon and Martin Luther King. Friction between Robinson and Wilkins—and between Robinson and the NAACP—

came to a head in 1962, after the Albany campaign and just after Robinson was elected to baseball's Hall of Fame in his first year of eligibility. The rift was, in a sense, triggered by Robinson's election.

Incredible as it seems, when the vote was to be announced in January, Robinson had his doubts that he would make it. When the votes of the baseball writers were counted, he had been named on 124 of 160 ballots, just over the 75 percent he needed for election. There were columns and stories explaining why the vote was so close—Robinson, after all, had never been a diplomat with the press; he had had one too many quarrels with one too many important people; and his numbers weren't *that* overwhelming: a .311 career average without big power stats or base-stealing totals gave more than enough cover to those who would not or could not acknowledge an achievement that could not be measured in numbers alone.

Robinson was genuinely overwhelmed by the honor. "I feel so strongly and deeply about being a member of the Hall of Fame," he wrote in his brand-new *Amsterdam News* column, "that I almost am at a loss to explain those feelings to readers. . . . I just want to say that if this can happen to a guy whose parents were virtually slaves, a guy from a broken home, a guy whose mother worked as a domestic, from sunup to sundown for a number of years; if this can happen to someone who, in his early years, was a delinquent, and who learned that he had to change his life—then it can happen to you . . . out there who think that life is against you."

Robinson backed up these sentiments by renewing his commitment to the cause in the most timely way he could think of. He decided to use the occasion of a testimonial dinner in his honor to raise money: not for the NAACP, but for Martin Luther King and the SCLC's voter registration project in the South.

Roy Wilkins, invited to be an "honorary chairman" of the event, was furious. Aside from the loss of potential income to the SCLC, Wilkins was especially peeved that Robinson was allowing King's group to take credit for voter registration efforts that in no way matched those of the NAACP. Wilkins wrote to the dinner's organizer, Al Duckett:

"I understand Mr. Robinson's loyalties in this matter, and I am happy to cooperate on that basis. It does seem to us a little strange here that through a publicity technique the impression is being created that the voter registration drive in the South is strictly an SCLC affair.

". . . I mention this . . . to indicate how we must feel when we run into the impression on all sides, created by a type of publicity, that implies that the registration job being done in the South is being executed by the SCLC."

Wilkins's outburst was by no means a solitary expression of sour grapes. Jack Greenberg, the longtime head of the NAACP Legal Defense Fund, wrote dinner chairman Floyd Patterson shortly thereafter:

"Without questioning the worthiness of the purpose of the dinner, I must say it places me in a slightly awkward position in that while I am delighted and honored to pay tribute to Jackie Robinson, and while I admire and applaud the work of Dr. King of the Southern Christian Leadership Conference, I am, to an extent, embarrassed by the fact that this is part of a fund raising appeal for but one of a group of organizations doing identical work in connection with voter registration."

King, on the other hand, though skilled in the art of nonviolence, knew how to skewer a political opponent as well as anyone. Weeks after Wilkins and Greenberg let loose their complaints, King wrote to Wilkins, who in the end knew he could not turn down an honorary post for the dinner.

"Dear Roy," King wrote on May 28, "We did not want too much time to pass before saying to you personally how grateful we are for your enthusiasm in accepting an Honorary Chairmanship for the Hall of Fame Dinner in honor of Jackie Robinson to be held at the Waldorf-Astoria, July 20, 1962. As you already know, Mr. Robinson has graciously agreed that all proceeds from the dinner will be contributed toward our work in the South. You cannot imagine how great a boost this will give our program."

Robinson's standing in the NAACP by this point was uncertain. Though he continued to head efforts like the Freedom Fund drive, his presence on the board had become perfunctory. He missed many meetings. The minutes indicate that on those occasions when he did attend, he had little or nothing to say. This was not because of a lack of interest but because he had come to see, as had a number of the younger members at that time, including Percy Sutton, that the organization was ossified, run from the top by Wilkins and his close aides, who were invariably timid and conservative on matters of policy and involvement.

The quarrel over the dinner was only part of a widening disagreement between Robinson and Wilkins over who and what Robinson represented in the NAACP and in the movement in general.

During the Albany campaign, Robinson's relationship with Nelson Rockefeller had became much stronger. Rockefeller had by then made a concerted effort to back Martin Luther King both personally and organizationally. He had wined and dined King, brought him aboard his private jet, hosted private parties for him. When Jackie Robinson became chairman of the drive to rebuild the burned churches of Terrell County, Rockefeller was the single largest contributor to the campaign, offering a check of $10,000. At Robinson's Hall of Fame Dinner at the Waldorf, Rockefeller aide Hugh Morrow was dispatched to set up a meeting with Wyatt Walker, King's chief of staff, so Rockefeller would be better able to keep abreast of developing issues in the campaign.

King was impressed with Rockefeller. Wyatt Walker believed he was by far the most sensitive of all white politicians on matters of race in the country, and that his sensitivity went beyond political opportunism. "He was genuinely a Christian, I think his commitment was deep in his religious mooring. Look," said Walker, "the philanthropy of that family is interesting. They employed twenty-one public relations specialists to keep their names *out* of the news when they gave, just the opposite of what opportunists do."

Unlike Martin Luther King, who had to preserve a delicate "purity" in relation to any establishment political figure, Robinson was free to do as he pleased. Robinson was already identified as a Republican. If Dr. King was unable to openly align himself with a likely presidential candidate who might best serve the movement, Jackie Robinson could—and in defiance of Roy Wilkins and his lagging leadership of the NAACP.

Robinson used his column in the black press to boost Rockefeller even before his candidacy was out in the open. By early 1962, Rockefeller had written Robinson thanking him for articles praising his administration and its record on civil rights. By midyear, Robinson was "Jackie" to Rockefeller, someone in whom he was willing to share a confidence (or at least its appearance), even someone whose advice he sought. On April 4, 1962, Rockefeller wrote Robinson thanking him for recommending Robert T. Delany to the State Commission on

Human Rights. In June, Rockefeller wrote Robinson at length concerning New York State's participation in the centennial observation of the Emancipation Proclamation. Robinson at the time was the New York State director of the American Negro Emancipation Centennial Authority, one of dozens of honorary, largely ceremonial positions he occupied over the years. Though Rockefeller was only touching base on a formality, he went out of his way to remind Robinson that aside from creating legislation to build a shrine for the state's copy of the Proclamation, his administration, as a matter of "great and historic concern," was committed to equality of opportunity.

Apart from being a dais guest and speaker at Robinson's Hall of Fame Dinner, Rockefeller also joined Robinson and Dr. King at a September dinner commemorating the Emancipation anniversary. A month later, Rockefeller, full of great plans for a state office complex to be built in Harlem, was invited by Robinson to join him for Sunday services at the Antioch Baptist Church on 125th Street. Afterward, the governor was escorted by Robinson on a walking tour along Lexington Avenue. Rockefeller later thanked Robinson for the day in a formal note on October 23.

But Robinson's public connection to the Republican Party and its candidates, while it helped Dr. King, continued to compromise his position within the NAACP. And even more importantly, it solidified the growing impression (something Wilkins, with some small sense of irony, was in a position to criticize) that he was a political conservative, or worse: in the streets and in polite conversation, Jackie Robinson was ever more casually being referred to as an Uncle Tom.

CHAPTER THIRTY-FIVE

The Hall of Fame ceremony took place on Monday, July 23, 1962, on a day perfect in sentiment, though the weather did not cooperate. The view of the world from the steps of the Cooperstown Hall and library was of a small town where baseball's roots could be savored. From the speaker's podium came a testament to the greatness of the game and to its irresistible democratic character. The clouds on the horizon eventually blew up into a storm, wiping out the Hall of Fame exhibition game for that year between the Yankees and the Milwaukee Braves.

But everyone, from those honored to those watching and waiting, knew something about the day's ironies and glories.

One New Yorker, a youngster then, remembers feeling lost when he was crushed against a side door of the museum by crowds of waiting people. Then, suddenly, the door opened, and instead of being trampled underfoot, he was face-to-face with his hero, Jackie Robinson.

"Everything was so gray and dark, I had been pushed to the side, and I had dropped the baseball glove I was carrying," remembered this city resident who wished to remain anonymous. "Jackie Robinson caught my eye, must have seen me slip, and he stopped. Everybody stopped. He bent over and picked me up, asked if I was all right. I said yes, of course. He reached over and handed me my glove. He smiled. I'll never forget that smile as long as I live. I asked him if he would autograph my glove. He did, and went on his way. I have that glove to this day."

In his acceptance speech, Robinson called three people to his side —his mother, his wife, and Branch Rickey, who he said had been like a father to him through the first years of trouble.

But in the award ceremony, which also honored Edd Roush and Bob Feller, it was never mentioned that Feller had originally asked not to share the same platform with Robinson. Likewise, no mention was made of Robinson's continuing unhappiness over baseball's inability to find room for a single black coach, manager, or front-office executive.

As triumphant as his entry into the Hall was, Robinson's energies were being taxed to the utmost. Apart from his continuing everyday labors with Chock Full o'Nuts, his attention was constantly fixed on the unfolding battles in the South. He kept up an extensive schedule of talks, interviews, and personal appearances, and his poor health alarmed those close to him. Anyone who saw him now noticed that his hair had become almost snowy white, that his gait was slower, the bulk of his body more easily recognizable as fat. He had a minor heart attack in this period—not disclosed to the public—which kept him briefly bedridden and which, even more, indicated the alarming toll of the everyday pressures he had endured for so long.

In late 1962, right around the time when he was being feted as a Hall of Famer, Robinson got into a public dispute with a small group of black nationalists who were picketing a newly opened, Jewish-owned Harlem fast-food store. The store, part of a chain, was seen by the nationalists as unfair competition for local black merchants. Pickets outside the new restaurant chanted anti-Semitic slogans, and Robinson came down heavily against the nationalists—though not as heavily as Roy Wilkins, who this time rushed to Robinson's aid with rhetoric that somehow made things worse.

In a telegram to Robinson that was later issued as a press release by the NAACP, Wilkins asserted that "Negroes cannot use the slimy tool of anti-Semitism or indulge in racism, the very tactics against which we cry out when they are employed against us.

"Black dictatorship and religious persecution are as vicious and despicable as white dictatorship and religious persecution.

"The basic battle will not be won by noisemakers and name-callers and race-baiters, but by men and women mature emotionally as well as physically."

The quarrel, however, blew up into something much larger. The owner of the property that had been leased by the steak house was Frank Schiffman, the white owner of the Apollo Theater, Harlem's premier entertainment showcase. Schiffman's son, Bobby, was a golfing companion of Jackie Robinson's, and overnight the issue of picketing the steak house was broadened to include the Apollo Theater and later the Waldorf-Astoria, the site of the Hall of Fame dinner for Robinson.

A local black radio station, WWRL, picked up on the dispute, inviting Robinson and a well-known nationalist spokesman, Lewis Michaux, to debate one evening on a program moderated by host Leon Lewis.

"I've been in a number of heavy debates on radio and television, but never one as free-swinging and as brutally frank as the one with Michaux," Robinson said. "He accused me of taking the white man's side in a black argument. I retorted that it was wrong for any group, of whatever color, to agitate hatred, to use religious prejudice to resolve a dispute. Mr. Michaux labeled me a flunky for whites, and I responded by calling him a bigot."

Some months later, in the early part of 1963, Robinson got into a much nastier public quarrel with Harlem congressman Adam Clayton Powell Jr. Powell, a Democrat, was the most powerful member of the black political establishment and had long been a subtle and skilled intermediary between his constituency and Washington. In Wyatt Walker's opinion, Powell was "the most productive public official in this century for common people." He knew the game, and enjoyed its privileges, as well as anyone, all the while planting himself firmly on the side of civil rights and the revolution it was inspiring from below.

At the juncture where he and Robinson came to loggerheads, Powell, according to biographer Charles Hamilton, was casting around for an issue. He had been eclipsed by fiercer activists. His fiery speeches denouncing segregation paled alongside the actions being taken around the country that had nothing to do with him. As chairman of a powerful House committee, he couldn't openly attack President Kennedy for dragging his feet on civil rights, because to do so, said Hamilton, "was to jeopardize [his standing] by possibly chilling relationships [with the White House]."

Instead, Powell selected "go-slow" groups in the civil rights movement as targets, groups like the NAACP. In a speech in a crowded Baptist church in Washington, Powell said, "The white man has given the Negro just about all he intends to give him. From now on we will win only what we intend to fight for. There is no future for the Negro man except what he fights for. Now this may sound like black nationalism—and maybe it is!"

Following that speech, widely reported in the black press, Powell stood side by side with Malcolm X on an outdoor platform at a Harlem rally and bitterly attacked the NAACP and the Urban League. Powell was no follower of Malcolm, but he knew the time had come to make common cause as far as he was able. "I don't agree with some of the things Malcolm X preaches and he doesn't agree with some of the things I preach," Powell cried. "But one of the things I am very close to agreeing almost completely with is Malcolm X's analysis of our present national Negro organizations."

Whatever problems Robinson had with the direction and leadership of the NAACP, his loyalty to the organization made it impossible for him to turn his cheek at this kind of assault. The NAACP issued its response and Robinson offered one as well. But where a press release from the NAACP got lost in the day's traffic, Robinson's words brought traffic to a halt.

He replied to Powell and incidentally—but far more significantly— to Malcolm X. In an "open letter" to Powell, published in the *Amsterdam News,* Robinson lambasted Powell for his "vicious attacks upon the National Association for the Advancement of Colored People, your intemperate and ill-advised suggestion that the Negro people boycott the NAACP because of the participation in its affairs of white people and your rallying call to the Negro people to support Malcolm X and the Black Muslims."

Robinson leaned on the horn when it came to Malcolm: "You know, also, in spite of the fact that you and I share deep respect for Minister Malcolm X as an individual, that the way pointed by the Black Muslims is not the true way to the solution of the Negro problem. For you are aware—and you have preached for many years— that the answer for the Negro is to be found, not in segregation or in separation, but by his insistence upon moving into his rightful place, the same place as that of any other American within our society."

What Robinson might not have appreciated—or cared about—was what light his criticism of Malcolm placed him in. It was still early in the game, the course of the struggle was far from clear, and someone he felt was an incendiary without a real program might be an obstacle to victory. In the strength of his commitment to integration, which went far beyond any organizational commitments, Robinson knew he stood in the mainstream, shoulder to shoulder with Martin Luther King.

All through the early months of 1963, unfolding events in Birmingham captured national and international headlines. The SCLC's campaign there, initially modest, had been dramatically expanded, largely due to the heavy-handed repression employed by Police Chief Eugene "Bull" Connor, backed up by state forces dispatched by Governor Wallace. Film footage and photographs of police dogs and water cannons exploding into crowds of demonstrators were flashed across the country and around the world.

At the beginning of May, Robinson joined with a white businessman, Noel Marder, in forming a Birmingham fund-raising and support group, Back Our Brothers. Shortly after raising initial sums of money, Robinson decided that he wanted to do more. He later said that watching scenes of police brutality against defenseless people in Birmingham moved him to go to Birmingham himself. On May 12, the motel that King and some SCLC associates were staying in was bombed—as was the home of A. D. King, King's brother. Robinson told his family that he could not stand by any longer, that he wanted to be physically present with King in Birmingham. His children innocently asked if they could accompany him. He told them they could not.

Robinson arranged a spur-of-the-moment trip and was accompanied by his friend Floyd Patterson. When he got to Birmingham, he and Patterson were driven from the airport into town by Wyatt Walker, who seemed nervous about who might be following them. Robinson asked to be shown the bomb damage at the Gaston Motel. When he and Patterson walked around in the rubble-strewn lobby just beneath the quarters where King had been staying, Robinson tightened, the anger in him visible and vocal.

"The people who did this are animals," he told Walker.

Robinson's ultimate destination was a local church, the site of almost daily nighttime rallies organized by the SCLC. The rallies had become larger, more fervent, and more dangerous as police and vigilante repression grew.

Robinson spoke to a packed church with Dr. King at his side. Whatever he had prepared to say, he discarded. His words tumbled out, driven by emotion, by the fury he had been containing through the day:

"When we think about the little kids being tossed from one side of the street to the other by the tremendous force of this hose, when we think about . . . this picture just sickens me, this big brave policeman down here with his knee in the throat of this lady. And the problem of this is that this same picture of the dogs and of this policeman with his knee in the throat of this lady is a picture that's being portrayed throughout the world!"

Robinson's high voice shook with excitement, full of scorn and irony. He praised those who were packed into the church, who had been out on the streets day after day. "Many people in this world, which is made up of four-fifths colored people, are looking at you and admiring your courage. And I want to say to you that just looking at all of you out here, that the inspiration of your togetherness, your actions, your songs, you just don't know what it means to guys who have come down from New York!"

He added, with almost a touch of wistfulness in his voice, "I just wish the same kind of enthusiasm that is shown right here in this church tonight could be shown to Negroes throughout America, because they would have a much deeper, much more sincere desire to get involved in our struggle."

Above all, Robinson was there to support King. Backing this great leader was a moral and emotional choice even before it was a political one—which it also was.

"When we talk like this," Robinson said, "it reminds me of this person who bought this home and who went out in the backyard and started cultivating his yard, and all of a sudden instead of weeds it began to bear vegetables and the flowers began to bloom awfully pretty. And all of a sudden the neighbor came over and said the Lord has been good to you, and the man said, 'Yes, the Lord has been good to me, but you should have seen this field before I tried to plow it.' "

The punch line was anticipated by the crowd, which rose to its feet, applauding and shouting its approval. But the story wasn't finished. "That's what I say to Dr. King," Robinson shouted. "The Lord certainly has been good to you, Dr. King, he has been good to all of us. But before Dr. King came down here and started to inspire people to stand up for their rights, you couldn't sit down and discuss integration. God is certainly wonderful, I certainly put my faith in Him, but in my humble opinion, God helps those who help themselves!"

The cheering that greeted Robinson went beyond paying court to his celebrity. His words were clear and to the point, the message of uplift honed to simple, practical teaching that gave those listening courage for the next day and the day after in the streets and jails.

King and his associates knew that Robinson was as dedicated and constant as any soldier in the ranks. They never questioned the drift of his politics. Where he stood, what he did, who his allies or enemies were in the establishment, were all facets of the same struggle, strands in a single tapestry that they were all creating day by day, improvising as they went along.

If anyone believed that Robinson's commitment to the movement was tempered by his attachment to the Republican Party, they should have paid attention to his response to President Kennedy's televised address on civil rights in June. Kennedy, according to his aides, decided virtually without consultation, even against advice to the contrary, to speak to the nation and the world following events in Birmingham. The decision to go before the cameras was so spontaneous that his speechwriters didn't have time to prepare a complete text. The speech, most historians agree, was the most passionate he ever gave on civil rights.

"Are we to say to the world—and much more importantly, to each other—that this is the land of the free, except for Negroes, that we have no second-class citizens, except Negroes, that we have no class or caste system, no ghettos, no master race, except with respect to Negroes?" Kennedy seemed to understand exactly the terms of the struggle taking place. "We face, therefore, a moral crisis as a country and a people. A great change is at hand, and our task, our obligation, is to make that revolution, that change, peaceful and constructive for all."

King, who just as surely as Jackie Robinson, had mistrusted Kennedy, praised him without restraint. The speech, he wrote, was "one of the most eloquent, profound, and unequivocal pleas for Justice and the Freedom of all men ever made by any President."

Robinson wired Kennedy the very night of the speech, using similar language. "Thank you for emerging as the most forthright President we have ever had and for providing us with the inspired leadership that we so desperately needed."

In his syndicated column in the *Amsterdam News,* Robinson underscored that "as consistent readers of this column know, I have been highly critical of this Administration and its handling of the civil rights issue.

"I must state now that I believe the President has come through

300

with statesmanship, with courage, with wisdom and absolute sincerity.

"Speaking as one person, I can honestly say that Mr. Kennedy has now done everything I hoped he would do."

But even as Kennedy spoke, it was all too clear that what was playing itself out on the streets had a life of its own, beyond the reach of anyone's leadership. On that same June night, Medgar Evers, the NAACP field secretary in Mississippi, was murdered as he stepped from his car outside his home.

The commitment of the Kennedys to finally break the centuries-old deadlock, to use the full power of the federal government to advance the cause, could not change the reality that resistance to that change was deeper and more volatile than anyone could predict. The anger and frustrations produced in reaction to a largely peaceful revolution had such force that they could sweep aside anyone at a moment's notice.

Robinson, as grieved now as he had been elated only days before, wired Kennedy again just before departing for Evers's funeral in Mississippi, demanding that protection for civil rights leaders, especially Martin Luther King, be given by the federal government. He warned of "a holocaust" to follow if King were harmed. He seemed almost desperate in the tone of his prompting.

On August 28, a little more than two months after Evers's murder, more than 250,000 people turned up in Washington to hear Martin Luther King's famous "I Have a Dream" speech, rallying the nation to pass a comprehensive civil rights bill. Hope was in the air as well as in King's words. But like a shadow or a Greek chorus, Malcolm X turned up for the occasion along with every other civil rights leader in the country.

Sometime after the crowds at the Lincoln Memorial began dispersing, Bruce Llewellyn, a well-connected Harlem businessman, was making his way back to his motel. He was accompanied by a cousin, a New York state senator, and by Raymond Jones, the Tammany Hall leader. In the parking garage of the motel, the men were surprised when they encountered Malcolm, who, they had assumed, would have skipped an occasion like the March.

"Malcolm says to us, 'Where have you guys been?' We say, 'We've just come back from the march,' " Llewellyn said. "Then he just smiled slightly. Malcolm says to us, 'You think any of that bullshit is gonna change anything?' "

On September 15, less than a month after the great outpouring, a bomb destroyed the Sixteenth Street Baptist Church in Birmingham, killing four little girls. The explosion of rage and grief that followed could do nothing to change what had happened. Three decades later, it may be clearer that the martyrdom of the children, while never wished for, was foreseen in the wisdom of King's philosophy of nonviolent resistance. However much he admired King and believed in his approach, however, Robinson could not temperamentally begin to accept what had happened.

"Jack and I were the ones Dr. King always joked about, saying we were definitely not nonviolent types—and he was right," Marian Logan said. Robinson immediately set out for Birmingham. "Jack went down there and walked over the rubble of the church," remembered Logan, who accompanied him. "I can see him standing there with his fists shaking, trying to control his fury."

Robinson also set out immediately to organize a fund-raising effort to rebuild the church. In late September, he put together a major street-corner rally in front of the Theresa Hotel on 125th Street. Peter Bailey attended the rally and remembered what happened:

"The person who seemed to have put the rally together was Jackie Robinson. Now, when he broke into baseball, he was my childhood hero, but I kind of forgot about that when he became very hostile to Brother Malcolm, and I switched my allegiance.

"Malcolm X was the first speaker. I guess maybe eight or nine other speakers spoke—including Eartha Kitt, who was at the Apollo Theater at the time—and when it was over, Jackie Robinson thanked everyone for coming. And the crowd started yelling, 'We want Malcolm X.' They kept saying, 'We want Malcolm X,' and they wouldn't leave. And Jackie Robinson kept saying, 'Well, the rally's over and everybody should go home.' And then the crowd started getting really belligerent. And they were jumping on cars and stopping traffic, and Brother Malcolm—who had been kind of leaning up against the Chock Full o'Nuts, which was right there at the bottom of the Hotel Theresa —got up on the platform again and said to the crowd, 'Brothers and sisters, let's don't do this. And we've had it and I think everyone should now go home.' And immediately the crowd just quieted down and moved on out. They just faded away. . . . I had never seen anything like that before.''

Jackie Robinson, who had single-handedly pried open the door to everything that was now taking place, was swept aside as casually as a scrap of old newspaper.

In less than two months, the entire nation would be dealing with the assassination of a president—and the opening of a very different era. For Jackie Robinson, personally and politically, that moment was far more consequential than it was for the millions of others traumatized across the nation.

CHAPTER THIRTY-SIX

On the afternoon of Friday, November 22, 1963, at about the time bullets were slamming into the president of the United States in Dallas, Jackie Robinson was at a local racetrack in New York. Most Americans alive at the time know where they were when they heard news of the assassination; the public moment was a private one too, because of the import of what had happened. Because Jackie Robinson could not go anywhere without being recognized, he had no such private moment. An anonymous reporter came across Robinson at the racetrack and placed him there in his account of the day. William Black, Robinson's employer, either read or heard about the report, confirmed it, and then asked for Robinson's resignation from Chock Full o'Nuts.

The decision to fire Robinson, while seemingly capricious, actually was not. Robinson had long since outlived his usefulness to Black. The job he performed, handling personnel problems, was minor in terms of corporate responsibility; Robinson's position could easily be filled by someone else who was not a public or political figure.

For some time, Robinson's performance at Chock had been wearing on his employers' nerves. Only some of it had to do with his political allegiances. "He was a very decent guy at all times," said Martin Slater, a company vice president at the time. "He was a pleasure to be around because he had no airs whatsoever. Anyone would feel comfortable coming up to him and talking with him." But he also seemed to go out of his way to favor blacks in hiring and firing, said Slater. Another person close to the company, who did not wish to be named, mentioned one case in particular: "There was an employee who urinated in a janitor's sink. He was caught and was sent in to see Jackie Robinson. The door was closed and everybody assumed when it opened again, the guy would walk out as an ex-employee. Instead, he kept his job and, so far as anyone knew, was not even reprimanded."

Whatever Black's racial sensibilities, he also had a compulsive, almost obsessive need for cleanliness. "One of Mr. Black's innovations was that you were never allowed to touch the food; in front of customers you always had to use wax paper," Martin Slater said. "Mr. Black used to make midnight trips to different stores; he'd get up on a chair and run a cloth napkin around on the inside rim of the coffee urns to see that they had been properly cleaned. Old coffee oils can ruin fresh coffee." Whenever Black shook hands with someone, Slater said, "he used to wash his hands immediately afterwards."

It was hard to work for Black, whether someone was a server at a lunch counter or a company president. There were four different presidents in four years at one stretch during those years. Black provided a generous benefits package to his employees along with liberal amounts of time off. "There were not only pension and health plans that were in advance of other companies," Slater said, "but all employees had a full day off with pay on their birthdays. No other companies did that." Perhaps, but in return, loyalty had to be absolute, and policy decisions were never to be questioned.

Robinson's letter of resignation, dated January 27, 1964, expressed regret, cordiality, and gratitude. It was the standard cover, Martin Slater said, for a firing in the business world.

"The decision I must make is a most difficult one, but under the circumstances I have no other choice," Robinson wrote Black. "My seven years at Chock have been most rewarding. I am grateful for the opportunity of knowing you and learning from you things I am certain will be very beneficial to me. I wish the company continued success. If I can be of service to this end, please let me know—I sincerely mean this.

"Because there may be publicity connected with my leaving the Company, I suggest a meeting with you and Burt Watson for the purpose of discussing how [to] handle the official announcement by Chock."

For his part, Robinson had been wanting out of Chock for some time anyway. Friends acknowledged that he had been disturbed for years at having to be the one to "catch flak" for the company's non-union hiring practices. And then the grumbling over his alleged favoritism in handling employee problems had upset him no end.

"Jackie called me one day very disturbed," said Wyatt Tee Walker. "William Black brought somebody in who was supposed to work under Jackie, but who reported directly to Black. He called me and talked to me for a long time—and he was really in pain. What did I think he should do?

"I was so awestruck that Jackie Robinson would call me to get counsel about what he should do. I told him that I would quit . . . that what was happening was an insult to your personhood. It was an odd arrangement. Bill Black wanted Jackie Robinson as a toy, but he did not respect him as a man."

But Robinson, much as he might have wanted to leave, had hung on for economic reasons. He had vainly been looking around for another job. For a while, before the Birmingham campaign heated up, he believed he had something. He had located a wealthy liberal New York businessman, Owen Cummings, and got him interested in a one-stop funeral business—funeral parlor, chapel, religious services, burial arrangements, cemetery, in a single package—in Atlanta, the home of the SCLC. "I found a piece of land where there was a railroad siding that was unused, and I did Jackie up a memo or two about what he should do," said Wyatt Walker. "You get the funeral, you get the plot, you have uniform headstones so you don't have to get involved in any of the complications." Walker, also looking to increase his income, would have been the person in charge in Atlanta, as well as the presiding minister. But the deal fell through, as did a number of other prospects, and when Robinson finally left Chock, he had nothing lined up, only his celebrity—which did not pay the bills.

The absence of a job was as much an internal as an external burden. Much as his pride had kept anyone from seeing that he had been fired, pride also interfered at home when it came to Rachel's career. Her postgraduate studies led to work, and Robinson did not want her to be the family's support and said so. Robinson acknowledges that he was pleased when his wife got her advanced degree in psychiatric nursing, but then, "when she actually began to go to work every day, my annoyance and resentment began to show."

Rachel was not about to give up what it had taken her so many years to earn—nor was she about to minimize the advantages she could now bring to her family in the face of her husband's difficulties.

Robinson's children also were suddenly tilted on that precarious edge where he now found himself. It was as though he had awakened with a start to realize that over the years he had not spent much time at home, that he had devoted himself far more to other people's children than to his own. He came and went more as a force, a power, than as an everyday presence. He says that at the dinner table, Rachel protected him from family quarrels and troubles:

"She remembers my discussions about my daily—and, to me, vital —experiences; they left the children with little to say and made them feel that their activities would seem insignificant in comparison with mine. She felt that [youngest son] David identified with reports about 'how the day had gone,' but that Jackie [Jr.] felt it would be demeaning if he bragged about the fifty cents he had earned doing a school chore for someone when his father had made five hundred dollars."

Just around the time his father lost his job, Jackie junior ran away from home. Robinson says there was no warning, no single precipitating event he could point to. His son had been shifted from school to school, public and private. He had a long history of report-card failures and "troublemaking"—and therapy—which Robinson essentially left for his wife to handle.

Jackie junior, said any number of friends, bore the burden of a name he should never have been given. Under any circumstances, it was hard being the son of a famous man, harder still to bear his name. He was a gifted athlete, said Jackie senior, but his son's gifts made it inevitable that his father, much as he honestly wanted to give him room for his own life, pushed him.

"I remember we were in Connecticut one day and Jack was out on the front lawn with Jackie junior," said Marian Logan. "They were by the batting cage. Jackie was no more than thirteen, fourteen. Jack was so angry because Jackie just didn't want to play. Jack wanted to coach him and Jackie junior just didn't want him to. Jack said to me, 'He's got such good reflexes, he can do this and he can do that,' and I tried to tell him, 'Look, maybe he just doesn't want to.' "

Robinson's friendship with Logan, which involved shared work for Martin Luther King, was unusually close. Logan was one of just a handful of people in whom Robinson was willing to confide. That was true when it came to Jack junior.

"Oh, I told him he should never have named him Jackie Robinson Jr., that it was a terrible thing to do to a child when the father's such a big and famous somebody. And Jackie junior just could do nothing right. And so we'd get into it. Big Jack thought, 'You can hit the ball, you can hit the ball, you're just not trying.' And I'd go into that thing about his maybe not wanting to and he'd cuss me out and tell me, 'That's my son, of course he wants to.' And I'd come back, 'No, *you* want him to.' "

Logan laughed as she remembered.

"Oh, he would fuss with me, we'd fuss. I'd cuss him out and he'd cuss me out. Never cussed in front of the children, never cussed in front of Rachel. She never heard that stuff and I'd tell her, 'I just took him out to the backwoods so he could call me all those names.' Rae would say to me, 'My husband doesn't talk like that!' 'Don't tell me!' I'd say—and we'd laugh, Jack and me."

When Jackie junior ran away from home, both his parents were shocked and bewildered. But the Logans were not surprised—because Jackie junior came to stay with them, on the condition that they not reveal his whereabouts.

In the spring of 1964, Jackie junior resolved some of his immediate problems by joining the army. "He told us that he hoped to pull himself together, get the discipline he knew he needed badly, and establish his own identity," Robinson said. "He was seventeen and he believed all the stories he heard about the opportunity the army gave enlistees to travel."

Within a year, Jackie junior was in Vietnam.

As if his family and employment situations were not stressful enough, Robinson was forced to deal with the festering public quarrel he had been having with Malcolm X. In the period following the Kennedy assassination, and before he too faced a personnel problem of his own when he was "silenced" by Black Muslim leader Elijah Muhammad, Malcolm had responded to the attacks Robinson had been making on him over the past months, especially the "open letter" Robinson had directed to Adam Clayton Powell Jr.

Malcolm fired off an open letter to Robinson, condemning him for a history of selling out to white interests as though all along he had been nothing more than a privileged slave. His great baseball achievement was a sellout to a white boss, Branch Rickey. White bosses had made him kowtow to HUAC, getting him to denounce Paul Robeson, who, Malcolm said, "had these guilty American whites frightened silly." But Malcolm's most pointed barbs had to do with Robinson in the present. He was still selling out to whites, having been alone among black leaders to support Richard Nixon. "Very few Negroes," Malcolm asserted, "were dumb enough to follow your MISLEAD. . . . You never give up. You are now trying to lead Negroes into Nelson Rockefeller's political camp."

To Malcolm, Robinson was weak, shifty, sneaky, and even venal. The real reason Robinson was willing to support Rockefeller, Malcolm wrote, was that the governor was holding out the promise of appointing him boxing commissioner of New York State. "Does this have any bearing on your efforts to get Negroes into Rockefeller's camp? Just who are you playing ball for today, good friend?"

Malcolm's blast made it impossible for Rockefeller to appoint Robinson to any kind of job, an unfortunate development to be sure. Robinson, perhaps more aware than anyone of the trip wire Malcolm had hit, fired back a long and often rambling rebuttal. He was proud of the "white bosses" he had worked for and he had absolutely nothing to apologize for in his present political connections. Yes, he had supported Nixon in 1960—and if he had it to do all over again, he'd do the same.

"As for Governor Rockefeller, I sincerely hope that whatever contribution I can make to his campaign . . . will be meaningful," Robinson said, trapping himself in ways he might later have wished he had not. "I don't know where you went to school, Malcolm. If you attended virtually any Negro college, I venture to say that a Rockefeller helped make your education possible."

Robinson did have a real criticism to make. Malcolm, he said, had asserted that "Negroes . . . are dying for freedom to please the white man." No, Robinson said, "we feel our stake in America is worth fighting for. Whom do you think you are kidding, Malcolm, when you say that Negro leaders ought to be 'thankful' that you were not personally present in Birmingham or Montgomery after racial atrocities had been committed there? The inference seems to be that you would have played some dramatic, avenging role. I don't think you would have.

"I think you would have done exactly what you did after your own Muslim brothers were shot and killed in Los Angeles. You left it to the law to take its course."

This "debate" between two powerful African-American voices was followed avidly in the black press, while it was virtually ignored in the white media. The effect it had on Robinson's public standing is hard to determine, but it seemed to further isolate him at a time when he had to have felt more uncertain than ever about where he was going, what he was doing, and how and where he fit in.

With his son off to the army, with no job in view, Robinson almost inevitably turned to politics—to Republican Party politics. Nineteen sixty-four was again a presidential election year. As much as in 1960, he still believed that the creation of a climate favorable to civil rights in *both* political parties was necessary and worth fighting for.

Control of the Republican Party was a real issue. The Goldwater wing of the party, with its hostile and reactionary views on race, was now a potent force. Regardless of what Malcolm or anyone else said, Nelson Rockefeller was a very different kind of Republican, promising a different kind of leadership on matters of race.

Robinson settled both his immediate employment and political problems by volunteering to work for the Rockefeller campaign. Rockefeller, delighted to have someone as prestigious as Robinson in his camp, immediately offered him a position as an assistant campaign manager, which Robinson accepted with alacrity and gratitude.

CHAPTER THIRTY-SEVEN

Nelson Rockefeller was no Nixon. In fact, he was like no other white politician Robinson had ever met. Something about him went beyond his race, his family, his vast wealth. No doubt Robinson was flattered to have the attention of someone so important, especially at that time, but it was not flattery but the force of Rockefeller's personality that made Robinson and many others believe in the man, believe that his rather ordinary liberal credentials on race were extraordinary.

Percy Sutton, the longtime Democratic Party stalwart, remembers Rockefeller as "a very special man. He was a glad-hander, a level-headed, warm, compassionate rich man, who could get anything he wanted from either house of the legislature because he knew how to bargain with people and how to make them feel good. . . . He came with a sense of royalty about him. When he'd want to convince you of something, he'd invite you up to his estate, he'd say, 'Bring your wife with you.' I'd tell him, 'Governor, there are people down in Harlem who don't like you.' 'Bring 'em all,' he'd say, and he'd laugh and he'd say, 'Come on, you want to do the right thing, don't you?' And there'd be all that lavish food, all of that. How do you say no to a man who gave it all away so easily?"

Evelyn Cunningam, the former special assistant to Rockefeller who served as Jackie Robinson's assistant in the campaign and later, remembered that the force of Rockefeller's personality went far beyond glad-handing. As powerful as he was, he was also vulnerable, and not afraid to show it. At the time Cunningham was hired, she believed her job interview with Rockefeller would be postponed because his son Michael was missing on a wilderness expedition, and because the newspapers were then filled with headline stories about the governor's impending divorce from his first wife, Mary.

"However, the meeting wasn't called off, and I knew in fifteen minutes this man had chosen a total stranger to open up to, to bare his soul to," Cunningham said. "Rockefeller told his secretary, please bring us some tea—and we sat there for three hours. There were no notes to take, it was nothing like that. He told me about his divorce, about Michael, his money, his thoughts about government. I learned about his brothers, the family history. I knew about the money they had poured into schools they created, but I knew nothing about Mary —that she didn't like politics, didn't like being out there shaking hands with people. He didn't use the word *divorce* or *unhappy* but just pointed these things out. He told me Michael was his favorite child, something a parent will almost never say, even though they have those feelings. Told me his brother Mark was the philosopher of the family and that one day he was going to show David how to be a banker. Maybe he confided in me like that because he sensed that I knew something about the family history, but I don't know. I do know that I was very flattered.''

She was also convinced that Rockefeller was sincere in his commitment to civil rights. And in this regard, the commitments he made to individuals, such as Jackie Robinson, carried that same weight of conviction and vulnerability.

"He really made Jackie feel like he was his equal—he was in awe of people like Jackie," Cunningham said, "he considered them far greater achievers than he. . . . Nelson Rockefeller often said, 'Jackie Robinson makes me feel like a human being, because he tells me the truth—most people don't. They tell me what they think I want to hear.' ''

For his part, Robinson was just as sensitive to Rockefeller. "I remember one time that after Jackie was quoted about something in the *New York Times* that he thought might have hurt Rockefeller, he called me up at five o'clock in the morning and said, 'My God, did you see the *Times?*' He was so frightened that he had hurt the governor. My suggestion was that he call him before he got to the office, which is what he did. Jackie said the governor laughed and said, 'Jackie, I've been through so much with the press. This is not important. You and I both know there's no split between us.' And he was right.''

But the closer Robinson got to Rockefeller, the more he was drawn into the whirl of party machinations. Whatever he was as a man, the force of Rockefeller's personality and all his charm went into the building and maintaining of power. He was a Republican, and through him Jackie Robinson's ties to the party became inevitably deeper. Even if he didn't consider himself by philosophy and inclination any more a Republican than a Democrat, he now had a place in a way that he had never had before. He was in a position where others in the party referred back to him, wanting to be on *his* good side.

One day, Evelyn Cunningham remembers, Robinson got a long-distance call at his midtown campaign office—from Barry Goldwater. Goldwater was upset about some especially harsh comments that Robinson had made about him in his column. Goldwater wanted to fly up to New York to meet with him. Would that be all right?

"Jackie told me they made it for breakfast because 'I don't want anybody to see me with him.' But here it was, Goldwater making plans to come all the way up to New York just to meet with Jack— that was something that occurred to him after he hung up," she said.

Robinson did meet Goldwater the next morning for breakfast, only their meeting carried on longer than expected.

"He didn't come back at lunchtime; in fact, he didn't come back to the office and I almost died," Cunningham said. "What happened? The next day, I noticed he was not going to volunteer anything—and I'm mad, very mad at Jackie Robinson then. I said, 'Oh, so what happened at breakfast?' He said, 'You know, Ev, that's not a bad guy. In fact, he and I agree on a lot of things. Not a bad guy.' "

This meeting, which would have cost Robinson every last shred of reputation in the liberal community if it had ever become public knowledge, was also recalled by Barry Goldwater:

"I took the advantage of telephoning him one day and informing him that I would be in New York within a few days, and, if he wasn't busy and wanted to, I would like to have lunch with him. He said that he would. We met at the hotel where I was staying, it was cordial, there was no evasiveness on either of our parts. . . . We discussed the very thing that brought us together, my feeling about the black man. I told him that when I was on the City Council in Phoenix, I helped to desegregate the restaurants, and then the Air Terminal, and when I was Chief of Staff of the Air National Guard, I desegregated that. I never believed in segregation and I passed that on to him."

But Robinson was no more taken in by Goldwater than Goldwater by Robinson. Both men had political commitments to keep—and miles to go before the nomination. Robinson's commitments meant that he spent endless hours on the phone, going to meetings, talking to potential delegates, trying to talk up a candidate who was unable to attract significant support in the black community, and who, perhaps because he was too liberal, perhaps because public knowledge of his marital difficulties had been too damaging, was in a hopeless position in the national Republican Party. Robinson's efforts ultimately brought him head-to-head with hooting, jeering delegates at the Republican National Convention when Nelson Rockefeller tried to speak. Robinson almost got into a fistfight on the convention floor. After the nomination of Goldwater, there was no place for Robinson or what he stood for in the party, either. As much as he had briefly found himself a home, he was once again on the outside looking in.

Robinson's work for Rockefeller ended almost as quickly as it began—at least for a time. In his *Home Plate* column of August 29, he announced his intention to support President Johnson in the upcoming election, urging black voters who were wary of Johnson's past indifference to civil rights to vote for him anyway.

"I beg and implore every Negro citizen who is against Goldwater not to aid and abet his campaign by staying home from the polls," he wrote.

It is impossible to determine from his writings or from any of his public remarks if Robinson was fully aware of the Rubicon his party had crossed in this election campaign. It seems clear today that if there was ever a chance to build a base of support in the Republican Party to keep the Democrats from taking the black vote for granted, it was lost in that landmark election.

In any case, Robinson's mind was already elsewhere. With the presidential landslide under way in the autumn of 1964, the ongoing and unending war against racial injustice remained. Earlier that summer, on August 4, the mangled bodies of three civil rights workers had been discovered in a Mississippi swamp. Like others around the world, Robinson had been sickened. Unlike many others, he had immediately determined to do something about it.

Days after the bodies of James Chaney, Michael Schwerner, and Andrew Goodman were located, Jackie Robinson, architect Paul Willen, and James Farmer, the head of CORE, announced that they were cochairing a drive to raise $25,000 for the building of a new memorial community center in Meridian, Mississippi. The bulk of the money came from the annual Afternoon of Jazz concert the Robinsons held every year to benefit civil rights causes.

314

During that same presidential-election summer and fall, riots broke out in New York and elsewhere. A major riot occurred in Harlem in mid-July and soon spread to other areas, including the huge Bedford-Stuyvesant ghetto in Brooklyn. Rioting also broke out upstate, in Rochester, forcing Rockefeller to dispatch National Guard troops to quell the disorder.

Robinson, with perhaps an added sense of urgency from the growing racial violence in the country, increasingly turned his attention to the creation of a predominantly black-owned bank, multiracial in its operation, to provide the sort of economic boost not offered by other banks or by government programs to low-income people.

The original idea for the bank, which would be located in Harlem, was not Robinson's but that of Dunbar McLaurin, a Harlem businessman. Robinson was at first reluctant to become personally involved because of his lack of banking experience, but he soon became the bank's champion. Long before other black leaders stressed the irreducible importance of economics in changing the racial landscape, Robinson grasped its significance perfectly.

"Black people were coming to the point where they would be crying out in behalf of Black Power, but it was pathetic to realize how little we knew of money," he said. "During the postbaseball years, I became increasingly persuaded that there were two keys to the advancement of blacks in America—the ballot and the buck. If we organized our political and economic strength, we would have a much easier fight on our hands."

Increasingly, the discussions Robinson had with Dunbar McLaurin drew him into the day-to-day planning for the bank's eventual operation. Robinson agreed to become the chairman of the board, while McLaurin would be its president. The position of chairman, at least as it was first envisioned, was unsalaried, but it meant a commitment of more than prestige and name. Robinson's goal was to do whatever he could to see that the bank succeeded. He committed himself to attending all board meetings, and to interceding with authorities from Governor Rockefeller, who became a strong supporter, to anyone else either in or out of government.

Unfortunately, the plans for the new bank quickly became mired in internal conflict. Robinson and others on the board saw that McLaurin was the wrong choice for chief executive officer. A mercurial self-promoter, he spent lavishly on parties, entertainment, and other expenses before there were covering funds. Robinson reluctantly but firmly led a successful move to replace McLaurin, even though it meant pushing back the bank's opening date. The new president was William R. Hudgins, an old friend of Robinson's with considerable banking experience; he had been associated for years with another Harlem bank, the Carver Savings and Loan. At the time, he seemed to be the ideal choice.

For Robinson, all the while cognizant of his professional inexperience, the goal was to win a fight that had to be carried on without equivocation if it was to succeed. The bank, after all its preliminary troubles, opened its doors for business on December 21, 1964. For Robinson, especially after the bitter experiences of the past summer, it was a triumph.

But the victory, though significant, was limited. For almost the entire year following, Dunbar McLaurin and a group of dissident stockholders waged a sometimes noisy, always unsettling—and public —effort to take back control of the bank from the Robinson faction. The campaign failed, but it took its toll. In Harlem, the publicity fanned the flames of suspicion. Nationalist groups, even as Robinson's group was winning its proxy fight with McLaurin, staged protests on 125th Street, distributing literature charging that the bank was just another white scheme in blackface designed to subjugate the community.

Much as he tried to stay a step ahead, Robinson now seemed to be doing his best just to keep up. In early 1965, President Johnson announced a massive escalation of the war in Vietnam—which swept Jackie Robinson's son into combat among hundreds of thousands of others. The War on Poverty suddenly became a pointless and arid dispute over whether the nation could afford both guns and butter. Instead of money and opportunity flowing into urban areas, increasing unrest manifested itself in a seemingly endless cycle of marches, protests, and riots. Money for loans, and cooperation with other banks and institutions, became more difficult. In this same year, Robinson suffered another heart attack—a more serious one than he had had in 1962.

And he still did not have a job that provided a paycheck. Rachel, not he, was now the family breadwinner. An effort to start an insurance company failed; other job possibilities flared up but went nowhere. Robinson frequently strolled on 125th Street, stopping to greet passersby, chatting, enjoying the warmth that still seemed to attach to his celebrity. But he was very much a man who had slipped from view. Though his column in the *Amsterdam News* continued, his views on politics and even race were now largely ignored. A physically large and imposing man, his gait had become noticeably slowed by the circulatory complications of his diabetes. In the political world, he had slowed to the point of becoming almost inert. In terms of influence, he had become almost invisible. If Robinson perceived these changes, as he surely must have, whatever anguish this brought did not in the least deter him. It may have been mainly willpower that drove him now, like a fighter blinded and confused, struggling to his feet to continue the fight. But unlike that fighter with his mind scrambled and only his heart sustaining him, Robinson knew the dimensions of the fight as clearly as ever. It was just that he had no control, where once he had been in the center, knowing, despite the uncertainties and punishments that buffeted him, that he was a moving force. As he once had been more widely, he was still a "spokesman," though he now spoke only for a small and very loosely associated group of people, many with widely diverging viewpoints and interests, who in one way or another were clustered around a single, fragile Harlem institution, the Freedom National Bank. Robinson understood the need for such a foothold in the economic system far better than those who derided his efforts as tokenism. He knew better than anyone that someone had to blaze a trail if a community was to have a lasting piece of the action.

CHAPTER THIRTY-EIGHT

Though the bank did manage to open and, over time, expand its operation, its troubles did not quickly ease. The board's original idea was to raise money through the sale of stock to the community. Sixty thousand shares of stock were to go on sale, at $25 per share, to local residents. The board anticipated that the offering would be quickly sold-out. It was not. In order to complete the capitalization, Freedom's officers had to secure a loan of $478,000 to purchase more than nineteen thousand unsold shares. The loan did not come from within the community but from the Irving Trust Company. The deal made it possible to open the bank, but put it on the edge—even as its services were eagerly and heavily patronized.

Robinson and Hudgins, the new president, were each vigorous promoters. Robinson never lost an opportunity to tell people, publicly and privately, how vital the bank's role was in an industry that routinely turned its back on minorities.

"Our people take pride in progressive steps in business," Robinson told readers of his column. "The establishment of an institution such as Freedom National adds something to their sense of 'somebodiness.' . . . In my humble opinion, Freedom National is not just another local bank. It is symbolic of the determination of the Negro to become an integral part of the mainstream of our American economy. . . .

"If Freedom National succeeds, it will set an example which will result in new banks all over the country—banks which are color-blind and banks which have as resources not only their reserve funds, but also the support of the masses of the Negro people."

Hudgins was another kind of booster. He set out to make sure that investments grew, that large corporations that did business in Harlem also carried accounts at the bank. His thinking was that as these mainstream accounts grew, so would the community's confidence in the bank.

Both men accomplished their objectives. "In 1960," according to *Business Week,* "there were only 10 black-owned banks in the U.S.

318

with total assets of $58 million.'' In the decade following, after the creation of Freedom, the nation's largest black-owned bank, the number grew to twenty-five with over $350 million in assets. The idea's time had come. It caught on even against the grain of the day's prevailing rhetoric, which denounced business and businessmen as all part of the same exploitative machinery, and, more significantly, at a time when guns, not butter, commanded the marketplace.

Hudgins did not have the ear of black communities—but he commanded respect in the business world. Slowly, big names with big accounts placed money in Freedom. HARYOU-ACT, the community development program created as part of the Johnson administration's War on Poverty, placed its funds with Freedom. So did Con Ed, the giant New York utility. General Motors, Ford, Chrysler, and others, including Hunt Foods, also had accounts.

The bank's assets grew from $1.25 million when it opened to almost $42 million six years later, tops among all black-owned banks.

The rapid growth of the bank created its own set of problems. In early 1966, Hudgins spurred the opening of a branch office of Freedom in Bedford-Stuyvestant in Brooklyn. The move provoked another threatened lawsuit by dissident shareholders, objecting to a change in the bank's governing regulations that would allow it to sell an additional thirty thousand shares of stock to help finance the move, which everyone knew would be costly. The growth of the bank's assets was not, even then, related to its profits. In the first three months of 1966, Hudgins reported profits of only $4,356, compared to a loss of $9,126 in all of 1965. But still, at the time, moving through uncharted waters on a maiden voyage, the ship at least seemed to be in good hands and on course.

In early 1966, while he was still chairman of the board of Freedom Natioinal Bank and still searching around discreetly for a job, Robinson was appointed a special assistant to Governor Rockefeller. It represented something of a political rebirth.

Rockefeller, following the Goldwater debacle and looking to rebuild his coalition for another presidential run in 1968, had been quietly assembling a staff of special assistants from the black community, each one to work in different problem areas. Dr. Arthur Logan had been appointed to work in the area of drug addiction and rehabilitation; his professional connections to lawyers and doctors were espe-

319

cially valued. Wyatt Walker had been appointed as a special troubleshooter because he had assisted Dr. King and was known for his organizing skills and his ability to work the roughest neighborhoods. Sandy Ray, Robinson's old friend and counselor, the pastor of Brooklyn's Cornerstone Baptist Church and a statewide official in the black Baptist church, helped on church matters. Sam Singletary and Evelyn Cunningham also were part of this "kitchen cabinet."

But the offer to Robinson was almost an afterthought—at least according to Wyatt Walker: "Once I was ensconced, Al Duckett revealed to me that Jackie had complained, 'Gee whiz, I've been helping the governor and I don't have no post.' So that's when he became a special assistant for community affairs."

The man who was really in charge of the day-to-day operations of the kitchen cabinet was Rockefeller's chief of staff, Alton Marshall. Marshall served as a kind of alter ego for Rockefeller, but he had his own view of things. A seasoned political in-fighter, he was highly knowledgeable about the workings of government and the subtleties of political relationships.

Marshall viewed Jackie Robinson as a straight shooter, utterly sincere but "a little plodding." His main virtue was, as Evelyn Cunningham had also pointed out, his ability, because of the great celebrity he had as an admired baseball star, "to go in and talk to Nelson Rockefeller" as no one else in the group or from the black community could.

Robinson's job was to take what celebrity he had left and go out in the public. Much more than the others, who each had target constituencies, he was "a part of the government apparatus," Marshall said, a liaison to both the black and white communities. "He was a bird dog, and then he was also a stand-in for the governor when he couldn't attend different functions," said former New York governor Malcolm Wilson, who was then Rockefeller's lieutenant governor.

Marshall believed Robinson was passionately interested in ideas but that he wasn't ever an original thinker. "There's one very important aspect to this," Marshall said. "He was Jackie Robinson the baseball player who really seriously substantially had become interested in the racial problem. He was not endorsing Nike shoes and saying, 'Oh, by the way, let's do something about race.' The significance was that he wanted to do whatever he could to be a nurse to whatever activities there were."

Robinson worked out of the governor's city office, a brownstone on West Fifty-fifth Street, attached by a passageway to the family home on Fifty-third Street. Unlike the other special assistants, Robinson came and went not from the community but from the governor's office. His workday was notable because he never assumed that he had a sinecure.

He was usually the first one at work in the morning and the last to leave at night, noted Evelyn Cunningham. "There were events and dates all the time," she said. "He was constantly getting requests for photographs and autographs, and, oh, yes, he was a phone freak."

He continued to enjoy his strolls down 125th Street, but the fire directed at him for being an "Uncle Tom," for being Rockefeller's "house Negro," became increasingly intense. He worked on his own speeches and nearly always seemed to deliver them without reading them, without having to look down at the text or into a teleprompter. "He was very good at talking about Nelson Rockefeller, his boss. It came out very real and sincere," Cunningham said. "He was no political hack." Robinson rarely alluded to his baseball career in his speeches. Business, yes, and civil rights nearly always. "And he usually took questions, not too many, from the audience. He got feisty whenever he got a negative question, and he wasn't the least bit frightened by a hostile person," said Cunningham.

Robinson had a goal in mind: putting Nelson Rockefeller in the White House in 1968. It did not matter now if it was harder to appear in public or that nationalists more easily pilloried him or that to the great majority of those out protesting he seemed like a figure from another era. Those who were close to him, members of his family, his friends, saw better than anyone that he was his own man, doing just what he felt he should be doing.

Still, at home—when he was home—his family, like the rest of society, seemed to have receded from him. Jackie junior was away, and his daughter, Sharon, was about to enter college and was very much taken with the words, dress, and political style of the newer, younger black leaders who were increasingly paying attention to their African roots rather than to any white political leaders.

Rachel Robinson was a professor at Yale. At one point, after an article appeared in *Life* magazine, she made a point of denying to a curious coworker that she was Jackie Robinson's wife. At least two of Robinson's children, uncomfortable with their father's dominating celebrity, also denied that they were related to him as well at different points in their lives.

Other members of Robinson's family reacted to his celebrity differently. Rachel's mother, who had been living with the family for years, often used the name Robinson in social situations, even though her name was Isum. Robinson's brother-in-law, Chuck Williams, an executive with Schenley Distilleries, used his friendship with his famous relative in an attempt to influence Martin Luther King regarding a boycott of grape growers by Cesar Chavez and the United Farm Workers of America. A March 15, 1966, telegram from Robinson to King in Atlanta read:

> *Imperative that you meet with my brother-in-law, Charles T. Williams, Vice President of Schenley Distilleries Co., regarding the California Delano Grape Strike. I think there are some facts you would like to know which shows both sides of the situation. I hope that you will set up an appointment at your earliest convenience. I know that you will give him every consideration.*

> *Jackie Robinson*

Robinson's relationship with King, while remaining friendly and supportive, had by now also become more distant. For years, the FBI had been conducting a surveillance campaign against King in an effort to discredit him. As part of that campaign, the FBI spread rumors about King's having extramarital affairs with white women. At one point, Jackie Robinson phoned Wyatt Walker about the rumors.

"There had been a couple of times when he called me about some of these spurious stories being spread about Dr. King," Walker said, "but then there was one time in particular when there was a check that turned up written to some lady who had done some stenographic work. Dr. King gave her, I remember it, a fifteen-dollar check. An hour's work or whatever. He was very disturbed that someone could make out that this was for her sexual services. I told him, 'Come on, Jackie, Dr. King wouldn't give her a check if he hired her for that.' Somebody was just trying to spoil his admiration for Dr. King. I think Jackie had the check, the photostated copy of the check."

Even if Robinson was satisfied, how had he come into possession of a photostated copy of a check written by King? The only reasonable guess was that the government had sought out Robinson, fed him compromising information, and that he had chosen to act on it.

A far more serious breach with King developed over the Vietnam War. King through much of 1966 had resisted pressure to come out strongly against the war. But the pressure, from within and without, was unrelenting, and in the beginning of 1967, King's vocal opposition to the war grew, as did his active participation in protests against it. It soon became clear—to the dismay of people like Jackie Robinson —that King was linking opposition to the war in Vietnam with the struggle against racism at home.

In April 1967, King took part in the gigantic Spring Mobilization against the war in New York City, marching in the lead column of protesters with Benjamin Spock and Harry Belafonte. In another line of marchers was Stokely Carmichael, who led a group of younger, more militant dissidents who carried Viet Cong flags. King's speech ended with the chant, "Stop the bombing! Stop the bombing!" The huge crowd at the U.N. Plaza echoed his call, joining the chant.

Robinson says he agonized over King's stand against the war as his position became stronger through late 1966 into 1967. In early May 1967, weeks after the Spring Mobilization—and only weeks before his troubled son Jackie junior, who had been recently wounded in the war, was scheduled to be released from the army—Robinson attacked King in another of those "open letters" he reserved for black leaders with whom he found himself in major disagreement.

"Is it fair," he asked King, "for you to place all the burden of the blame on America and none on the Communist forces we are fighting? You suggest that we stop the bombing. It strikes me that our President has made effort after effort to get both sides to the peace table. Why should we take the vital step of stopping the bombing without knowing whether the enemy will use that pause to prepare for greater destruction of our men in Vietnam? . . . Why do you seem to ignore the blood that is on their hands and speak only of the 'guilt of the United States'? . . . . I am confused, Martin. I am confused because I respect you deeply. But I also love this imperfect country. I respectfully ask you to answer this open letter and give me your own point of view."

King's point of view did not require an open-letter response to Jackie Robinson—an irony perhaps more telling than anything. King did personally phone Robinson because he was an old friend and explain his opposition to the war. Robinson acknowledged the depth, forcefulness, and sincerity of King's argument. Perhaps the break between them was healed, though Robinson's explanation for why he chose the form of an open letter in which to attack King—he had a press deadline he could no longer postpone—seemed lame at best, and in any case, it hardly represented a ripple on the surface of King's political life.

During this same period, Robinson had a final falling out with Roy Wilkins and the leadership of the NAACP. At its annual winter convention in 1966, delegates loyal to Wilkins were once more elected, once again insuring control of the board. Robinson—again publicly rather than privately—attacked Wilkins, denouncing him and his "dictatorship" in an early 1967 *Amsterdam News* column.

Wilkins responded angrily but with icy precision. In a personal letter, specifically marked "not for publication," on February 8, 1967, he said that Robinson's charges about dictatorship were laughable. Other organizations, such as SCLC, SNCC, and CORE, were smaller and far more top-down than the NAACP. Another charge of Robinson's—that the organization had taken money from the Ford Foundation, thereby compromising its ability to speak and act on behalf of the black community—was equally ridiculous, Wilkins said; only a fraction of the organization's income for the preceding year had come from Ford, and as far as taking money from whites was concerned, "all other civil rights organizations have depended upon the general public (which means white people) for their funds. Thus the hateful remark about Jews, made in Mt. Vernon by a local CORE officer at a school board meeting sheared instantly $200,000 from the CORE income. Dr. King was dependent upon mail solicitations and his own personal appearances. SNCC depends on various contributors, mostly white."

But as clinically as Wilkins attempted to rebut Robinson's attack, he could not conceal a sense of fury that had been accumulating for years.

"One of these days before you are seventy," he said, "some down-to-earth wisdom will find its way into your life. If it does nothing else except stop you from believing that 'because I see it this way I have to say it,' it will have done a great service.

"The basis of informed comment is not simple, self-serving personal re-affirmation but truth arrived at through reasoning, not feeling.

"If you had played ball with a hot head instead of a cool brain, you would have remained in the minors. You need that cool brain in the weighing of issues in the critical area of civil rights."

Robinson wrote back to Wilkins a week later. He was not about to back down or to offer even a nod of reconciliation: "I have to laugh when you talk of down-to-earth wisdom. When I speak it's because I know what I'm doing. I'm sorry the truth hurts so much. I really don't have to answer to you for what I have done and I certainly will not apologize. . . .

"I don't intend to get into a further hassle with you. Whenever I feel criticism of you, the N.A.A.C.P. or any other organization is justified—expect it."

The exchange continued. Robinson meant his criticism to be public —whether or not Wilkins thought it came from a hot head rather than a cool brain—and Robinson's view of the NAACP was shared by many other younger, impatient members.

"The Association needs new blood," he told Wilkins. "It needs young men with new ideas and a mind of their own. Unfortunately I don't think this is true of the present Board."

That Robinson became politically estranged from old friends and supporters who were too far out front, and also from others who seemed to be dragging their feet, is painfully and irreducibly ironic. This torturous isolation cannot be fully explained by the buffeting Robinson took in the political crosswinds, or even by a peculiar combination of circumstances beyond his control. It is reminiscent of his later years on the Dodgers: a teammate and friend, yes, but a bit distant because of his unrelenting focus on the cause he represented. In the end, Robinson's isolation was even more personal than political —and nowhere was that more visible than in the relationship he had with his eldest son, Jackie junior.

In June, Jackie junior was discharged from the army, finishing his three-year hitch. He was deeply troubled. By his own admission, Jackie junior had not only been wounded in combat, he had also become a drug addict in Vietnam, a heavy user of marijuana, sometimes dipped in opium. Jackie junior said that as he increasingly used drugs, his aggressive feelings sharpened. He remembered riding through villages stoned, pointing his pistol—but not shooting—at staring villagers. He estimated that about one-fourth of his unit smoked heavily, while almost three-quarters used pot "irregularly."

It is likely that Robinson knew something about his son's drug problems at the time but denied them. When Jackie junior was shipped back to the States from Vietnam after being wounded, Marian Logan remembers that the Robinsons went to visit their son in Colorado. His rehab there, she was sure, had to do with drugs. At one point he was in the stockade for going AWOL, probably on a drug binge. Logan said, "He was supposed to be in a rehab place, then when they thought he was all clear with it, he came home—but he wasn't."

All that Robinson was sure of was that his son, his namesake, when he returned to Connecticut at the beginning of the summer of 1967, was someone whose life seemed hopelessly adrift. Jackie junior found it impossible to live at home, or to share much of what he was thinking and feeling with his parents, particularly with his famous father. The simplest of personal needs, like finding a job, seemed out of reach. In Connecticut, sometimes living on the street, sometimes with friends, Jackie junior drifted into a life of crime. He got a gun, later acknowledging that to support his continuing drug habit he carried it with him when he broke into houses and robbed people. His new friends were hardened criminals, pushers, and prostitutes. In New Haven and sometimes in New York City, he frequented dives and flytraps, the likely gathering places not only for the lost and forgotten but for those working undercover for the police.

Whatever Robinson may have been telling himself about his son blew apart on the night of March 4, 1968. Jackie junior was picked up on a street corner in a run-down section of Stamford at 2:15 A.M. He was carrying several glassine bags of heroin, a stash of marijuana, and a .22-caliber pistol.

The Robinsons were awakened at home and summoned to the police station. Entering the station house through a knot of reporters, Rachel Robinson and daughter Sharon were in tears. Robinson ultimately faced reporters and told them some of the details of the arrest and its background.

He had seen his son in a holding cell, he said, and it was obvious to him that he was high "on some kind of drug beyond marijuana." He acknowledged that his son had been addicted for some time and that he had had arguments with him over marijuana: "I told him that marijuana, which he admitted smoking, can lead to the stronger things."

A $5,000 bond was posted and Jackie junior was released, with the family pledging to stick by him and see him through real rehabilitation.

"I guess I had more of an effect on other people's kids than I had on my own," was all Robinson could bring himself to say to reporters. His son's problems, however, did more to change his thinking about the racial struggle in the country than almost all of the public battles Robinson had been involved in before.

CHAPTER THIRTY-NINE

Robinson had a little over three years left with his son. In the final years of his life, he was preoccupied with his son's recovery. Because he blamed himself for negligence in raising him, he altered his way of looking at the world around him, philosophically and emotionally, so he could better see through the eyes of a young person like Jackie Robinson Jr.

Despite what he had said in despair to reporters that night in Stamford, he and, especially, his wife had always known that their son had problems. They had moved him from school to school when he was a youngster in an effort to find a place where he might finally feel a sense of belonging.

When Jackie junior was a teenager, Kenneth Clark, the eminent psychologist and a family friend, recalls that the parents consulted with him. "They talked a great deal with me about him, about the difficulties he had coping with the fact that he was Jackie Jr. This was something they, Jack and Rachel, had to come to terms with. . . . What they were hoping for was what any parent would hope for—stability, acceptance, a positive role."

Robinson hoped that a real drug rehabilitation program might now be the key. After Jackie junior was arrested, he was initially placed in the custody of the State Commission of Adult Probation, which agreed that he could be treated in a mental hospital in New Haven rather than going to jail. The court agreed to a two-year delay in prosecution. This let the Robinsons keep tabs on the care being offered; Rachel worked nearby and was able to monitor the help her son was getting.

It apparently wasn't much.

Jackie junior told his parents the program was worthless, that the hospital was for mental patients, not people with drug problems. He was eventually moved into a program run by Daytop, Inc., first at a facility on Staten Island, then for a longer haul at Seymour, Connecticut. Robinson says that his son went through hell drying out, but that he did and emerged two years later not only clean but strengthened by the mutual support system provided by Daytop residents.

Robinson, perhaps as a way of trying to draw closer to his son, perhaps because he was disturbed by what his son had been through, paid far more public attention to the drug problem than he had in the past. He inquired about the status of drug treatment and research in Connecticut; he devoted columns to the nature and consequences of addiction and the negligence of authorities as they related to young, inner-city children.

One month after the arrest of Jackie junior, Martin Luther King Jr. was assassinated in Memphis. In America's black communities, the murder triggered nights of rioting and violence along with angry questioning and finger-pointing. Whatever his distance from King at that point, Robinson saw the slaying as an assault on everything he had worked for and believed in. In a long, emotional column in the *Amsterdam News,* he recalled the night King's home had been bombed during the Montgomery bus boycott and King's sermon following it, which cited the biblical parable of Joseph and his brothers. The parable spoke of the will of God, which gave man freedom but also the choice to commit evil. God, though all good, was a God of two wills, King had preached; he "sometimes suffers evil in order to change the hearts and minds of men"—as Joseph did, after he went to Egypt.

The great sermon King had preached, Robinson hoped, would also apply now. "Perhaps what God had done in Montgomery," Robinson wrote, "allowed some bombs to fall, allowed some property to be destroyed so that the white community could feel the necessity for reconciliation. . . . Perhaps this will happen today in America. Perhaps after the raging emotions quiet down; perhaps after the streets of our cities are no longer haunted by angry black people seeking revenge."

Later, Robinson was a guest aboard Nelson Rockefeller's private plane which carried a group of mourners to the funeral in Atlanta. He still could not contain his grief and anger, but there was a focused and pointed change in the way he thought about what had taken place. Writing a month later, he acknowledged that federal authorities were probably doing all they could to apprehend King's killer or killers, but added, "There is no doubt in my mind that many, many whites wanted to see Dr. King silenced to death. How deeply they will regret the day. For, as Brooklyn's Rev. George Lawrence, one of Dr. King's aides and intimate friends, told a group of whites at a Brooklyn meeting the other day, 'You killed your best buddy.' "

When Robert Kennedy, no political friend of Robinson's, was murdered in June, Robinson noted that "American society, whose white rulers spend so much time cautioning black people to be nonviolent, is one of the most violent 'civilizations' on the map. And the rest of the world knows it."

In his own political work, Robinson's efforts for Nelson Rockefeller were going nowhere. It was clear early in the 1968 campaign that the New York Governor would not capture the Republican nomination. Robinson blasted the likely Republican nominee, Richard Nixon, declaring he would never vote for him and that his election would imperil the nation. Soon after, Robinson signed on to the Humphrey campaign.

This was an awful period in Robinson's life. Everything he feared most seemed to be converging all at once: his son was fighting drug addiction, the civil rights leader he most believed in had been slain, cities were in flames across the country, and the candidate who had cost him so much credibility was marching to the White House. It would have been easy for him to pull back, to leave the fight to others after decades of exhausting struggle. Yet at this point Robinson found common cause with one of the most radical elements of the entire movement, the Black Panther Party.

To the surprise of some, Robinson publicly associated himself with party members who were arrested in New York and were subsequently roughed up in the hallway of the Brooklyn Courts Building by 150 off-duty cops.

Robinson blasted the police for brutality in his *Amsterdam News* column and praised the Panthers for the way they comported themselves after the attack:

"Instead of taking to the streets to retaliate, these young brothers took their complaint to City Hall where one of the Black Panther leaders, David Brothers, bared his mutilated back to give mute and horrible proof of the kind of brutality which would be the accepted thing under the 'law and order' philosophy of Richard Nixon and that other Richard—Daley."

Robinson followed up the words by holding at least one meeting following the assault with Panther leaders at their Brooklyn headquarters in an effort to set up some kind of communication between them and the police. The Muslim newspaper, *Muhammad Speaks,* quoted Robinson as saying that he too "could have become a Black Panther as a teenager." The goals of the Panthers, he said, were no different from those of other major civil rights groups. "The Black Panthers seek self-determination, protection of the Black community, decent housing and employment and express opposition to police abuse."

His view of white America as expressed in this article was consistent with things he was now saying elsewhere: "There has to be a willingness to sit down and develop a dialogue. They have to recognize that Black people aren't asking for people to give them anything. We want to develop pride and dignity in ourselves and we can't do it on relief. . . . There are not enough people around who give a damn about what is going on as far as the Black man is concerned."

Robinson's much more pointed, much more ethnocentric view of what was happening around him was also reflected in his day-to-day life. When Robinson left his job as special assistant to Governor Rockefeller to campaign for Hubert Humphrey, he believed that a paying job with Rockefeller would be waiting for him later on. No such position was ever offered—a source of bitterness to both Robinson and his wife.

"Rachel was especially bitter about Nelson Rockefeller," Evelyn Cunningham said. "I've tried in every way I can to sort out the facts from the fiction with her, but she feels that Nelson just let Jackie down by not giving him a big appointment, a big job or something when he kind of needed one."

Robinson's disappointment had another dimension. Robinson had put all his Republican Party hopes in Rockefeller; he was one of three white men—Branch Rickey and William Black were the others—with whom Robinson had had decisive relationships in his life. And while he claimed that all of these men were "hardheaded, practical men" who never did anything out of "misplaced emotion," his disappointment with Rockefeller was keenest because the hope he had placed in him was greatest. Rockefeller wound up as a party loyalist, supporting Nixon in the general election, tolerating positions that seemed to be a betrayal of what he stood for.

With the election over, the landscape was bleak. Evelyn Cunningham recalled, "He was just floundering personally and professionally.

Nothing was happening for him.'' Eventually he became involved in
a restaurant chain, Sea Host. He was named a vice president, but the
position and the chain went nowhere. Sea Host declared bankruptcy
in 1970.

Marian Logan remembers that through this period, Robinson had a
city apartment at 33 W. Ninety-third Street, not far from where she
lived. Like Cunningham, she believed he was floundering, but his
attitude about it was almost cavalier.

"He came down here all the time,'' Logan said. "He'd sit down
and I'd say, 'What are we involved in now?' 'Well, we're in the
seafood thing.' There was a store up on One Hundred and Twenty-
fifth Street, then it was something called Holiday Magic, which was
cosmetics, creams, and stuff. I used to end up having to invite a few
ladies in and do makeup on them and hope they'd wind up buying the
products. Jackie put me in charge, set me up, and then he'd go off
laughing, you know. I got mad one time; I said, 'Jack, you know I've
lost eight thousand dollars in this venture so far,' and he would just
laugh. Arthur and Rachel just said, let him go on—they'd tell us we
knew what we were doing."

While Robinson seemed to be fading from view, he was not yet
forgotten. Nineteen seventy was also the year when the baseball
player Curt Flood decided to challenge baseball's reserve clause,
which allowed owners to bind players to one team under provisions
of a special anti-trust exemption provided by Congress. When Flood's
lawyers, Marvin Miller and former Supreme Court Justice Arthur
Goldberg, looked around for prominent people who might be willing
to testify in support of their case, they contacted Jackie Robinson.

"We thought of only a few names,'' Miller said. "Jim Brosnan was
one because he had written a good critical book about baseball; Hank
Greenberg was another. And Jackie Robinson came to mind.

"I called Robinson cold. I didn't know what his reaction would be,
but he was more than willing to testify. I warned him that he had once
taken a position favoring the owners back in the fifties and that he
would surely be cross-examined about it. It didn't phase him in the
least. The testimony would be very unpopular, I said. It didn't matter
at all. Robinson said he was older and wiser than he was back then
and he would be glad to help."

Miller described the shock of seeing Robinson—white haired, walking slowly with a cane. But the testimony he gave, Miller said, was strong, "up front and he didn't bat an eye when he was challenged. He was a very good witness for us."

Robinson testified that though he continued to favor some kind of control by teams over players, he was unequivocal in his support of Flood. "Anything that is one-sided is wrong in America. The reserve clause is one-sided in favor of the owners and should be modified to give the player some control over his own destiny," Robinson said. "If the reserve clause is not modified, I think you will have a serious strike by the players."

Though Flood ultimately lost his suit, Robinson's remarks were more than supportive—in his view of the determination of the players as a group, he was all too prophetic.

Robinson was still chairman of the board of the Freedom National Bank, but that further ensnared him in bitterness and controversy. Gradually, he came to view the work of Bill Hudgins, the bank's president and his long-standing friend, with suspicion, eventually moving against him and forcing his resignation, as he had Dunbar McLaurin's.

Robinson says in his autobiography that even as "a novice in banking and financial matters, it was becoming obvious . . . that we were not being cautious enough with the processing of loan applications . . . that we had a tendency to favor friends."

Then, over time, others confirmed his suspicions. Someone Robinson describes as "one of the most powerful men in Wall Street circles" warned him, "If you want to save Freedom National Bank, the only way you are going to be able to do it is to take it over and clean house." One day, leaving the bank, Robinson ran into an in-house attorney and a former employee who told him the same thing.

Robinson says that he finally confronted his old friend, with the help of bank employees who provided him details of Hudgins's mismanagement.

The "one-man" investigation of Hudgins cost him terribly, Robinson says. "I found myself losing sleep at nights. . . . It happened that during this period I was having a very serious health crisis. My breathing had become constricted at times to the extent that I could not bear the pressure. I was having trouble with my legs and my doctors were unable to pinpoint the problem, unable to tell me there was a direct relationship to my diabetes. The more involved I got with the bank problems, the sicker I got.''

Hudgins was eventually forced to step down as president, temporarily replaced by Bob Boyd, the former L.A. Rams football player. Though never indicted, never even asked to give up his association with the bank (he was subsequently named vice chairman of the board), questions about Hudgins's integrity were ineradicably planted.

For his part, Hudgins, today a vigorous man in his late eighties who heads a small mortgage business of his own, denies any wrongdoing. The problem, he says, was Robinson, not him. ''Jackie was a star, a celebrity, and was accustomed to the treatment the celebrities get, but the bank started doing very well and people let it be known that they would be interested, and I think that was a little hard for Jackie to swallow. I think the popularity and esteem that I developed out of this venture was sort of rolling over him and he didn't like it. I was absolutely amazed when the board and Jackie took the position they did.''

Hudgins evaded Robinson's assertions that he was making loans to friends. The charge of not being cautious enough was a curious one, he pointed out, since the bank was set up to provide loans for applicants other banks routinely turned down. ''That was the whole idea of Freedom,'' he said.

But when Robinson came to him with the specific allegation of making bad loans to personal friends, Hudgins says he thought his answer satisfied Robinson: ''He sat down and said, 'I just met a guy on the street and he told me you were making loans to your friends and he had applied to you for a loan and you had turned him down.' Now I knew Robinson for some time and he was a really decent guy, so I asked for this guy's name, the person he'd been talking to, and then I called the loan office and had them bring up his file.''

Hudgins had the file read to Robinson; it carefully detailed why the loan application had been turned down—for sound reasons. ''The man owed several people money, several institutions money—and he had failed to live up to his obligations. It was clear he was ambitious and that his ethics were a little short—just the kind of person you would reject. . . . Jackie apologized to me then. I said, 'Jackie, I'm faced with a lot of this. This is a community bank, the bank was organized to help the people of areas like Harlem, Bed-Stuy, Jamaica, and wherever blacks were thought to be overlooked. You know that and I know that.' I think Jackie just lost sight of that when he came to see me."

Hudgins thought Robinson shot from the hip, that he reacted to random anecdotal asides and that he did not have the real knowledge to separate fact from fiction. He was in a leadership role, but deferred to others to fill in his opinions with knowledge. "I'm sure of that," Hudgins said. "You could tell from the way Jack deported himself at board meetings. He didn't really take the leadership position. You could distract his thinking if you walked up to him and started talking about golf or something. He just didn't have the depth of the subject matter. . . . There was a lot of innocence in Jackie. I don't perceive him as being a vicious person, but I do think there was innocence there."

Hudgins never specifically answered the question about making loans to friends. Bruce Llewellyn, who ultimately became both the bank's chairman and president, said:

"The charges were basically that Hudgins was taking money under the table for making loans, was making self-serving loans to his brother-in-law and others, and that anyone who wanted to get financial assistance from the bank had to pay him off. The controller of the currency—Clinton Rumer, I think—took a look and came back and told Hudgins either you resign or they were going to bring charges—and it was preferable that he resign because Freedom then was the only major black bank, et cetera." Hudgins denied the accusations, saying that he "did not want to dignify those lies with an answer" but that they represented "a gross untruth."

But Llewellyn's view of Robinson was, in important respects, similar to Hudgins's. He saw that Robinson lacked a business background, that he had no real knowledge of the bank or its workings.

"I had the sense that he was trying to be a businessman and I think that basically he wasn't," Llewellyn said. "You know, it's very difficult to be a businessman if you don't have the training or have any background of real experience in it, and his whole experience had been with Chock Full o'Nuts . . . human resources . . . and that's not making any decisions. . . . I think the problem was that he really didn't know that much, in terms of the inner workings of the bank. I think it came as a great shock to him that day when employees came to him and said, 'Listen, you gotta do something about this guy who's the president.' But, you know, he was everybody's hero. He was mine. They'd stop him on the street, One Hundred and Twenty-fifth Street, and one day they stopped him and told him what was going on in the bank.''

The mounting troubles in his life made Robinson seem almost like Job to those who knew him. From his deteriorating health to his disintegrating dreams to the heart-wrenching problems of his eldest son, he seemed like a man summoned as much to hold on to his faith as to an everyday life that sustained him. And yet he did both. But none of his woes in any way prepared him for what was now to come. For beyond his own trials, even any tests of faith or of his body's defenses against age and illness, was the most elemental challenge of all: the death of a firstborn child.

CHAPTER FORTY

According to his father and others who knew him, Jackie Robinson Jr. successfully completed his rehabilitation program at Daytop Village. His recovery was so complete that he turned his energies into helping others similarly plagued walk the same walk he had made. He talked the talk as well: Jackie junior became a Daytop counselor and one of its stronger public advocates. As spring 1971 inched toward summer, he was immersed in organizing activities for that year's Afternoon of Jazz, the proceeds of which were to go entirely to Daytop.

He seemed to have finally reached a balancing, even a closeness, with his father and his world. In the second week of June 1971, three years after his treatment at Daytop began, Jackie junior spoke at a church in Bedford-Stuyvesant; at the local pastor's urging, he included a biblical parable that might appeal to youthful parishioners —that of the prodigal son. He seemed uncomfortable with it, more interested in talking directly about his experiences in the streets. But in the end, he got around to the theme. "My father was always in my corner," he said. "I didn't always recognize that and I didn't always call on him, but he was always there."

Four days after Robinson Jr.'s sermon, on June 16, 1971, in the early-morning hours, he was driving alone at the wheel of his 1969 MG along the Merritt Parkway in Connecticut. The car, according to one report, was traveling so fast that it "spun out of control, smashed into an abutment, and severed several guardrail posts before crashing to a halt. Jackie junior was killed instantly. He was pinned underneath the small car, his neck broken, when police arrived at 2:21 A.M."

Marian Logan remembers that she was awakened in the middle of the night with the news and that she and her husband got into their car, picked up one of the Robinson children, David, and Rachel's mother, and then immediately drove up to Connecticut.

"Rae was up in New Hampshire, at some class. Sharon and Jack drove up together to tell her what happened. She hadn't heard it," Logan said. "When they got back and pulled into the driveway, you could hear Rachel screaming, screeching like a banshee; all the way

337

up to the house, she screamed, screamed, screamed. When she got out of the car, she began running around the house, up and down the fields and everything. Jack got out of the car and said, 'I have to go get her.' But he couldn't see to do it. Arthur said to him, 'Leave her alone, she'll wear out better that way.'

"And then poor Jack . . . that was the first time I ever saw him . . . he broke down and cried in my arms. That was the first time I ever saw him break in my life."

By then, Robinson was old and blind and barely able to walk, though he was only fifty-two years old. It was thought by many that his son's death was the blow that killed him too, but it was not. No one can measure a parent's grief at the loss of a child or even the more uncertain process of healing, but Robinson carried wounds and blows as if they were part of the configuration of the neurons and synapses that defined him.

The Afternoon of Jazz concert for Daytop was held as scheduled, as a tribute Jackie junior. Evelyn Cunningham believed that Robinson, for all his pain and bitterness, was at home, at peace, in the setting of that festival, walking slowly from guest to guest, stopping to chat, being a host. She believed that in some way all the hurt and disappointment finally freed him to be himself.

Cunningham recalls that he was "mellow and even expansive" at the outing, which drew thousands and featured the top musicians in the field, such as Duke Ellington and Ella Fitzgerald, all of whom still seemed to crave Robinson's company and basked in the light of his role as a fighter and pioneer.

"All the famous musicians by then were dying to be a part of it for no money," Cunningham said, "and there it was at the beautiful home on the slanting lawn, and he went from tree to tree: 'Hi, you enjoying yourself? Why don't you get in the shade where it'll be more comfortable for you.' It was amazing to me to see. . . . He was very interested in people, and in a personal way that he never seemed to be before. In other words, what I saw was that he was wearing his grief and his immortality with a kind of acceptance and grace. 'Yes, I am Jackie Robinson,' he seemed to be saying. 'I am famous, it's been hell for me, but so what, let me give something back of myself.' "

Another visitor at that summer's festival was a little-known singer and longtime friend of Robinson's, Jim Randolph, who was scheduled to be part of the day's program. Randolph had met Robinson years before, when he was a young, aspiring singer. His career had never panned out, professional troubles followed him, but he was determined to continue no matter what. Robinson had always been impressed by that—even more so that afternoon. The promoters of the concert tried to bump him from the card to get to superstar Roberta Flack more quickly. Robinson interceded—forcefully.

"He told the people running things that if I wasn't in the show, there wouldn't be a show," Randolph said. "I'll never forget the way he stood by me. And under what circumstances."

Within months of his son's death, Robinson gradually moved back out into the world he knew, once again turning his attention to politics, this time to quarrel with his old friend Nelson Rockefeller over the use of force to put down a prisoners' rebellion at the Attica prison in upstate New York.

Robinson was bitterly disappointed by Rockefeller's actions in quelling the uprising that September, in which scores of inmates were killed in a police assault. The Attica prison population was predominantly black. Both the revolt and the ultimate response to it demonstrated the racial chasm in the country that Robinson had once hoped Nelson Rockefeller would be able to help bridge.

The inmates asked to see Wyatt Walker, still an aide to Rockefeller at that point, during the revolt. He was flown up to the prison and was allowed into one of the burned-out cellblocks to talk to the prisoners.

"They were not really rioting," he said. "They took over the prison because they couldn't take a shower but once a week and couldn't get a roll of toilet paper. I mean, you don't treat animals like that. But Rockefeller didn't ask me or Jackie Robinson or anyone else who might have been able to give him an answer, instead he turned for advice to Norman Hurd and Bobby Douglass, a Princeton-trained lawyer. He did that because of his breeding as a member of the dominant community. Nelson Rockefeller did add plenty to the governorship. But his greatest weakness was that he was a white man."

Robinson said the same thing more politely. He revealed that he met with Rockefeller "and voiced my concerns. I told him I was beginning to wonder if he was the same Rockefeller." He acknowledged that Rockefeller used his "best judgment" over Attica, "but that he took the advice of people he really believed in. I think he

should have gone to Attica in person, but others close to him said it
would not help.''

Robinson undertook two major projects in the months following.
One was the writing of his last autobiography, *I Never Had It Made;*
the other was the start-up of a new business enterprise, the Jackie
Robinson Construction Corporation, designed to build low-cost housing, using investments from both private and government sources.

In the autobiography, among other things, he made his peace with
Malcolm X. The hajj to Mecca, he said, had been impressive, because
in it Malcolm had seen the possibility of cooperation between the
races. Robinson found it "ironic, that just as he seemed to be rising
to the crest of a new and inspired leadership, Malcolm was struck
down, ostensibly by the hands of blacks. His murderers quieted his
voice but clothed him in martyrdom and deepened his influence.''

But no time was really left for the making or settling of quarrels,
the undertaking or leaving of projects. It was amazing that he finished
his book and that the construction company actually got to the point
of ground-breaking, since Robinson's energies were by now being
consumed almost completely by his illness. He came and went among
friends with the slowest of steps, caught up not in flames of controversy but in his body's consuming cauldron. His pleasures, as before,
were golf and the track, but anyone in his company knew that even
the simplest physical tasks—swinging a golf club, walking from one
place to another—were almost impossible for him.

Robinson was a regular among friends at lunchtime in Harlem. Kiah
Sayles, an old friend of Robinson's and an associate at the new construction company, was often at his side, walking him to one of two
spots, Jacques's or the Red Rooster, on Seventh Avenue, where a
table was waiting.

"This was not really Jackie's lifestyle," said Sayles's widow,
Deane, "but he felt very comfortable with Kiah.''

Sayles was something of a boulevardier, everyone's friend, someone, Mrs. Sayles said, "who made other people feel better." At lunch,
a leisurely time among some of the area's "lawyers and doctors and
businessmen," Robinson sat around amidst drinks and jokes, neither
drinking nor joking but, Mrs. Sayles said, "enjoying himself.''

Robinson's blindness always came as a shock to others. In April
1972, Robinson joined many of his old Dodger teammates at Gil Hod-

ges's funeral. He didn't recognize his old friend Pee Wee Reese, sitting just a row away. "When I said hello, he apologized," Reese recalled. "Pee Wee, I just can't see," Robinson explained.

Mrs. Sayles remembered one evening she and her husband spent with the Robinsons not long before he died. Toward the end of the evening, said Mrs. Sayles, "Rachel insisted that Jackie go get the car. Kiah was very upset because he knew how bad Jack's eyesight was. He said, 'Rachel, that's all right, I'll get the car.' But Jack said, no, he'd go and get it. But Kiah followed him anyway, because he did not want him driving at night. As they were leaving, Jack walked straight into a door because he couldn't see it."

And what sight remained was getting worse. Doctors could not prevent further loss of his vision because of the constant hemorrhaging behind the eyes. Laser treatments to fuse ruptured capillaries failed. Eventually Robinson couldn't even distinguish the food on his plate.

"Three days before he died," Marian Logan said, "I remember he was staying over at the little apartment on Ninety-third Street. And I walked into the apartment and I said, 'Jack, here's your dinner.' I said, 'Chicken's at six o'clock, greens are at three o'clock,' whatever else there was at nine o'clock on the plate—you know. He said, 'Put on the light.' The light was on and it was as bright as it could be in there. I just said, 'yeah, okay.' "

On October 15, 1972, just prior to the second game of the World Series between the Reds and the A's in Cincinnati, Robinson was honored by baseball on the occasion of the twenty-fifth anniversary of his first season. To those in the stands and in the press box, it was a rare on-field glimpse of a man who had long ago put baseball behind him. (That same summer he had attended a ceremony at Dodger Stadium—his first—when his uniform number was officially retired.)

In his remarks to the crowd at Riverfront Stadium, it was clear why he had had so little to do with baseball over the years—and why he might have been so willing to testify against the game's owners on behalf of Curt Flood. He was extremely pleased to be there, he said, "but I will be more pleased the day I can look over at the third-base line and see a black man as manager."

Just moments before he made those farewell remarks, Robinson was standing around in a runway behind the stands, waiting to be introduced. Pee Wee Reese and Joe Black were with him. Reese had not seen Robinson since Gil Hodges's funeral and—somewhat nervously, Joe Black remembered—asked Robinson about his vision problems.

Robinson shrugged and said, "Ah, you know, the sugar went to my eyes, they're gonna make special glasses, steel beams or something, thick as magnifying glass. I don't know. The left eye just floods with blood, the right eye I can see images. But that's not the main thing. I'm gonna go into the hospital and have my leg amputated."

"That's just what he said," Joe Black recalled, "like he's talking about apples and oranges. Pee Wee said, 'Whaddaya talking about?' Jack says, 'Watch when I walk, I sort of drag this leg—all the time it feels like electric shocks going through it.' Pee Wee gets real upset, says, 'Can't they do something?' He says, 'Naw, the sugar—they figure they'd cut it and that would stop it. And I'll take awhile and get an artificial leg and I'll learn to walk and I'll play golf, and you know what, Pee Wee?' 'What?' he says. 'I'll still beatcha.'

"Then they called us and we went up."

At around 6 A.M. on the morning of October 24, 1972, just nine days later, Robinson had a massive heart attack at his home in Stamford. He was pronounced dead in the ambulance on the way to the hospital less than an hour later.

EPILOGUE

The tributes for Jackie Robinson were led by the president of the United States, Richard M. Nixon, who praised Robinson's courage and who said that his sense of "brotherhood and brilliance on the playing field brought a new human dimension not only to the game of baseball but to every area of American life where black and white people work side by side."

Among the principal honorary pallbearers at Robinson's funeral service at New York's Riverside Church were New York Governor Nelson Rockefeller and NAACP chief Roy Wilkins.

The magnificent old pseudo-Gothic cathedral just across the way from Grant's Tomb looked especially elegant on that sun-splashed late-October day. Crowds lined the streets outside, and buses of schoolchildren were brought in for the occasion.

Rachel Robinson entered the cathedral with her eyes shut, her face puffy with grief. The weight of her anguish was such that she seemed unable to walk on her own. Her son David and another person appeared to be carrying her to her place in the front pews near the blue and silver casket adorned only with a single decoration of American Beauty roses.

The high and mighty were there in numbers, of course. Though the president himself could not make it, one of his advisers, Robert Finch, did. R. Sargent Shriver, New York Mayor John Lindsay, A. Philip Randolph, Bayard Rustin, baseball commissioner Bowie Kuhn, Joe Louis, Dick Gregory, Hank Aaron, and scores of other luminaries took up at least one-third of all the seating available in the cathedral. But at Rachel Robinson's request, the remainder of the seats, principally those in the upstairs sections, went to ordinary people, to residents of neighboring Harlem, to schoolchildren, to those who had been bused in for the day.

Of course, many of Robinson's old Dodger teammates were there —Newcombe, Gilliam, Pee Wee Reese, Carl Erskine, Roy Campanella. The actual pallbearers, the ones who gripped the carrying rails and lifted the remains of their friend out of the church, included bas-

ketball star Bill Russell, Larry Doby, Monte Irvin, Joe Black, Ralph
Branca, childhood friend Ray Bartlett, and Dr. Arthur Logan. These
pallbearers, because they knew Robinson well, became the special
focus of the swarms of media people waiting for one last and appropriate farewell story.

Monte Irvin stopped and told a reporter, "What I remember was
him saying to me one time shortly after he quit baseball that his pains
had disappeared. When he was playing, he was having stomach pains
and he never told anybody about them. Maybe they were psychoso-
matic or maybe he was so full of nervous tension, but he always had
that pain in his gut and look what he was able to do despite it."

Another reporter, looking for another angle, queried the hearse
driver and a man named Patterson who was there to organize the
motorcade afterward.

"I tried to get out of this job, it's too much work," he told the
reporter, who then used the remark to remind readers that no task
was too much for Jackie Robinson.

Wyatt Walker delivered one of the eulogies. At the request of the
family—Sharon Robinson in particular—the principal eulogy was delivered by Jesse Jackson, the thirty-one-year-old minister who had
been an associate of Martin Luther King's in the SCLC and who
now headed his own organization, the Chicago-based PUSH (People
United to Save Humanity). Robinson, at the end of his life, had been
its honorary first vice president.

Jackson told the mourners that Robinson was not so much a ballplayer as a chess player: "He was the black knight and he checkmated
bigotry!" Jackson reminded his listeners that progress did not roll on
wheels of inevitability, that "person and personality" were required
to change things.

A life is marked by two dates with a dash in between, Jackson
continued. "It is in that dash, between those dates, where we live.
For everyone," he said, his preacher's cadence catching the crowd,
"there is a dash of possibility, to choose the high road or the low
road, to make things better or make things worse."

Members of the congregation spontaneously responded, "That's
right! That's right! Say it like it is!"

"On that dash he snapped the barbed wire of prejudice," Jackson
cried, "in that dash he carried with him the gift of new expectations."

Robinson "stole home" from all those who had tried to stop him. "Call me nigger, call me black boy, I don't care," Jackson said. "I told Jesus it will be all right if I change my name! No grave can hold that body down because it belongs to the ages!"

The decorous crowd erupted as though it were a gigantic revival meeting.

Then Roberta Flack, her voice soaring in the high reaches of the building, sang the spiritual "I Told Jesus It Will Be All Right If I Change My Name." The benediction was rendered and then, led by the hearse waiting outside, began a long journey through the streets of the city.

The cortege proceeded slowly down to 125th Street, into central Harlem. The celebrities and family members sat huddled in their long cars as the procession passed crowds of people lining both sides of the roadways. A scheduled stop before the Freedom National Bank turned into a crowding and milling around, passersby stopping, people waving from open windows. Then the procession finally moved on, winding its way through the most blasted parts of the city, pausing again in Brooklyn, in Bedford-Stuyvesant, this time at a site associated with the new Jackie Robinson Construction Corporation. Again crowds pushed and shoved to get closer to the hearse, to the limousines with their tinted windows preserving the anonymity of the famous and the family members within.

Eventually the line of cars passed the last crowds who stood on the sides of the busy expressway leading out to the city's airports. The motorcade turned into the Cypress Gardens Cemetery, full of mausoleums and headstones more densely packed than the tenements of the living left behind.

In a surprisingly modest grave, barely marked, only upgraded years later, Jackie Robinson was laid to rest—alongside his son, Jackie junior.

In the more than two decades since his death at the age of fifty-three, time has done little to diminish his baseball achievement. He played with such verve, drama, and personal dignity that it seems impossible that any player coming through the door that he opened could possibly forget him—but the reality is, especially in a culture where history is too often measured in minutes not years, that forgetfulness is common, a blank slate even more common.

"I don't know anything about Jackie Robinson," said Ken Griffey Jr. several years ago, when he was launching his own special major league career. Barry Larkin, the Reds' superb shortstop, confessed that he knew Robinson was the first black player in baseball, "but if he were a shortstop, I'm sure I would want to know more about him."

Of course, some modern players do remember, even if what they remember is only the open door, not the man who walked through it. The White Sox superstar Frank Thomas acknowledged, "I don't know much about Jackie Robinson at all, I just know he gave all of us a chance. I heard he was a helluva ballplayer because it took a helluva ballplayer to break in back then. He had to be a really fine man to go through the things he went through." The Red Sox slugger Mo Vaughn wears Robinson's number 42 in his honor.

Memory has a way of becoming fixed in rituals of official respect—in commemorative postage stamps, bronze plaques, and anniversaries—so that the living heart of the achievement is lost. Those who lived and shared Robinson's time with him are all too aware of what he accomplished and why that accomplishment, from the very beginning, went far beyond the ball field. The "black knight" Jesse Jackson eulogized opened the chessboard for others in many areas. Hank Aaron, surviving his own corner of abuse and danger to break Babe Ruth's lifetime home run record, said that he "never dreamed of the big leagues until Jackie broke in with the Dodgers in 1947." He called Robinson "the Dr. King of baseball."

The first black player on a U.S. Olympic basketball team, Don Barksdale, said Robinson paved the way for him. The first black professional football player signed by the Cleveland Browns, Bob Willis, credited Robinson with inspiring him, as did Althea Gibson, the Wimbledon tennis champion in 1957, the basketball greats Bill Russell and Kareem Abdul Jabbar, and of course Arthur Ashe. Joe Louis, who had himself carried the burden of other people's dreams, acknowledged before he died, "Jackie is my hero. He don't bite his tongue for nothing. I just don't have the guts, you might call it, to say what he says. And don't talk as good either, that's for sure. But he talks the way he feels."

But if time has spread its sand of forgetfulness among our contemporaries, it only makes more poignant what took place on the ground, in plain view, so many (and so few) years ago. James Farmer, the civil rights leader and former director of CORE, actually found a virtue in being forgotten. "Oh, shucks," he said, "being forgotten is perfectly all right. You can have an impact and then years later people won't know who you are—but your work is still done. Right now, I visit college campuses, and I mention the name of A. Philip Randolph—and they say, 'A. Philip *who*?' Well, Randolph would smile at that and say, 'Well, I did my work.' And so did Jackie Robinson. The work lives on."

Farmer recalled that Robinson's work went beyond sports to the civil rights movement. Because Farmer himself had served for a time in the Nixon administration, he was acutely conscious that any involvement in Republican Party politics could easily create confusion—especially when trying to match the whole of Jackie Robinson's life with its easier-to-understand baseball phase.

"The curious thing was that a black person who moved in and out of Republican politics was lambasted, but the white person who did that wasn't," Farmer said. "Pat Moynihan was counselor to Nixon in the White House, and in his speech on resigning he praised Nixon to the hilt—and yet he became the darling of the left, right, and center." The late Floyd McKissick, the activist minister and a friend of Farmer's, only half-jokingly explained that plantation politics was to blame. "Don't you understand that, man," Farmer recalled him saying, "when you entered the Nixon administration, you left the plantation. Moynihan never left the plantation because he never came from no damn plantation!"

Far more serious to Farmer was all that remained unfinished. The state of race relations in the country today, in his mind, was related to the success of the civil rights revolution and its larger failure.

"I think the leadership of the fifties and sixties was too simplistic; we confused two terms—*segregation* and *racism*—when they really were different," he said. "Even Thurgood [Marshall], right after the Brown decision, was addressing a board meeting of the NAACP. According to Wilkins, he said, 'It's almost over now, we're almost over the hump.' But he would have been the first in his later years to acknowledge that we . . . had not even approached the hump."

Whatever wound there was in becoming a black Republican, this other one of being an "integrationist" was somehow even more painful, because even as the goal was increasingly achieved, the sense of

347

personal disenchantment grew stronger. The struggle to break segregation was only one part of the fight, not the fight itself. Integration, in the end, was only an ideal, like liberty or justice. It was never recognized that once integration had taken place, racism could persist.

Robinson's commitment to white and black cooperation was both practical and ideological. But emotionally, temperamentally, he was a committed "race man" from the day he received his first insult and decided he would fight back. His view of cooperation was surely complicated by his later lifestyle, by his family's needs. But he, unlike other committed integrationists—as reflected in his address, his attire, and his interests in banking, business, and the Republican Party—saw beyond the ideal of integration to self-sufficiency, to economic power rather than goodwill as a means to reach equality. That was not because he sold out, but because he never lost the sense of where he came from and what he had learned along the way.

Robinson's historic role is more important than his being the first black baseball player or, later, his becoming "a spokesman rather than a leader." He was, at first, a pioneer, and as such he prepared the way for other athletes—and for everyone else looking to tear down the walls. He was the figure who made civil rights a *popular* issue before anyone took to the streets or talked about programs, bills, or social action. Robinson was a link, and a crucial one, between despair and a movement. He is a far more important figure than he is given credit for in this country's civil rights movement.

Robinson no doubt suffered because whether he was a spokesman or a leader, he did not do enough homework to take charge of an issue when he could have. He thus became a person others could exploit, even if they could not push him around. It is hard to measure the exact amounts of sincerity and cynicism that went into Nelson Rockefeller's use of Robinson; it is easier to measure those components when employed by Richard Nixon. It is most difficult of all to measure the ways in which Martin Luther King used Robinson. King, it seems clear, believed it was urgent to have a civil rights presence in both political parties, as did Jackie Robinson. And it also seems clear that, as a matter of necessity, King kept himself above the fray for the sake of, as one associate put it, "purity." Whatever the facts, the suspicion lingers that he was actually the motivating force urging Robinson into the Republican camp. In any case, all that mattered to Robinson was getting results.

348

What, finally, was his accomplishment? How should he be seen today—beyond his being "the first" or even being an overlooked "link"? Roger Wilkins, an assistant attorney general in the Johnson administration and a longtime civil rights activist, said that Robinson's major achievement was that he changed the way black people thought about themselves—and then the way whites thought about blacks.

"Robinson was not simply carrying the whole race on his shoulders —which he was—he was driving the consciousness of black capacities more deeply into American culture than any black person had ever done previously," he said.

And, in Wilkins's mind, it was peculiarly related to baseball.

"You could ignore the other blacks who had become prominent in the thirties and forties as people who were doing things that were peripheral, whether it was Marian Anderson, Joe Louis, or Jesse Owens . . . but there was nothing more *American* than baseball. . . . And here's this guy, all by himself, in lonely competitive dignity day after day shattering the myth that blacks couldn't excel. It wasn't a sprint, he did it over the slow, languid pace of a baseball season where people can have streaks and then fall apart, under the severest pressure that any human being ever had to endure in that game. And it seems to me that his feat—it didn't matter who you were—if you were Hugo Black or Bill Douglas or Felix Frankfurter sitting there on the Supreme Court, you knew what Jackie was doing. If you were Harry Truman sitting in the White House, you knew what Jackie was doing. If you were Bull Connor down in Birmingham, you also knew. Jackie forced people, all people, to reconsider their assumptions about race."

Robinson was asked to carry more than any single human being should, and probably the price he paid was the brevity of his life. But the most certain facet of his nature was that, once given an opportunity, he could no more avoid what he had to do, no matter the damages nor even the compromises, than if he had been handpicked by Fate.

It did not matter if it was South Africa, South Carolina, or the south Bronx, the issue was always the same, and Robinson, in his way, was eternally, universally committed. The world he saw, from the moment he understood that he had a chance to make an impact on it, was one where walls of race and caste might come down and be replaced by new relationships, even, in the case of Africa, new nations. In a recent letter to the *New York Times,* George M. Hauser, a founding member of CORE and executive director of the American Committee on Africa, listed the Americans he believed were most influential in supporting South Africa's antiapartheid movement. He listed Robert Kennedy, Eleanor Roosevelt, Hubert Humphrey, Martin Luther King —and Jackie Robinson.

"If he had done nothing else in his life after 1947," Roger Wilkins said, "he would be entitled to be an American legend. But then he went on and had a very distinguished career. Moreover, having completed that, the man then went on and defined his heart. He could have engaged in trivial pursuits the rest of his life and he did not, so that it does not matter what other people thought or whether he was the leader of the band or anything else, what really mattered was the depth of his commitment to a cause which lots of people who get rich and famous forget all about.

"He never did."

A NOTE ON SOURCES

Very early in the research stage of this book, it was made clear to me that Rachel Robinson would neither consent to be interviewed nor permit me access to the archives of the Jackie Robinson Foundation. For a time, I considered abandoning the project altogether. But as I continued to do research and to interview people, including some who believed they were even taking a chance in talking to me against Mrs. Robinson's wishes, my own purposes in writing this biography became clearer.

I was never interested in Jackie Robinson as a tabloid figure. I couldn't have cared less who he slept with or whether or not he was a saint or a softy, but I was and am immensely interested in who he was out in the open, and what he accomplished—and did not accomplish —amongst us all. That story is a national possession in the same way that Martin Luther King's or Malcolm X's is; it is a story equally owned by all people who have been affected by the history of racism in this country and by the determined efforts of people like Robinson to make a difference. It is also one, fortunately, with an abundant record, public and private, to draw from.

I was most fortunate in finding people close to Robinson, including some members of his family, friends and acquaintances from his childhood, college classmates, members of his military units, teammates, workmates, and friends and colleagues from the civil rights movement, whose insights and remembrances gave me the opportunity to write about a complex and original human being rather than one built out of newsprint and marble. To those people, especially, I owe a debt of enormous gratitude. My deepest wish is that they will find confirmed in these pages the confidence they placed in me.

Frequently cited books, periodicals, and newspapers will be referred to by abbreviations in the notes section as follows:

JRS—The Jackie Robinson Story by Arthur Mann

NHM—I Never Had It Made by Jackie Robinson and Alfred Duckett

Rowan—*Wait Till Next Year* by Carl T. Rowan and Jackie Robinson

MOS—Jackie Robinson: My Own Story as told to Wendell Smith

Tygiel—*The Great Experiment* by Jules Tygiel

SN—The Sporting News

NYT—The New York Times

NYP—The New York Post

AN—Amsterdam News

BW—Business Week

WP—Washington Post

VP—Papers of John Vernon, unpublished. National Archives, Washington, D.C.

NOTES

Prologue

9–10 An account of the game and exchange between Rickey and a reporter in *Time*, Sept. 22, 1947, p. 74.

Chapter One

14 "No other state in the union": W. E. B. Du Bois, *The Souls of Black Folk* (1903; Penguin ed., 1989), p. 96.

15 "Chimney . . . still stands, without marking plaque": description of family birthplace in detail, art. by Ed Grisamore in *Macon Telegraph*, June 23, 1993.

15–18 Sasser family history quoted from int. with Marvin Sasser, Albany, Ga.

18 "There were thirteen of us": Willa Mae Walker int.

Chapter Two

22 "supportive mother": Harvey Frommer, *Rickey and Robinson* (New York: Macmillan, 1982), p. 20.

24 "Their door was never locked": Jack Gordon int.

25 "True hell": Jessie Maxwell Wills int.

26 "We were raising some horses": int. in Frommer, p. 24.

Chapter Three

28 "When Marbles": in Frommer, p. 22.

29 "At lunchtime": Bartlett int.

29 "There weren't signs in the neighborhood": Hasagawa int.

30 "I remember, even as a small boy": Jackie Robinson and Alfred Duckett, *I Never Had It Made* (New York, 1972), p. 18.

31 "Whenever there was a newsreel": Gordon int.

Chapter Four

35 "We used to play a game": *Christian Science Monitor*, Sept. 26, 1977, p. 11.

36 "Nipped . . . in the last stride": ibid.

37 "The morning of the day": Glickman int.

38 "As far as I can remember": undated 1976 int. with Blaine Newnham in *Portland* (Oreg.) *Register-Guard*.

Chapter Five

41 "I was in the ninth grade": Takayama int.

43 "I saw Jackie": *The Duke of Flatbush* (Zebra, 1988), p. 25.

45 "I can conceive": *Notes of a Native Son* (New York: Beacon, 1957), p. 71.

Chapter Six

49 Ray Bartlett's story and the details of the recruiting offers: Carl T. Rowan with Jackie Robinson, *Wait Till Next Year* (New York, 1960), pp. 43–44.

49 "I tried to influence him to enroll": MR in *Ebony*, July 1957.

49 "Spaulding . . . told . . . Mann": Arthur Mann, *The Jackie Robinson Story* (New York, 1950), p. 52.

50 "Clutches of competing schools": Rowan, p. 44.

51 "job as busboy": *JRS*, p. 64.

52 "forty thousand of them would be black": Woody Strode and Sam Young, *Goal Dust* (Lanham, Md., 1990), p. 62.

53 "contests in the Coliseum": Strode, op. cit., p. 57.

54 Strode believes Robinson to be "on guard": ibid., p. 89.

55 "the tough Bruin halfback": Rowan, p. 55.

56 Wilbur Johns, "Jackie had another great night": *JRS*, p. 61.

56 "If Jackie hadn't played football": ibid., p. 59.

57 "team practiced in great secrecy": Strode, op. cit., pp. 96–97.

58 "The Beverly Hills": ibid., pp. 98–99.

58 "He told Roger Kahn": *The Boys of Summer* (Signet, 1973), p. 356.

58 "dress up when we traveled": Strode, op. cit., p. 74.

Chapter Seven

62 "He was cocky, arrogant, conceited": *NHM*, pp. 22–23.

62 "You can't replay a single minute": JRS, p. 72.

63 "could fend off . . . subtle prejudices": Rowan, p. 60.

63 "dance at the Biltmore": ibid., pp. 62–63.

64 The offer from school officials to help pay expenses to allow him to graduate is explained by JR in *Look* magazine, "Your Temper Can Ruin Us," the third in a three-part series, Feb. 15, 1955, pp. 81–82.

64 "Rachel . . . ardent about the importance of college": *NHM*, p. 23.

65 "The Jim Thorpe of his race": Rowan, p. 66.

66 "peering out a porthole": *JRS*, pp. 84–85.

66 "iconoclast in him": Frommer, op. cit., pp. 33–34.

66 "a most uneasy man": Rowan, p. 69.

67 "Sole means of support": ibid.

67 "Rachel . . . chided him": ibid.

Chapter Eight

68 JR's induction order in *VP*.

69 Details concerning JR's induction physical and other army-related matters were obtained by FOIA request and furnished under the heading "Official Statement of the Military Service of Jack R. Robinson, Service Number 01 031 586." The official file had been furnished to JR on May 21, 1958.

70 "admitted to OCS": Rowan, p. 70.

70 "One day we were out at the field": Reiser in *Bums*, Peter Golenbock, (New York, 1984), p. 152.

71 "let's be reasonable, Lieutenant": Rowan, p. 73.

71 "several officers present": Gary int.

72 A description of the Alexandria incident is in *Liberators: Fighting on Two Fronts*, Lou Potter with William Miles and Nina Rosenblum (New York, 1992), pp. 73–75.

73 "In eight years of playing football": Bates int.

74 "Officers . . . rarely so honest": Rowan, p. 76.

75 "He was kind of aloof": Williams int.

75 "Primarily interested in Jackie": Gary int.

75 "used to sit with us . . . goldbricking": McConnell int.

Chapter Nine

78–86 Sources for the general background of Robinson's court-martial, including the situation regarding transportation on the base, are drawn from already cited interviews, "The Court Martial of Jackie Robinson" by Jules Tygiel, in *American Heritage*, September 1984, p. 34ff.

78–86 The North Carolina incident, ibid., p. 36.

78 The incident involving Joe Louis and Sugar Ray Robinson is noted in *Liberators*, op. cit., p. 124.

79 Robinson's statements, unless otherwise noted, are drawn from the official court-martial transcript, which includes written pretrial statements as well as direct testimony. The "Record of Trial and Accompanying Papers" was obtained under an FOIA request. The report is dated August 2, 1944, and is assigned the document number 262476.

79 Statement to Ed Reid, *WP,* August 26, 1949.

79 "pretty, peach-skinned girl": Rowan, p. 90.

81 Robinson's letter to the NAACP as well as the "anonymous" letter are in NAACP papers, L.C.

83 Trial length, background of army thinking, see Tygiel, *American Heritage, op. cit.*

84 "My letter was timed to reach": *NHM,* p. 35.

84 "honorably relieved from active duty": Official Statement of . . . Service," op. cit.

85 "Medical discharge": Rowan, p. 93.

85 "Not suitable material": Rachel Robinson interview in *Legends,* Art Rust Jr. (New York), p. 93.

85 "said her husband had been dishonorably discharged": int. with Rust.

85 "The intermediate one": Rosenthal int.

Chapter Ten

87 "He, Smith, contacted Monarchs owner, J. L. Wilkinson": John B. Holway, *Voices From the Great Black Baseball Leagues* (New York, 1992), pp. 283–84.

87 "they responded rather quickly": *NHM,* p. 35.

88 "she sent back his ring and bracelet": ibid., p. 25.

88 "He was not immune to soldierly diversions . . ." Robinson's army medical records indicate that, at least on one occasion, he was treated for venereal disease. See papers of John Vernon, privately collected, National Archives, Washington, D.C.

89 "Neither the technique nor the circumstances": Rowan, p. 93.

89 "Can't we postpone it": ibid., p. 94.

90 "Robinson hit .350 through the season": *JRS,* p. 103.

90 "Jackie had one-third ability and two-thirds brains": Holway, op. cit., p. 103.

91 "Robinson . . . learned from Cool Papa Bell": Donn Rogosin, *Invisible Men: Life in Baseball's Negro Leagues* (New York, 1983), pp. 85–86.

92 "We went to school on a team": Janet Bruce, *The Kansas City Monarchs* (University of Kansas Press, 1985), p. 101.

93 "players have to make the jump between cities": *Ebony,* June 1948.

93 "Renfroe told Jules Tygiel": Jules Tygiel, *Baseball's Great Experiment* (New York, 1983), p. 63.

Chapter Eleven

96 *"Worker* calling for fans to write": Jan. 25 and 28, 1943.

97 Article comparing Olmo to DiMaggio: *Worker,* Mar. 18, 1943.

97 "The first Puerto Rican ever to make the Dodgers": ibid., Mar. 30, 1943.

98 "Petitions were being circulated everywhere": ibid., Apr. 11, 1943. The text of the petition addressed to Rickey is included.

98 "Rightful place in the big leagues": ibid., Dec. 17, 1943.

98 "in a separate article, featured thumbnail sketches of the players": ibid., Dec. 1943.

99 *Worker* coverage of winter baseball meetings, including "over-the-transom" report of Robeson's speech, Dec. 3–6, 1943.

100 Int. with Sam Lacy, Baltimore, 1993.

Chapter Twelve

102 "Listen, Smith, it burns me up": *NHM*, p. 99.

102 "Sam told us what a joke that so-called tryout was": Grace int.

103 "More for your cause": Rickey quoted in Tygiel, p. 46.

104 Six-part plan in *JRS*, p. 12.

104–105 The Thomas story is in Mann, pp. 29–30.

105 "I am quite sure that Mr. Rickey didn't say what the reporters enlarged upon": Thomas note in Mann Papers, Library of Congress, Washington, D.C.

107 "Have you got a girl?" *NHM*, p. 42.

107 "he acted out a series of one-man dramatic scenes": *Look*, Feb. 15, 1955, p. 83.

107 "You tar-baby son of a bitch": Rowan, pp. 117–18.

107 For details of the "legendary meeting" see Tygiel, p. 67.

One tantalizing story about Robinson around this time is related in Benjamin Davis Jr.'s autobiography, *Communist Councilman from Harlem*. According to Davis, when Robinson signed his pact with the Dodgers in August, a small reception was given for him, "attended by about 25 trade union, Negro, progressive and Communist leaders." Among those present, said Davis, was Paul Robeson. "[Robinson] commended Robeson for his contributions to the struggle and said a few kind words to me. . . . We were happy because we felt he was aware of the long struggle put up by his own people and by the labor and progressive movement to achieve this symbolic triumph." No one has ever said how Davis, Robeson, or anyone else knew that Robinson had actually signed with the Dodgers as early as August 1945, and no corroborating evidence for this meeting has turned up; if it did take place, the strong likelihood is that Robinson himself was involved in passing on the information—in spite of the stricture laid down by Rickey, that it be kept secret.

NOTES

Chapter Thirteen

109 Holtzman account: *Chicago Tribune*, Apr. 11, 1993.

109 Radcliffe's reputation as yarn-spinner: Holway, op. cit., pp. 169–70.

109 "on June the thirteenth, we went to Newark": Radcliffe int.

113 "Good enough to die for his country": Tygiel, p. 69.

113–114 Rickey's letter to Mann: Mann papers.

Chapter Fourteen

116 "In the papers the next day, they reported that I had been cool": *Jackie Robinson: My Own Story* as told to Wendell Smith, (New York, 1948), p. 28.

116 "I can only say I'll do my very best": *NYT*, Oct. 24, 1945.

116 "The *New York Times* noted": ibid.

117 "Dick McCann of the *Washington Times-Herald*": JRS, p. 129.

117–118 "We question Rickey's statements that he is another Abraham Lincoln": Tygiel, p. 74.

118 "Father Devine will have to look to his laurels": *JRS*, p. 127.

118 Edgar T. Rouzeau and Ludlow Werner: *Herald*, Oct. 25, 1945.

118–119 "Mike Gold noted": *Worker*, Oct. 26, 1945.

120 "But signing Jackie like they did still hurt me deep down": Satchel Paige, *Maybe I'll Pitch Forever* (New York, 1961), p. 151.

120 "When we got down there, Robinson didn't look too good": Holway, op. cit., p. 267.

Chapter Fifteen

127 "The food was something of an embarrassment to Rachel": Rowan, 130–32.

128 "I felt like weeping": ibid., 134–35.

129 "The white Montreal players": *SN*, Mar. 14, 1946.

130 "anything could happen anytime to a Negro": *MOS*, p. 67.

130 "just throw the ball around and hit a few": ibid., p. 69.

132 "Robinson claims he heard voices of encouragement": *MOS*, p. 78.

133 "he demands a fair chance and fair play": ibid., p. 79.

134 "he and his wife wound up going to the same black movie theater": Rowan, p. 146.

Chapter Sixteen

135 *Daily News . . . Daily Mirror*, Apr. 19, 1946.
141 "although JR made only one hit in three games": Mann papers.
142 *"Pittsburgh Courier* writer Sam Maltin described the scene": *MOS*, pp. 109–10.

Chapter Seventeen

145 "In November 1946, the publication *Fraternal Outlook*": the publications and organizations mentioned and their "communist" connection are contained in Robinson's FBI file, portions of which were released under an FOIA request. An updated summary report is dated Aug. 24, 1969.
146 "to date no copy of it has ever surfaced": Tygiel, pp. 80–81.
146 "However well-intentioned the use of Negro players": *JRS*, p. 134.
147 "This is the part I don't think anybody knows about ": *Washington Star-News*, Oct. 27, 1972.
148 "Come prepared to hear Mr. Rickey": *JRS*, p. 164.
148 "the biggest threat to his success—is the Negro people themselves!": ibid., p. 162.
149 "You'll strut. You'll wear badges": ibid., p. 163.

Chapter Eighteen

151 The meeting at Joe's Restaurant: Red Barber, *1947: When All Hell Broke Loose in Baseball* (New York, 1982), pp. 49–50 and 64.
152 Durocher "wouldn't have been able to spell *equality* much less preach it' ": Harold Parrott, *The Lords of Baseball* (New York, 1976), 208–9.
152 "I won't play with the black sonuvabitch": Bragan int.
154 Dixie Walker's letter to Rickey: Rickey papers, Library of Congress, Washington, D.C.
156 "Robinson laughed in Smith's face": *MOS*, p. 121.
156 "I thought you were carrying a watermelon on each hip": Roy Campanella, *It's Good to be Alive* (New York, 1959), pp. 131–32.

Chapter Nineteen

161 "The American Creed represents the national conscience": Gunnar Myrdal, *An American Dilemma* (New York, 1944), p. 23.
161 "Behind all outward dissimilarities": ibid., p. 1023.

163 "Robinson went hitless but distinguished himself in the field": Barber, op. cit., p. 153.

164 "hate poured forth from the Phillies dugout": *NHM*, p. 71.

164 "You yellow-bellied cowards": ibid., p. 73.

165 "the St. Louis Cardinal strike . . . remains an extremely elusive topic": Tygiel, p. 186.

165 "The Chicago Cubs . . . actually took a strike vote": Hank Wyse int.

166 "I could hear the Cincinnati players screaming at Jackie": Barney interview in Golenbock, op. cit., p. 193.

166 "Usually I didn't show Robbie the hate mail": Parrott, op. cit., p. 190.

168 "The woman with whom we shared the apartment seemed to entertain friends constantly": Rowan, p. 191.

168 "the most lucrative draw in baseball since Babe Ruth": Tygiel, p. 189.

169 "In city after city, Robinson showed skeptical critics": ibid.

169 "I tried again and again to get him to talk about the problems he was meeting": Parrott, op. cit., p. 199.

169 "Roger Kahn . . . says that Robinson specifically told him": Roger Kahn, *The Era* (New York, 1993), pp. 48–49.

Chapter Twenty

172 "The game resumes. Robinson starts to dance off the third-base line": Bill Reddy quoted in Golenbock, op. cit., p. 432.

172–173 For more on the Greenberg episode, see *MOS*, pp. 146–47.

173 "Robinson himself said the incident took place in Braves Field": *Look*, Feb. 8, 1955.

174 "Robinson said that he was nearly overcome with rage": Rowan, p. 188.

174 "I wasn't trying to think of myself as being the Great White Father": *NYT*, July 17, 1977.

175 "Only my opinion, but I think Rickey did it for money": Branca int.

175 "Branca called a meeting in Chicago": Black int.

177 Accounts of the Borough Hall celebration and, also, of Jackie Robinson Day: *JRS*, pp. 197–98.

Chapter Twenty-one

179–180 All letters in Mann papers.

181 "God, I was working two jobs at that time": Sutton int.

181 "I met him on the radio": Dee int.

182 "Bankhead . . . was a frightened black man from Tennessee": Irving Rudd and Stan Fischler, *The Sporting Life* (New York, 1990), p. 82.

187 "Arthur Mann said that Robinson had already agreed to testify": *JRS*, p. 211.

187 "Both Rickey and Veeck reinforced the opinion": Tygiel, p. 225.

Chapter Twenty-two

188 "Jake Pitler will see to it": *JRS*, p. 205.

192 "I do know . . . that—more than once—my father told me that he remarked to Robinson": Stokes Jr. int.

194 "The failure of organized baseball to follow Rickey's lead": Tygiel, p. 225.

194 "The first contribution of Jackie Robinson": Branch Rickey with Robert Riger, *The American Diamond*, p. 47.

195 "Paul Robeson was quoted in an AP dispatch": Martin Bauml Duberman, *Paul Robeson* (New York, 1989), p. 342.

195 "a de facto double standard when it came to blacks": Victor S. Navasky, *Naming Names* (New York, 1980), p. 187.

Chapter Twenty-three

197 "Throughout the almost four years": Committee on Un-American Activities, House of Representatives, *Hearings Regarding Communist Infiltration of Minority Groups—Part 1*, pp. 425–26.

197 "The Negro population, etc.": ibid., p. 428.

199 "I confess that I was miffed": Granger to Rickey, Aug. 29, 1950, in Mann Papers.

199 "informer Manning Johnson specifically cited the group": ibid., p. 518.

200–201 The text of Robinson's remarks to HUAC are in HR *Hearings*, op. cit., pp. 481–82.

Chapter Twenty-four

205 "We used to have this thing": Satlow int.

207 Reese turning over a rock at the Atlanta airport: Lester Rodney int.

207 "Yeah, we were afraid when we got to Atlanta": Rosenthal int.

209 "It was a decoy which only Robinson knew": *NYT Magazine*, Sept. 18, 1949, p. 17.

208 "Jackie just reached over and pulled down the shade": Rosenthal int.

210 "I started to appreciate him when I put myself into his shoes": quoted in "Tribute to Robinson," Dan Coughlin, undated article in *Cleveland Plain Dealer,* in Robinson collection, Hall of Fame Library, Cooperstown.

210 "He was Jackie Robinson's friend": Roger Kahn, *The Boys of Summer* (New York, 1973), pp. 288–89.

Chapter Twenty-five

212 For the Van Cuyck episode, see Rowan, pp. 236–37.

213 "The sportswriter who seemed to be doing his best to make me revert": *NHM,* p. 106.

216 "The two Rickeyphiles O'Malley detested": Golenbock, op. cit., p. 336.

216 "Bringing Jack into organized baseball was not the greatest thing": ibid., p. 339.

Chapter Twenty-six

220 "Reese hoisted a fly": see Campanella, op. cit., p. 154.

223 "Even an enormously sympathetic writer like Roger Kahn": Kahn, *Boys,* p. 362.

223 "Adventure. Adventure. The man is all adventure": ibid., p. 358.

224 "you'd almost have to say that the personality of this team centered around Jackie": Erskine int.

225 "Hey, Jackie, here's some black pussy for you": Newcombe int.

Chapter Twenty-seven

231–232 The report on Cox is in Mann papers, dated Jan. 30, 1949.

232 "It raised for him the infinitely barren prospect": Kahn, *Boys,* pp. 167–68.

235 " 'I don't even know how to swim,' Jackie said": Newcombe int.

237 "Jackie Robinson made it possible for me": Walker int. King is more widely on record: "You will never know how easy it was for me because of Jackie Robinson." Cited most recently in *Fan: A Baseball Magazine,* September 1994, p. 30.

Chapter Twenty-eight

239 "A knee crashed into Williams's lower spine": Kahn, *Boys,* p. 361.

241 Robinson . . . "irked that Campy, a Negro with children": Rowan, p. 261.

242 Irving Rudd called the evening "one of the great, glorious nights of Dodger history": Golenbock, op. cit., p. 506.

242 "Publicist Rudd remembers that Roy Campanella": ibid., p. 507.

Chapter Twenty-nine

251 "Robinson said that before his meeting with Black, he had discussed with Rachel": Rowan, pp. 278–79.

252 "Horace Stoneham, the President of the Giants": *Look*, Jan. 22, 1957, p. 92.

253 "I was so often advised": text of Robinson speech in NAACP papers, Library of Congress, Washington, D.C.

254 "Mr. Wilkins asked me to head the drive": *NHM*, p. 138.

254 "gave me a check made out to the NAACP that was in five figures": ibid.

255 Copy of the letter to King: NAACP papers.

256 Williams's confidential report to Wilkins: NAACP papers.

Chapter Thirty

258 "Campanella, said Young, blasted Jackie for being a clubhouse loudmouth": Rowan, p. 324.

260 Text of Robinson's letter to Nixon, Mar. 19, 1957: NAACP papers.

261 Nixon reply to JR, Mar. 19, 1957: Nixon Vice-Presidential Papers, Nixon Library, San Clemente, Calif.

262 Text of Freedom Fund Chicago speech, July 14, 1957: NAACP papers.

263 Nixon reply to JR, Jan. 23, 1958: Nixon papers.

264 JR speech to Detroit convention, June 30, 1957: NAACP papers.

265 Text of Robinson's remarks on *Viewpoint*, the Sunday religious program, Dec. 14, 1957: Nixon papers.

Chapter Thirty-one

267–268 Text of Robinson's address in Jackson, Feb. 16, 1958: NAACP papers.

270–271 JR's column: *NYP*, Apr. 7, 1958.

Chapter Thirty-two

273 "That was really how Jack and I got together": Logan int.

276 Humphrey letter to Robinson, Feb. 16, 1960, in Hubert H. Humphrey Papers, Minnesota Historical Society, St. Paul, Minn.

276 Timilty's account is in a photo request to White House chief of staff Lawrence F. O'Brien, in Kennedy Papers, John F. Kennedy Memorial Library, Boston, Mass.
278 Kennedy letter to JR: *NHM*, p. 149.
278 For more on Nixon's courtship of JR: ibid., p. 148.
279 Taylor meetings with JR and JFK: Taylor int.

Chapter Thirty-three

281 JR leave from Chock and *Post: NYP*, Sept. 8, 1960.
281 ". . . great Northern 'liberals' and . . . Southern liberals,": *AN*, Jan. 6, 1962.
283 Nixon letter to JR: *NYP*, June 10, 1960.
284 For a detailed account of the attempts to free King, see Taylor Branch, *Parting the Waters* (New York, 1988), pp. 351ff.
285 Memo from Thompson to Rockefeller: Rockefeller Archive, Pocantico Hills, N.Y.
286 JR letter to Wilkins and the reply: NAACP papers.

Chapter Thirty-four

288 Baldwin's letter to his nephew: James Baldwin, *The Fire Next Time* (Vintage ed., 1993), pp. 9–10.
289 "Reviews of King's performance in Albany": Branch, op. cit., p. 631.
290–291 Wilkins to Duckett, Apr. 25, 1962: NAACP papers.
291 Greenberg to Patterson, May 23, 1962: NAACP papers.
291 "Dear Roy": King to Wilkins, NAACP papers.

Chapter Thirty-five

295 Texts of the telegram, July 16, 1962, and of the press release, July 20, 1962: NAACP papers.
296 "I've been in a number of heavy debates": *NHM*, pp. 161–62.
296 "Powell . . . was casting around for an issue": Charles Hamilton, *Adam Clayton Powell, Jr.* (New York, 1991), p. 359.
297 "I don't agree with some of the things Malcolm X preaches": ibid., p. 360.
297 Text of the open Letter: NAACP papers.
300 Kennedy's speech and King's reaction: Branch, op. cit., p. 824.
301 "Malcolm says to us": Llewellyn int.

302–303 Peter Bailey's account: Hampton and Fayer, eds., *Voices of Freedom* (New York, 1990), p. 256.

Chapter Thirty-six

304 "He was a pleasure to be around": Slater int.

306 "I was so awestruck": Wyatt Walker int.

306 "When she actually began to go to work every day": *NHM*, p. 171.

309 "Just who are you playing ball for today, good friend?": *AN*, Nov. 30, 1963.

309 Robinson's reply to Malcolm: *AN*, Dec. 14, 1963.

Chapter Thirty-seven

311 "However, the meeting wasn't called off": Cunningham int.

313 "I took advantage of telephoning him one day": Goldwater letter to author, Sept. 3, 1993.

315 "Black people were coming to the point where they would be crying out": NHM, pp. 195–96.

Chapter Thirty-eight

318 "Our people take pride": *AN,* Jan. 1, 1965.

318 "In 1960 . . . there were only 10 black-owned banks": *BW*, Dec. 5, 1970.

320 "There's one very important aspect to this . . . he was Jackie Robinson the baseball player": Marshall int.

322 Western Union telefax from JR to MLK: King Archive, Atlanta, Ga.

323 Account of the 1967 Spring Mobilization: David Garrow, *Bearing the Cross* (New York, 1986), pp. 556–57.

323 Text of Robinson's open letter to King: *NHM*, pp. 224–25.

324 Wilkins to JR, Feb. 8, 1967: NAACP papers.

325 JR's reply to Wilkins, Feb. 15, 1967: NAACP papers.

325 "The Association needs new blood," JR to Wilkins, Feb. 20, 1967: NAACP papers.

325–327 Robinson Jr.'s own account of his drug problems is given in *NHM*, pp. 239–46.

Chapter Thirty-nine

328 "They talked a great deal with me about him": Clark int.

329 "Perhaps what God had done in Montgomery": *AN*, Apr. 13, 1968.

329 "There is no doubt in my mind that many, many whites wanted to see Dr. King silenced to death": *AN*, May 18, 1968.

330 "American society . . . is one of the most violent 'civilizations' on the map": *AN*, June 15, 1968.

330 "Instead of taking to the streets to retaliate": *AN*, Sept. 21, 1968.

331 The article from *Muhammad Speaks*, Oct. 4, 1968, is also contained in Robinson's FBI file.

332 "He came down here all the time": Logan int.

332 "We thought of only a few names": Marvin Miller int.

332 "Anything that is one-sided": reported in *NYT*, May 22, 1970.

333 it was becoming obvious . . . that we were not being cautious enough": *NHM*, p. 202.

333 "I found myself losing sleep at nights": ibid., p. 205.

Chapter Forty

337 The car "spun out of control, smashed into an abutment": *New York Daily News*, June 17, 1971.

339 "They were not really rioting": Walker int.

339–340 "I think he should have gone to Attica in person": *NHM*, pp. 220–21.

340 Robinson found it "ironic, that just as he seemed to be rising to the crest": ibid., p. 194.

341 "When I said hello, he apologized": *NYP*, Nov. 27, 1972.

Epilogue

344 "I tried to get out of this job, it's too much work": reported by Dave Anderson, *NYT*, Oct. 28, 1972.

346 "I don't know about Jackie Robinson," said Ken Griffey Jr.: reported by Ira Berkow, *NYT*, Dec. 10, 1989.

346 Frank Thomas acknowledged, "I don't know much about Jackie Robinson. . . . I just know he gave all of us a chance": Thomas int.

346 Hank Aaron . . . said that he "never dreamed of the big leagues": *NYT*, Apr. 13, 1987.

346 "Jackie is my hero. He don't bite his tongue for nothing": ibid.

347 "Oh, shucks," he said, "being forgotten is perfectly all right": Farmer int.

349 "Robinson was not simply carrying the whole race": Wilkins int.

SELECTED BIBLIOGRAPHY

Allen, Maury. *Jackie Robinson: A Life Remembered.* Franklin Watts, 1987.

Aptheker, Herbert. *A Documentary History of the Negro People in the United States.* 4 vols. Citadel, 1992.

Baldwin, James. *Notes of a Native Son.* New York: Beacon, 1955, 1957.

———. *The Fire Next Time.* New York: Dial, 1963.

Barber, Red. *1947: When All Hell Broke Loose in Baseball.* New York: Da Capo, 1982.

Barney, Rex with Norman L. Macht. *Rex Barney's Thank Youuuu.* Tidewater Publishers, 1993.

Bennett, Lerone Jr. *Before the Mayflower: A History of the Negro in America, 1619–1964* (revised ed.). Penguin, 1966.

Bragan, Bobby. *You Can't Hit the Ball with the Bat on your Shoulder.* The Summit Group, 1992.

Branch, Taylor. *Parting the Waters: America in the King Years 1954–1963.* New York: Simon and Schuster, 1988, Touchstone, 1989.

Bruce, Janet. *The Kansas City Monarchs: Champions of Black Baseball.* U. of Kansas Press, 1985.

Campanella, Roy. *It's Good to be Alive.* New York, 1965.

Chadwick, Bruce. *When the Game was Black and White: The Illustrated History of Baseball's Negro Leagues.* Abbeville Press, 1992.

Davis, Benjamin Jr. *Communist Councilman from Harlem.* International Publishers, 1969.

Duberman, Martin Bauml. *Paul Robeson: A Biography.* New York: Ballantine, 1989.

Du Bois, W.E.B. *The Souls of Black Folk.* A. C. McClurg and Co., 1903. Penguin, 1989.

———. *Black Reconstruction In America 1860–1880.* Meridian, 1964. Edwards, Bob. *Fridays with Red.* New York: Simon and Schuster, 1993.

Frommer, Harvey. *Rickey and Robinson.* New York: Macmillan, 1982.

Foner, Philip S. *Paul Robeson Speaks.* Citadel, 1978.

Garrow, David J. *Bearing the Cross: Martin Luther King and the Southern Christian Leadership Conference.* New York: Morrow, 1986.

———. *The FBI and Martin Luther King, Jr.* W. W. Norton, 1981.

Halberstam, David. *The Summer of '49.* New York: Morrow, 1989.

Hamilton, Charles V. *Adam Clayton Powell, Jr.* Atheneum, 1991.

Hampton, Henry and Steve Fayer. *Voices of Freedom: An Oral History of the Civil Rights Movement from the 1950's through the 1980's.* Bantam, 1990.

Holway, John B. *Voices from the Great Black Baseball Leagues.* New York: Da Capo, 1992.

Honig, Donald. *A Donald Honig Reader.* New York: Fireside, 1988.

———. *The Plot to Kill Jackie Robinson.* Signet, 1993.

Kahn, Roger. *The Boys of Summer.* Signet, 1973.

———. *The Era.* New York: Ticknor and Fields, 1993.

King, Martin Luther, Jr. *Why We Can't Wait.* Harper and Row, 1963, Signet, 1964.

Lipman, David. *Mr. Baseball: The Story of Branch Rickey.* New York, 1966.

Mann, Arthur. *The Jackie Robinson Story.* New York: Grosset and Dunlap, 1950.

———. *Branch Rickey: American in Action.* New York, 1966.

Miller, Marvin. *A Whole Different Ball Game: The Sport and Business of Baseball.* Birch Lane Press, 1991.

Myrdal, Gunnar. *An American Dilemma.* New York, 1944.

Navasky, Victor. *Naming Names.* Viking, 1980, Penguin 1981.

Paige, Satchel. *Maybe I'll Pitch Forever* (as told to David Lipman). New York: Grove, 1961.

Parrott, Harold. *The Lords of Baseball.* New York: Praeger, 1976.

Potter, Lou, et. al. *Liberators: Fighting on Two Fronts in World War II.* Harcourt, Brace, Jovanovitch, 1992.

Rickey, Branch with Robert Riger. *The American Diamond.* New York: Simon and Schuster, 1965.

Robinson, Jackie. *My Own Story* (as told to Wendell Smith). New York: Greenberg, 1948.

——— and Al Duckett. *I Never Had it Made.* New York: Putnam, 1972.

———. *Baseball Has Done It.* New York, 1964.

——— with Carl Rowan. *Wait Till Next Year.* New York: Random House, 1960.

Rogosin, Donn. *Invisible Men: Life in Baseball's Negro Leagues.* New York: Atheneum, 1985.

Rudd, Irving. *The Sporting Life.* New York: St. Martin's, 1990.

Rust, Art Jr. *Legends.* McGraw-Hill, 1989.

———. *Get That Nigger off the Field.* New York: Delacorte, 1976.

Snider, Duke with Bill Gilbert. *The Duke of Flatbush.* New York: Zebra, 1988.

Strode, Woody with Sam Young. *Goal Dust.* Madison Books, 1990.

Tygiel, Jules. *Baseball's Great Experiment: Jackie Robinson and His Legacy,* New York: Oxford, 1983.

West, Cornell. *Race Matters.* Beacon, 1993.

Wilkins, Roy, with Tom Matthews. *Standing Fast: The Autobiography of Roy Wilkins.* Viking, 1982.

ACKNOWLEDGMENTS

It is is impossible to adequately thank all those who contributed to the making of this book. Many of those I want to thank most will find their names in place in the text. I was helped enormously by friends and family and people I met only in the context of doing a book about Jackie Robinson. All my friends at Out to Lunch offered support, suggestions, hard-to-find materials as well as constant good cheer over the last three years. A special thank you to Lee Lowenfish. It is generally held that library staffs are there to serve, but anyone who has had the good fortune to work at the Hall of Fame library in Cooperstown, or at the Library of Congress, or at the Schomberg Center in New York, will understand immediately how much more is offered beyond any call of duty. The same goes for my editor, Jeff Neuman, who in the most personal and exacting way made his labor my special reward and support. Thanks to David Garrow, Pete Golenbock, Don Honig, Larry Ritter, Bruce Keys at the King Library, Bill Kaplan, Lorraine Springsteen, Harold Oakhill, Ted Karns, Sy Preston, Paige Morton Black, Paul Wormser, and Tony Greiner. Thanks to Ivan Siff for the hours and the wheels. To Maggie Siff and Bill Harrington for the hours and the digging. Special thanks also to Don Kaplan at the Brooklyn Public Library and John Vernon at the National Archive, who both went out of their way to provide me with invaluable help and material assistance along the way.

INDEX

Belafonte, Harry, 277, 323
Bell, Cool Papa, 91, 121
Benson, Gene, 91, 120, 121–23
Benswanger, William, 96
Berra, Yogi, 228
Bethune, Mary McLeod, 126, 252
Bigotry, 170
Birmingham, 297–98, 302
Black, Joe, 140, 175, 218–19, 223, 224, 235, 236, 341, 342, 344
"Black knight." See Jackson, Jesse
Black Muslims, 297
Black Panthers, 72, 288, 330
  goals, 331
Black Power, 315
Blacks. See African-Americans
Blackwell, Ewell, 176
Black, William, 246, 254, 276, 282, 304, 305
  hiring Robinson as public relations coup, 249–50
Blindness, 340
Bombings, 298, 302
Bostic, Joe, 95, 102
Boston Red Sox, 102
Boudreau, Lou, 182
Boycotts, 259, 268, 322
Boyd, Bob, 334
Boys of Summer. See Brooklyn Dodgers
Boys of Summer, The (Kahn), 210
Bragan, Bobby, 152, 153
Bramham, W. G., 118
Branca, Ralph, 173, 174–75, 344
Branch, Taylor, 277, 289
Braves, 170, 217, 245
Breadon, Sam, 147, 165
Breard, Stan, 131
Brecheen, Harry "the Cat," 176
Brock, Lou, 172
Brooklyn Dodgers, 9, 94, 96, 151–60, 200, 204–5
  acceptance of Puerto Rican player, 97
  in Dominican Republic, 186
  exhibitions in Latin America, 152
  and New York Giants, 238–46
  Robinson signs contract with, 106
Brookside Park, 46, 47
Brosnan, Jim, 332

Brothers, David, 330
Brown, H. Rap, 288
Brown-Sharkey-Isaacs Law, 270
Brown v. Board of Education, 230–231, 256
Brown, Willard, 90, 186
Bruce, Janet, 91
Bruins, 52, 60. See also UCLA
  Robinson's first season with, 55–56
Bruton, Billy, 245
Bums (Golenbock), 216
Bunche, Ralph, 260
Bus transportation, segregated, 78–80, 128
Butts, Pee Wee, 91

Cairo, Georgia, 13, 18
California Committee on Un-American Activities, 146
California Delano Grape strike, 322
Campanella, Roy, 96, 114, 120, 144, 155, 186, 188, 190, 207, 220, 242, 258
  Most Valuable Player award, 222
Campanis, Al, 137, 138
Camp Breckinridge (Kentucky), 84, 87, 88
Camp Claiborne (Louisiana), 72, 78
Camp Hood (Texas), 71–72, 77, 78
Cantor, Leo, 54
Card playing, 58, 173, 210
Carmichael, Stokely, 288, 323
Carver, George Washington, 252
Carver Savings and Loan, 316
Casey, Hugh, 174
Cavaretta, Phil, 165
Central High School, integration of, 263
Chandler, A. B. "Happy," 147, 157, 164, 212
Chaney, James, 314
Chapman, Ben, 163
Chase Hotel (St. Louis), 167, 234–235
Chavez, Cesar, 322
Chester, Hilda, 204
Chicago Cardinals, 52
Chicago Cubs, 165
Chicago Defender (newspaper), 95, 100

and death of brother Frank, 50
death of, 342
early athletic accomplishments, 41–42
as early target of HUAC, 184
early years, 28–34
elected to NAACP National Board of Directors, 267–73
fan letters, 179–81
first major league hit, 163
greatest defensive play, 221–22
health problems, 272, 333–34
induction physical, 69
junior college years, 44–48
marriage of, 125
military service, 68–77
petition against, 152, 154
relationship with Rachel Isum, 88–89, 112
relieved from active duty, 84–85
resignation from Chock Full o'Nuts, 304–5
retirement, 249
as role model, 192
senior year at UCLA, 60–67
signs on with William Black, 250
as special assistant to Governor Rockefeller, 319
suffers nervous exhaustion, 140
as supporter of Nixon, 277–80, 281–87
as ultimate team player, 55
unpredictable moods of, 46–47
weight problems, 186, 188
as youth director at Harlem YMCA, 190–91
Robinson, Jackie, Jr., 307–8, 325–327, 328–29
death of, 337
drifting into life of crime, 326
drug addiction problems, 325
Robinson, Jerry, 16
Robinson, Mack, 35–40, 49, 64
athletic scholarship, 40
banning of, from school sports, 35
as role model for Jackie, 39
Robinson, Mallie, 16, 17–18, 20–27
and house on Pepper Street, 21–24
as powerful influence on her children, 25–26

Robinson, Rachel, 61–63, 67, 167, 205, 216, 224, 306, 316, 321, 331
and death of Jackie, 343
on Jackie's discharge, 85
quest for good family living, 232–233
Robinson, Sharon, 344
Robinson, Sugar Ray, 78
Rockefeller, Nelson, 270, 285, 292, 309, 310, 311–13, 330, 331, 339, 343, 348
commitment to civil rights, 312
Rockefeller, Winthrop, 270
Rodney, Lester, 95
Roeder, Bill, 212
Roe, Preacher, 154, 231
Rogan, Bullet Joe, 90, 123
Rogers, William P., 263
Role model, Robinson as, 191–92
Rookie of the Year, Robinson as, 177
Roosevelt, Eleanor, 126, 282
Roosevelt Stadium (Jersey City), 244
Rose Bowl, 41, 57
Rosenthal, Harold, 85, 204, 207, 208, 213, 218, 223
Roush, Edd, 294
Rouzeau, Edgar T., 118
Rowan, Carl, 20, 33, 55, 62, 85
Rowe, Billy, 126, 128–29, 134
Rudd, Irving, 182, 242
Ruffing, Red, 87
Rumer, Clinton, 335
Russell, Bill, 344, 346
Rust, Art, Jr., 85
Rustin, Bayard, 343

Sain, Johnny, 171
St. Louis Browns, 186
St. Louis Cardinals, 165, 170, 173, 225
Sam Houston College, 89
Sanford, Florida, 130–31, 133
San Francisco Seals, 194
Sasser, Jim, 15–17
Sasser Plantation, 15
Satlow, Sarah, 205
Satlow, Stephen, 205
Sayles, Kiah, 340, 341
Schenley Distilleries Co., 322
Schiff, Dorothy, 282